Lecture Notes in Computer Science   10623

Commenced Publication in 1973
Founding and Former Series Editors:
Gerhard Goos, Juris Hartmanis, and Jan van Leeuwen

More information about this series at http://www.springer.com/series/7408

Simone Cavalheiro · José Fiadeiro (Eds.)

Formal Methods: Foundations and Applications

20th Brazilian Symposium, SBMF 2017
Recife, Brazil, November 29 – December 1, 2017
Proceedings

 Springer

Editors
Simone Cavalheiro (iD)
Universidade Federal de Pelotas
Pelotas
Brazil

José Fiadeiro (iD)
Royal Holloway, University of London
Egham
UK

ISSN 0302-9743   ISSN 1611-3349   (electronic)
Lecture Notes in Computer Science
ISBN 978-3-319-70847-8   ISBN 978-3-319-70848-5   (eBook)
https://doi.org/10.1007/978-3-319-70848-5

Library of Congress Control Number: 2017959597

LNCS Sublibrary: SL2 – Programming and Software Engineering

Printed on acid-free paper

This Springer imprint is published by Springer Nature
The registered company is Springer International Publishing AG
The registered company address is: Gewerbestrasse 11, 6330 Cham, Switzerland

Preface

This volume contains the papers presented at SBMF 2017: the 20th Brazilian Symposium on Formal Methods. The conference was held in Recife, Brazil, from November 29 to December 1, 2017.

The Brazilian Symposium on Formal Methods (SBMF) is an event devoted to the dissemination of the development and use of formal methods for the construction of high-quality computational systems, aiming to promote opportunities for researchers with an interest in formal methods to discuss the recent advances in this area. SBMF is a consolidated scientific–technical event in the software area. Its first edition took place in 1998, reaching the 20th edition in 2017. The proceedings of the last editions have been published in Springer's *Lecture Notes in Computer Science* series as volumes 5902 (2009), 6527 (2010), 7021 (2011), 7498 (2012), 8195 (2013), 8941 (2014), 9526 (2015), and 10090 (2016).

The conference included three invited talks, given by Ana Cavalcanti (University of York, UK), Christoph Benzmüller (University of Luxembourg, Luxembourg; Freie Universität Berlin, Germany; and Saarland University, Germany) and Patrícia Machado (UFCG, Brazil). A total of 16 papers were presented at the conference and are included in this volume. They were selected from 37 submissions that came from 16 different countries: Australia, Belgium, Brazil, Canada, China, Colombia, France, Germany, India, Ireland, Norway, Portugal, Spain, Sweden, the UK, and the USA. The Program Committee comprised 46 members from the national and international community of formal methods. Each submission was reviewed by three Program Committee members. Submissions, reviews, deliberations, decisions, as well as the compilation of these proceedings were all handled via EasyChair, which provided excellent support throughout the whole process.

We are grateful to the Program Committee and to the additional reviewers for their hard work in evaluating submissions and suggesting improvements. We are very thankful to the general chair of SBMF 2017, Gustavo Carvalho (UFPE), and the local organization team, who made everything possible for the conference to run smoothly, and to CIn-UFPE for kindly hosting the event. SBMF 2017 was organized by the Federal University of Pernambuco (UFPE), promoted by the Brazilian Computer Society (SBC), and sponsored by the following organizations, which we thank for their generous support: CAPES, CNPq, CIn/UFPE, FACEPE and UFPE. Finally, we would like to thank Springer for agreeing to publish the proceedings as a volume of *Lecture Notes in Computer Science*.

November 2017

Simone Cavalheiro
José Fiadeiro

Organization

Local Organizers

Gustavo Carvalho	UFPE, Brazil
Sidney Nogueira	UFRPE, Brazil

Program Chairs

Simone Cavalheiro	UFPel, Brazil
José Fiadeiro	Royal Holloway, University of London, UK

Steering Committee

Christiano Braga	UFF, Brazil
Simone Cavalheiro	UFPel, Brazil
Márcio Cornélio	UFPE, Brazil
José Fiadeiro	Royal Holloway, University of London, UK
Thierry Lecomte	ClearSy Systems Engineering, France
Narciso Martí-Oliet	Universidad Complutense de Madrid, Spain
Leila Ribeiro	UFRGS, Brazil
Bill Roscoe	University of Oxford, UK

Program Committee

Aline Andrade	UFBA, Brazil
Luís Barbosa	Universidade do Minho, Portugal
Christiano Braga	UFF, Brazil
Michael Butler	University of Southampton, UK
Sérgio Campos	UFMG, Brazil
Ana Cavalcanti	University of York, UK
Simone Cavalheiro	UFPel, Brazil
Márcio Cornélio	UFPE, Brazil
Andrea Corradini	Università di Pisa, Italy
Jim Davies	University of Oxford, UK
Ana De Melo	USP, Brazil
David Deharbe	ClearSy Systems Engineering, France
Ewen Denney	SGT/NASA Ames, USA
Clare Dixon	University of Liverpool, UK
Rachid Echahed	CNRS and University of Grenoble, France
José Fiadeiro	Royal Holloway, University of London, UK
Luciana Foss	UFPel, Brazil
Rohit Gheyi	UFCG, Brazil

Stefan Hallerstede	Aarhus University, Denmark
Reiko Heckel	University of Leicester, UK
Rolf Hennicker	Ludwig-Maximilians-Universität München, Germany
Juliano Iyoda	UFPE, Brazil
Thierry Lecomte	ClearSy Systems Engineering, France
Michael Leuschel	University of Düsseldorf, Germany
Patrícia Machado	UFCG, Brazil
Rodrigo Machado	UFRGS, Brazil
Marcelo Maia	UFU, Brazil
Narciso Martí-Oliet	Universidad Complutense de Madrid, Spain
Tiago Massoni	UFCG, Brazil
Álvaro Moreira	UFRGS, Brazil
Anamaria Martins Moreira	UFRJ, Brazil
Alexandre Mota	UFPE, Brazil
Arnaldo Moura	UNICAMP, Brazil
David Naumann	Stevens Institute of Technology, USA
Daltro José Nunes	UFRGS, Brazil
José Oliveira	Universidade do Minho, Portugal
Marcel Vinicius Medeiros Oliveira	UFRN, Brazil
Fernando Orejas	UPC, Spain
Arend Rensink	University of Twente, The Netherlands
Leila Ribeiro	UFRGS, Brazil
Augusto Sampaio	UFPE, Brazil
Leila Silva	UFS, Brazil
Adenilso Simão	USP, Brazil
Neeraj Singh	University of Toulouse, France
Sofiene Tahar	Concordia University, Canada
Jim Woodcock	University of York, UK

Additional Reviewers

Bonifácio, Adilson	Klein Galli, Jaqueline
Brenas, Jon Hael	Lahiouel, Ons
Gawanmeh, Amjad	Salehi Fathabadi, Asieh
Helali, Ghassen	Souza, Marlo

Contents

Refinement and Verification

Semantics and Languages

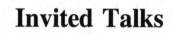

Invited Talks

Formal Methods for Robotics: RoboChart, RoboSim, and More

Ana Cavalcanti[(✉)]

Department of Computer Science,
University of York, York YO105GH, UK
Ana.Cavalcanti@york.ac.uk

A report from 2014 indicates that "The UK Government has identified 'eight great technologies' which will propel the UK to future growth"; one of them is robotics and autonomous systems. Currently, robotics is at the heart of the UK economic plans (www.tinyurl.com/mtut23s). A 13 billion pounds global market is predicted for 2025 (www.tinyurl.com/nyf64av). A limiting factor, however, is safety. The UK Technology Strategy Board reports that we are sitting on a "robotics goldmine" (www.tinyurl.com/o2u2ts7), but "Regulation and certification will also be a vital part of RAS deployment...".

Although many factors are involved in establishing safety of a robotic system, software poses a key challenge for design and assurance (www.tinyurl.com/o2u2ts7). Full verification is beyond the state of the art due to the complexity of models and properties for decision-making systems. Lack of customised techniques and tools means that, in spite of the modern outlook of the applications, the current practice of software engineering for robotics is outdated.

Main players in industry like Microsoft, Amazon, and Facebook have started using formal methods to improve their products [13]. What is routine in many engineering disciplines, that is, use of tools and techniques justified by mathematical principles, is becoming feasible for software developers.

The practical use of formal methods in many specific areas of application is, however, still an open challenge that is being tackled by scientists and engineers worldwide. What we propose is to face this challenge in the exciting area of development of controller software for mobile and autonomous robots.

The importance of Software Engineering has been recognised by the robotics community. There is an open-access journal on the subject (Journal of Software Engineering for Robotics - www.joser.org/). A premier conference in the area, the IEEE/RSJ International Conference on Intelligent Robots and Systems (IROS), has organised a Special Session on Robotics Software Engineering last year. Several domain-specific languages are available in the literature [9], but, by far and large, their focus is support for programming and simulation. Modern verification techniques have not been widely explored, with a few notable exceptions [1,4,5,7]. Applications of general-purpose formal techniques have shown the value that they can add to robotics. Due to lack of specialisation and difficulties with automation, however, the cost involved and scalability achieved do not indicate a clear prospect of wide practical application.

© Springer International Publishing AG 2017
S. Cavalheiro and J. Fiadeiro (Eds.): SBMF 2017, LNCS 10623, pp. 3–6, 2017.
https://doi.org/10.1007/978-3-319-70848-5_1

As part of a five-year EPSRC project, called RoboCalc (www.cs.york.ac.uk/Circus/RoboCalc), we are developing a framework for modelling and simulation of mobile and autonomous robots. We have devised RoboChart [8], a graphical domain-specific language from which we can generate CSP [11] mathematical models automatically. As opposed to other languages for robotics, RoboChart targets software design, rather than simulation. RoboChart has an associated tool, called RoboTool, that supports graphical modelling and automatic generation of CSP scripts, and is integrated with the model checker FDR4 [6].

We are also designing RoboSim, a graphical language to describe simulations. It makes it possible to verify a simulation with respect to a RoboChart model. We are also extending RoboChart to deal with systems comprising a collections of robots and tackle the important area of swarm robotics. The RoboCalc framework will ensure that models and simulations are consistent, and properties established by analysis and simulation are preserved in the robotic platform. This will cover timed, continuous, and probabilistic properties.

RoboChart and RoboSim provide a solid foundation to deal with the engineering of software for robotics. They are notations akin to those already in widespread use, but enriched with facilities that enable use of modern verification techniques. Further work, however, is needed to realise their full potential to the economic benefit of industry and to encourage adoption.

Current practice in robotics is normally based on standard state machines [2,3,10,12], without formal semantics, to specify the robot controller only. The environment is either not explicitly considered or described in English. The state machine that gives an abstract account of the robot controller guides the development of a simulation, but no rigorous connection between them is established. For implementation in a robotic platform, ad hoc adjustments are normally required to cater for the reality gap between the simulation and actual environment. Here, different running conditions may be considered for testing. There is no rigorous approach for the use of simulation and testing. Numerous iterations of (re)development and testing, tool dependency, and low-level programming are prevalent, with impact on cost, maintainability, and reliability. This is outdated even when compared with practice in other safety-critical domains.

RoboChart and RoboSim address the issues of principled modelling, verification, and sound simulation generation. Beyond the scope of RoboCalc, however, are a model-based framework for sound and automated testing of robotic systems. This is essential to ensure that the simulations generated from RoboChart models are used in an effective and cost-efficient way.

Another major hurdle for safety assurance is the highly complex environments in which critical robotic applications work; examples are autonomous vehicles and home-assistance robots. A safety argument needs to ensure absence of undesirable behaviour in all possible environments. Currently, however, even characterising all valid scenarios is not feasible using existing tools.

In the agenda for future work, we ought to consider testing based on simulations, with full control of the robots and their environment, and tests for use on robots operating in the real world. We need sound test generation and execution techniques to support systematic and automated simulation experiments.

We will also investigate the design of a modelling language that can identify essential properties of the environment in which a robotic system is expected to work. It needs to support verification by simulation via automatic generation of explicit environment specifications for use with simulators, by deployment testing via automatic generation of test cases, and by proof of properties considering all environments for which a robotic system is suited.

The challenges are (1) a rich semantic model to underpin sound and systematic testing techniques; (2) test generation based on timed, probabilistic, and hybrid models for the robots and their environment; (3) tractability for a variety of simulation tools; (4) design of a language that is accessible by practitioners, supports abstraction in the modelling of environments, and has a formal semantics; (5) techniques for model-based generation of simulation environment definitions or programs for use with a variety of simulators; (6) techniques for model-based generation of environment definitions for use in tests; and (7) techniques for proof-based verification of properties.

Our vision is a 21st-century toolbox for robot-controller developers. In this toolbox, a developer can find unambiguous diagrammatic notations to specify models for the environment, the robotic platform, and the controller. For commonly used environments and robotic platforms, the toolbox includes a range of ready-made models. Because these models are precise, there is no scope for misunderstanding and, most importantly, the toolbox includes techniques for desirable properties of the models: deadlock freedom, speed limits, and so on.

Since the technique for validation that robot controller developers favour nowadays is simulation, in the 21st-century toolbox, there are tools for automatic generation of these simulations. The ingenuity of the developer is now focused in the optimisation of the simulation and of the associated deployed code. Because the languages used for simulation and programming are high-level, the results are tool independent, and can be deployed in a variety of robotic platforms. Moreover, the toolbox provides techniques to generate tests automatically, for use with the simulation and the deployed system. Test drivers support the use of simulations described in RoboSim running on top of customised simulators, or off-the-shelf tools like Simulink and Webots.

With the 21st-century toolbox, the costly cycles of iterations of design and testing, with problems found very late, even just at deployment time, are reduced. Moreover, the developer can demonstrate that the controller produced satisfies essential properties established during modelling. Software for mobile and autonomous robot is cheaper and more reliable.

Acknowledgements. The work mentioned is a collaboration with colleagues at the University of York and Universidade Federal de Pernambuco: André Didier, Wei Li, Alvaro Miyazawa, Alexandre Mota, Pedro Ribeiro, Augusto Sampaio, Jon Timmis, and Jim Woodcock. Work on testing has been extensively discussed with Rob Hierons. The author's work is funded by the EPSRC grant EP/M025756/1, and INES, grants CNPq/465614/2014-0 and FACEPE/APQ/0388-1.03/14. No new primary data was created as part of the study reported here.

References

1. Abdellatif, T., Bensalem, S., Combaz, J., de Silva, L., Ingrand, F.: Rigorous design of robot software: a formal component-based approach. Robot. Auton. Syst. **60**(12), 1563–1578 (2012)
2. Brunner, S.G., Steinmetz, F., Belder, R., Domel, A.: Rafcon: a graphical tool for engineering complex, robotic tasks. In: IEEE/RSJ International Conference on Intelligent Robots and Systems, pp. 3283–3290 (2016)
3. Dhouib, S., Kchir, S., Stinckwich, S., Ziadi, T., Ziane, M.: RobotML, a domain-specific language to design, simulate and deploy robotic applications. In: Noda, I., Ando, N., Brugali, D., Kuffner, J.J. (eds.) SIMPAR 2012. LNCS (LNAI), vol. 7628, pp. 149–160. Springer, Heidelberg (2012). https://doi.org/10.1007/978-3-642-34327-8_16
4. Fleurey, F., Solberg, A.: A domain specific modeling language supporting specification, simulation and execution of dynamic adaptive systems. In: Schürr, A., Selic, B. (eds.) MODELS 2009. LNCS, vol. 5795, pp. 606–621. Springer, Heidelberg (2009). https://doi.org/10.1007/978-3-642-04425-0_47
5. Foughali, M., Berthomieu, B., Dal Zilio, S., Ingrand, F., Mallet, A.: Model checking real-time properties on the functional layer of autonomous robots. In: Ogata, K., Lawford, M., Liu, S. (eds.) ICFEM 2016. LNCS, vol. 10009, pp. 383–399. Springer, Cham (2016). https://doi.org/10.1007/978-3-319-47846-3_24
6. Gibson-Robinson, T., Armstrong, P., Boulgakov, A., Roscoe, A.W.: FDR3 - a modern refinement checker for CSP. In: Tools and Algorithms for the Construction and Analysis of Systems, pp. 187–201 (2014)
7. Kapellos, K., Simon, D., Jourdant, M., Espiau, B.: Task level specification and formal verification of robotics control systems: State of the art and case study. Int. J. Syst. Sci. **30**(11), 1227–1245 (1999)
8. Miyazawa, A., Ribeiro, P., Li, W., Cavalcanti, A.L.C., Timmis, J.: Automatic property checking of robotic applications. In: The International Conference on Intelligent Robots and Systems (2017)
9. Nordmann, A., Hochgeschwender, N., Wigand, D., Wrede, S.: A survey on domain-specific modeling and languages in robotics. J. Softw. Eng. Robot. **7**(1), 75–99 (2016)
10. Pembeci, I., Nilsson, H., Hager, G.: Functional reactive robotics: an exercise in principled integration of domain-specific languages. In: 4th ACM SIGPLAN International Conference on Principles and Practice of Declarative Programming, pp. 168–179. ACM (2002)
11. Roscoe, A.W.: Understanding Concurrent Systems. Texts in Computer Science. Springer, London (2011)
12. Wachter, M., Ottenhaus, S., Krohnert, M., Vahrenkamp, N., Asfour, T.: The armarx statechart concept: graphical programing of robot behavior. Front. Robot. AI **3**, 33 (2016)
13. Woodcock, J.C.P., Larsen, P.G., Bicarregui, J., Fitzgerald, J.S.: Formal methods: practice and experience. ACM Comput. Surv. **41**(4), 1–36 (2009)

Recent Successes with a Meta-Logical Approach to Universal Logical Reasoning (Extended Abstract)

Christoph Benzmüller[1,2]([✉])

[1] University of Luxembourg, Esch-sur-Alzette, Luxembourg
[2] Freie Universität Berlin, Berlin, Germany
c.benzmueller@gmail.com

The quest for a most general framework supporting universal reasoning is very prominently represented in the works of Leibniz. He envisioned a scientia generalis founded on a characteristica universalis, that is, a most universal formal language in which all knowledge about the world and the sciences can be encoded. A quick study of the survey literature on logical formalisms suggests that quite the opposite to Leibniz' dream has become reality. Instead of a characteristica universalis, we are today facing a very rich and heterogenous zoo of different logical systems, and instead of converging towards a single superior logic, this logic zoo is further expanding, eventually even at accelerated pace. As a consequence, the unified vision of Leibniz seems farther away than ever before. However, there are also some promising initiatives to counteract these diverging developments. Attempts at unifying approaches to logic include categorial logic algebraic logic and coalgebraic logic.

My own research draws on another alternative at universal logical reasoning: *the shallow semantical embeddings (SSE) approach.* This approach has a very pragmatic motivation, foremost reuse of tools, simplicity and elegance. It utilises classical higher-order logic [21] as a unifying meta-logic in which the syntax and semantics of varying other logics can be explicitly modeled and flexibly combined (cf. [3] and the references therein). Off-the-shelf higher-order interactive and automated theorem provers [6] can then be employed to reason about and within the shallowly embedded logics.

Respective experiments have e.g. been conducted in **metaphysics**. An initial focus thereby has been on computer-supported assessments of modern variants of the *ontological argument for the existence of God*, where the SSE approach has been utilised in particular for automating variants of higher-order (multi-)modal logics [8].

In the course of these experiments (cf. [13–18] for details), my prover LEO-II [9] detected an previously unnoticed inconsistency in Kurt Gödel's [25] prominent variant of the ontological argument, while the slightly modified variant by Dana Scott [31] was verified in the interactive proof assistants Isabelle/HOL [29] and Coq [19]. Further modern variants of the argument have subsequently been studied with the approach, and theorem provers have even contributed to the clarification of an unsettled philosophical dispute [12].

© Springer International Publishing AG 2017
S. Cavalheiro and J. Fiadeiro (Eds.): SBMF 2017, LNCS 10623, pp. 7–11, 2017.
https://doi.org/10.1007/978-3-319-70848-5_2

Another, more ambitious study has focused on Ed Zalta's *Principia Logico-Metaphysica* (PLM) [37], which aims at a foundational logical theory for all of metaphysics and the sciences. This includes mathematics, and in this sense it is more ambitious than Russel's Principia Mathematica. The semantical embedding of PLM in HOL has been very challenging, since in addition to its size, its foundational theory is complicated: the PLM is based on hyperintensional higher-order modal logic S5 defined on top of a relational (as opposed to a functional) type theory that comes with restricted comprehension principles (the use of full comprehension in the PLM has been known to cause paradoxes and inconsistencies [30]). The PLM has meanwhile been successfully encoded in Isabelle/HOL by my student Daniel Kirchner [26]. As an unexpected highlight of this project, Kirchner, supported by the Isabelle/HOL system, detected an previously unnoticed issue: a deeply rooted and known paradox is reintroduced in PLM when the logic of complex terms is adjoined to PLM's specially-formulated comprehension principle for relations. Kirchner is now using the framework to support Zalta in fixing this issue.

Other logics, for which the SSE approach applies, and which are relevant for theoretical philosophy, include quantified conditional logics and multi-valued logic [4, 5, 34].

Motivated by the successful experiments on the ontological argument, and supported by my research group at Freie Universität (FU) Berlin, I have set-up a worldwide new *lecture course on computational metaphysics* [36], which has received FU Berlin's central teaching award in 2015/16. Student projects originating from this course have led to impressive new contributions (cf. [1, 24, 26]; further papers are submitted), including Kirchner's already mentioned embedding of the PLM in HOL, a computer-assisted reconstruction of an ontological argument by Leibniz and a verification of (main parts of) prominent textbooks by Fitting [22] and Boolos [20]. A key factor in the successful implementation of the course has been, that a single methodology and overall technique (the SSE approach) was used throughout, enabling the students to quickly adopt a wide range of different logic variants in short time within a single proof assistant (Isabelle/HOL). The course concept seems in fact well suited to significantly improve interdisciplinary, university level logic education.

Another interesting application area for the SSE approach is **mathematics**, where e.g. the proper treatment of partiality and undefinedness in computer-formalisations constitute unsettled challenges. *Free logic* [28, 32] adapts classical logic in a way particularly suited for addressing them. Free logics have interesting applications, e.g. in natural language processing and as a logic of fiction. In mathematics, free logics are particularly suited in application domains such as category theory or projective geometry (e.g. morphism composition in category theory is a partial operation). In a collaboration with Dana Scott, I have shown that free logics can be elegantly embedded and automated in HOL [10]. Utilising this embedding, we have conducted an exemplary *theory exploration study in category theory* [11], in the course of which theorem provers have revealed a previously unnoticed technical flaw (constricted inconsistency resp. missing axioms) in a prominent category theory textbook [23].

The SSE approach is, of course, relevant also for **artificial intelligence and computer science**. For example, the knowledge and belief of intelligent agents can be modelled with *epistemic and doxastic logics*, which are directly amenable to the SSE approach, since they are just particular modal logics. To demonstrate this, prominent AI puzzles about knowledge and belief, including the well known wise men puzzle, have been successfully automated [3,35]. Moreover, the semantic web *description logic* ALC is just a reinvention of basic multi-modal logic K and, hence, the SSE approach is immediately applicable to it. *Access control logics* have applications e.g. in computer security; again the SSE approach applies [2]. Further ongoing work e.g. adresses *intuitionistic modal logic* [27] and predicate dynamic logic.

In summary, the SSE approach is the most widely applied universal logical reasoning approach to date. Note, however, the difference to Leibniz' original idea (and to various strands of related work). Instead of a single, universal logic formalism, the SSE approach supports many different competing object logics from the logic zoo. No ontological commitment is thus enforced at the object logic level (e.g. the approach well supports both classical and intuitionistic object logics, and can even combine them [7]). The concrete selection of (a range of) object logic candidates is typically determined by the specific requirements of the application at hand. Only at meta-level a single, unifying logic is provided, namely HOL (or any richer logic incorporating HOL). By unfolding the embeddings of the object logics, problem representations are uniformly mapped to HOL. This way Leibniz' vision is realised in an indirect way: *universal logical reasoning is established (only) at the meta-level in HOL*.

References

1. Bentert, M., Benzmüller, C., Streit, D., Woltzenlogel Paleo, B.: Analysis of an ontological proof proposed by Leibniz. In: Tandy, C. (ed.) Death and Anti-Death. Four Decades after Michael Polanyi, Three Centuries after G.W. Leibniz, vol. 14. Ria University Press (2016)
2. Benzmüller, C.: Automating access control logics in simple type theory with LEO-II. In: Gritzalis, D., Lopez, J. (eds.) SEC 2009. IAICT, vol. 297, pp. 387–398. Springer, Heidelberg (2009). https://doi.org/10.1007/978-3-642-01244-0_34
3. Benzmüller, C.: Combining and automating classical and non-classical logics in classical higher-order logic. Ann. Math. Artif. Intell. (Special Issue Computational logics in Multi-agent Systems (CLIMA XI)) **62**(1–2), 103–128 (2011)
4. Benzmüller, C.: Automating quantified conditional logics in HOL. In: Rossi, F. (ed.) IJCAI 2013, pp. 746–753. AAAI Press (2013)
5. Benzmüller, C.: Cut-elimination for quantified conditional logic. J. Philos. Logic **46**(3), 333–353 (2017)
6. Benzmüller, C., Miller, D.: Automation of higher-order logic. In: Gabbay, D.M., Siekmann, J.H., Woods, J. (eds.) Handbook of the History of Logic. Computational Logic, vol. 9, pp. 215–254. North Holland, Elsevier (2014)

7. Benzmüller, C., Paulson, L.: Multimodal and intuitionistic logics in simple type theory. Logic J. IGPL **18**(6), 881–892 (2010)
8. Benzmüller, C., Paulson, L.: Quantified multimodal logics in simple type theory. Logica Univ. (Special Issue on Multimodal Logics) **7**(1), 7–20 (2013)
9. Benzmüller, C., Paulson, L.C., Sultana, N., Theiß, F.: The higher-order prover LEO-II. J. Autom. Reasoning **55**(4), 389–404 (2015)
10. Benzmüller, C., Scott, D.: Automating Free Logic in Isabelle/HOL. In: Greuel, G.-M., Koch, T., Paule, P., Sommese, A. (eds.) ICMS 2016. LNCS, vol. 9725, pp. 43–50. Springer, Cham (2016). https://doi.org/10.1007/978-3-319-42432-3_6
11. Benzmüller, C., Scott, D.S.: Axiomatizing category theory in free logic (2016). arXiv, http://arxiv.org/abs/1609.01493
12. Benzmüller, C., Weber, L., Woltzenlogel Paleo, B.: Computer-assisted analysis of the Anderson-Hájek controversy. Logica Univ. **11**(1), 139–151 (2017)
13. Benzmüller, C., Woltzenlogel Paleo, B.: Gödel's God in Isabelle/HOL. Archive of Formal Proofs (2013). (Formally verified)
14. Benzmüller, C., Woltzenlogel Paleo, B.: Automating Gödel's ontological proof of God's existence with higher-order automated theorem provers. In: Schaub, T., Friedrich, G., O'Sullivan, B. (eds.) ECAI 2014. Frontiers in Artificial Intelligence and Applications, vol. 263, pp. 93–98. IOS Press (2014)
15. Benzmüller, C., Woltzenlogel Paleo, B.: Interacting with modal logics in the coq proof assistant. In: Beklemishev, L.D., Musatov, D.V. (eds.) CSR 2015. LNCS, vol. 9139, pp. 398–411. Springer, Cham (2015). https://doi.org/10.1007/978-3-319-20297-6_25
16. Benzmüller, C., Woltzenlogel Paleo, B.: The inconsistency in Gödel's ontological argument: a success story for AI in metaphysics. In: Kambhampati, S. (ed.) IJCAI 2016. vol. 1–3, pp. 936–942. AAAI Press (2016)
17. Benzmüller, C., Paleo, B.W.: The ontological modal collapse as a collapse of the square of opposition. In: Béziau, J.-Y., Basti, G. (eds.) The Square of Opposition: A Cornerstone of Thought. SUL, pp. 307–313. Springer, Cham (2017). https://doi.org/10.1007/978-3-319-45062-9_18
18. Benzmüller, C., Woltzenlogel Paleo, B.: Experiments in Computational Metaphysics: Gödel's proof of God's existence. Savijnanam: scientific exploration for a spiritual paradigm. J. Bhaktivedanta Inst. **9**, 43–57 (2017)
19. Bertot, Y., Casteran, P.: Interactive Theorem Proving and Program Development. Springer, Heidelberg (2004)
20. Boolos, G.: The Logic of Provability. Cambridge University Press, Cambridge (1993)
21. Church, A.: A formulation of the simple theory of types. J. Symbolic Logic **5**, 56–68 (1940)
22. Fitting, M.: Types, Tableaus, and Gödel's God. Kluwer, Amsterdam (2002)
23. Freyd, P.J., Scedrov, A.: Categories. North Holland, Allegories (1990)
24. Fuenmayor, D., Benzmüller, C.: Automating emendations of the ontological argument in intensional higher-order modal logic. In: Kern-Isberner, G., Fürnkranz, J., Thimm, M. (eds.) KI 2017. Lecture Notes in Computer Science, vol. 10505, pp. 114–127. Springer, Cham (2017). https://doi.org/10.1007/978-3-319-67190-1_9
25. Gödel, K.: Appx. A: Notes in Kurt Gödel's Hand. In: Sobel [33], pp. 144–145 (1970)
26. Kirchner, D.: Representation and partial automation of the principia logico-metaphysica in Isabelle/HOL. Archive of Formal Proofs (2017). formally verified with Isabelle/HOL

27. Lachnitt, H.: Systematic verification of the intuitionistic modal logic cube in isabelle/hol. Bachelor Thesis at the Freie Universität Berlin, Institut für Informatik (2017)
28. Lambert, K.: Free Logic. Selected Essays. Cambridge University Press, Cambridge (2012)
29. Nipkow, T., Wenzel, M., Paulson, L.C. (eds.): Isabelle/HOL. LNCS, vol. 2283. Springer, Heidelberg (2002). https://doi.org/10.1007/3-540-45949-9
30. Oppenheimer, P.E., Zalta, E.N.: Relations versus functions at the foundations of logic: type-theoretic considerations. J. Log. Comput. **21**(2), 351–374 (2011)
31. Scott, D.: Appx. B: Notes in Dana Scott's Hand. In: Sobel [33], pp. 145–146 (1972)
32. Scott, D.: Existence and description in formal logic. In: Schoenman, R. (ed.) Bertrand Russell: Philosopher of the Century, pp. 181–200. George Allen & Unwin, London (1967). (Reprinted with additions. In: Philosophical Application of Free Logic, edited by K. Lambert. Oxford Universitry Press, 1991, pp. 28–48)
33. Sobel, J.: Logic and Theism. Cambridge U. Press, Cambridge (2004)
34. Steen, A., Benzmüller, C.: Sweet SIXTEEN: automation via embedding into classical higher-order logic. Logic Logical Philos. **25**, 535–554 (2016)
35. Steen, A., Wisniewski, M., Benzmüller, C.: Tutorial on reasoning in expressive non-classical logics with Isabelle/HOL. In: Benzüller, C., Rojas, R., Sutcliffe, G. (eds.) GCAI 2016. EPiC Series in Computing, vol. 41, pp. 1–10. EasyChair (2016)
36. Wisniewski, M., Steen, A., Benzmüller, C.: Einsatz von Theorembeweisern in der Lehre. In: Schwill, A., Lucke, U. (eds.) Hochschuldidaktik der Informatik: 7. Fachtagung des GI-Fachbereichs Informatik und Ausbildung/Didaktik der Informatik. Commentarii informaticae didacticae (CID), Universitätsverlag Potsdam, Potsdam, Germany (2016)
37. Zalta, E.N.: Principia logico-metaphysica (2016). draft version, preprint https://mally.stanford.edu/principia.pdf

Formal Methods Integration and
Experience Reports

Abstract State Machines and System Theoretic Process Analysis for Safety-Critical Systems

Farah Al-Shareefi$^{(\boxtimes)}$, Alexei Lisitsa, and Clare Dixon

Department of Computer Science, University of Liverpool,
Liverpool L69 3BX, UK
{F.M.A.Al-Shareefi,lisitsa,cldixon}@liverpool.ac.uk

Abstract. The Abstract State Machine (ASM) method is a formal specification and modeling technique that allows us to specify computational systems at the required abstraction level and facilitates formal analysis and verification. System Theoretic Process Analysis (STPA) is a semi-formal hazard analysis method that aims to identify safety requirements emerging from the analysis of potential interactions among components and inadequate control in the system's design. In this paper, we combine these two techniques to develop a methodology capturing both the formal representation of ASM with the ability to generate safety properties from the STPA hazard analysis. This has the advantages of verifying the STPA requirements in a formal way, and giving insights for the improvement of the ASM specification, depending on these requirements. We illustrate our methodology by applying it to an insulin pump control system case study, showing what safety issues it highlights.

Keywords: Abstract State Machines · System Theoretic Process Analysis · Temporal logic · Validation · Verification

1 Introduction

Due to the increasing adoption of software in safety critical systems, together with their potential failure, it has become imperative to develop safe and efficient systems before deployment. We address this issue by combining a particular formal method with the results of a particular safety analysis technique.

Within the existing variety of formal methods, the Abstract State Machine (ASM) method can seamlessly direct the development process of computational systems, from capturing the requirements to practical implementation [11]. Several modeling and analysis tools have been developed for ASMs. In this paper, we have chosen the set of interoperable tools integrated in a meta modelling framework called ASMETA [9], which includes automatic tools for the editing [13], validation [12], and verification [6] of ASM models. These tools help the modeler to develop an appropriate model for the functional requirements.

System Theoretic Process Analysis (STPA) is a safety analysis technique from the safety engineering domain [19]. It was developed to analyse complex modern systems that involve interactions between their software, hardware,

© Springer International Publishing AG 2017
S. Cavalheiro and J. Fiadeiro (Eds.): SBMF 2017, LNCS 10623, pp. 15–32, 2017.
https://doi.org/10.1007/978-3-319-70848-5_3

human and environment components. This technique uses a non-linear accident causation model for the whole system, where the failure of interaction between the system's components or component failures can lead to unsafe states. It has been demonstrated that this technique is able to identify a wide range of hazard causes and safety requirements in a semi-formal manner [24]. Recently, the STPA technique has been used, in [1,3], as an integrated tool with verification activity by supplying it with the formulated safety requirements. However, the formalization process of safety requirements is both cumbersome and does not accurately capture some of the temporal aspects of the requirements.

In this paper, we present a methodology for developing correct and safe critical systems, that is based on the ASM method, the STPA technique, and temporal logic. It starts with modelling the system in the AsmetaL (ASMETA Language) to obtain an accurate mathematical representation. Then, using the AsmetaV validation tool, the model validation process is applied to ensure that it meets the functional requirements. Next the STPA technique is utilized to elicit safety requirements. These requirements are formalized into Linear Temporal Logic (LTL) that can be verified against an AsmetaL model using the AsmetaSMV verification tool.

The methodology is illustrated through the Insulin Pump Control System (IPCS) [23]. This system is chosen because its design provides a plausible level of complexity for research, and its safety aspects are still under scrutiny.

The main contributions of this paper are: a systematic methodology for developing safety critical systems through combining ASM with STPA, with the target of developing safe specifications, and adequate and concise temporal formalizations of the STPA requirements.

The rest of the paper is organized as follows: Sect. 2 is an overview of the tools and techniques of our methodology. Section 3 presents our case study. In Sect. 4, we describe our methodology. The application of this methodology is explained in Sect. 5. In Sect. 6, we evaluate our methodology. Section 7 discusses the related work. Section 8, finally, concludes the paper.

2   Background

2.1   Abstract State Machines

Abstract State Machines (ASMs), were originally introduced by Gurevich [15] as a versatile and extended way of representing Finite State Machines, where unstructured control states are replaced by multi-sorted first order structure states. Using ASMs, the modeler can specify the system from a high-level of abstraction, called a ground model, to the required detailed one [11]. ASM is based on abstract states, to model the system's structure, and on transition rules, to model the system's dynamic behavior. An ASM state is denoted by a pair (location, location value). The location is represented by an n-ary function name and its list of first-order terms, while the location value is a value assigned to that location. The ASM locations or functions can be *static*, which never change during any run of the machine, or *dynamic*, which may be changed by the environment or by machine updates. The dynamic functions are also differentiated between *controlled* (read and write by the machine), and *monitored* (read by the machine and write by the environment).

Changing an ASM state is performed by a control logic rule that has the following format: "if *Condition* then *Update*". This rule is invoked at the current state to produce the subsequent state. In addition to if-then, there is a set of rule constructors, such as par (parallel execution of the grouped rules), choose (non deterministic selection) and switch case (extension of the control logic rule).

A set of tools have been developed around ASMs to support the ASM method, and to help the developer in performing different analysis activities within the same development platform. These tools are included in a meta modelling framework called ASMETA (ASM mETAmodelling)[1] [9]. The ASMETA tools that have been utilized in this paper are as follows: (1) The ASMETA Simulator (AsmetaS) tool [13], which executes ASM models that are written in ASMETA Language (AsmetaL). (2) The ASMETA Validator (AsmetaV) tool [12] which validates AsmetaL specifications by scenarios written in ASMETA validation language, named Avalla. Avalla expresses the execution for a scenario in an algorithmic manner via a set of constructs: set (determine the values for monitored functions), check (inspect the machine state), step (perform one transition into another state), and step until (perform several transitions). The AmetaV tool captures any violation of Avalla scenario by producing only success or fail validation verdicts. (3) The ASMETA SMV (AsmetaSMV) model checker tool [6] which is for formal verification of ASMs. The inputs for this tool are the AsmetaL model and temporal properties, which can be written in either LTL or CTL. The AsmetaSMV translates these inputs into the NuSMV model checker. In this paper, we will use only LTL properties. The propositional and future-time connectives that are available for writing LTL properties in AsmetaL are: ! (not), iff ('if and only if', $\leftrightarrow$), and ($\land$), or ($\lor$), implies ($\rightarrow$), x ('next state', $\bigcirc$), g ('globally', $\square$), and u(p, q) ('until', p U q).

2.2   System Theoretic Process Analysis

System Theoretic Process Analysis (STPA) is a hazard analysis technique that was proposed by Leveson [17] to address safety as a control problem. It considers the system's component interaction and dynamic behavior, rather than considering component failure only.

Typically, in this technique, the system is deemed as a safety control loop which consists of a controller, actuator, sensor and controlled process. The controller includes a model of the process it is controlling, in order to identify the requisite control action to be issued. The actuator executes this action on the controlled process, and the sensor returns the current status data about the controlled process to the controller. The analysis through STPA focuses on identifying the context and timing conditions that affect the action to make it a hazardous action.

---

[1] http://asmeta.sourceforge.net/.

Implementation of this technique is outlined in five steps [18], as follows: (1) Identify system analysis fundamentals by determining expected accidents, and the potential hazards that can lead to these accidents. (2) Identify unsafe control actions under different timing conditions (provided at any time, provided too early/too late, not provided), as well as determining the controller process model (a set of environmental and system variables) which can contribute to providing the control action. (3) Ask an expert to determine which control action, with which combination of values taken by the environmental and system variables, and under which timing conditions, is a hazardous action. (4) Translate the hazardous control actions into safety requirements. (5) Determine the potential causes of each unsafe control action depending on the expert. In our work, we will focus on the first four steps.

3   Case Study: The Insulin Pump Control System

The Insulin Pump Control System (IPCS) is a therapeutic system used to improve diabetes treatment. The problem with traditional treatments is the possibility of taking an insulin overdose or insufficient dose due to focusing only on the current glucose value and ignoring the last insulin injection time. It has been chosen as a case study for software analysis of safety-critical systems in [23]. The IPCS works in three different modes: automatic, manual, and switching off. In the automatic mode, the software controller can implement one of the following two activities at a time: running (performed every 10 min) or testing (performed every 30 s). In addition, the software controller resets the cumulative dose to 0 every 24 h. The running activity starts with sensing the current glucose value, then it analyses this value by comparing it with two saved values (10 and 20 min prior) to calculate the required dose. Before delivering the dose, it does a safety check, considering the maximum daily dose and maximum single dose. During the delivery of the dose, the controller sends pulses equivalent to each unit of the delivered dose. Within the running activity, the warning alarm must be run when the received glucose value is less than the minimum safe limit, the available insulin is less than or equal to four maximum single doses, or delivering the dose will exceed the maximum daily dose. The testing activity involves detecting any hardware unit failure (sensor, battery, needle, insulin reservoir) to suspend the IPCS work and to run the failure alarm. In the manual mode, the system will deliver the dose manually, hence the software controller will not perform safety checking, but it will update the quantity of the available insulin and the cumulative dose. The complete requirements are documented and specified in the Z language in [22], and part of the specification is provided in [23].

4   The Proposed Methodology

Our proposed methodology is based on: AsmetaL, AsmetaV, AsmetaSMV, STPA, and temporal logic. Using this methodology, we aim to guide the modeller to improve the ASM model, depending on the detection of any violations to the functional and safety requirements via the validation and verification tools, and to provide the verification tool with the STPA requirements in a formal way.

Figure 1 shows an overview of our methodology which includes the following ' steps: (1) Modelling the system using the AsmetaL to capture the system's requirements. (2) Validating that the AsmetaL model satisfies the functional requirements, which relate to the user needs about the system through using the AsmetaV tool. This tool allows construct particular scenarios describing the interactions between the system and its environment. The AsmetaV tool reads a scenario written by the user in Avalla, and invokes the AsmetaS tool to simulate this scenario and checks if the AsmetaL model satisfies this scenario or not. In the event that any of these scenarios are not satisfied, the AsmetaL model must be modified. (3) Eliciting safety requirements for the system via STPA. (4) Formalizing the elicited STPA safety requirements into LTL specifications using the formula in Sect. 5.4 that captures the four STPA timing requirements of control actions. (5) Verifying that the AsmetaL model satisfies the formulated STPA safety requirements. If any of these requirements are not satisfied, then a counter example will guide the modeller to improve the AsmetaL model.

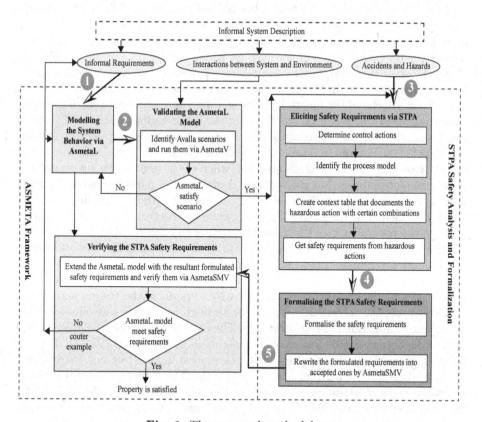

Fig. 1. The proposed methodology

5   Methodology Applied to IPCS Case Study

In this section, we apply our methodology to the IPCS case study.

5.1   Modeling the System Behavior via AsmetaL

In this stage, we present an abstract model or what is called a ground model, for the IPCS, written in AsmetaL[2]. The ground model is shown in Code 1. Through this model, we want to show how AsmetaL specifies the issues that have not been addressed by [22], such as switching between the system operation mode (automatic, manual, or switching off) at any state by the user, and timing details of the software controller activities: setting the cumulative dose to 0, running, and testing, which occurring at different times: 24 h, 10 min, 30 s, respectively. We do not discuss the following in detail: the switching off and manual operating modes, and the running activity stages, which include sensing the glucose value, analysing it, calculating the insulin dose, checking the calculated dose and delivering it, since they are explained in [22,23].

In the AsmetaL model, we first define several data types, followed by a number of functions, as discussed below. Finally a number of rules are defined to show how the IPCS works. We declared the btn monitored function that represents the operation mode of the system, which can be ON (automatic mode), MANUAL (manual mode), or OFF (switching off mode). The transition from any state into another one in the model is derived by the btn function in the r_main rule. We also declared the function cS whose value represents the state of the software controller, which can be SNS (sensing the current glucose value), ANLSCAL (analysing the current glucose value and calculating the dose), SFTCK (safety checking for the computed dose before delivering it), DLVR (delivering the dose), or TST (testing). The value of cS function, when the system works automatically (btn=ON), determines what the software controller can perform during the running activity or can exclusively perform the testing activity. Running activity, which is modelled by the r_run rule, starts when the controller state is sns. If it is so, then the controller gets the value from the sensor via the valS function, and the state of the controller is set to ANLSCAL. After calculating the dose, the value of cS function becomes SFTCK. Following safety checking for the computed dose, the cS value changes into DLVR. After delivering the dose, the running activity is finished and the cS function turns into TST to perform the testing activity.

Performing the testing activity will be through inspecting the values for the iA, ndl, rsv, fl functions in the r_test rule. The iA function is the available insulin value, which must not be less than the maximum single dose (mSD=4). The rsv function records whether the reservoir has presented (PRS) or not (NOT), and the same role for the ndl function of the needle. The fl function shows if there is a failure in any hardware unit, such as the sensor, pump, needle, or battery. Showing hardware units failure in one rather than several monitored functions

---

[2] All the rules for the refined model are available online at http://cgi.csc.liv.ac.uk/~hsfalsha/Insulin_Pump_Control_System.html.

helps to keep the model size small. If any of the monitored functions indicate a failure, then the system must be put in a suspension state by updating the value of the controlled function spn to true, and at the same time a command must be given to the alarm through the alarmCommand function.

```
asm insulinpump                                   rule r_test=
signature:                                           if (fl=true) or (rsv=NOT) or (ndl=NOT)
   domain Seconds subsetof Integer                       or (iA<mSD) then
   domain Dose subsetof Integer                       par
   domain ThirtyC subsetof Integer                      spn:=true
   domain TenC subsetof Integer                         alarmCommand:=true
   domain InsulinRange subsetof Integer              endpar
   enum domain ControllerState={SNS,                 endif
       ANLSCAL, SFTCK, DLVR, TST}                 rule r_sense=
   enum domain Button={ON, OFF, MANUAL}              if exist $x in Dose with $x=valS then
   enum domain Present={NOT, PRS}                       par
   monitored pas:Seconds->Boolean                      cR:=valS
   monitored valS:Dose                                 cS:=ANLSCAL
   monitored mD:Dose                                 endpar
   monitored fl:Boolean                              endif
   monitored ndl:Present                          rule r_run=
   monitored rsv:Present                             switch cS
   monitored btn:Button                                case SNS: r_sense[]
   controlled cR:Dose                                  case ANLSCAL: cS:=SFTCK
   controlled cS:ControllerState                       case SFTCK: r_safetycheck[]
   controlled spn:Boolean                              case DLVR: cS:=TST
   controlled alarmCommand:Boolean                   endswitch
   controlled manualD:Dose                        rule r_autoperating=
   controlled iA:InsulinRange                        if spn=false then
   controlled sC30:ThirtyC                             par
   controlled mC10:TenC                                if sC30=1 and cS!=TST then
   domain Seconds={30}                                    r_run[]
   domain ThirtyC={1..20}                              endif
   domain TenC={1..144}                                if sC30>=1 and sC30<=19
   domain Dose={0..35}                                 and cS=TST then
   domain InsulinRnge={0..100}                            if pas(30)=true then
   function mSD=4                                          par
   function mDD=25                                           r_test[]
rule r_manualdelivering=                                     sC30:=sC30+1
   if updateiACommand=false then                           endpar
      if iA<=100 then //This must be modified             endif
         if exist $md in Dose with ($md=mD and          endif
            ($md>=1 and $md<=5)) then                  if sC30=20 then
            par                                           if pas(30)=true then
               manualD:=mD                                  par
               updateiACommand:=true                           cS:=SNS
            endpar                                            sC30:=1
         endif                                               if mC10=144 then
      endif                                                     par
   else                                                           mC10:=1
      par                                                         cD:=0
         iA:=iA-manualD                                        endpar
         updateiACommand:=false                              else
      endpar                                                   mC10:=mC10+1
   endif                                                     endif
rule r_safetycheck=                                       ...
par                                                    endpar
   cS:=DLVR                                        rule r_ceasing= .....
   if comD=0 then                                 main rule r_Main =
      dD:= 0                                          switch btn
   else                                                 case ON:r_autoperating[]
      if (comD+cD)>mDD then                             case MANUAL: r_manualdelivering[]
         dD:=mDD-cD        -                            case OFF:r_ceasing[]
      else                                           endswitch
      if (comD+cD)<mDD then//No equality          default init s0:
         if (comD<=mSD)then                           function sC30=1
            dD:=comD                                  function mC10=1
         else                                         function cS=SNS
            dD:=mSD                                    function spn=false
         endif                                        function iA=100
      endif                                           function cD=0
   .....                                              function updateiACommand=false
```

Code 1. The AsmetaL ground model for IPCS

Executing the testing and running activities are also restricted by time (30 s and 10 min). This is carried out by guards in the r_autoperating rule. As there is no tool to deal with time within the ASMETA framework, we treat time in an abstract manner. To achieve this, we use the controlled function sC30 to represent the number of 30 s cycles in 10 min. The maximum value for this function is 20. As the controller performs the running activity every 10 min and the testing activity every 30 s (but running and testing can not take place at the same time), one of these 20 cycles is for running and the other cycles are for testing. During the running activity, the controller sets the cumulative dose cD to 0 every 24 h. We use the controlled function mC10 to represent the number of 10 min cycles in 24 h (its maximum value is 144). When this function reaches 144 and the sC30 function reaches 20, then the controller will set the cumulative dose to 0. Furthermore, we deal with increasing these functions in an abstract manner via the boolean monitored function pas(30). This means, when the pas(30)=true, some function should be increased, and at the same time, some activity should be performed. For example, if sC30=20 and 30 s has passed since the last update of sC30 to 20, then the running activity must be started by changing cS into SNS, sC30 becomes 1, and at the same time mC10 is checked. If it has reached 144, it is set to 1, otherwise it is increased to the next value. If 30 s has passed since the last update of sC30 to a value within 1–19, then the testing activity must be performed and sC30 is increased to the next value.

5.2　Validating the AsmetaL Model

This stage attempts to validate the AsmetaL model by running particular Avalla scenarios, and obtaining a fail/success outcome. The scenario describes the identifiable interactions between the system and its environment to represent informal functional requirements. In the IPCS, the interactions are represented by the current glucose value and the delivered dose. We identify 14 scenarios that correspond to the delivered dose quantity requirements. From these scenarios, we only discuss the scenario that has a fail verdict (see Code 2). Code 2 is the scenario that is written in Avalla as input to the AsmetaV tool. This scenario corresponds to the following requirements: if the cumulative dose does not exceed the maximum daily dose, and the computed dose itself is less than or equal to the maximum single dose, then the delivered dose is equal to the computed dose.

```
//setting the initial 250 states       check spn=false;
set btn:=ON;                            set btn:=ON;
set valS:=22;                           step
step                                    check cS=SNS;
check cR=22 and cS=ANLSCAL;             set btn:=ON;
step until cS=TST;                      set valS:=34;
check cD=22;                            step
set btn:=ON;                            check cR=34 and cS=ANLSCAL;
set pas(30):=true;                      step
set fl:=false;                          check comD=3 and comD+cD<=25
set rsv:=PRS;                           and comD<=mSD;
set ndl:=PRS;                           step
step until sC30=20;                     check dD=comD;
```

Code 2. The scenario that has a fail verdict

The scenario in Code 2 can be described as follows: the system is operating in automatic mode, the current glucose value is 34, the previous glucose value from 10 min earlier is 22, the cumulative dose is equal to 22, there is no suspension situation, the computed dose is 3 units, and the requirement that must be checked is: the delivered dose should be equal to the computed dose.

The simulation of the scenario in Code 2 is illustrated in Fig. 2. In this figure, we use the following abbreviations: vdct (verdict), succ (succeed). The comD and dD functions represent the computed dose and the delivered dose, respectively. The simulation shows that we obtain the succ verdict for: the first received glucose value (22), the cumulative dose, no suspension, the second received glucose value (34), the sum of the computed dose and the cumulative dose equals the maximum daily dose (25), and the computed dose is less than the maximum single dose (4), while a fail verdict is obtained at state 283, due to missing the equality operator in the safety condition on the computed dose before delivering it (see r_safetycheck rule in Code 1). This condition checks whether the summation of the computed dose plus the cumulative dose is greater or less than the maximum daily dose, but it does not checks the equality situation $((comD(3)+cD(22))=mDD(25))$. Therefore, the delivered dose is not calculated and we obtained a fail verdict. Thus, we have shown that ignoring the equality testing in the [22] specification may lead to a serious issue in the IPCS.

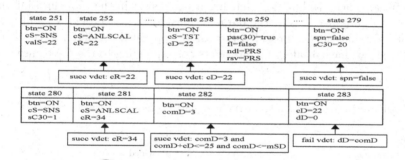

Fig. 2. Simulation of the scenario shown in Code 2

5.3   Eliciting Safety Requirements via STPA

Next we employ the STPA technique for eliciting the safety requirements of the IPCS, and it consists of the following steps:

- Indicating the main expected accidents, e.g. damage to the patient's eyes or kidneys if the required insulin dose is not taken.
- Identifying the possible hazards that can lead to the previous accidents, such as the user's unawareness of warning or failure conditions.
- Determining the actions issued by the controller that can lead to hazards in the previous step, such as: run the alarm, update the available insulin, deliver the dose.

- Identifying the process model for the controller. We define this as a set of monitored and controlled functions of the AsmetaL model. Each member of this set consists of a function name and its values, e.g., the process model that affects the run warning alarm action is: {btn=(ON, OFF, MANUAL), spn=(true, false), cR=($\geqslant$sMin, <sMin), cS=(SNS, ANLSCAL, SFTCK, DLVR), nP=(0, 1, 2, 3, 4), iA=(>4×mSD, $\leqslant$4×mSD), sCC=(>mDD, $\leqslant$mDD)}. Where the meaning of cR is the current reading of glucose, sMin is the minimum safe limit (6), mDD is the maximum daily dose, sCC is the summation of the computed and cumulative doses, and nP is the number of pulses issued by the controller to deliver the insulin.
- Evaluating the combination of function values for each control action under four contexts: 'provided', 'provided too early', 'provided too late' and 'not provided'. The evaluation process is performed through asking a question to an expert of the following form: if the controller receives a certain combination of function values, will (provide, provide too early/too late, not provide) the action in the next state by the controller lead to a hazard? The results of the evaluation are documented in Table 1. This Table is only for the run warning alarm. The no/fun answer represents no actual hazard will happen, but there is a flaw with the system function, e.g. it is not hazardous if the alarm action is provided earlier than realizing that the current glucose is less than the minimum safe limit.
- Translate each combination that has a yes answer in the table into informal safety requirements using the phrases "must" (for 'not provided') and "must not" (for 'provided', 'provided too early', 'provided too late'. According to Table 1, we have 6 safety requirements corresponding to the 6 yes answers.

Table 1. The context table for the run alarm action with warning conditions

| Process model | | | | | | | Hazardous action? | | | |
btn	spn	cR	cS	nP	iA	sCC	Provided	Provided too early	Provided too late	Not provided
ON	false	any	DLVR	=0	$\leqslant$4mSD	any	no	no/fun	yes	yes
ON	false	any	DLVR	>0 and $\leqslant$4	$\leqslant$4mSD	any	no/fun	no/fun	no/fun	no
ON	false	any	DLVR	=0	>4mSD	any	no/fun	no/fun	no/fun	no
ON	false	any	SNS	any	any	any	no/fun	no/fun	no/fun	no
ON	false	any	SFTCK	any	any	$\leqslant$mDD	no/fun	no/fun	no/fun	no
ON	false	any	SFTCK	any	any	>mDD	no	no/fun	yes	yes
ON	false	<sMin	ANLSCAL	any	any	any	no	no/fun	yes	yes
ON	false	$\geqslant$sMin	ANLSCAL	any	any	any	no/fun	no/fun	no/fun	no
ON	true	any	any	any	any	any	no/fun	no/fun	no/fun	no
MANUAL	any	any	any	any	any	any	no/fun	no/fun	no/fun	no
OFF	any	any	any	any	any	any	no/fun	no/fun	no/fun	no

5.4   Formalizing the STPA Safety Requirements

Here we formalize the elicited requirements. The formalization steps are:

- Determine the combination of the function values that have yes answers in the 'not provided' condition only. The purposes for this are: to ensure that the action is provided with these combinations, and to avoid repetition, e.g. the combination that has a yes answer when the action is 'not provided' is the same as that which has a yes answer when the action is 'provided too late'. Regarding Table 1, the combinations that have been identified are: (1) btn=ON, spn=false, cS=DLVR, nP=0, and iA$\leqslant$4mSD. (2) btn=ON, spn=false, cS=SFTCK, and sCC>mDD. (3) btn=ON, spn=false, cS=ANLSCAL, and cR<sMin.
- Formulate these combinations, using the following formula:

$$\Box((com_{i1} \vee com_{i2} \vee ...com_{in}) \leftrightarrow \bigcirc(CA_i)) \tag{1}$$

Where: CA_i is the ith control action, com_{in} is the nth combination that relates to the ith action, and the formula informally means that the control action is always provided in the next state, if and only if one of the determined combination occurs. The $\leftrightarrow$ operator puts a strong condition on providing the action, i.e. the action will not be provided with another combination or later/earlier than satisfying the determined combination. Furthermore, employing the $\leftrightarrow$ and $\vee$ operators helps to reduce the number of properties to be verified (6 safety requirements are reduced to only 1).
- Rewriting the formulated requirements into ones accepted by the AsmetaSMV tool via its propositional and future-time connectives.

5.5   Verifying the STPA Safety Requirements

This stage is intended to verify the resultant formulated requirements against the AsmetaL model, to improve it. As we here use the AsmetaSMV tool, we rewrite the resultant formulated requirements into other ones accepted by this tool. We will present only the verification results from the AsmetaSMV tool, for the properties that are not met, as follows:

- LTLSPEC   g(((**btn=ON and spn=false and cS=dlvr and nP=0 and iA<=4mSD**) or (btn=ON and spn=false and cS=SFTCK and sCC>mDD) or (btn=ON and spn=false and cS=ANLSCAL and cR<sMin)) iff x(alarmCommand=true)). This property informally means that the warning run alarm action is always provided in the next state if and only if one of the warning combinations occurs. The bold font for the first combination in this property indicates that this combination is the reason for the unsatisfied property. In Fig. 3 we show the failing trace for providing the run alarm action when the available insulin quantity is equal or less than 4 maximum single

doses. The new abbreviation that we use in this figure is: pR (previous glucose reading). From state 1.1, onwards the system is operating under the automatic mode shown by the value ON. At state 1.1, there is no alarm action (alarmcommand=false) and the insulin quantity is 18 (iA=18). At state 1.2 the controller receives the current glucose value (cR=22) from the sensor (valS=22), and it computes the dose at state 1.3 (comD=(22(cR)-14(pR))/4(mSD)). Delivering the dose starts at state 1.4, and at state 1.5 it finishes and the available insulin becomes 16 which is equal to (4×(maxSingleDose=4)). The loop starts at state 1.6 showing that the run alarm action is not provided (alarmCommand=false), when iA=16. This happens because the initial version of the AsmetaL model relies on the specification in [22], which does not consider running the alarm at cautionary situations for the available insulin quantity.

– LTLSPEC g((btn=MANUAL and iA<=100 and mD!=0) iff x (updateiACommand=true)). Where the mD is the manual dose, and the property informally means that the action of updating the available insulin according to the manual dose is always provided in the next state, if and only if the system works under the manual mode, the available insulin is less than or equal the capacity (100 units), and there is a manual dose. In Fig. 4 we provide a failing trace for providing the update available insulin action when the system is in manual mode. From state 1.1 onwards, the system is in the manual mode via the value MANUAL. At state 1.1, the insulin quantity is 10 (iA=10), the manual dose is 6, and updating the available insulin action is not provided (updateiACommand=false). At state 1.2, the action is provided and has been executed at state 1.3 through changing the value of iA to 4. The loop starts at state 1.3 showing that insulin quantity is not updated, when the iA=4 and the mD=5. The loop arises from a lack of a constraint, in the [22] specification, on the available insulin before delivering the manual dose (see r_manualdelivering rule in Code 1). This constraint must check if the available insulin is equal or greater than the maximum manual dose (5) before delivering it[3].

State	1.1	1.2	1.3	1.4	1.5	1.6	1.7
btn	ON	ON	ON	ON	ON	ON	ON
cS	SNS	ANLSCAL	SFTCK	DLVR	DLVR	TST	TST
valS	22	22	22	22	22	22	22
iA	18	18	18	17	16	16	16
cD	3	3	3	3	5	5	5
cR	14	22	22	22	22	22	22
pR	14	14	14	14	14	22	22
nP	0	0	2	1	0	0	0
comD	0	0	2	2	2	0	0
dD	0	0	0	2	2	0	0
alarmCommand	false	false	false	false	false	false	false

Fig. 3. Failing trace for the running alarm action when the available insulin is equal to the 4 maximum single doses

---

[3] All the modified specifications are available online at http://cgi.csc.liv.ac.uk/~hsfalsha/Insulin_Pump_Correct_Version.txt.

State	1.1	1.2	1.3	1.4	1.5
btn	MANUAL	MANUAL	MANUAL	MANUAL	MANUAL
iA	10	10	4	4	4
mD	6	6	5	5	5
updateiACommand	false	true	false	true	false

Fig. 4. Failing trace for updating the available insulin action when the manual dose is greater than the available insulin

6 Evaluation

In this section, we present two comparisons. The first is comparing results of the development procedure for the IPCS, in [23] with ours. The second is between the formalization process for the STPA requirements of [3] and ours.

With regard to the development methodology for IPCS, we can compare our methodology's results with the results in [23]. Our methodology starts with specifying the system via AsmetaL, while [23] employs the Z language for specification. Our specification tries to represent the timing aspects for the system via using an abstract time representation, while the [23] specification uses the input variable clock? to obtain the current time, but it does not specify how the implementation of RUN and TEST schemas responds to this variable. In our methodology, we use the validation and verification tools to develop a safe system, whereas [23] utilizes the safety arguments method for performing manual verification. This method starts with an unsafe state, then all paths in the system code must be proven to be contradictory to this state. This method does not address the unsafe conditions determined by our methodology, which includes: (1) The patient does not take the automatic dose when the sum of the computed dose and the cumulative dose equals the maximum daily dose. (2) The system can deliver a manual dose even if it exceeds the available insulin. (3) The system does not give an alarm if the insulin reservoir is less than the sum of 4 maximum single doses. We believe that these unsafe conditions are not highlighted by other methods.

Regarding the formalization process for the STPA requirements, in [3] four types of safety requirements have been elicited and formalized, which are:

- The control action must always be provided at the next state (without being too early or too late) when a combination occurs. It has been formalized as:

$$\Box (Com_{ij} \rightarrow \bigcirc (CA_i)) \tag{2}$$

  Where: CA_i is the ith control action, and Com_{ij} is the jth combination that relates to the ith action. Such formula is formulated for each combination presented in a line of context table with a yes answer in the 'not provided' column.
- The control action must always be provided no later than a certain combination occurrence. This requirement is elicited according to the combination line with a yes answer in the 'provided too late' column of the context table.

The corresponding safety property is formulated as:

$$\Box((Com_{ij} \rightarrow CA_i) \wedge \neg(Com_{ij} \ U \ CA_i)) \tag{3}$$

The authors of [3] claim that this formalization of the requirement "the software controller should always (...) not provide a control action CA_i too late while the occurrences of the critical set of combinations has become previously true in the execution path." However, a simple semantic analysis does not support their claim. Indeed, the right hand side of conjunction ensures that either (1) no action occurred, or (2) an action should be occurred, such that at some point before that a combination should not hold, which is different from the statement of the claim.

– The control action must always be provided not earlier than the occurrence of a combination. This requirement is elicited according to the combination line with a **yes** answer in the 'provided too early' column of the context table. Regarding safety requirement is formulated as:

$$\Box((CA_i \rightarrow Com_{ij}) \wedge \neg(CA_i \ U \ Com_{ij})) \tag{4}$$

The authors of [3] claim that this formalization of the requirement "a software controller should always (...) not provide control action CA_i before the occurrence of critical combinations set (...) still not become true in the execution path and that it well provides the CA_i when the combination of (...) holds." Now again, a simple semantic analysis does not support their claim. Furthermore, the left hand side of conjunction can not be ensured when the control action emerges from more than one combination.

– The control action must always not be provided when a combination occurs. It has been formalized in the following form:

$$\Box(Com_{ij} \rightarrow \neg CA_i) \tag{5}$$

This formalization is formulated for each combination line with a **yes** answer in the 'provided' column of the context table.

In our approach all these requirements are captured by a single formula (1): $\Box((com_{i1} \vee com_{i2} \vee ...com_{in}) \leftrightarrow \bigcirc(CA_i))$. In this formula, the if and only if, always, and or operators strict providing the control action only with the determined combination of the function values, not with another one. Furthermore, the biconditional (if and only if) operator ensures that when one of the determined combinations is satisfied then the control action is provided in the next state (not too late), and when the control action is provided, then one of the determined combinations must be satisfied at the previous state (the action is not provided earlier than satisfying the combination).

7   Related Work

Here, we discuss related work that uses hazard analysis techniques, formal methods, or both for analysing safety-critical systems. In [25], an integrated approach for combining the results of Fault Tree Analysis (FTA) and Failure Mode and Effects Analysis (FMEA) techniques into the requirements specification. The FTA results are the identification of combinations of component failures, while the FMEA identifies the failure modes and the minor errors that lead to component failure. That paper uses statecharts to bridge the semantics gap between the results of safety analysis and software requirements. In [21], a method for formalizing and verifying the safety requirements elicited by the FTA technique, is presented.

The safety analysis techniques that have been used for eliciting safety requirements in these papers rely mainly on component failure, and only partially on unintended interactions between system's components. Leveson [19] presents the STPA technique to identify the safety requirements for inadequate control actions that affect whole system functions and its components' behavior. According to STPA, the accidents do not simply arise from sequences of component failures, rather, they arise when the safety constraints related to the functional interactions among system components are not enforced. In [1,3] the authors propose a software safety verification methodology based on the STPA technique to elicit the safety requirements and verify them to identify software risks. First, they elicit and formalize the STPA requirements (with respect to providing and not providing actions) into LTL properties and they verify them based on an SMV manual constructed model. Next they formalize the STPA requirements (with respect to providing actions too early and too late), and they build a safe behavior model of a software controller constrained by the STPA results with UML statechart, as well as they provide an algorithm to transform the safe model into an input model of the NuSMV model checker. However, the formalization process does not reflect the requirements for too early/late actions. In our work, we reformulate the four STPA requirements ('provide', 'provide too early', 'provide too late', and 'not provide') into one formula capturing these requirements, and we exploit ASMs to model the functional behavior of the system and we do not constrained the ASM model by STPA results. We choose ASM method as it supports several characteristics, including: flexibility in modelling any algorithm at an appropriate level of abstraction, and feasibility of being used in an automatic and tool supported manner during the system development process. Furthermore, ASMs have simple and well-defined formal semantics [11].

The advantages of using formal methods for developing safety-critical systems have been shown in [14]. In [26] a Structured Object-Oriented Formal Language (SOFL) is adopted to build a formal specification for the IPCS. That paper shows that the SOFL provides an effective means to allow the developer to take a gradual process to build a formal specification for the system, but it does not show how to verify or validate the resulted specifications. In [16], timed automata is chosen to model the railyard interlocking system, and UPPAAL model checker is used to verify the safety properties of that system. On one hand, UPPAAL, unlike ASM, lacks structuring mechanism to achieve abstraction [20], and on the other hand, UPPAAL does not fully support CTL model checking [10]. In [5,8], it is shown how the ASM method serves in supporting the design, validation, and verification activities within the ASMETA framework. However, in this work the verification of safety requirements is guided only by the modeller experience, not by a safety analysis technique. Our approach utilizes the same framework (ASMETA) for developing systems, but we employ the STPA procedure for deriving the safety requirements.

8 Conclusion and Future Work

In this paper, we combine the ASM method and STPA technique in a development methodology. Our methodology shows how functional requirements validation and STPA requirements verification help us to modify the ASM specification. We have demonstrated how to capture the four STPA requirements adequately via using disjunction and if and only if operators in our formalization for the requirements. The next step will be formalizing and generalizing the STPA requirements in terms of Allen's interval algebra [4].

We have shown how the timing aspects for the IPCS have been modelled in an abstract manner. We modelled the start point of the controller activities via using two controlled functions mC10 and sC30, and we modelled the time passing since last activity by a boolean monitored function pas. This abstract handling specifies when the activity starts but it ignores dealing with durative action, while a certain activity is performed, e.g. run alarm for 10 s during running activity. In the future, we hope to use improved abstractions to deal with timing aspects.

In the specification analysis presented here, we did not consider the static analysis for the completeness and consistency properties. In the future work, we are going to address this by applying the AsmetaMA tool [7] to the specification.

To further our methodology we intend to design an algorithm to automate the part of eliciting STPA requirements. Although an automatic tool has been proposed to achieve this [2], it seems only to work for up to 6 variables in a process model for the software controller. Hence, we plan to make the integration between ASM and STPA automatic, without the need for user input.

Acknowledgments. We gratefully acknowledge Dr. Paolo Arcaini for his advice on ASMETA framework.

References

1. Abdulkhaleq, A., Wagner, S.: Integrated safety analysis using systems-theoretic process analysis and software model checking. In: Koornneef, F., van Gulijk, C. (eds.) SAFECOMP 2015. LNCS, vol. 9337, pp. 121–134. Springer, Cham (2015). https://doi.org/10.1007/978-3-319-24255-2_10
2. Abdulkhaleq, A., Wagner, S.: XSTAMPP: an extensible STAMP platform as tool support for safety engineering. In: 2015 STAMP Workshop. MIT, Boston. Stuttgart University (2015)

3. Abdulkhaleq, A., Wagner, S.: A systematic and semi-automatic safety-based test case generation approach based on systems-theoretic process analysis. arXiv preprint arXiv:1612.03103 (2016)
4. Allen, J.F.: Maintaining knowledge about temporal intervals. Commun. ACM **26**(11), 832–843 (1983)
5. Arcaini, P., Bonfanti, S., Gargantini, A., Mashkoor, A., Riccobene, E.: Formal validation and verification of a medical software critical component. In: 2015 ACM/IEEE International Conference on Formal Methods and Models for Codesign (MEMOCODE), pp. 80–89. IEEE (2015)
6. Arcaini, P., Gargantini, A., Riccobene, E.: AsmetaSMV: a way to link high-level ASM models to low-level NuSMV specifications. In: Frappier, M., Glässer, U., Khurshid, S., Laleau, R., Reeves, S. (eds.) ABZ 2010. LNCS, vol. 5977, pp. 61–74. Springer, Heidelberg (2010). https://doi.org/10.1007/978-3-642-11811-1_6
7. Arcaini, P., Gargantini, A., Riccobene, E.: Automatic review of abstract state machines by meta-property verification. In: NASA Formal Methods Symposium, pp. 4–13. NASA (2010)
8. Arcaini, P., Gargantini, A., Riccobene, E.: Modeling and analyzing using ASMs: the landing gear system case study. In: Boniol, F., Wiels, V., Ait Ameur, Y., Schewe, K.-D. (eds.) ABZ 2014. CCIS, vol. 433, pp. 36–51. Springer, Cham (2014). https://doi.org/10.1007/978-3-319-07512-9_3
9. Arcaini, P., Gargantini, A., Riccobene, E., Scandurra, P.: A model-driven process for engineering a toolset for a formal method. Softw. Pract. Exp. **41**(2), 155–166 (2011)
10. Behrmann, G., David, A., Larsen, K.G.: A tutorial on UPPAAL. In: Bernardo, M., Corradini, F. (eds.) SFM-RT 2004. LNCS, vol. 3185, pp. 200–236. Springer, Heidelberg (2004). https://doi.org/10.1007/978-3-540-30080-9_7
11. Börger, E., Stärk, R.: Abstract State Machines: A Method for High-Level System Design and Analysis. Springer, Heidelberg (2003). https://doi.org/10.1007/978-3-642-18216-7
12. Carioni, A., Gargantini, A., Riccobene, E., Scandurra, P.: A scenario-based validation language for ASMs. In: Börger, E., Butler, M., Bowen, J.P., Boca, P. (eds.) ABZ 2008. LNCS, vol. 5238, pp. 71–84. Springer, Heidelberg (2008). https://doi.org/10.1007/978-3-540-87603-8_7
13. Gargantini, A., Riccobene, E., Scandurra, P.: A metamodel-based language and a simulation engine for abstract state machines. J. UCS **14**(12), 1949–1983 (2008)
14. Gerhart, S., Craigen, D., Ralston, T.: Experience with formal methods in critical systems. IEEE Softw. **11**(1), 21–28 (1994)
15. Gurevich, Y.: Evolving algebras 1993: Lipari guide. In: Börger, E. (ed.) Specification and Validation Methods, pp. 9–36. Oxford University Press, Inc. (1995)
16. Khan, U., Ahmad, J., Saeed, T., Mirza, S.H.: On the real time modeling of interlocking system of passenger lines of Rawalpindi Cantt train station. Complex Adapt. Syst. Model. **4**(1), 17 (2016)
17. Leveson, N.: A new accident model for engineering safer systems. Saf. Sci. **42**(4), 237–270 (2004)
18. Leveson, N., Thomas, J.: An STPA Primer, Cambridge (2013)
19. Leveson, N.G.: A new approach to hazard analysis for complex systems. In: International Conference of the System Safety Society (2003)
20. Ouimet, M., Berteau, G., Lundqvist, K.: Modeling an electronic throttle controller using the timed abstract state machine language and toolset. In: Kühne, T. (ed.) MODELS 2006. LNCS, vol. 4364, pp. 32–41. Springer, Heidelberg (2007). https://doi.org/10.1007/978-3-540-69489-2_5

21. Santiago, I.B., Faure, J.M.: From fault tree analysis to model checking of logic controllers. IFAC Proc. **38**(1), 86–91 (2005)
22. Sommerville, I.: Insulin Pump – Z schemas. http://iansommerville.com/software-engineering-book/files/2014/07/Insulin-Pump-Z-schemas.pdf
23. Sommerville, I.: Software Engineering, 9th edn. Addison Wesley, Boston (2010)
24. Thomas, J.: Extending and Automating a Systems-Theoretic Hazard Analysis for Requirements Generation and Analysis. Ph.D. thesis, Massachusetts Institute of Technology (2013)
25. Troubitsyna, E.: Elicitation and Specification of Safety Requirements. In: Third International Conference on Systems (ICONS 2008), pp. 202–207. IEEE (2008)
26. Wang, J., Liu, S., Qi, Y., Hou, D.: Developing an insulin pump system using the SOFL method. In: 14th Asia-Pacific Software Engineering Conference (APSEC 2007), pp. 334–341. IEEE (2007)

From Scenarios to Timed Automata

Neda Saeedloei[1][(✉)] and Feliks Kluźniak[2]

[1] Southern Illinois University, Carbondale, USA
neda@cs.siu.edu
[2] Logic Blox, Atlanta, USA
feliks.kluzniak@logicblox.com

Abstract. We describe a new method of synthesizing a formal model for real-time systems from scenarios. Scenarios, formally defined as *Timed Event Sequences*, together with *mode graphs* are used to describe behaviors of real-time systems. Given a set of Timed Event Sequences and a mode graph, our synthesis method constructs a *minimal, acyclic*, timed automaton that models the specified aspects of the system. We formalize criteria that a set of scenarios must satisfy in order to make it feasible to generate such an automaton.

Keywords: Formal models · Scenarios · Timed automata

1 Introduction

Model-based design has been used as an effective approach to the process of designing, analysis, and verification of complex systems. The process can greatly benefit from building a formal model, i.e., one that is expressed in a formal language with well-defined semantics. An important advantage of modeling is that one obtains insight into how a physical realisation of the system would behave in the real world.

A formal model can be used as a high-level "prototype": it can be experimented with and iteratively improved. (The cost of doing so is significantly lower than that of experimenting with and improving a real implementation of the system.) Depending on how the model is constructed, such experimentation usually takes the form of either formally deriving logical conclusions, or of automatic simulation. The overall purpose is to obtain a validated model, i.e., one whose "behavior" does indeed comply with the desired behavior of the modeled system. The insight mentioned in the preceding paragraph arises out of the necessity of formulating very clear criteria for (or examples of) desirable and undesirable behaviors.

While the use of model-based design is promising and rapidly growing, a major problem is the lack of good formal requirements, which are the starting point in building a model. System requirements are often incomplete, ambiguous

---

The preliminary research was carried out while the first author was at the University of Minnesota, Duluth.

S. Cavalheiro and J. Fiadeiro (Eds.): SBMF 2017, LNCS 10623, pp. 33–51, 2017.
https://doi.org/10.1007/978-3-319-70848-5_4

or very low level. Incomplete requirements cannot be used for building realistic systems, as some parameters and functionalities are missing and must be guessed. Real-time systems, in particular, are often safety-critical systems, and unspecified behaviors and missing cases cannot be tolerated. Ambiguous requirements must be made more precise before the formal model is complete (and the act of analysing and attempting to model ambiguous requirements can be very helpful in detecting the ambiguities). Finally, very low level requirements are difficult to understand and reason about, so tend to be less useful for modeling purposes. It is exactly the unavailability of satisfactory requirements specifications that makes modeling such an important step in the process of constructing a system.

In this paper we focus on two important questions: (1) how to express requirements, and (2) how to obtain formal models of real-time systems from requirements. Our formal models will take the form of timed automata [1].

We propose a new method for synthesizing a timed automaton model of a real-time system from *scenarios*. A scenario can be viewed as a description of a set of *partial* behaviors of a real-time system during a time interval: it describes not only the events that occur in the system, but also the timing relations among the events. All behaviors "allowed" by a particular scenario must satisfy the same time constraints.

The events in a scenario include both the system's internal events and its interactions with users or the environment. A set of scenarios can capture the important aspects of the required system behaviors, and be the starting point for constructing a formal model of the system.

We introduce *Timed Event Sequences (TES)*[1] to describe scenarios formally, precisely, and at a high level of abstraction. We also use *mode graphs* (others have called them "mode diagrams" [8]) to specify the events that are possible at various points in the history of the system. Our scenarios, together with mode graphs, can be viewed as high level descriptions of real-time systems. As such, they are easy to understand and use by practitioners who utilise scenarios to elicit system requirements. The other alternative would be to build timed automata directly. But people who provide information about the requirements will not always be comfortable with timed automata: for some of them mode graphs and scenarios might be easier to handle (this observation seems to have motivated different work by others [8]).

Our method constructs a timed automaton from a set of TES and a mode graph. The constructed automaton is an *acyclic*[2] automaton with a minimum number of locations, which captures all those behaviors of the system that are described by the set of TES. All the possible runs of the constructed timed automaton are possible behaviors of the system in the sense of being runs of the mode graph. The principal value of the constructed automaton is that it caters for the time constraints introduced in the scenarios.

---

[1] We will use the abbreviation for both the singular and the plural form of the term.

[2] The acyclicity of our automaton does not prevent it from being used as a timed automaton with infinite runs, as will be explained in Sect. 6.

Our goal of synthesizing timed automata with a minimal number of locations is motivated by the fact that the "state explosion problem" has been a major challenge in model checking concurrent systems [5].

We construct *acyclic* timed automata, because the conventional formalism of timed automata does not allow inclusion of variables other than clocks. By allowing cycles the formalism would have to be extended in order to express a limit on the number of iterations (e.g., the number of attempts to enter a PIN).

From a bird's eye perspective, our approach can be described as follows:

1. A mode graph $\mathcal{M}$ defines the universe $B_{\mathcal{M}}$ of all the possible behaviors of the system: these are, roughly, the runs of $\mathcal{M}$ when treated as a finite automaton.
2. A scenario A imposes timing constraints on certain kinds of concrete behaviors, thus defining $Allowed(A) \subset B_{\mathcal{M}}$: the set of those possible behaviors that are allowed by A.
3. Two scenarios, A and B, together define the set of allowed behaviors as $Allowed(A) \cap Allowed(B)$.
4. The constructed timed automaton exhibits behaviors that are allowed by all the scenarios and are described by some of them. If the set of exhibited behaviors is smaller than expected, then either the constraints in some scenarios are too strict, or certain kinds of behaviors have not yet been specified. The activity of specifying a system must of necessity be iterative: that is why the automaton must be constructed automatically.

2   Timed Automata

We now present a brief overview of timed automata [1].

For a set C of clock variables, the set $\Phi(C)$ includes *clock constraints* of the form $c \sim a$, where $\sim \in \{\leq, \geq, <, >, =\}$, $c \in C$, and a is a constant in the set of rational numbers, $\mathbb{Q}$.

A *timed automaton* is a tuple $\mathcal{A} = \langle E, Q, Q_0, Q_f, C, R \rangle$, where

- E is a finite alphabet;
- Q is the (*finite*) set of locations;
- $Q_0 \subset Q$ is the set of initial locations;
- $Q_f \subseteq Q$ is the set of final locations;
- C is a finite set of *clock* variables;[3]
- $R \subseteq Q \times Q \times E \times 2^C \times 2^{\Phi(C)}$ is the set of transitions of the form $(q, q', e, \lambda, \phi)$, where the set $\lambda \subseteq C$ is the set of clocks to be reset with this transition, and ϕ is a set of clock constraints over C.

A time sequence $\tau = \tau_1 \tau_2 \ldots$ is an infinite sequence of (time) values $\tau_i \in \mathbb{R}^{\geq 0}$, satisfying two requirements:

- *Monotonicity*: τ increases strictly monotonically, i.e., $\tau_i < \tau_{i+1}$ for all $i \geq 1$.
- *Progress*: For every $t \in \mathbb{R}^{\geq 0}$, there is some $i \geq 1$ such that $\tau_i > t$.

---

[3] We will follow the usual convention and use "clocks" instead of "clock variables".

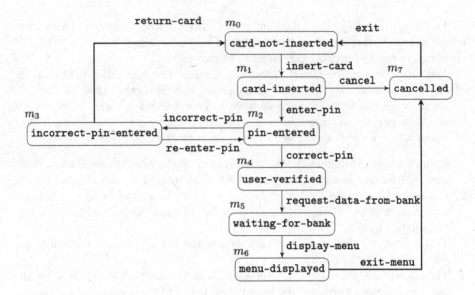

Fig. 1. A mode graph corresponding to the ATM

A *timed word* over an alphabet E is a pair (σ, τ) where $\sigma = \sigma_1 \sigma_2 ...$ is an infinite word over E and τ is a time sequence.

A *clock interpretation* for a set C of clocks assigns a value in $\mathbb{R}^{\geq 0}$ to each clock; that is, it is a mapping from C to $\mathbb{R}^{\geq 0}$. We say that a clock interpretation ν for C satisfies a set of clock constraints ϕ over C iff every clock constraint in ϕ evaluates to true after replacing each clock variable c with $\nu(c)$.

For $\tau \in \mathbb{R}, \nu + \tau$ denotes the clock interpretation which maps every clock c to the value $\nu(c) + \tau$. For $Y \subseteq C$, $[Y \mapsto \tau]\nu$ denotes the clock interpretation for C which assigns τ to each $c \in Y$, and agrees with ν over the rest of the clocks.

A run ρ of $\mathcal{A}$ over a timed word (σ, τ) is an infinite sequence of the form

$$\rho : \langle q_0, \nu_0 \rangle \xrightarrow[\tau_1]{\sigma_1} \langle q_1, \nu_1 \rangle \xrightarrow[\tau_2]{\sigma_2} \langle q_2, \nu_2 \rangle \xrightarrow[\tau_3]{\sigma_3} \cdots$$

with $q_i \in Q$ and $\nu_i \in [C \mapsto \mathbb{R}^{\geq 0}]$, for all $i \geq 0$, satisfying two requirements:

- $q_0 \in Q_0$, and $\nu_0(c) = 0$ for all clocks $c \in C$;
- for every $i \geq 1$ there is a transition in R of the form $(q_{i-1}, q_i, \sigma_i, \lambda_i, \phi_i)$, such that $(\nu_{i-1} + \tau_i - \tau_{i-1})$ satisfies ϕ_i, and ν_i equals $[\lambda_i \mapsto 0](\nu_{i-1} + \tau_i - \tau_{i-1})$.

3   Specifying Scenarios

We will now describe our representation of scenarios. We will use the initial behavior of an Automatic Teller Machine (ATM) to illustrate some terms and definitions.

Intuitively, a scenario describes a set of partial behaviors of a system during a time interval. We use mode graphs to describe *all* the possible behaviors of a system. A mode graph (cf. [8]) is a deterministic state machine that describes the high level behavior of a system. Modes can be viewed as visible states of a system. A transition is triggered by an event allowable in the current mode and brings the system to a new mode. For example, Fig. 1 shows the mode graph that outlines the initial behavior of the ATM controller and a potential customer (user). The transition from *pin-entered* to *user-verified* is triggered by a *correct-pin* event.

Scenarios are used to put various constraints on certain behaviors of a system. Examples of constraints include time constraints on certain events or constraints on the number of occurences of some events, e.g., a limit on the number of times a PIN can be re-entered.

We use Timed Event Sequences to formally represent scenarios. A Timed Event Sequence (formally defined in Sect. 4) contains:

- The initial and the final mode of the specified scenario.
- A sequence of timed events. We assume each event occurs at some time w, shown by the *wall clock* when the event occurs. An event may be augmented with a set of time annotations that impose restrictions on relations between the time of the event and the times of some earlier events in the scenario.

Figure 2 shows two scenarios, which specify the ATM's initial behavior. Scenario 1 describes behaviors in which the user enters an incorrect PIN, and then the correct PIN in the second attempt. It includes a sequence of seven timed events, along with the initial and the final modes. Initially the mode of the system is m_0 (*card-not-inserted*). After inserting the card at time t_0, the user enters the PIN at time $w > t_0$, such that the time difference between the two events, i.e., $w - t_0$ is within $[5, 60]$ seconds. Upon receiving the PIN, the ATM notifies the user that the PIN was incorrect. The user then enters another PIN within $[5, 60]$ seconds since inserting the card. Once the user is verified (mode m_4), the system displays the menu within the next 5 seconds. The new mode at this point is m_6 (*menu-displayed*). Please note that t_j, where $0 \leq j \leq 7$, is used to denote the time of leaving mode m_j (most recently).

Scenario 2 describes behaviors in which the user enters the correct PIN on the first try. The time annotations are a subset of those in scenario 1.

It is easy to see that each of these scenarios allows an infinite number of slightly different behaviors: a scenario directly captures the salient features of a class of allowable behaviors.

4   A Formal Description of Mode Graphs and TES

Mode Graphs. A *mode graph* is a tuple $\mathcal{M} = (M, m_0, m_f, \Sigma, T)$, where M is a finite set of modes, m_0 is the initial mode, m_f is the final mode (which can be identical to m_0), Σ is a set of events, and $T : M \times \Sigma \rightarrow M$ is a transition function. The latter will be represented as a set of transitions, i.e., triples of the

```
card-not-inserted
(insert-card, {})
(enter-pin,{w − t₀ ≥ 5, w − t₀ ≤ 60})
(incorrect-pin, {})
(re-enter-pin,{w − t₀ ≥ 5, w − t₀ ≤ 60})
(correct-pin, {})
(request-data-from-bank, {})
(display-menu, {w − t₄ ≤ 5})
menu-displayed
```

```
card-not-inserted
(insert-card, {})
(enter-pin,{w − t₀ ≥ 5, w − t₀ ≤ 60})
(correct-pin, {})
(request-data-from-bank, {})
(display-menu, {w − t₄ ≤ 5})
menu-displayed
```

            Scenario 1   Scenario 2

Fig. 2. Two scenarios showing two alternative sets of initial behaviors of the ATM

form (m_i, e, m_j), where m_i and m_j, are modes in M, and e is an event in Σ. We assume events are unique in the mode graph: for an event $e \in \Sigma$, there is at most one transition in T that is labelled with e.[4]

A *run* r of $\mathcal{M}$ is a (possibly infinite) sequence of the form $r : s_1 \xrightarrow{e_1} s_2 \xrightarrow{e_2} s_3 \xrightarrow{e_3} \ldots$ (where $s_1 = m_0$ and $s_i \in M$), such that for every $i \geq 1$ there is a transition in T of the form (s_i, e_i, s_{i+1}). Any contiguous subsequence of a run is called a *partial run* (so a run is also a partial run).

We define $source(e) = m$, if $(m, e, n) \in T$, for any mode $n \in M$.

If m and n are modes in M, then m *dominates* n if and only if all paths from the initial mode to n pass through m [9]. We denote the *dominance relation* on M by $\succeq$: $m \succeq n$ iff m dominates n (we also say that n is dominated by m). We write $m \succ n$ to denote that $m \succeq n$ and $m \neq n$. ($\succeq$ is a partial order.)

We extend the definition of dominated modes to *dominated events*: an event e is *dominated* by mode m iff $m \succeq source(e)$. For example, in Fig. 1, *card-not-inserted, card-inserted, pin-entered, user-verified* and *waiting-for-bank* are all the dominating modes of *waiting-for-bank*. The event *display-menu* is dominated by all the modes that dominate *waiting-for-bank*.

Let $V = \{t_1, t_2, ..., t_n\}$ be a set of time variables, such that $|V| \geq |M|$.

To each mode m_i of M that appears in a scenario we assign $t_i \in V$, which is interpreted as the time of leaving m_i. If there is a cycle involving mode m_i, then t_i corresponds to the time of the *most recent* event occurrence at m_i *in that scenario* (since the most recent visit at m_0). For example, if a scenario for the mode graph of Fig. 1 describes an iteration between modes m_2 and m_3, then t_2 corresponds to the time of the most recent notification of an incorrect PIN in the scenario.

We use $\Phi(V)$ to denote the set of *time annotations* of the form $w − t_j \sim a$, where w is the time currently shown by the global wall clock, t_j is a time variable in V, $\sim \in \{\leq, \geq, <, >, =\}$, and a is a constant in the set of rational numbers.

Timed Event Sequences. Given a mode graph $\mathcal{M} = (M, m_0, m_f, \Sigma, T)$, a *Timed Event Sequence* ξ is a tuple of the form $\langle m^{initial}, \Psi, m^{final} \rangle$, where $m^{initial}$

---

[4] This is just a convenient convention, not a real restriction.

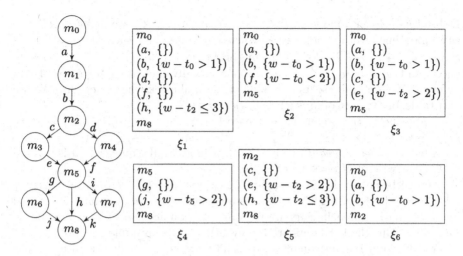

Fig. 3. A mode graph and a few TES

and m^{final} are in M, and Ψ is a *non-empty* sequence of timed events of the form (e_k, ϕ_k), $1 \le k \le n$, where $e_k \in \Sigma$, and $\phi_k \in 2^{\Phi(V)}$ is a set of time annotations associated with e_k. $m^{initial}$ and m^{final} are the first and last modes of ξ.

We define $initial\_mode(\xi) = m^{initial}$ and $final\_mode(\xi) = m^{final}$. We also define $events(\xi)$ to be the sequence $e_1 e_2 \ldots e_n$ of events in ξ.

Compatibility with Mode Graph. A TES $\xi = \langle m^{initial}, \Psi, m^{final} \rangle$ is *compatible with* $\mathcal{M}$, if

- for $events(\xi) = e_1 \ldots e_n$, there exists a partial run $s_1 \xrightarrow{e_1} s_2 \ldots \xrightarrow{e_n} s_{n+1}$ of $\mathcal{M}$, such that $s_1 = m^{initial}$, $s_{n+1} = m^{final}$ and $s_i \in M$, for $1 \le i \le n$;
- for a timed event (e_k, ϕ_k) in Ψ and time annotation $w - t_a \sim b \in \phi_k$, t_a corresponds to the time of the most recent event e_j that occurred before e_k in ξ, such that $s_j = m_a$ and $m_a \succ s_k$.

The second requirement means that a time annotation accompanying an event e can refer *only* to the times of previous events which originated in modes that dominate e. This fundamental *dominance assumption* guarantees that all time variables are *well-defined* (i.e., each time variable used in a time annotation on a transition is being defined on every path that reaches the transition).

This notion is best illustrated by an example. In the mode graph of Fig. 3, each mode m_i is associated with time t_i. In scenario ξ_1, the time annotation on event h refers to the time of leaving m_2, which dominates h. Hence, t_2 is well-defined regardless of the path taken from m_0 to m_5.

If h were annotated with a reference to t_3, t_3 would not be well-defined, as m_3 does not dominate h: if m_5 were reached through m_4, t_3 would be undefined.

Observe that the TES ξ_2 of Fig. 3 is not compatible with the mode graph of Fig. 3, as the sequence abf does not correspond to a partial run of the mode graph. The rest of the TES in Fig. 3 are compatible with the mode graph.

Behaviors. Given a mode graph $\mathcal{M} = (M, m_0, m_f, \Sigma, T)$, we define a *behavior* as a finite timed word (e, w) over Σ, where $e = e_1 e_2 e_3 ... e_n$, such that there exists a run $m_0 \xrightarrow{e_1} s_2 \xrightarrow{e_2} s_3 \xrightarrow{e_3} \ldots \xrightarrow{e_n} m_f$ of $\mathcal{M}$ (in which m_0 and m_f occur only once), and $w = w_1 w_2 w_3 \ldots w_n$ is a monotonically increasing sequence of real numbers. Each w_i represents the value of the wall clock when e_i occurs. We use $B_{\mathcal{M}}$ to denote the set of all such behaviors.

A non-empty contiguous subsequence $(e_k...e_m, w_k...w_m)$ of a behavior $\mathcal{B} = (e, w)$ is *covered* by a TES ξ iff $e_k...e_m = events(\xi)$.

A behavior $\mathcal{B}$ is *relevant* to TES ξ iff it includes a subsequence that is covered by ξ. Otherwise, it is *irrelevant* to ξ.

All the behaviors in $\mathcal{B}_1 = \{(abceik, w_1 w_2 w_3 w_4 w_5 w_6) \mid \forall_{1 < i \leq 6}\ w_i > w_{i-1}\}$ are relevant to ξ_3 of Fig. 3, as their subsequence $(abce, w_1 w_2 w_3 w_4)$ is covered by ξ_3. Similarly, the behaviors are relevant to ξ_6 on account of the subsequence $(ab, w_1 w_2)$. But the behaviors are irrelevant to ξ_4, for example.

A behavior $\mathcal{B}$ is *covered* by a set of TES, Ξ, iff $\mathcal{B}$ can be partitioned into a series of non-empty contiguous subsequences, such that each subsequence is covered by a *different* ξ in Ξ. (Different, to avoid unwanted loops.)

All the behaviors in $\mathcal{B}_2 = \{(abcegj, w_1 w_2 w_3 w_4 w_5 w_6) \mid \forall_{1 < i \leq 6}\ w_i > w_{i-1}\}$ are covered by the set $\{\xi_3, \xi_4\}$ of TES in Fig. 3.

We define $Covered(\Xi) = \{\mathcal{B} \in B_{\mathcal{M}} \mid \mathcal{B} \text{ is covered by } \Xi\}$.

A behavior $\mathcal{B} = (e_1 e_2 \ldots e_n, w_1 w_2 \ldots w_n)$ is *allowed* by a TES ξ iff, for every non-empty contiguous subsequence $(e_k \ldots e_m, w_k \ldots w_m)$ of $\mathcal{B}$ that is covered by ξ, the following holds: for every $k \leq i \leq m$, $w - t_j \sim a \in \phi_i$ in ξ evaluates to true when w is replaced by w_i and t_j by the time of leaving mode m_j (for the last time before e_i in this covered subsequence). The dominance assumption ensures that the latter will be well-defined.

Notice that a behavior that is irrelevant to ξ is allowed by ξ.

All the behaviors in $\mathcal{B}_3 = \{(abceh, w_1 w_2 w_3 w_4 w_5) \mid (\forall_{1 < i \leq 5}\ w_i > w_{i-1}) \wedge w_2 - w_1 > 1 \wedge w_5 - w_3 \leq 3\}$ are allowed by ξ_3, ξ_5 and ξ_6 in Fig. 3. The behaviors in $\mathcal{B}_3$ are allowed also by ξ_4, as they are irrelevant to ξ_4.

The set of behaviors allowed by a TES ξ is denoted by $Allowed(\xi) \subset B_{\mathcal{M}}$.

With a slight abuse of notation, we define the set of behaviors allowed by Ξ as $Allowed(\Xi) = \bigcap_{\xi \in \Xi} Allowed(\xi)$.

5 Synthesis of Timed Automata from Scenarios

Given a mode graph $\mathcal{M}$ and a set of TES, Ξ, the objective is to build a timed automaton $\mathcal{A}$, such that each behavior that is allowed and covered by Ξ corresponds to a run of $\mathcal{A}$, and vice versa. The automaton should contain the smallest possible number of locations.

Observe that the constructed timed automaton cannot, in general, be replaced by a suitably annotated mode graph. For instance, if the original mode graph contains a cycle to allow multiple attempts to enter a PIN, just adding time annotations would not let us express that the number of attempts must not exceed three, and that all must take place within a given time. That would require adding extensions to the conventional formalism of timed automata.

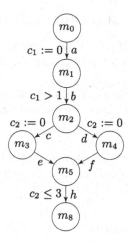

Fig. 4. A timed automaton

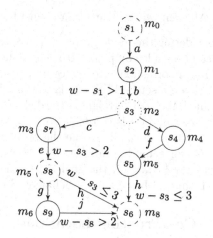

Fig. 5. A TAG synthesized from $\{\xi_1, \xi_3, \xi_4, \xi_5, \xi_6\}$ of Fig. 3

As another example consider the mode graph and the set of TES $\Xi_1 = \{\xi_1, \xi_5\}$ of Fig. 3. The goal is to construct an automaton, which captures *all* and *only* those behaviors that are both covered and allowed by Ξ_1. Annotating the "relevant" parts of the mode graph with appropriate time constraints, and hence obtaining the automaton of Fig. 4, for instance, would create unsatisfactory results: the automaton would also "show" the behaviors in $\{(abceh, w_1 w_2 w_3 w_4 w_5) \mid \forall_{1 < i \leq 5} \, w_i > w_{i-1}\}$ which are clearly not covered by Ξ_1.

A requirement of the synthesis algorithm is that the overall automaton have only one initial location and one final location. Moreover, the automaton should be *connected*: each location must be reachable from the initial location and there must be a path from each location to the final location.

We introduce five criteria that a set of TES must satisfy in order to make generation of such an automaton feasible. A set of TES that complies with these criteria is called *complete*.

Given a mode graph $\mathcal{M} = (M, m_0, m_f, \Sigma, T)$, a set Ξ of TES is *complete* if:

1. Every $\xi \in \Xi$ is compatible with $\mathcal{M}$.
2. For every $\xi \in \Xi$, either $initial\_mode(\xi) = m_0$ or there exist $\xi_1, \xi_2, ..., \xi_j \in \Xi$, such that $\xi_j = \xi$ and:
   - $initial\_mode(\xi_1) = m_0$,
   - $initial\_mode(\xi_k) = final\_mode(\xi_{k-1})$, for each ξ_k, $1 < k \leq j$.
3. For every $\xi \in \Xi$, either $final\_mode(\xi) = m_f$ or there exist $\xi_1, \xi_2, ..., \xi_j \in \Xi$, such that $\xi = \xi_1$ and:
   - $final\_mode(\xi_j) = m_f$,
   - $final\_mode(\xi_{k-1}) = initial\_mode(\xi_k)$, for each ξ_k, $1 < k \leq j$.
4. For every $\xi \in \Xi$, $initial\_mode(\xi) \neq final\_mode(\xi)$. Moreover, there is no sequence of TES $\xi_1, ..., \xi_j$ such that $\xi = \xi_1$, $final\_mode(\xi_{k-1}) = initial\_mode(\xi_k)$ for $1 < k \leq j$, and $final\_mode(\xi_j) = initial\_mode(\xi)$.

5. All occurrences of an event e must have (textually) identical time annotations.

Considering the mode graph of Fig. 3, the set $\Xi_1 = \{\xi_1, \xi_5\}$ is not complete. But it can be made complete, either by removing ξ_5 or by adding ξ_6. The automaton of Fig. 4 corresponds to the complete set of TES $\Xi_2 = \{\xi_1, \xi_5, \xi_6\}$.

Given a set of TES, checking that the set is complete (based on the criteria defined above) is straightforward. In the rest of the paper, we assume that the given set of TES is complete.

Next, we formally define the problem.

Given a mode graph $\mathcal{M} = (M, m_0, m_f, \Sigma, T)$ and a complete set of TES $\Xi = \{\xi_1, \xi_2, ..., \xi_n\}$, the goal is to construct an acyclic, minimal automaton $\mathcal{A}$ such that: $\mathcal{A}$ has a run on behavior $\mathcal{B}$ iff $\mathcal{B} \in Allowed(\Xi) \cap Covered(\Xi)$.

6   Constructing Locations and Transitions

Our synthesis method is implemented in two major steps. First, the timed events in each $\xi_i \in \Xi$ along with the mode graph $\mathcal{M}$ are used to build a graph, which we call a *time-annotated graph*. The graph consists of nodes[5] connected by time-annotated transitions. Second, clocks are allocated and time annotations are rewritten in terms of these clocks: the result is a timed automaton $\mathcal{A}$.

Before describing our method, we formally define *time-annotated graphs*. Let P be a set of labels, e.g., atomic propositions, etc.

A *time-annotated graph* (*TAG*) is a tuple $G = \langle E, Q, q^0, q^f, R, L \rangle$, where

- E is a finite alphabet;
- Q is the (*finite*) set of nodes;
- $q^0 \in Q$ is the initial node;
- $q^f \in Q$ is the final node;
- $R \subseteq Q \times Q \times E \times 2^{\Phi(Q)}$ is the set of transitions of the form (q, q', a, ϕ), where ϕ is a set of time annotations of the form $w - s \sim a$, where $s \in Q$;
- $L : Q \to P$ is a total function that maps each node to a label.

When we construct a time-annotated graph from a set of scenarios and a mode graph $\mathcal{M} = (M, m_0, m_f, \Sigma, T)$, we will use $E = \Sigma$ and $P = M$.

The first step of our synthesis is preceded by a preprocessing step in which the following three tasks are performed on the set of TES Ξ:

1. For each TES $\xi = \langle m^{initial}, \psi_1 \ldots \psi_n, m^{final} \rangle$, if there is a sequence of TES $\xi_1, \ldots, \xi_j$ in Ξ, such that $events(\xi) = events(\xi_1) \oplus \cdots \oplus events(\xi_j)$ (where $\oplus$ concatenates sequences), then ξ is removed from Ξ.
   Intuitively, if a TES ξ can be broken up into several parts, each of which is a TES in Ξ, then ξ can be safely discarded.
2. For each TES ξ, both the first and the last element of ξ (which name the initial and final modes) is "marked" as a *Join*. In the constructed graph a *Join* will correspond to a node that may have several incoming transitions and several outgoing transitions.

---

[5] The nodes will be the locations of the synthesized automaton.

3. For each TES ξ_i, if there is no TES ξ_k, $k \neq i$, such that $final\_mode(\xi_i) = final\_mode(\xi_k)$, the final element of ξ_i (which names the final mode) are marked as *Fork* (i.e., not a general *Join*: the corresponding node cannot have more than one incoming transition).

After the preprocessing step is performed, Algorithm 1 constructs the nodes and transitions corresponding to the first TES, ξ_1, thus obtaining the initial TAG, G_1. It then repeatedly takes a partial TAG G_k (constructed so far) and integrates a new TES ξ_{k+1} with G_k to obtain the augmented graph G_{k+1}.

As the algorithm constructs the corresponding nodes and transitions of each ξ_i, it also labels the nodes. A newly constructed node q is labelled with mode m_j, i.e., $L(q) = m_j$, if there is a transition on event e from node s to q such that $L(s) = m_i$, and $(m_i, e, m_j) \in T$. Moreover, the algorithm sets the status of each node in the constructed graph. The status of q will be set to *Open* ($Open_f$), if m_j is a *Join* (*Fork*) in ξ_i; otherwise it will be set to *Closed*.

Every time the algorithm chooses a new TES ξ, it takes one whose initial mode is already represented by a node s whose status is not *Closed*. It then tries to identify a common prefix between $events(\xi)$ and the sequence of events in a path beginning at s. In doing so, the algorithm avoids merging (i) a *Closed* node q in the graph, where $L(q) = m$, with a mode m that is a *Join* in ξ, and (ii) an *Open* node q in the graph, where $L(q) = m$, with mode m, if m is not a *Join* in ξ. This avoids introduction of new behaviors that are not covered by Ξ. For example, consider the set of TES $\{\xi_1, \xi_5\}$ in Sect. 5. We already mentioned that the automaton of Fig. 4 is not correct for this set. This is because the node corresponding to mode m_2 in the automaton is *Closed*, but is merged with a *Join* in ξ_5.

Criterion 2 on ensures that, as long as Ξ is not empty, it will always contain at least one TES such that there is a node s in the constructed graph such that $L(s) = initial\_mode(\xi)$ and the status of s is not *Closed*. So the algorithm will terminate.

Procedure *rename* deserves a comment. When the current node is q and a timed event (e, ϕ) of some ξ is processed, we rename t_j in $w - t_j \sim a \in \phi$ to s, where s is the latest predecessor of q in G, such that $L(s) = m_j$. Since ξ is compatible with the mode graph, that predecessor must be one of the states that were visited during the integration of ξ, hence there is no possibility of two paths joining between s and q, hence the "latest predecessor" is well-defined.

Figure 5 shows the time-annotated graph constructed by Algorithm 1 from the mode graph and the set $\{\xi_1, \xi_3, \xi_4, \xi_5, \xi_6\}$ of TES in Fig. 3. Circles in dashed and dotted lines indicate *Open* and $Open_f$ nodes, respectively. Note that the path ab corresponds to the common prefix of ξ_1, ξ_3 and ξ_6, as mode m_2 in ξ_6 is not a *Join*, but a *Fork* (task 3 of the preprocessing step).

The graph, G, built by Algorithm 1 has the following properties:

1. It is acyclic: we never introduce a transition from a node to its predecessor.
2. By construction, every scenario corresponds to a partial path in the graph, and every path can be partitioned into partial paths that correspond to scenarios.

Algorithm 1. Building nodes and transitions with time annotations

---

Input   : A mode graph $\mathcal{M} = (M, m_0, m_f, \Sigma, T)$, and a complete,
             non-empty set of TES $\Xi = \{\xi_1, ..., \xi_n\}$
Output: Time-annotated graph $G_n = \langle E_n, Q_n, q^0, q^f, R_n, L_n \rangle$

$k := 0;$ $E_0 := \emptyset;$ $Q_0 := \emptyset;$ $R_0 := \emptyset;$ $L_0 := \emptyset;$
create a new node s: $Q_0 := \{s\};$
set the status of s to *Open*;
add label m_0 to node s: $L_0 := \{(s, m_0)\};$
while $\Xi \neq \emptyset$ **do**

    $E_{k+1} := E_k;$ $Q_{k+1} := Q_k;$ $R_{k+1} := R_k;$ $L_{k+1} := L_k;$
    choose a $\xi = \langle m^{initial}, \psi \ldots \psi_l, m^{final} \rangle$ in Ξ, such that there is a node s in
        Q_{k+1} whose status is not *Closed* and $L_{k+1}(s) = m^{initial};$
    $\Xi := \Xi \setminus \{\xi\};$
    $s_c := s;$ // s_c always indicates the current source
    $j := 1;$
    // Identify a common prefix:
    while $j \leq l \wedge \psi_j = (e, \phi) \wedge (m, e, m') \in T \wedge m'$ *is not a Join in* $\xi \wedge$
        $(s_c, q, e, rename(s_c, \psi_j, G_{k+1})) \in R_{k+1} \wedge q$ *is not Open* **do**
        $s_c := q;$
        if $j = l$ **then**
          set the status of q to *Open$_f$*; // status of m^{final} in ξ
        $j := j + 1;$
    // Create the rest of the nodes and transitions (if any):
    while $j \leq l$ and $\psi_j = (e, \phi)$, where $(m, e, m') \in T$ **do**
        $\phi' := rename(s_c, \psi_j, G_{k+1});$
        if $j = l$ and there is a node $q \in Q_{k+1}$ such that
          $L(q) = m'$ and q is Open **then**
          create a new transition $r := (s_c, q, e, \phi');$ // last transition for ξ_i
        else
          create a new node q: $Q_{k+1} := Q_{k+1} \cup \{q\};$
          add label m' to node q: $L_{k+1} := \{(q, m')\} \cup L_{k+1};$
          create a new transition: $r := (s_c, q, e, \phi');$
          if $j = l$ **then**
            if *the status of* m^{final} *in* ξ *is Fork* **then**
              set the status of q to *Open$_f$*;
            else
               set the status of q to *Open*;
          else
            set the status of q to *Closed*;
            $s_c := q;$
        $R_{k+1} := \{r\} \cup R_{k+1};$ $E_{k+1} := E_{k+1} \cup \{e\};$
        $j := j + 1;$
    $k := k + 1;$
$q^f := f$, where f is the node with no outgoing transitions; // property (6)

Procedure rename(location q, timed event (e, ϕ), TAG G)

$\phi' := true$;

foreach $w - t_i \sim a \in \phi$ **do**

$\quad \phi' := \phi' \wedge w - s \sim a$, where s is the nearest predecessor of q in G such that
$\quad L(s) = m_i$;

Return ϕ';

---

3. By construction, several nodes in G might be labelled m, but only one of them will not be *Closed*.
4. For every ξ added to the graph the node that corresponds to *initial_mode*(ξ) is already in the graph. So the partial path corresponding to ξ will be connected to the graph at node s, i.e., every node will be reachable from the initial one.
5. The order in which the TES are selected from Ξ does not affect the shape of the constructed graph. By property 3 at most one node with a label m is not *Closed*. We connect TES only on nodes that are *Open* or *Open$_f$*, and the merging of prefixes does not depend on ordering.
6. There must be at least one node with no outgoing transitions, because the graph is finite and acyclic. Each such node is labelled with m_f, because the set of TES is complete (criterion 3 on implies that a node whose label is not m_f must have outgoing transitions). But by property (3) at most one node with label m_f is not *Closed*. So all the TES whose final mode is m_f must join at this node. Therefore the final node is unique.
7. Property 6 and criterion 3 on imply that the final node can be reached from all the other nodes in the graph.
8. When one considers the labels of the nodes, every run of G is also a run of the mode graph. This is because a transition from s to q is introduced only if there is a transition from $L(s)$ to $L(q)$ in the mode graph.

The TAG constructed by the algorithm might not yet be minimal: there might exist paths ending in the same (*Open*) node that have common suffixes. Such common suffixes should be merged, with appropriate attention given to the status of nodes in order to avoid introduction of new behaviors: the process is very similar to that of merging prefixes.

The resulting automaton (Sect. 7) will be minimal, in the sense that merging any two nodes or transitions would create a cycle or introduce a new behavior.

7   Building the Target Timed Automaton

Algorithm 1 generates the locations and time-annotated transitions of the overall timed automaton in the form of a TAG. The next step of our synthesis method is to transform this TAG to the final automaton. For this, the time annotations of the graph must be replaced by clock operations, i.e., clock resets and clock constraints. There are three tasks: (i) determining the number of clocks required, (ii) identifying transitions at which each clock must get reset and adding the

---

Algorithm 2. Generating clock resets and constraints

    Input : A time annotated graph $G = \langle E, Q, q^0, q^f, R, L \rangle$
    Output: A timed automaton $A = \langle E, Q, q^0, q^f, C, \Theta \rangle$

    $C := \emptyset; \quad \Theta := \emptyset; \quad clock\_assign := \emptyset;$
    foreach *transition* $(q_1, q_2, e, \phi) \in R$ **do**
        foreach *time annotation* $w - s \sim a \in \phi$ **do**
            if $(s, c_i) \notin clock\_assign$, *for some clock* c_i **then**
                create a new clock c_i: $C := C \cup \{c_i\}$;
                $clock\_assign := clock\_assign \cup \{(s, c_i)\}$;

    foreach *transition* $r = (q_1, q_2, e, \phi) \in R$ **do**
        $\lambda := \emptyset; \quad \delta := \emptyset;$
        if $(q_1, c_i) \in clock\_assign$, *for some clock* c_i **then**
            $\lambda := \{c_i\}$;
        foreach *time annotation* $w - s \sim a \in \phi$ **do**
            $\delta := \delta \cup \{(c_j \sim a)\}$, where $(s, c_j) \in clock\_assign$

---

resets, (iii) rewriting the time annotations of the graph as clock constraints. The three tasks mentioned above are performed by Algorithm 2.

The dominance assumption and our construction ensure that in the constructed TAG every path leading to a transition r annotated with $w - s \sim a$ must have previously passed through location s. Therefore, the clock assigned to s is *well defined*, i.e., it will always be initialized (reset) before it is used for the first time.

The number of clocks allocated by this algorithm may be greater than strictly necessary. Moreover, some of the resets may be redundant. A method for computing an optimal allocation of clocks, too involved to present here, is described in another paper [13].

After the construction is completed, we identify the final location with the initial location. This allows runs to be infinite. The dominance assumption ensures that the value of a clock from a previous iteration will not be used before it is reset in the current iteration.

From property 2 on it follows that the set of runs of the final automaton will correspond exactly to all those behaviours in $B_{\mathcal{M}}$ that are covered by Ξ. Each such behaviour will also be allowed by Ξ. This follows from our assumption that all the occurrences of a particular event in the members of Ξ have exactly the same time annotations: our construction ensures that all the supbaths in the automaton that correspond to those partial behaviours that are relevant to a particular scenario will have equivalent constraints.

Figure 6 shows the minimal TAG and the automaton synthesized from the two TES in Fig. 2. Without the optimization step mentioned at the end of Sect. 6 the automaton would include two additional states and two more transitions.

8   The Class of Synthesized Timed Automata

Each of our synthesized timed automata has the following properties:

- It has a unique initial location, q^0. There is a path from q^0 to every location.
- Each clock c_j is always reset upon leaving a unique state s_j.
- A clock constraint on a transition r that leaves a state s can refer only to a clock that has been reset upon leaving a state that dominates s.

We call the class of such timed automata TA_{DS}. All automata in TA_{DS} share some interesting properties. These properties allowed us to formulate a clock allocation algorithm whose results are, for all practical purposes, optimal: the details are discussed in another paper [13] (its theoretical underpinings are examined elsewhere [12]). The pivotal role of the dominance assumption makes the class TA_{DS} somewhat restricted, but it can be used to model interesting properties of real-time systems, e.g., safety properties such as *bounded-response* and *bounded-invariance*.

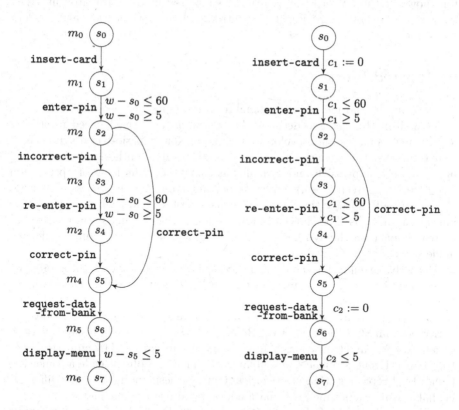

Fig. 6. The synthesized TAG and the automaton for the initial behavior of the ATM

For instance, Fig. 7 shows a variant of a monitor automaton [10], which checks the property that "a is always followed by b within at most 10 time units".

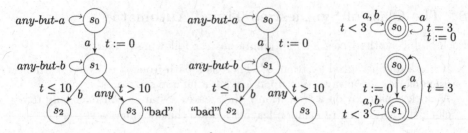

Fig. 7. Bounded response   **Fig. 8.** Bounded invariance   **Fig. 9.** Periodic behavior

Figure 8 shows an automaton that checks a bounded-invariance property that "b will never occur within 10 time units after a's occurrence".

Periodic behaviors can also be specified quite easily. For instance, the automaton shown at the top of Fig. 9 [1] can be simulated by an automaton in TA_{DS} (shown at the bottom of Fig. 9), by introducing a new location and a silent transition.

9   Related Work

Synthesizing formal models of systems from scenarios has been an active area of research in the last two decades. The research has been focused mostly on formalizing scenarios and developing techniques for scenario-based synthesis of formal models. For scenarios to be used in automatic synthesis methods, they must be both expressive and formal. Choosing the right level of abstraction for representing scenarios is a very important step in this process. Scenarios should formally specify the high level behavior of systems, without going into unnecessary details. The choice of formalisms for representing scenarios also has a great impact on the synthesis method that will be used for building formal models from them.

Recently, Event Sequence Charts (ESCs) have been proposed for expressing scenarios of systems, and a method for synthesizing finite state machines from ESCs has been introduced [8]. Our TES are different from ESCs: ESCs use the notion of monitored, term and controlled variables along with modes, all borrowed from SCR (Software Cost Reduction) [8]. The relation between various actions in ESCs and transitions of mode diagrams are specified by numeric labels. Our Timed Event Sequences accompanied by mode graphs provide a somewhat higher-level representation of scenarios. Our synthesis method is also different, in that it constructs timed automata and not finite state machines.

Various extensions of Message Sequence Charts (MSCs) with time constraints have been proposed for describing scenarios for real-time systems [3]. Different notations for modeling time and expressing timing requirements are used in each of these extensions, e.g., timers with reset and time-outs, and delay intervals for events and activities [2]. UML features sequence diagrams: timing constraints are included by drawing message arrows or by including timing markers [11].

Most of the work on scenario-based synthesis of formal models has been focused on synthesizing state machine models [6, 15, 16]. While the resulting models are useful for reasoning about the overall behavior of systems, they are less useful for reasoning about time and behavioral properties related to time.

To the best of our knowledge the problem of constructing timed automata from a set of scenarios has been addressed only by Somé et al. [14]. However, it is not very clear how clocks, clock resets, and clock constraints are generated, and to which transitions the clock resets are assigned. Moreover, the use of contradictory scenarios may cause "unwanted non-determinism" in the constructed automata, which seems undesirable. The authors use the concept of "characteristic conditions" for generating locations and identifying identical locations, but the concept is not formally defined: in particular, it is not obvious whether clock constraints are also considered as characteristic conditions. Moreover, arbitrary variables (e.g., a variable that counts the number of attempts for entering a PIN) are allowed in the constructed automata: this is beyond the conventional formalism of timed automata, which can feature only clock variables [1].

By contrast, in our approach we formally define a set of criteria for a complete set of scenarios from which a synthesis to a timed automaton is possible. We use modes, which are formally defined, as location labels, and use these labels for identifying identical locations. Our algorithm precisely determines the transitions along which each clock must be reset and the transitions where clock constraints must be added.

There has been also some work in scenario-based synthesis of *parametric* timed automata [7], where scenarios with parametric timing constraints in the form of upper and lower time bounds are considered. Allowing parametric constraints in scenarios makes the corresponding synthesis methods difficult to scale up to larger problems, though there are some indications that this might not be a problem in practice [4].

10 Conclusions

We presented a new technique for specifying the required behaviors of real-time systems in terms of a mode graph and a set of scenarios, and of generating a timed automaton from these scenarios.

Intuitively, scenarios put time constraints on the possible partial behaviors of systems. We have used *Timed Event Sequences* to formally describe scenarios.

We have presented a synthesis method for generating a minimal, acyclic timed automaton from a set Ξ of such scenarios, provided that Ξ satisfies our completeness requirements (see Sect. 5). Each behavior allowed by a scenario in Ξ can be viewed as a run of this timed automaton. Moreover, every run of the automaton corresponds to a behavior that is both covered and allowed by the set of scenarios (see Sect. 4).

Our algorithm for constructing a timed automaton comprises two steps. The first step is to generate a time-annotated graph which includes the locations and transitions of the target timed automaton, where transitions are augmented with time annotations from scenarios. Having constructed the skeleton of the target timed automaton, the algorithm performs the second step: clock allocation. The time annotations are used to determine the number of clocks and their reset locations in the target timed automaton, and then to transform the time annotations to clock constraints. The clock allocation algorithm presented here is not optimal: the description of a more sophisticated version is presented in another paper [13].

Acknowledgements. The authors would like to thank one of the anonymous referees of an earlier version of the paper for detailed and helpful comments.

References

1. Alur, R., Dill, D.L.: A theory of timed automata. Theor. Comput. Sci. **126**(2), 183–235 (1994)
2. Alur, R., Holzmann, G.J., Peled, D.: An analyzer for message sequence charts. In: Margaria, T., Steffen, B. (eds.) TACAS 1996. LNCS, vol. 1055, pp. 35–48. Springer, Heidelberg (1996). https://doi.org/10.1007/3-540-61042-1_37
3. Ben-Abdallah, H., Leue, S.: Timing constraints in message sequence chart specifications. In: Mizuno, T., Shiratori, N., Higashino, T., Togashi, A. (eds.) FORTE 1997. IFIP, vol. 107. Springer, Boston (1997). https://doi.org/10.1007/978-0-387-35271-8_6
4. Cimatti, A., Palopoli, L., Ramadian, Y.: Symbolic computation of schedulability regions using parametric timed automata. In: RTSS (2008)
5. Clarke, E.M., Klieber, W., Nováček, M., Zuliani, P.: Model checking and the state explosion problem. In: Meyer, B., Nordio, M. (eds.) LASER 2011. LNCS, vol. 7682, pp. 1–30. Springer, Heidelberg (2012). https://doi.org/10.1007/978-3-642-35746-6_1
6. Damas, C., Lambeau, B., Roucoux, F., van Lamsweerde, A.: Analyzing critical process models through behavior model synthesis. In: Proceedings of the 31st International Conference on Software Engineering, pp. 441–451. IEEE Computer Society (2009)
7. Giese, H.: Towards scenario-based synthesis for parametric timed automata. In: Proceedings of the 2nd International Workshop on Scenarios and State Machines: Models, Algorithms, and Tools (SCESM), Portland, USA (2003)
8. Heitmeyer, C.L., Pickett, M., Leonard, E.I., Archer, M.M., Ray, I., Aha, D.W., Trafton, J.G.: Building high assurance human-centric decision systems. Autom. Softw. Eng. **22**(2), 159–197 (2015)
9. Lengauer, T., Tarjan, R.E.: A fast algorithm for finding dominators in a flowgraph. ACM Trans. Program. Lang. Syst. **1**(1), 121–141 (1979)
10. Nicolescu, G., Mosterman, P.J.: Model-Based Design for Embedded Systems, 1st edn. CRC Press Inc., Boca Raton (2009)
11. Rational Software: Unified Modeling Language, version 1.1, September 1997
12. Saeedloei, N., Kluźniak, F.: Clock allocation in timed automata and graph colouring. http://www2.cs.siu.edu/~neda/report3.pdf
13. Saeedloei, N., Kluźniak, F.: Optimal clock allocation for a class of timed automata. http://www2.cs.siu.edu/~neda/report2.pdf

14. Somé, S., Dssouli, R., Vaucher, J.: From scenarios to timed automata: building specifications from users requirements. In: Proceedings of the Second Asia Pacific Software Engineering Conference, pp. 48–57. IEEE Computer Society (1995)
15. Uchitel, S., Brunet, G., Chechik, M.: Synthesis of partial behavior models from properties and scenarios. IEEE Trans. Softw. Eng. **35**(3), 384–406 (2009)
16. Uchitel, S., Kramer, J., Magee, J.: Synthesis of behavioral models from scenarios. IEEE Trans. Softw. Eng. **29**(2), 99–115 (2003)

Graph Grammar Extraction from Source Code

Lucio Mauro Duarte$^{(\boxtimes)}$ and Leila Ribeiro

Institute of Informatics, Federal University of Rio Grande do Sul (UFRGS),
15.064, Porto Alegre, RS 91.501-970, Brazil
{lmduarte,leila}@inf.ufrgs.br

Abstract. We present an approach for the extraction of Graph Grammars (GGs) from Java source code. A GG consists of an initial graph, describing the initial state of a system, and a set of rules, modeling the possible changes of state. We generate a GG based on execution traces collected from annotated code, following the main ideas from an existing approach for extracting Labelled Transition Systems (LTS) based on context information (combination of block of code, values of attributes, and evaluated path conditions). Since GGs are data-driven, in contrast to the action-based formalism of LTS, we have adapted the existing technique to focus on data information. The approach is partially supported by a tool and the generated GGs can serve as input to existing analysis tools. We illustrate the approach with a case study and compare the resulting GG with a GG manually created by an expert for the same system.

Keywords: Graph Grammars · Model extraction · Model analysis

1 Introduction

Formal behavior models are important artefacts for the development of software systems. They not only provide a precise way of describing the expected behavior of systems, but can also serve for several purposes, such as program documentation, understanding, and analysis. *Model extraction* [14] offers the possibility of (semi-)automatically generating models from existing implementations. Hence, it eases the burden of building models from scratch and also allows the application of techniques of model analysis to systems already in use.

In this work, we discuss a model extraction approach to construct *Graph Grammars* (GG) [19] from existing Java code. GG is a generalisation of Chomsky grammars from strings to graphs. Graphs are a very natural means to explain complex situations on an intuitive level and graph transformation rules may be used to capture the dynamic aspects of systems. The basic idea is to model the states of a system as graphs and describe the possible state changes as rules that transform the graph describing the current state into a new graph, representing the new state. Due to their declarative nature, GGs are well suited for the specification of a wide variety of applications [11].

This work is partially supported by CNPq/Brazil.

S. Cavalheiro and J. Fiadeiro (Eds.): SBMF 2017, LNCS 10623, pp. 52–69, 2017.
https://doi.org/10.1007/978-3-319-70848-5_5

Our approach follows the main ideas of an existing extraction approach [10] that generates Labeled Transitions Systems (LTS) [15] from Java source code, which is based on *contexts*. Contexts are identified in execution traces and abstract a combination of control flow information and values of attributes, thus merging static and dynamic information to create a program state. In [17], we proposed an adaptation of the LTS extraction approach to be used for the extraction of GG. In contrast to the action-based, operational semantics of LTS, which is more suited for model checking [2], GG is declarative and data-driven, which allows a different view of the system and, thus, enables the use of other types of verification techniques, such as theorem proving [6], and tools, such as Groove [18] and AGG [20].

In the proposed approach, the main difficulty was the large number of rules that would be generated. To a large extent, this was due to the fact that GG is data-driven but the extraction technique takes into account not only information about data but also about control flow. Although the number of rules does not affect analysis results on the extracted GG, a large set of rules may hinder model visualization, increase the time for running analyses, and even make the model intractable in the available tools. Thus, in this paper, we revisit the extraction process, proposing improvements to the approach, including optimization strategies that allow the merging/elimination of rules without affecting the behavior of the extracted models, whilst reducing the number of rules. We have (partially) implemented the approach to generate the resulting grammar in the format used by the AGG tool. We apply the approach to a case study and compare the resulting GG to a GG manually created by an expert for the same application. The comparison shows that, apart from abstractions that the expert introduces in their models, these models and the extracted GG represent the same behavior, considering analyses carried out using tool support.

The article is organized as follows: Sect. 2 revises the main concepts of model extraction and Graph Grammars; Sect. 3 describes the details of the approach and the methods used for mapping traces ·with context information to GG rules; Sect. 4 presents the proposed optimization strategies; in Sect. 5, we discuss related work; finally, in Sect. 6, some results, status of the work and future work are presented.

2   Background

2.1   Model Extraction

Model extraction [14] is a reverse engineering technique used to obtain a model from an implementation of a system. Existing model extraction approaches can be classified according to the type of information they use. Approaches based on *static information* (such as [13,14]) build models considering only information collected directly from the source or compiled code. This information generally includes control flow information. They provide a complete view of the system behavior, however analyses on the model may have to deal with many false alarms due to behaviors that seem possible statically but are actually infeasible when the system runs. Models constructed based on *dynamic information* (such as [3, 16, 21]), on the other hand, consider only feasible behavior, since they are inferred from observed execution traces. The drawback is that each trace is collected in isolation and there is usually not enough information on how to safely (i.e., without introducing invalid behaviours) combine these samples of execution into one single, general model.

The approach proposed in [10] to extract *Labelled Transition Systems (LTS)* [15] from code belongs to a *hybrid category*, where static and dynamic information are combined [12]. This combination is obtained using the abstraction of *contexts*, which includes control-flow and data information. A context represents a specific situation during system execution, including the point of code being executed and the current valuation of program variables (attributes). Using contexts, it is possible to safely merge multiple traces of execution, as each context is unique during execution. The approach is partially supported by the *LTS Extractor (LTSE)* tool, which creates a *context table* to store information about all identified contexts during trace analysis, assigning an ID number to each one of them (*CID*), and converts traces to *context traces*, which are sequences of identified contexts (CIDs) and the names of actions that happened in between them. Action names are obtained based on the names of executed methods or from specific annotations in the code, called *user-defined actions* [8], which allows a user to represent their own types of actions, other than method-related actions. Based on the context table and traces, the tool constructs an LTS model: each context in the table corresponds to a state and each two consecutive contexts in the traces represent a state transition; action names become transition labels and transitions with no labels are silent transitions. For detailed information on this approach, the reader is referred to [9].

2.2   Graph Grammar

Graphs are structures that consist of a set of nodes and a set of edges. Each edge connects two nodes of the graph, one representing a source and another representing a target. *Graph Grammars* (GG) [11, 19] is a formal, intuitive method for modelling concurrent and distributed systems using graphs and graph transformations. The basic idea is that system states are represented by graphs and state transitions are described by transformation rules, which may create/delete/preserve nodes and/or edges.

A *Graph Rule* $r : L \rightarrow R$ describes a relationship between two graphs. It consists of: a *left-hand side (LHS) L*, which is a graph describing items that must be present for this rule to be applied; a *right-hand side (RHS) R*, describing items that will be present after the application of the rule; and a *mapping from LHS to RHS r*, which is a (partial) graph homomorphism mapping items that will be preserved by the application of the rule (a homomorphism between graphs is a pair of mappings of nodes and edges that is compatible with source and target of edges). Items that are in the LHS and are not mapped to the RHS are *deleted*, whereas items that are in the RHS and are not in the image of the mapping from the LHS are *created*. We assume that rules do not merge items, that is, r is injective. A GG is defined by an initial graph, representing the initial state of a system, and a set of rules. Its behavior is defined by the successive application of rules to the states of the system. The application of a rule to a particular graph is called *derivation step* and is only performed if an occurrence (image) of the LHS of the rule exists in the system graph. We use typed graphs with attributes, i.e. graphs that may have different types of nodes and edges and may have values of data types associated to nodes. For formal definitions, see e.g. [19].

In this work, we propose to extract a GG from Java code. Thus, the generated rules will have a specific format, similar to Object-Based Graph Grammars [7]. Objects are represented by attributed nodes, references to other objects are represented by edges. Methods are modelled by messages that represent the method's call and return whereas the effect of the execution of the method is described by rules. Each rule may describe a behavior of at most one object (since objects are autonomous), and treat at most one message (representing the execution of a call or return of a method). In this paper we use rectangles to represent nodes and attributes are drawn inside the nodes.

An example of a GG corresponding to a Java code shown in Fig. 1 is depicted in Fig. 2. This GG was manually created from the code. The application simulates a traffic lights system that alternates between a green light and a red light. The *TrafficLights* GG has two kinds of nodes: a system node (TL) and a message node (representing method calls/returns and commands). The system node has two attributes: one boolean variable (isGreen), which models whether the lights are currently green or not, and an integer opt, that contains the result of the read command (which is used to switch the traffic light from green to red and vice versa, and to end the execution). In the initial state of the system (graph Ini), there is a node TL in which the attributes are initialized and a message node representing that the do loop of the code should be executed. Rule Read represents the start of the do-loop, triggering the read command, that may have three different outcomes, described by three distinct rules: ReadGreen models the input of number 0, ReadRed the input of number 1, and ReadEnd the input of number 2. Rules that describe the behavior for red lights are analogous to the green lights and are thus omitted in Fig. 2. The remaining rules model how the actual change of traffic light color occurs (according to the given code). Note that, whenever a method is called, a corresponding message is created, and a message to indicate the end of method execution is also created.

3   Approach

As mentioned before, we follow the same initial steps of the LTS extraction approach [10] and then use the resulting information to generate a GG. Figure 3 presents the basic steps of our approach, where the boxes represent the different phases and the arrows indicate the sequence of steps. The initial input is the source code of the application, which is annotated to collect context information. In Step 1, the instrumented code is executed to produce traces; in Step 2, the

```
class TrafficLights {                                          break;
private static final int GREEN = 0;                        }
private static final int RED = 1;                        } while (opt != END);
private static final int END = 2;                       }
private static boolean isGreen;
                                                        private void greenLights () {
  public TrafficLights (CommandReader c) {                isGreen = true;
    isGreen = false;                                      changeColour ("green");
    int opt = - 1;                                      }
    do {
      opt = c.readCommand ();                           private void redLights () {
      switch (opt) {                                      isGreen = false;
        case GREEN :                                      changeColour ("red");
          if (!isGreen)                                 }
          greenLights ();
            break;                                      private void
                                                          changeColour (String newColour) {
        case RED :                                        // Turns on the necessary light
        if (isGreen)                                    }
        redLights ();                                 }
```

Fig. 1. Source code of the running example.

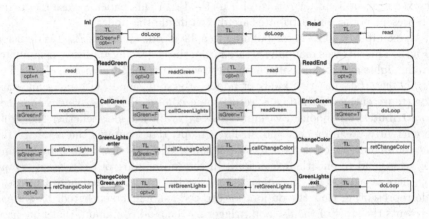

Fig. 2. Graph Grammar for the traffic lights system.

collected traces are fed to the LTSE tool for context identification, generating the context table and the set of context traces; in Step 3, the context table and traces serve as inputs to our tool, called GGExtractor, producing GG rules. The rules are produced in the input format of the AGG tool [20], where analyses such as conflict and dependency detection can be executed.

Next, we present each step of the approach in more detail. We will use the traffic lights application presented in Fig. 1 to illustrate the process.

3.1   Step 1: Generating Traces

We use the TXL language [4] to instrument the code and include the necessary annotations to produce context information. These annotations follow the same rules applied in the original approach [10]. The execution of the instrumented code produces traces. Each trace is a sequence of annotations, where

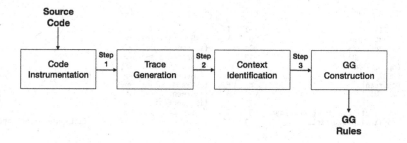

Fig. 3. Overview of process flow of our approach.

each annotation contains the block of code executed, identified by a type (repetition, selection, method call, method body, etc.) and an ID number (can be seen as an abstract program counter), a condition (if any) tested and its value, the value of a set of selected program variables, and the current call stack (names of methods still in execution). The set of variables used determines the level of abstraction of contexts, which means that including more program variables refines the model [10]. The call stack is mainly used to identify other actions happening whilst a method is still running, such as in the case of a method that calls another method. It is also important when representing concurrent systems, especially if they implement some blocking mechanism.

3.2   Step 2: Identifying Contexts

The execution traces are then processed by the LTSE tool, creating the context table and the context traces. The LTSE tool combines the results of the analysis of multiple traces of a particular component into a single model, hence the model represents a generalization of the set of observed behaviours. Figure 4 presents part of the context table (CT) generated for our running example based on a set of 4 traces. It contains, for each identified context: a context ID (CID), which is a number used to identify each different context (column S); the control predicate (condition) tested for that context (column P); the block of code ID (column ID) executed in that context; the value of the control predicate (column V); the values of the attributes (column A), and the state of the call stack (column CS). For instance, context 3 is defined by a command block in which the predicate *(opt!=END)* is tested, its value is true, the attribute value *(isGreen)* is false, the BID is 10, and the call stack is empty. Any change in at least one of these values causes the identification of a different context. For example, context 4 has similar information, but the value of the predicate is false at this point, indicating that the system is running within a new context. Note that all traces of a system always start at an initial context (INITIAL) and that, in case of contexts related to method calls, the associated predicate is the name of the method and its value is always set to *true*.

Figure 5 shows a fragment of one of the context traces produced for the traffic lights application. CIDs are prefixed with a # and the sequence of contexts

CID	P	ID	V	A	CS
0	INITIAL	-1	T		◇
1	c.readCommand	0	T	{isGreen=false}	◇
2	Integer.parseInt	1	T	{isGreen=false}	◇
3	(opt != END)	10	T	{isGreen=false}	◇
4	(opt != END)	10	F	{isGreen=false}	◇
5	(RED)	9	1	{isGreen=false}	◇
6	(isGreen)	8	F	{isGreen=false}	◇
7	(GREEN)	9	0	{isGreen=false}	◇
8	(! isGreen)	7	T	{isGreen=false}	◇
9	call.TrafficLights.greenLights	3	T	{isGreen=false}	◇
10	TrafficLights.greenLights	11	T	{isGreen=false}	<call.TrafficLights.greenLights>

Fig. 4. Example of a context table.

#0	call.changeColour.enter
#1	#12
c.readCommand.enter	changeColour.enter
c.readCommand.exit	changeColour.exit
#2	call.changeColour.exit
#7	greenLights.exit
#8	call.greenLights.exit
#9	#13
call.greenLights.enter	#14
#10	c.readCommand.enter
greenLights.enter	c.readCommand.exit
#11	#15

Fig. 5. Example of context trace.

(from top to bottom, left to right in the figure) follows the order of the information recorded in the original trace, transforming each annotation into the CID assigned to the corresponding context when it was included in the CT. The names not preceded by a # are action names. Action names representing internal method calls are prefixed with the word *call*; action names representing calls to methods of other classes are prefixed with an identifier (e.g., c); and the execution of method bodies are described using only the method name. The suffix *enter* is used to denote the action representing the beginning of the execution of the method call/body, whereas the suffix *exit* represents the its termination. This allows us to know when some other method call/body was executed while a previous method call/execution was in process.

3.3 Step 3: Constructing the GG

Our approach proposes a mapping from the CT and set of context traces to GG rules. This translation is automated by a tool we have developed, called GGExtractor [17]. This process is based on the analysis of *context sequences*, which is a sequence of elements $(x, ..., y)$ from a context trace where the elements of the sequence are either a CID or an action name. In a context sequence, the first and the last elements are CIDs and the elements in between are action names. Therefore, a context sequence identifies a possible transition between two contexts and the actions that happen in this transition. We create one or more rules (depending on the number of actions) to describe each context sequence. We also consider the contents of the call stack to identify pending actions, representing actions that come from a previous transition.

Each rule is a tuple $r = (L_{state}, L_{msg}, R_{state}, R_{msg})$, where L_{state} is the state (context) represented in the LHS of the rule, L_{msg} is the message (action name) present in the LHS of the rule, and R_{state} and R_{msg} are the same elements but for the RHS of the rule. L_{msg} and R_{msg} can assume the value ϵ, representing an empty list of actions. We divide the analysis of this rule creation process into the cases presented below, where c_1 and c_2 are CIDs representing contexts C_1 and C_2, respectively, a and b are action names, and cs is the call stack:

1. **Sequence (c_1, c_2)**: Indicates a change of context with no action, hence, it is mapped to a rule $\mathbf{r} = (\mathbf{C_1}, \epsilon, \mathbf{C_2}, \epsilon)$;
2. **Sequence (c_1, a, c_2)** and **CS** $= \langle \rangle$: Indicates a transition with an action a, with no pending action, hence it is mapped to a rule $\mathbf{r} = (\mathbf{C_1}, \epsilon, \mathbf{C_2}, \mathbf{a})$;
3. **Sequence (c_1, a, c_2)** and **CS** $= \langle b \rangle$: Indicates a transition with an action a, with a pending action b, hence it is mapped to a rule $\mathbf{r} = (\mathbf{C_1}, \mathbf{b}, \mathbf{C_2}, \mathbf{a})$;
4. **Sequence (c_1, a, b, c_2)** and **CS** $= \langle \rangle$: Indicates a transition with two actions a and b, with no pending action, hence it is mapped to rules $\mathbf{r_1} = (\mathbf{C_1}, \epsilon, \mathbf{C_1}, \mathbf{a})$ and $\mathbf{r_2} = (\mathbf{C_1}, \mathbf{a}, \mathbf{C_2}, \mathbf{b})$;
5. **Sequence (c_1, a, b, c_2)** and **CS** $= \langle c \rangle$: Indicates a transition with actions a and b, and a pending action c, hence it is mapped to two rules that describe a sequence: $\mathbf{r_1} = (\mathbf{C_1}, \mathbf{c}, \mathbf{C_1}, \mathbf{a})$ and $\mathbf{r_2} = (\mathbf{C_1}, \mathbf{a}, \mathbf{C_2}, \mathbf{b})$.

The idea behind this mapping is that sequences of contexts indicate changes of state, hence they are represented, respectively, as the LHS and RHS of the rule. A single action name between two contexts indicates an action that occurs during the transition and, therefore, is represented as a message created by the rule. Two consecutive actions are modelled by a rule with messages, where one message is consumed and the next is created by the rule. Pending actions are treated as messages created in some previous rule and consumed by the current rule. In cases 4 and 5, intermediate rules are created in the same way as rule r_1 for each pair of actions. For instance, for a sequence (c_1, a, b, c, c_2) with $CS = \langle \rangle$, we would have rules $r_1 = (C_1, \epsilon, C_1, a)$, $r_2 = (C_1, a, C_1, b)$, and $r_3 = (C_1, b, C_2, c)$.

Figure 6 shows two rules that illustrate the mapping with our running example, using the CT and the trace shown in Figs. 4 and 5, respectively. In the first case, the change from context 8 to context 9, with no messages between them (case 1), resulted in a simple rule where the LHS represents the former context whereas the RHS represents the latter. In the second example, we have a single action that is placed in the form of a message in the RHS of the rule (case 2).

Note that the quality of the model heavily depends on the quality of the traces used to build it, as it happens with any other approach based on samples of execution. We do not use any particular technique for selecting the traces used to build the GG. However, we usually use test cases to produce the behaviours

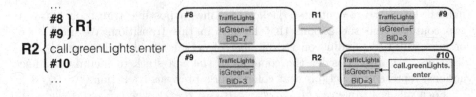

Fig. 6. Examples of rules generated by our algorithm.

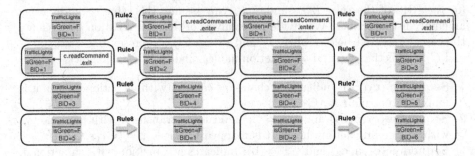

Fig. 7. Some generated rules

we would like to observe. Even though this may prevent the model from being complete, it is possible to customise it for specific purposes. Moreover, a complete model might not even be necessary, as some times only part of the code may need to be analysed. We also currently do not have a formal proof of the correctness of our mapping. However, based on visual inspection and analysis outcomes, the resulting GGs we have produced represent the behaviors observed in the corresponding traces and described in the code (given the level of abstraction). Our mapping (explained earlier) considers how to translate contexts to states of the GG, sequences of contexts to rules, and action names to messages. As GG is data-driven, we use context information to define states and messages to represent control-flow structures, such that selection structures are represented by multiple rules that can consume a certain message, whereas iteration structures are defined by rules or set of rules that can apply multiple times in a row.

For the TrafficLights code the algorithm generated 43 rules (42 actually represent behavior, as the first rule is just the initialization of variables). Some of these rules are presented in Fig. 7. This number is relatively large, considering the size of the code and that a manually generated GG for the same code has only 15 rules. Therefore, we provide, in the next section, two strategies to reduce the size of the generated set of rules.

4   Optimizing the Set of Rules

The aim of optimizing the set of rules is to obtain the smallest number of rules while preserving the overall observable effect, in terms of the variables of the original program. Since in this paper we did not present the formal definitions of GGs due to space limitations, we will only provide informal argumentation about the preservation of observable semantics of the optimizations. But, as another justification for the approach, at the end of this section we compare the grammar resulting from the optimizations with the grammar that was manually obtained for the traffic lights example, showing that they are very similar.

In order to build a more compact set of rules, we have to identify rules that could be either removed or merged with other rules, while keeping the same observable effect. We will provide two ways to perform this task: one based on method calls and another based on block IDs (BIDs). These two optimizations operate on different elements, thus they may be performed in any order (yielding the same resulting set of rules). Both optimizations are based on the conflicts and dependencies that exist between rules.

The notion of conflict and dependency between rules in GG is defined based on the items that a rule deletes, preserves, and creates. In the following, we will explain these notions in the context of rules generated from execution traces (i.e., this is not the general definition, but specific to our type of GG). Given two rules $r1 = (C1^L, msg1^L, C1^R, msg1^R)$ and $r2 = (C2^L, msg2^L, C2^R, msg2^R)$, where the BID of a context C is depicted by $BID(C)$, we define

(WCR) Weak conflict relation: $r1$ and $r2$ are in **weak conflict**, denoted by $r1 \rightarrow r2$ if both have the same BID, $r1$ does not change this BID and $r2$ changes it, i.e., $BID(C1^L) = BID(C2^L) = BID(C1^R)$ and $BID(C1^R) \neq BID(C2)^R$;

Conflict relation: $r1$ and $r2$ are in **conflict**, denoted by $r1 - r2$ if one of the following situations occur:

    (BCR) BID conflict: both have the same BID in the LHS, and both change it, i.e., $BID(C1^L) = BID(C2^L)$ and $BID(C1^L) \neq BID(C1^R)$ and $BID(C2^L) \neq BID(C2^R)$); or

    (MCR) message conflict: both delete the same message, i.e., $msg1^L = msg2^L$;

Dependency relation: $r2$ depends on $r1$, denoted by $r1 \dashrightarrow r2$, if one of the following situations occur:

    (BDR) BID dependency: $r1$ generates the BID that $r2$ needs, i.e., $BID(C1^R) = BID(C2^L)$ and $BID(C1^L) \neq BID(C1^R)$; or

    (BNR) message dependency: $r1$ creates the message for $r2$, i.e., $msg1^R = msg2^L$

Note that if two rules are in weak conflict they are not necessarily mutually exclusive, since it is possible to apply first rule $r1$ and then $r2$ (but not vice versa). If rules are in conflict they are mutually exclusive.

The graph that has as nodes the rules and as arcs the relations defined above is called **CPA graph** (CPA stands for *critical pair analysis*). The **BID-cpa graph** contains only arcs representing the context conflicts and dependencies

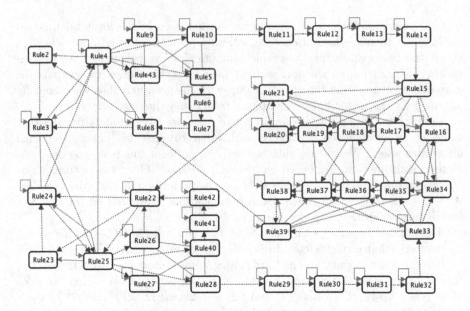

Fig. 8. CPA-graph of the generated TL grammar (Color figure online)

(**WCR**, **BCR** and **BDR**) whereas the **message-cpa graph** contains only arcs representing the message conflicts and dependencies (**MCR** and **MDR**). In a CPA graph, we say that a rule r is a **choice point** iff considering dependencies and conflicts based on the BID, there are more than one other rule that depend on r and these rules are mutually exclusive. A rule is a **merge point** iff considering dependencies based on the BID, r depends on more than one other rules.

Example 1. The CPA graph for the grammar automatically generated from the code of Fig. 1 is shown in Fig. 8. Solid (red) arrows denote weak conflicts (edges with no arrow tips denote conflicts) and dashed (blue) arrows denote dependencies. Rule4 is a choice point and Rule8 is a merge point.

4.1   First Optimization: Merging Rules

For this optimization we will identify sequences of rules with no observable effect and merge them into a single rule that has the effect of this sequence of executions. This is performed by the construction of the concurrent rule that summarizes the sequence. This is a standard construction in the theory of graph transformations, see e.g. [19], and it is well known that the application of the concurrent rule has the same effect that the application of its underlying rules. Therefore, we will identify sequences of rules that have no observable effect considering the variables of the program and the exchanged messages, such that no rule in these sequences is be a merge or choice point (thus, assuring that there is only one possible sequence in which these rules are present, and thus it is safe to substitute them by the corresponding concurrent rule).

Step 1: Select candidates for merging. A rule r is a candidate for merging if it satisfies all of the following conditions:

(i) r does not change the value of any attribute, except the BID;

(ii) r either creates or deletes some message, or does not contain messages;

(iii) r is not a choice point;

(iv) r is not a merge point.

Step 2: Partition the set of candidate rules. Each rule is grouped with the rule(s) that are dependent on it in the set of candidates (based on the BID).

Step 3: Construct concurrent rules. For each partition that has more than one rule in step 2, a concurrent rule is constructed and inserted in the set of rules, and the rules that belong to the corresponding partition are deleted from the set of rules.

Step 2 is well defined because, by the way the rules are constructed (from an execution of the original program), for each rule r that is in the set of candidates, there can only be at most one rule dependent on it in the set of merge candidates. This follows basically from to the fact that r is not a choice point (condition (iii)), that is, either there is at most one rule that depends on r or, if there are more, say $r1$ and $r2$, they are not mutually exclusive. In this situation, either $r1$ or $r2$, or none of them will be in the set of candidates.

Example 2. For the TL grammar, we get the following candidates for merging:

{Rule2, Rule5, Rule6, Rule7, Rule9, Rule10, Rule11, Rule12, Rule21, Rule23,

Rule26, Rule27, Rule28, Rule29, Rule30, Rule39, Rule40, Rule41,

Rule42, Rule43}

Note that Rule8 is not a candidate for merging because it does not satisfy condition (iv): it depends on three different rules (merge point). Rule4 is also not a candidate because rules that depend on it (Rule5, Rule9, Rule10 and Rule43) are mutually exclusive (choice point).

Then we obtain the following partitions:

{[Rule2], [Rule5, Rule6, Rule7], [Rule9], [Rule10, Rule11, Rule12], [Rule21], [Rule23], [Rule26], [Rule27], [Rule28, Rule29, Rule30], [Rule39], [Rule40, Rule41, Rule42], [Rule43]}

Rule2 and Rule21 are alone in partitions because no rule is dependent on them (Rule3 and Rule22, that depends on them, are not in the set of merge candidates).

Now we build concurrent rules. For example, rules Rule5, Rule6 and Rule7 (see Fig. 9) are substituted by rule R5+R6+R7.

Fig. 9. Concurrent rule

4.2 Second Optimization: Method Execution

For this optimization, we must build the message-cpa and the BID-cpa graphs. The former gives us the information about which rules generate messages that may be used by others (independent of the BID and attribute values), whereas the later relates rules based on the execution point (considering the BID). The aim of this optimization is to identify method executions that (a) have no observable effect, and (b) occur immediately when called (in case of concurrent systems, there may be a delay between a method call and its execution due to interleaving of processes). For the first case, we will remove the *enter/exit* tags of messages (removing also rules that create/delete these tags) and for the latter we will remove the *call* tags of method calls (removing also the rules that create/delete messages with such tags).

Step 1: Identify candidate method executions. Rules representing method executions that have no observable effect may take the forms (i) or (ii) in Fig. 10, where neither attributes nor the BID are changed. We construct sets $Cand_{(i)}$, of rules of type (i) and $Cand_{(ii)}$, of (triples of) rules of type (ii) – these sets must be disjoint, rules that appear in both should be kept only in $Cand_{(ii)}$. The union of these sets is called $Cand_{(i),(ii)}$. Rules representing method executions that occur immediately when called follow pattern (iii) depicted in Fig. 10, where there must be a chain of BID-dependent rules $R6 \to ... \to R7$, and no message *m.enter* is generated in the chain.

Step 2: Treat candidates with no observable effect.

1. For each method m that has some rule in the set $Cand_{(i),(ii)}$, let
   $Call_m$: set of all rules that are not in $Cand_{(i),(ii)}$ that generate *m.enter*, in case m is of type (i), or *call.m.enter*, in case m is type (ii);
   Ret_m: set of all rules that are not in $Cand_{(i),(ii)}$ that delete *m.exit*, in case m is of type (i), or *call.m.exit*, in case m is type (ii);
2. For each rule r in $Cand_{(i)}$ corresponding to method m, check that no rule that is not in $Cand_{(i),(ii)}$ is in conflict with r (this assures that there is no other executions of m that may be compromised by removing the enter/exit tags);
3. In case all rules rule in $Cand_{(i)}$ for a method call m pass the test, delete them from the set of rules and update all rules in $Call_m$, substituting *m.enter* by m, and all rules in Ret_m, substituting *m.exit* by m;
4. For each triple $(r1, r2, r3)$ in $Cand_{(ii)}$ corresponding to method m, check that no rule that is not in $Cand_{(i),(ii)}$ is in conflict with $r1$ (the rule that deletes *call.m.enter*);

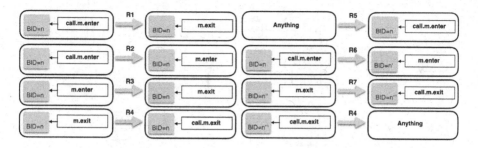

Fig. 10. Patterns (i) R1 (ii) R2, R3, R4 (iii) R5, R6, R7, R8

5. In case all rule triples in $Cand_{(ii)}$ that correspond to method calls to m pass the test, delete them from the set of rules and update all rules in $Call_m$, substituting $call.m.enter$ by m, and all rules in Ret_m, substituting $call.m.exit$ by m.

Step 3: Treat candidates that occur immediately. For each method m that has some rule in the set $Cand_{(iii)}$, construct the sets:
$Call_m$: set of all rules that are not in $Cand_{(iii)}$ that generate $call.m.enter$;
Ret_m: set of all rules that are not in $Cand_{(iii)}$ that delete $call.m.exit$.
Perform steps analogous to 4. and 5. below for the quadruples of $Cand_{(iii)}$.

The CPA graph of the resulting grammar is shown in Fig. 11 (green circles will be discussed below). We have a total of 20 rules instead of the 42 original rules.

Comparison. The manually generated grammar for the TL example has 15 rules (9 of which are shown in Fig. 2, the remaining 6 are analogous to the rules that handle green lights). We consider this as the optimum number of rules that faithfully represent the behavior of this program (since this grammar was manually generated by an expert inspecting the code). The grammar obtained following our algorithm has 20 rules for the same code. For a comparison with the manually generated grammar, we included in Fig. 11 the rules of this grammar in circles. For example, Rule4 of the generated GG corresponds to ReadGreen, rules Rule19 and Rule37 correspond to ChangeColor (rules that are duplicated in the generated grammar are marked with *). This duplication occurs because in the generation we consider the values of attributes, for example, Rule19 changes color when it is green. In the manually generated grammar, there is a generic rule that changes the color, no matter the current color. There are also rules of the generated grammar, such as the composed rule Rule10+Rule11+Rule12, that do not appear in the original grammar but we could not remove hem because it would change the conflict/dependencies relations and, thus, might change the behavior of the system (without manual inspection, it is not possible to determine whether this change is acceptable or not). But note that the automatically generated GG is quite close in the number of rules and has essentially the same behavior as the manually created GG.

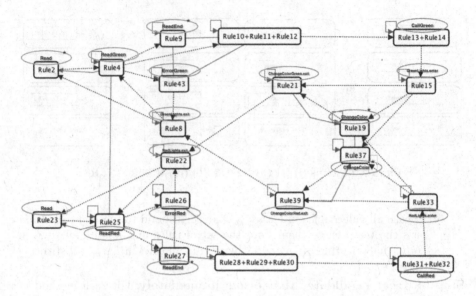

Fig. 11. CPA graph after Otimizations (Color figure online)

Another indication of correctness of the generated GG with respect to the
original code is its similarity with the LTS generated for the same code with the
LTSE tool [9]. The GG generated by our approach has 20 rules, and the LTS
has 23 states. By comparing the CPA graph of Fig. 11 with the LTS, we have
practically identical graphs, but the LTS has some extra nodes and transitions:
one for initialization and two because actions described by rules 13 and 14 (resp.
31 and 32) could not be merged in the LTS.

5   Related Work

Considering research specifically on the extraction of GG, the approach described
in [22] uses grammar inference from traces to construct nested hierarchical call
graphs from Java bytecodes. Their goal is to check this call graph against desired
properties, representing valid call sequences. Even though we also generate a GG
based on trace information, unlike their work, we take into account more than
just sequences of method calls, defining abstract states based also on data (values
of attributes). Thus, we explore the data-driven characteristic of the formalism
to achieve a description of a system behavior.

To the best of our knowledge, the approaches closest to ours are the ones
presented in [5] and [1]. In [5], the authors propose an approach for constructing
a GG from Java programs. However, the methodology used to translate from Java
to GG is based only on the source code and on the Java grammar. Moreover,
this translation can be applied to a very limited subset of the Java language or
require some conversion between program structures (e.g., while-do structures

are not allowed and must be replaced by calls of recursive functions). We do not require any modification in the original code apart from the introduction of the necessary annotations. Even though our models contain only those rules that can be inferred from the observed traces, which means that we cannot guarantee completeness, we only create rules that can actually occur. In [1] a technique is presented to extract rules from the observation of the transformations from an initial state to a final state of a system based only on traces. The goal is not to generate a model of a Java source code, but generate a model to explain a set of observations. Hence, they aim to create a model that could improve program understanding considering pre- and post-conditions of method executions. All preconditions become the LHS of a rule and the post-conditions become the RHS. To restrict the set of objects included in each rule, they need to identify which objects of the system are affected and/or required for a rule to be applied. This is not the case in our approach, as we build rules for each element of the system. Because we follow the idea of encapsulation, only the state of the object for which we are building the rule is visible, we only include objects referenced by this main object that are necessary to describe a state change. Moreover, we intend to produce models that (partially) describe the behavior of the system with the goal of applying analyses to detect real and potential problems as well as for program understanding and documentation.

6   Conclusions and Future Work

This article proposed a way to extract a model in terms of GG from Java code. The aim of this extraction is twofold: on the one hand, the model corresponding to code may serve as documentation and as basis for maintenance and evolution; on the other hand, analysis of this model may reveal properties and bugs of the code. The main difficulty in the extraction process was the large number of rules that were generated. To a large extent, this is due to the fact that GG is data-driven and since our extraction technique takes also executions into account, not only information about the application but also about control flow of executions was considered (for example, block identifier). Thus, we proposed optimisations for the extraction technique, leading to a considerable reduction in the number of generated rules. We have (partially) implemented the approach to generate the resulting grammar in the format used by the AGG tool.

As future work, we intend to evaluate the application of this technique to more complex software, such as concurrent systems, and also to large-scale applications. Since the LTS extraction approach allows a compositional construction of a model based on the models of each element of the system [9], we believe this part of the approach could also be adapted for GGs. In order to complement our work, we also plan to use the generated models to validate their corresponding implementations. The idea is to use the GG rules to construct test cases that could be run on the implementation to check whether those behaviors are valid.

References

1. Alshanqiti, A., Heckel, R.: Towards dynamic reverse engineering visual contracts from Java. Electron. Commun. EASST **67**, 1–12 (2014)
2. Clarke Jr., E.M., Grumberg, O., Peled, D.A.: Model Checking. MIT Press, Cambridge (1999)
3. Cook, J.E., Wolf, A.L.: Discovering models of software processes from event-based data. ACM Trans. Softw. Eng. Methodol. **7**(3), 215–249 (1998)
4. Cordy, J.R., Dean, T.R., Malton, A.J., Schneider, K.A.: Source transformation in software engineering using the TXL transformation system. Inf. Softw. Technol. **44**(13), 827–837 (2002)
5. Corradini, A., Dotti, F.L., Foss, L., Ribeiro, L.: Translating Java code to graph transformation systems. In: Ehrig, H., Engels, G., Parisi-Presicce, F., Rozenberg, G. (eds.) ICGT 2004. LNCS, vol. 3256, pp. 383–398. Springer, Heidelberg (2004). https://doi.org/10.1007/978-3-540-30203-2_27
6. da Costa Cavalheiro, S.A., Foss, L., Ribeiro, L.: Theorem proving graph grammars with attributes and negative application conditions. Theor. Comput. Sci. **686**, 25–77 (2017). https://doi.org/10.1016/j.tcs.2017.04.010
7. Dotti, F.L., Ribeiro, L., dos Santos, O.M., Pasini, F.: Verifying object-based graph grammars. Soft. Syst. Model. **5**(3), 289–311 (2006)
8. Duarte, L.M.: Behaviour Model Extraction using Context Information. Ph.D. thesis, Imperial College London, University of London, November 2007
9. Duarte, L.M., Kramer, J., Uchitel, S.: Using contexts to extract models from code. Softw. Syst. Model. **16**(2), 523–557 (2017)
10. Duarte, L.M., Kramer, J., Uchitel, S.: Towards faithful model extraction based on contexts. In: Fiadeiro, J.L., Inverardi, P. (eds.) FASE 2008. LNCS, vol. 4961, pp. 101–115. Springer, Heidelberg (2008). https://doi.org/10.1007/978-3-540-78743-3_9
11. Ehrig, H., Engels, G., Kreowski, H.J., Rozenberg, G. (eds.): Handbook of Graph Grammars and Computing by Graph Transformation, Applications, Languages, and Tools, vol. II. World Scientific, Singapore (1999)
12. Ernst, M.D.: Static and dynamic analysis: Synergy and duality. In: Workshop on Dynamic Analysis, Portland, OR, USA, pp. 24–27, May 2003
13. Henzinger, T., Jahla, R., Majumdar, R., Sutre, G.: Lazy abstraction. In: ACM Symposium on Principles of Programming Languages, pp. 58–70. ACM Press, Portland, January 2002
14. Holzmann, G., Smith, M.: A practical method for verifying event-driven software. In: International Conference on Software Engineering, pp. 597–607. ACM, New York, May 1999
15. Keller, R.: Formal verification of parallel programs. Commun. ACM **19**(7), 371–384 (1976)
16. Lorenzoli, D., Mariani, L., Pezze, M.: Inferring state-based behavior models. In: WODA 2006: Proceedings of the 2006 International Workshop on Dynamic Systems Analysis, pp. 25–32. ACM Press, New York (2006)
17. de Oliveira, M., Ribeiro, L., Mauro Duarte, L., Cota, E.: Specification of models based on contexts using graph grammars. In: 2013 2nd Workshop-School on Theoretical Computer Science (WEIT), pp. 129–134, October 2013
18. Rensink, A.: The GROOVE simulator: a tool for state space generation. In: Pfaltz, J.L., Nagl, M., Böhlen, B. (eds.) AGTIVE 2003. LNCS, vol. 3062, pp. 479–485. Springer, Heidelberg (2004). https://doi.org/10.1007/978-3-540-25959-6_40

19. Rozenberg, G. (ed.): Handbook of Graph Grammars and Computing by Graph Transformation: Foundations, vol. I. World Scientific, Singapore (1997)
20. Taentzer, G.: AGG: a graph transformation environment for modeling and validation of software. In: Pfaltz, J.L., Nagl, M., Böhlen, B. (eds.) AGTIVE 2003. LNCS, vol. 3062, pp. 446–453. Springer, Heidelberg (2004). https://doi.org/10.1007/978-3-540-25959-6_35
21. Walkinshaw, N., Taylor, R., Derrick, J.: Inferring extended finite state machine models from software executions. In: 20th Working Conference on Reverse Engineering (WCRE), pp. 301–310 (2013)
22. Zhao, C., Kong, J., Zhang, K.: Program behavior discovery and verification: a graph grammar approach. IEEE Trans. Softw. Eng. **36**(3), 431–448 (2010)

Applying a Formal Method in Industry: A 25-Year Trajectory

Thierry Lecomte$^{(\boxtimes)}$, David Deharbe, Etienne Prun, and Erwan Mottin

ClearSy, 320 Avenue Archimède, Aix en Provence, France
thierry.lecomte@clearsy.com

Abstract. Industrial applications involving formal methods are still exceptions to the general rule. Lack of understanding, employees without proper education, difficulty to integrate existing development cycles, no explicit requirement from the market, etc. are explanations often heard for not being more formal. Hence the feedback provided by industry to academics is not as constructive as it might be.

Summarizing a 25-year return of experience in the effective application of a formal method – namely B and Event-B – in diverse application domains (railways, smartcard, automotive), this article makes clear why and where formal methods have been applied, explains the added value obtained so far, and tries to anticipate the future of these two formalisms for safety critical systems.

Keywords: B method · Event-B · Integrated development environment · Code generation · Formal data validation

1 Introduction

Formal methods and industry are not so often associated in the same sentence as the formers are not seen as an enabling technology but rather as difficult to apply and linked with increased costs. In [11], the introduction of the B method and the Event-B language into several industrial development processes was witnessed with more or less success, even if new tools and new practices were available to ease acceptance in industry. At that time, these two formal methods had been backed by a number of research projects and non-trivial industrial applications.

Almost 10 years later, after several real size experiments in diverse application domains, the situation has slightly evolved. Some standards, like the D0-178C for aeronautics, are now accepting formal methods in their certification process with sometimes some restrictions on the perimeter where they are applied (unit testing replaced by unit proof for example). The newborn ISO 26262 automotive functional safety standard is also recommending the use of formal methods during development. On the opposite side, the Common Criteria 3.1 standard (compared to its version 2.3) has decreased the need for formal methods that are now only required at level 6+ and higher (instead of 5+ previously) while the maximum security is reached at level 7 (EAL). However, even if the standards have made some room for them, these methods haven't spread much out of the

© Springer International Publishing AG 2017
S. Cavalheiro and J. Fiadeiro (Eds.): SBMF 2017, LNCS 10623, pp. 70–87, 2017.
https://doi.org/10.1007/978-3-319-70848-5_6

railway sphere as it might have been expected. Their usage though have slightly evolved over the years as a reaction to industry needs in direct relation with fierce international competition.

This article presents in a first chapter the different ways B and Event-B were used for modeling software, systems and data, and for proving static and dynamic properties. In a second chapter, new technology and techniques are presented. Their tight combination is expecting to converge to a new, more automated way of developing safety critical applications that are not restricted to the railways.

2 Modeling

2.1 B for Software

The B Method was introduced in the late 80's to correctly design safe software. The main idea was to avoid introducing errors by proving the software while being built, instead of trying to find errors with testing after the software was produced.

Promoted and supported by RATP, B and Atelier B[1] have been successfully applied to the industry of transportation, through metros automatic pilots installed worldwide. Paris Meteor line 14 driverless metro is the first reference application with over 110,000 lines of B models, translated into 86 000 lines of Ada. No bugs were detected after the proof was completed, neither at the functional validation, at the integration validation, and at the on-site testing, nor since the beginning of the metro line operation (October 1998).

For years, Alstom Transportation Systems and Siemens Transportation Systems (representing a major part of the worldwide metro market) have been the two main actors in the development of B safety-critical software. Both companies have a product based strategy and reuse as much as possible existing B models for future metros. As an example, the Alstom Urbalis 400 CBTC (Radio communication based train control) equips more than 100 metros in the world, representing 1250 Km of lines and 25 % of the CBTC market.

2.1.1 Structure and Metrics

For such applications, B modeling is used for safety critical functions for both track-side (zone controller, interlocking) and on-board (automatic train pilot or ATP) software. The interlocking part has to avoid having two trains on the same track section. It computes boolean equations that represent the tracks status as seen from diverse sensors. The automatic pilot is mainly in charge of triggering the emergency brake in case of over-speed. It requires several functions such as the localization (*where is the train ?*) that involve several graph-based algorithms, and the energy control which computes the braking curve of the train, based on the geometry of the tracks (in particular the positive and negative slopes). Data types used are: integer for the energy control, booleans for the interlocking and tables of integer for the tracks.

A typical ATP software model is made of one top-level function executed every cycle.

---

[1] The tool implementing the B method.

```
variables :(types & properties & properties_train &
   (loc_trainLocated = TRUE =>
                 0 <= loc_locationUncertainty
                 & kine_kineInvalid = FALSE
                 & loc_train_track /= {}
                 & first(loc_train_track) = loc_ext2Block |-> oppositeDirection(loc_ext2Dir)
                 & !ii.(ii : 1..size(loc_train_track)-1 => loc_train_track(ii) : dom(sidb_nextBlock))
                 & !ii.(ii : 1..size(loc_train_track)-1 => sidb_nextBlock (loc_train_track(ii)) = loc_train_track(ii+1))
                 & #aa.(aa : 1..size(loc_train_track) & prj1(t_block,t_direction)(loc_train_track(aa)) = loc_ext1Block))
                 & loc_rearAbs    = { c_cabin1 |-> loc_ext2Abs, c_cabin2 |-> loc_ext1Abs, c_none |-> 0 }( io_frontEnd )
   )
)
```

Fig. 1. Example of a non-deterministic post-condition of a function

The specification of this function (see Fig. 1) is non-deterministic and is expressed as a large "variables become such as" substitution. The specification of the function, contained in the post-condition, is sufficiently abstract and different from the implementation[2] to avoid to prove the copy-paste from the specification to the implementation. This implementation imports 55 components. The complete B project is made of 233 machines (50 kloc[3]), 46 intermediate refinements (6 kloc) and 213 implementations (45 kloc), as well the handwritten code for non-safety critical parts (110 kloc). It also contains 3000 definitions reused among several components. 23,000 proof obligations are generated, 83 % of these of proved automatically, the remaining 17 % requires interactive proof. 3000 mathematical rules were added to ease the proof process, 85 % of these are proved automatically, the remaining 15 % requires human manual proof.

To date, the biggest B software is a XML compiler enabling the execution of safety critical embedded applications by an interpreter. More than 300,000 lines of Ada code are generated from B models, for this SIL4 T3-compliant (EN50128) program[4]. 300,000 lines do not represent the limit of the method as no bottleneck has been met until now. So the method is likely to scale up to larger, non-threaded software. A the other end of the scale, with platform screen doors controllers less demanding in term of computation, smaller applications are generated for both programmable logic controllers (PLC) and PIC32 microcontrollers, with a maximum of 64 KB in memory per software.

2.1.2   Organization and Acceptance

Since 1998, Atelier B has been slightly improved in order to obtain proven software more quickly:

– proof obligations (PO) contain traceability information (which parts of the B models have been used to obtain a PO), helping to better locate modeling errors and to improve modeling style
– a model editor allowing to navigate models (abstraction, refinement) and operations (caller, callee)

---

[2] Which contains the algorithm (statements, operation calls).

[3] Thousands lines of code.

[4] T3 means that the tool is able to generate a (faulty) binary program and as such requires a special attention in the safety process.

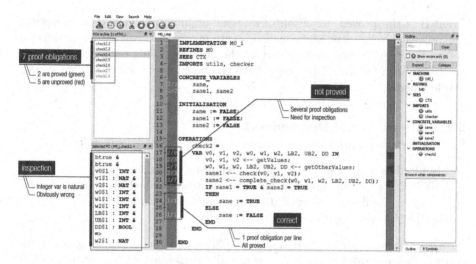

Fig. 2. Text-based model editor combining proof information with modeling

- a model editor merging model and proof (see Fig. 2) by displaying the number of proof obligations associated to any line of a B model, its current proof status (fully proved or not) and the body of the related proof obligations.
- a framework to automatically prove and review user added mathematical proof rules, that generates a report for the safety case.

From a human point-of-view, usual organization requires a local guru acting as a technical referee (usually - but not necessarily - a PhD) and a team of software engineers able to handle abstraction. Introductory B courses (B language, projects with B) and close support during the first months have been enough to set up development teams. The forthcoming MOOC on B[5] and a dedicated YouTube channel for Atelier B practitioners would speed up the learning process.

The B software development process is now well-oiled, accepted by certification bodies and several rail operators worldwide. Without being formally developed, Atelier B 3.6 was used for METEOR in 1998 while Atelier B 4.2/4.3 is used for Alstom Urbalis 400/500 product line. Atelier B 4.2 is at the core of the SIL4 certificate obtained for the platform screen-doors controller installed in 2017 in Stockholm (line Citybanan).

2.2 B for Systems

A broader use of B appeared in the mid '90s, called Event-B, to analyze, study and specify not only software, but also systems (system is here considered in its widest definition). It extends the usage of B to systems that might contain software, hardware and pieces of equipment, but also to intangible objects like process, procedure, business rule, etc. In that respect, one of the outcome of

---

[5] https://moocs.imd.ufrn.br.

Event-B is the proved definition of systems architecture and, more generally, the proved development of, so called, "system studies", which are performed before the specification and design of the software. This enlargement allows one to perform failure studies right from the beginning, even in a large system development.

2.2.1 Research and Development

Several European projects were required to set-up Event-B, among them:

- MATISSE aimed at providing a first definition of the language,
- PUSSEE specifically aimed at hardware/software embedded systems,
- Rodin for the development of the eponymous platform and
- DEPLOY for its deployment in the industry.

Several system studies from diverse application domains (banking, air traffic control, defense, satellites, etc.) were initially performed with Atelier B before naturally moving to the Rodin platform. The modeling of the Mazurkiewicz enumeration algorithm ands its proof during the project RIMEL[6] was the perfect demonstration of the suitability of Event-B for small, distributed systems. In 2008, during the certification for a smart-card microcircuit, Event-B was seamlessly integrated to Atelier B[7]. The supported language slightly differs from the one supported by Rodin but doesn't restrict its usability regarding target applications. Several EAL5+ (CC2.3) and EAL6+ (CC3.1) certifications were performed in France, Germany and Spain, and functional specification were proved to comply with security policies.

A follow-up project, FORCOMENT [2], was initiated with STMicroelectronics and aimed at providing a proven path from specification to VHDL. Specific proof obligations were added to ensure a deterministic behavior. Resulting VHDL was quite different from the one developed manually (similar numbers of gates, but architecture more easily analyzable) and went successfully through product test benches. However the technology failed to find its audience because of:

- (the complexity of) the input formalism,
- the necessity to specify the target system several tens of times (refinements) with different levels of detail,
- the time and the number of iterations[8] to converge to a final model,
- the obligation to allocate our best practitioners to complete the duty.

---

[6] http://rimel.loria.fr/.

[7] Because of the inability, at that time, for the Rodin platform to handle a model with 17 levels of refinement.

[8] Our maximum is 190 iterations and 5 major refactoring, many modifications having a slight impact on the structure of the model.

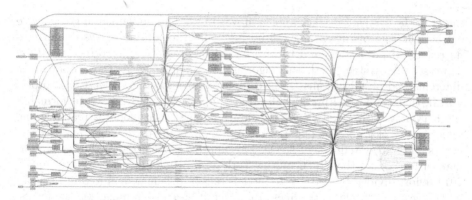

Fig. 3. All the dependencies between the sub-systems of a military vehicle analyzed with composys, and used for defining a non-trivial efficient integration testing policy. This drawing is for illustrating the complexity of the model.

2.2.2   Flat Specification

Event-B was also used as a descriptive language for behavioral specification (flat specification, no refinement), mainly for document generation, structural analysis (dependencies among variables) and model animation with application in the automotive (enhanced diagnosis – Peugeot), in the defense (military vehicles integration testing scheduling – CNIM) and in the railways (platform screen doors preliminary studies – RATP).

The main reason for not modeling with refinement was the complexity of the target systems and the level of detail required to perform an analysis that would have led to both practical and economical impossibilities (models too large to be handled by human modelers; too much effort to complete, if reachable). The Event-B models were sided by a dictionary containing natural language descriptions of the variables, events and substitutions, allowing for the automatic generation of document. Events were allocated to "sub-systems", allowing to analyze data-flows (see Fig. 3) between these sub-systems (where the variables are read/modified).

A dedicated tool, Composys [10], was developed and maintained to support this approach until 2012.

This approach was more aimed at finding ambiguities in the existing technical documentation, and at animating the specification than at proving a correct behavior and was finally abandoned.

2.2.3   Collection of Separate Models

Instead of developing a model of the whole signaling system , verbose, complex and not containing enough details[9] to ensure a definitive conclusion on the

---

[9] This demonstration requires for example to know the algorithm used for the odometer, to rediscover how the distance between signals and switches is computed based on the minimum curve radius, tunnel width, maximum slope, minimum train braking capability, etc.

safety of the system, another approach was tried. The fundamental goal was to extract the rigorous reasoning establishing that the considered system ensures its requested properties, and to assert that this reasoning is correct and fully expressed. At system level, this rigorous reasoning involves the properties of different kind of subsystems (from computer subsystems to operational procedures), that the formal proof shall all encompass. Event-B is used to formalize the reasoning with a collection of separate models: each model is readable and understandable by a non-expert and doesn't require to dig into hundreds of events and tens of refinement levels. This approach was used for the system formal verification for the CBTC of New York subway line 7 in 2012 and Flushing in 2014 (effort divided by two due to models reuse). It is now deployed in Paris for all the new automatic metro lines [15]. Even if based on refinement, the formal modeling effort is now manageable (each model is one or two pages long) and only requires engineers able to reason (not our best practitioners any more). The Event-B language as implemented in Atelier B in 2008 is still enough to support this modeling approach.

2.3   Formal Data Validation

The verification of a behavior, based on Event-B system specification or B software specification, is achievable by semi-automated proof. However the verification of static properties of parameters (that tune the system or the software) against properties may turn out to be a nightmare in case of large data sets (10,000+ items) and complex relationships among data, as the built-in Atelier B prover is not able to handle them properly. In the early 2000's data validation in the railways [8] used to be entirely human, leading to painful, error-prone, long-term activities (usually more than six months to manually check constantly changing[10] 100,000 items of data against 1,000 rules).

In 2003, this human process was made more formal while:

- formalizing data properties with the B mathematical language (set theory, first order logic)
- generating a B machine containing the properties (the data model) and instantiated with the data to verify,
- checking the correctness of the B machine

2.3.1   Rules

Properties, issued from international standards, national regulations, local practices, rail operator requirements, metro manufacturer constraints, are modeled as rules (see Fig. 4). The clause *WHERE* allows the selection and filtering of data[11]. The clause *VERIFY* specifies the conditions expected for all filtered signals. In case the predicates of this clause are not verified, an error message is displayed for each signal found.

---

[10] CAD data is replaced by real plant data, topology is modified after in situ testing, etc.

[11] That could be stored in files like JSON, Xml, Ecxel, CSV, TXT, etc.

```
FOR
        sig
WHERE
        sig : sys_sud_er::Signal &
        sig : dom(sys_sud_er::Signal__dptId) &
        sig : dom(ic::sys_sud_er::signal_geopoint) &
        ic::sys_sud_er::signal_geopoint(sig) : ic::sys_sud_er::zone_GPZone
(sys_sud_er::IXL_Core__singleZone(ixl))
THEN
        VERIFY
                sys_sud_er::Signal__dptId(sig) : ran(sys_sud_er::IXL_Core__signal(ixl))
        MESSAGE
                «The signal %1 belongs to IXL_Core %2 territory but is not referenced
                among its signals.»
                ARG sys_sud_er::Signal__name(sig) TYPE STRING
                ARG sys_sud_er::IXL_Core__name(ixl) TYPE STRING
        ENDVERIFY
ENDFOR
```

Fig. 4. Example of verification rule. Signals belonging to an interlocking territory are searched; such signals have to be linked to this interlocking. If not, an error message is displayed for each faulty signal found.

Most of the rules fit in one page, but some rules are really large, up to 10 pages, as they embed several small steps or they contain a lot of implicit information. To ensure compliance with safety standard, rules have to be cross-read and tested by independent engineers. A specific testing environment has been developed to ease to set up of testing scenarios demonstrating that a rule triggers a KO conclusion for all error classes.

2.3.2 Deployment

The PredicateB predicate evaluator was first used for checking the correctness. The PredicateB tool is a symbolic calculator able to manipulate B mathematical language predicates in order to animate a B formal model: constants and variables initial values are calculated, then operations are executed depending on enabling conditions and their substitutions. Symbolic values are scalars, sets, functions, etc. PredicateB has limited capabilities for non-deterministic computations and was replaced by ProB [9]. The ProB model-checker embeds several well performing heuristics for reducing search space (symmetry detection for example), is able to better handle non-deterministic substitution and to provide a more complete set of counter examples. It has been modified in order to produce a file containing all counter examples detected and slightly improved to better support some B keywords.

The major outcome of this decision to introduce formalities and to automate the verification [13] was a dramatic reduction of the validation duration from about six months of human verification to some minutes of computation (if we set aside the time to formalize verification rules). Since then the resulting tools (certified as T2 and T3 compliant, EN50128 standard) have been experimented

Table 1. Summary of the main tools used during the last 25 years for industrial projects. B/E/D columns refer to B language (B), Event-B language (E) and formal data validation (D) supports.

Tool	B	E	D	Usage	Availability
Atelier B	X	X		Modeling environment 100+ automatic metro lines	Free http://www.atelier.eu/en
ProB	X	X		Model-checker	Free https://www3.hhu.de/stups/prob
BMotionWeb	X	X		Model animator	Free http://wiki.event-b.org/index.php/BMotion_Studio
PredicateB		X		Model animator	Free https://sourceforge.net/p/rodin-b-sharp
PredicateB++		X		Model animator	Proprietary (ClearSy)
Rodin		X		Modeling environment	Free http://www.event-b.org/
DTVT			X	Data validation environment 20+ metro and tramway lines	Proprietary (Alstom)
Dave			X	Data validation environment Singapour metro line	Proprietary (General Electrics)
Ovado			X	Data validation environment Paris metro lines	Proprietary (RATP)

with success[12] on several metro lines worldwide for different metro manufacturers. In this context, more than 2,500 rules have been developed, cross-verified and applied. The French Railways (SNCF) is going to deploy these tools for the main lines to check new interlocking parameters for the 10 coming years, requiring the development of 2,500 more rules.

From a human point-of-view, usual organization requires engineers able to manipulate mathematical predicates and to understand railways signaling. A technical referee provides feedback and support on how to model certain tricky aspects like non-deterministic choices ("find a bijection such as ..."), quantified predicates, etc. The verification process is well accepted by certification bodies and by several rail operators worldwide, and is ready to be deployed in other industries with safety-critical constraints.

2.4   Adoption by Industry

From our experience, industry is not particularly interested in using formal methods except if it is required by the standards (1) or by the customers (2), or if it allows to speed up a process by an order of magnitude (3).

In our history, (1) is related to smartcard industry (Sect. 2.2.1), (2) is associated with Meteor/RATP (Sect. 2.1) and with L7/NYCT (Sect. 2.2.3), while (3) is represented by the formal data validation (Sect. 2.3).

In any case, a formal method without a proper tool support is useless. We have used several tools over the years (Table 1) that were applied in industrial

---

[12] Metro line fully and positively analyzed, results validated by certification body and independent expert.

settings. As such, formal data validation is much appreciated because as a V&V tool, it doesn't impact the development cycle (on the contrary of B for software development) and the verification phase is a "push-button" activity (once the formal data model is completed).

3   Convergence

We have seen from the previous chapter that B and Event-B have matured over the last decade and are addressing well safety-critical industry topics[13], at system level, at software level, and at configuration level. However using a formal method is not enough to demonstrate safety. For example, a software can't be SIL4-compliant by itself, even if it is developed with B. The hardware executing it has to be considered, especially its failure modes, and a sound specification at system level has to be elaborated accordingly. A safety demonstration requires a lot of experience, skills, time and energy to complete successfully.

We present in this chapter several new features, linked with B, that are directly contributing to the safety demonstration and that would ease the development and the certification processes of safety-critical systems.

3.1   Low Cost High Integrity Platform

LCHIP[14] is a new technology, combining a complete software development environment based on the B language and a secured execution hardware platform, to ease the development of safety critical applications. It relies on several building blocks already used in certified railways products.

LCHIP relies on a software factory that automatically transforms function into binary code that runs on redundant hardware. The starting point is a text-based, B formal model that specifies the function to implement. This model may contain static and dynamic properties that define the functional boundaries of the target software.

This formal specification is then refined automatically into a B implementable model. Transformation rules are applied to the specification to gradually replace abstract variables and substitutions with concrete ones.

The implementable model is then translated using two different chains:

- Translation into C ANSI code, with the C4B Atelier B code generator (instance I1). This C code is then compiled into HEX[15] binary code with an off-the-shelf compiler.
- Translation into MIPS Assembly then to HEX binary code, with a specific compiler developed for this purpose (instance I2). The translation in two steps allows to better debug the translation process as a MIPS assembly instruction corresponds to a HEX line.

---

[13] Even if re-targeted to address more specific issues.

[14] A short form of Low Cost High Integrity Platform.

[15] A file format that conveys binary information in ASCII text form. It is commonly used for programming micro-controllers.

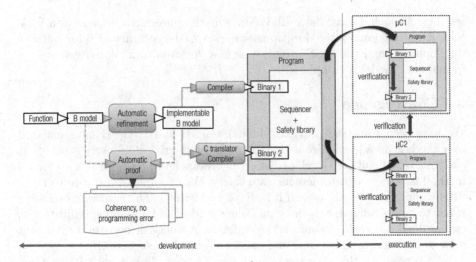

Fig. 5. The safe generation and execution of a function on the double processor.

3.1.1   Safety

These two different instances I1 and I2 of the same function are then executed in sequence, one after the other, on two PIC32 micro-controllers. Each micro-controller hosts both I1 and I2, so at any time 4 instances of the function are being executed on the micro-controllers. The results obtained by I1 and I2 are first compared locally on each micro-controller then they are compared between micro-controllers by using messages. In case of a divergent behavior (at least one of the four instances exhibits a different behavior), the faulty micro-controller reboots. The sequencer and the safety functions are developed once for all in B by the IDE design team and come along as a library. This way, the safety functions are out of reach of the developers and can't be altered. The safety is based on several features such as the detection of a divergent behavior, the detection of the inability for a processor to execute an instruction properly[16] and the ability to command outputs[17]. Memory areas (code, data for the two instances) are also checked (no overlap, no address outside memory range).

3.1.2   Target Software

The execution platform is based on two PIC32 micro-controllers and provides an available power of 100 MIPS. This processing power is sufficient to update 50k interlocking Boolean equations per second, compatible with light-rail signaling requirements. The execution platform can be redesigned seamlessly for any kind of mono-core processor if a higher level of performance is required. Similar secured platforms are operating platform-screen doors in São Paulo L15 metro

---

[16] All instructions are tested regularly against an oracle.

[17] Outputs are read to check if commands are effective, a system not able to change the state of its outputs has to shutdown.

and in Stockholm City line. The Brazilian one has been recently certified at level
SIL3 by CERTIFER on the inopportune opening failure of the doors.

The IDE provides a restricted modeling framework for software where:

- No operating system is used
- Software behavior is cyclic (no parallelism)
- No interruption modifies the software state variables
- Supported types are Boolean and integer types (and arrays of)
- Only bounded-complexity algorithms are supported (the price to pay to keep
  the refinement and proof process automatic)

The whole process, starting from the B model and finishing with the software
running on the hardware platform, is expected to be fully automatic with the
integration of the results obtained from some R&D projects[18]. In addition several
in-house projects have helped to optimize the automatic refinement process by
improving the refinement engine and by defining a subset of the B language,
Simple B.

3.1.3   Research and Development

LCHIP [12] is developed by the eponymous French R&D project. It is aimed
at allowing any engineer to develop a function by using its usual Domain Specific Language and to obtain this function running safely on a hardware platform. With the automatic development process, the B formal method will remain
"behind the curtain" in order to avoid expert transactions.

As the safety demonstration doesn't require any specific feature for the input
B model, it could be handwritten or the by-product of a translation process. So
several DSL are planned to be supported at once (relays schematic, grafcet)
based on an Open API (Bxml). The translation from relays schematic is being
studied for the French Railways with a strong focus on the feedback between
DSL and B: in case of unproven B proof obligations, it is mandatory to exhibit
its source in the DSL model.

The project reuses a number of building blocks such as the C4B[19] C code
generator extended to support PIC memory model, and the B to Hex binary file
in-house compiler supporting PIC32.

The IDE will be based on Atelier B 5.0, providing a simplified process-
oriented GUI. A first starter kit, containing the IDE and the execution platform,
will be publicly released by the end of 2017.

3.2   Proof Support Advances

3.2.1   Proof Support in Atelier B

A formal development demands that different aspects are verified using a mathematical proof. To this end, Atelier B produces automatically a number of proof

---

[18] To implement automatic refinement (ANR-RIMEL) and improve automatic proof
performances (ANR-BWARE).
[19] Atelier B C code generator.

obligations (POs). To assist the user in discharging POs, Atelier B has included a theorem prover since its inception. This "historical" theorem prover is an inference engine and an (extensible) rule database. It has been certified in the railway domain by expert review of both the inference engine and a core rule base. The architecture of the theorem prover is such that it can be used interactively, or automatically, at different force levels.

The user applies the theorem prover in batch to all the proof obligations, and is then left with a number of open POs. The remaining POs can be classified in three categories: valid, the theorem prover being unable to find the proof; unprovable, because the rule database is essentially incomplete; unprovable, because the user made a mistake in the formal development.

The top priority of the user is to ensure that there is no mistake, i.e., there is no PO of the last category. Visually inspecting the POs is often enough to detect most such errors, although there are also trickier mistakes that are only uncovered in the course of an interactive proof.

The user has then to discharge the unproved POs by interactive proof, and this is the most time-consuming task in a formal development. The prover of Atelier-B supports a number of commands to develop interactive proofs: hypotheses selection, case split, quantifier instantiation, equality rewriting, rule application, etc. A proof script is successful when the proof obligation has been shown valid. One a script is successful, it is saved in the project data base, and can be applied to other proof obligations. Actually, a script is often successful for more than one PO. To improve scripting capabilities and efficiency, the language has been enriched with pattern-matching constructs that enable more general proofs. However, we feel that the interactive proof process should be improved so that the user would only need to address "interesting" goals and sub-goals that require some human insight.

Since the specification language of the B method is undecidable, the user is allowed to write new rules to be taken into account by the inference engine. The risk of introducing inconsistencies is mitigated by two measures. The first measure consists in the inclusion of an alternative prover, based on tableaux, that is able to prove some of the rules automatically. The second measure applies to those rules that could not be proved automatically. It consists in the user writing a textual proof in natural language, that is then subject to validation by a third-party.

In the past year, Atelier B support for PO verification has been improved with two different tools, addressing this issue at different levels:

iapa (Interface to Automatic Proof Agents) for batch processing of POs;
drudges of the theorem prover for rapid processing of sub-goals in the interactive prover.

They are presented in turn in the following.

3.2.2   Iapa

The iapa extension for Atelier B gives access to a number of third-party provers to discharge POs [5]. In iapa, POs are not translated directly to the input format of these provers; instead the translation targets the format of a program verification platform that plays here the role of a gateway to such automatic provers, namely Why3 [3]. Each PO thus includes a prelude where the logic of the B expression language is formalized in Why3 [14]. The axiomatization of the B operators in Why3 has been fine tuned based on an industrial benchmark, resulting in significant improvement of the automatic proving capabilities in Atelier B on that benchmark [6].

As the proof obligations are produced automatically, they include all the hypotheses that are in scope at the point the PO is concerned about. It is often the case that the validity of the goal only depends on a small number of such hypotheses. However, at times, provers are not able to identify these relevant hypotheses and end up lost in the proof search space.

In order to address this issue, iapa includes a hypotheses selection functionality, where the user can identify a subset of the hypotheses, and only this subset is included in the proof obligation that is translated to Why3 and eventually processed by the provers. This functionality is available both through a graphical, point-and-click, interface and through a command line language. Subsets of hypotheses can be created according to the presence of some identifier or set of identifiers, then added to the proof obligation. Of course iapa also provides a function to extract a set of free identifiers from the goal or from some subset of hypotheses. These functionalities are built upon two kinds of entities that the user can create and manipulate: contexts (subsets of hypotheses) and lexicons

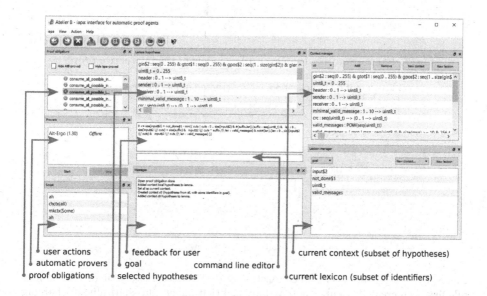

Fig. 6. An annotated screenshot of iapa

(subsets of identifiers). Full details are available in [5]; iapa is part of Atelier B starting from version 4.5.

3.2.3 Drudges of the Interactive Prover

The motivation for this functionality was born out of the feeling of frustration that the user of the interactive prover sometimes feels when she is faced with a seemingly trivial sub-goal, yet single command is able to discharge it. An example of such situation is when the current goal can be shown to be a consequence of the hypotheses using the theory of equality and propositional reasoning, but the terms involved are large or contain operators that get the automatic prover lost.

A general rule is that the less proficient the proof engine, the more efficient it is. So the rationale of the drudges of the interactive prover is to use automatic provers for simpler logics that are able to produce not only the result of the validity check, but also information on how they have reached their conclusion, and this information is then processed to produce guidance for the automatic prover of Atelier B.

Candidate drudges are provers that are either *proof producing*, or at least able to generate a so-called *unsat core*, i.e. a subset of the hypotheses that are actually used in the proof. Such functions have been standardized through at least two initiatives: TPTP [16] and SMT [1]. The drudges currently in the latter category only (veriT [4] and Z3 [7]), as they implement the unsat core functionality. Given the unsat core, a proof rule for the Atelier B prover can be produced automatically, compiled and applied to the current goal. The drudges

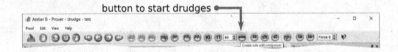

Fig. 7. Interface to the drudges in the window of the interactive prover

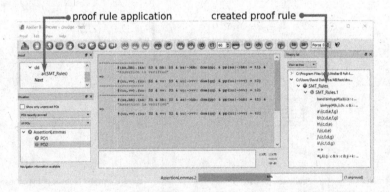

Fig. 8. State after the successful completion of the drudges : with a single click, a new rule has been created (right panel) and applied (left panel) automatically, discharging the goal.

are available as a single click on a new button in the tool bar of the interactive prover (see Fig. 7). If the drudges are successful, the current goal is automatically discharged and the proof rule is added to the rule base of the component (see Fig. 8).

4   Conclusion and Perspectives

4.1   Aimed at Industry

Introducing formal methods in industry is difficult. We have experienced this situation with B in almost all industries, with a wide range of arguments:

- "we do not want to change of development cycle"
- "we do not recruit PhD"
- "formal methods work for train in 1-D, but planes flight in 3-D"
- "trains and planes have professional drivers, but car drivers are mostly non-professional"
- "we are not able to understand your deliverable"
- etc.

The real chance for the B-method was the very difficult development of the automatic speed control system for rapid transit railways in Paris, SACEM, in 1977, and the decision by the RATP to promote the B-method for the development of the first driver-less metro Meteor in 1993.

Several new usages at system-level and at configuration level have emerged over the last decade, scaling up to industry-strength deployments and offering new verification means with increased levels of confidence. These techniques allow to better manage complexity when dealing with large systems. However, since 1994, B uses have been contained to a narrow scope of industrial software applications in the railways because of:

- the specific development cycle where unit and integration testing almost completely disappears,
- the mandatory ability to handle abstraction for efficient modeling,
- a specific code generator per target application to address hardware specifics.

The LCHIP technology, combined with improved proof performances and provers diversity, pave the way to an easier way of developing SIL4 functions (including both hardware and software). The platform safety being out of reach of the software developer, the automation of the redundant binary code generation process and the certificates already obtained for products embedding LCHIP building blocks, would enable the repetition of similar performances without requiring highly qualified engineers. The hardware platform is generic enough to host a large number of complexity-bounded industry applications, with a special focus on the IoT and nuclear energy[20] domains.

---

[20] In France several nuclear plants will have to be decommissioned in the coming years, requiring to develop supervision systems complying with current standards.

4.2 Challenges

Safety-critical systems are certainly privileged targets when considering the application formal methods. The risk to injure or kill people may entitle to consider more easily "exotic" development, verification or validation means. With the raise of the IoT and the "connect-anything-to-anything" paradigm, security adds a new dimension to analyze and being able to model and prove at the same time safety and security properties could facilitate the acceptance of formal methods in the forthcoming standards releases.

Every industry has its own challenges. Based on our experience, our advice is to know and understand very well a particular application domain, especially its problems and imagine a usage of your formal method, even for a tiny/very specific scope[21]. Aim for the most automated process as industry is very fond of any "push-button" tool[22] .

References

1. Barrett, C., Fontaine, P., Tinelli, C.: The SMT-LIB standard: version 2.5. Technical report, Department of Computer Science, The University of Iowa (2015). www.SMT-LIB.org
2. Benveniste, M.V.: On using B in the design of secure micro-controllers: an experience report. Electr. Notes Theor. Comput. Sci. **280**, 3–22 (2011)
3. Bobot, F., Filliâtre, J.C., Marché, C., Paskevich, A.: Why3: shepherd your herd of provers. In: Boogie 2011: 1st International Workshop on Intermediate Verification Languages, pp. 53–64. Wrocław, Poland, August 2011
4. Bouton, T., Caminha B. de Oliveira, D., Déharbe, D., Fontaine, P.: Verit: an open, trustable and efficient SMT-solver. In: Schmidt, R.A. (ed.) CADE 2009. LNCS (LNAI), vol. 5663, pp. 151–156. Springer, Heidelberg (2009). https://doi.org/10.1007/978-3-642-02959-2_12
5. Burdy, L., Déharbe, D., Prun, É.: Interfacing automatic proof agents in atelier B: introducing "iapa". In: Dubois, C., Masci, P., Méry, D. (eds.) Proceedings of the Third Workshop on Formal Integrated Development Environment, F-IDE@FM 2016. EPTCS, vol. 240, pp. 82–90. Limassol, Cyprus, 8 November 2016
6. Conchon, S., Iguernelala, M.: Tuning the Alt-Ergo SMT Solver for B Proof Obli-gations, pp. 294–297. Springer (2014). https://doi.org/10.1007/978-3-662-43652-3_27
7. de Moura, L., Bjørner, N.: Z3: an efficient SMT solver. In: Ramakrishnan, C.R., Rehof, J. (eds.) TACAS 2008. LNCS, vol. 4963, pp. 337–340. Springer, Heidelberg (2008). https://doi.org/10.1007/978-3-540-78800-3_24
8. Falampin, J., Le-Dang, H., Leuschel, M., Mokrani, M., Plagge, D.: Improving railway data validation with prob. In: Romanovsky, A., Thomas, M. (eds.) Industrial Deployment of System Engineering Methods, pp. 27–43. Springer, Heidelberg (2013). https://doi.org/10.1007/978-3-642-33170-1_4

---

[21] As such, LCHIP is a potential solution for small memory footprint safety-critical systems.

[22] Formal data validation is "usual" model-checking connected to a Domain Specific Language and traceability means to support certification.

9. Hansen, D., Schneider, D., Leuschel, M.: Using B and prob for data validation projects. In: Butler, M., Schewe, K.-D., Mashkoor, A., Biro, M. (eds.) ABZ 2016. LNCS, vol. 9675, pp. 167–182. Springer, Cham (2016). https://doi.org/10.1007/978-3-319-33600-8_10

10. Lecomte, T.: Safe and reliable metro platform screen doors control/command systems. In: Cuellar, J., Maibaum, T., Sere, K. (eds.) FM 2008. LNCS, vol. 5014, pp. 430–434. Springer, Heidelberg (2008). https://doi.org/10.1007/978-3-540-68237-0_32

11. Lecomte, T.: Applying a formal method in industry: a 15-year trajectory. In: Alpuente, M., Cook, B., Joubert, C. (eds.) FMICS 2009. LNCS, vol. 5825, pp. 26–34. Springer, Heidelberg (2009). https://doi.org/10.1007/978-3-642-04570-7_3

12. Lecomte, T.: Double cœur et preuve formelle pour automatismes sil4. 8E-Modèles formels/preuves formelles-sûreté du logiciel (2016)

13. Lecomte, T., Burdy, L., Leuschel, M.: Formally checking large data sets in the railways. CoRR abs/1210.6815 (2012)

14. Mentré, D., Marché, C., Filliâtre, J.-C., Asuka, M.: Discharging proof obligations from atelier B using multiple automated provers. In: Derrick, J., Fitzgerald, J., Gnesi, S., Khurshid, S., Leuschel, M., Reeves, S., Riccobene, E. (eds.) ABZ 2012. LNCS, vol. 7316, pp. 238–251. Springer, Heidelberg (2012). https://doi.org/10.1007/978-3-642-30885-7_17

15. Sabatier, D.: Using formal proof and B method at system level for industrial projects. In: Lecomte, T., Pinger, R., Romanovsky, A. (eds.) RSSRail 2016. LNCS, vol. 9707, pp. 20–31. Springer, Cham (2016). https://doi.org/10.1007/978-3-319-33951-1_2

16. Sutcliffe, G.: The tptp problem library and associated infrastructure. J. Autom. Reasoning **43**(4), 337 (2009)

Model Checking

Encoding Floating-Point Numbers Using the SMT Theory in ESBMC: An Empirical Evaluation over the SV-COMP Benchmarks

Mikhail Y.R. Gadelha[1]([envelope]), Lucas C. Cordeiro[2], and Denis A. Nicole[1]

[1] Electronics and Computer Science, University of Southampton, Southampton, UK
myrg1g14@soton.ac.uk, dan@ecs.soton.ac.uk
[2] Department of Computer Science, University of Oxford, Oxford, UK
lucas.cordeiro@cs.ox.ac.uk

Abstract. This paper describes the support for encoding C/C++ programs using the SMT theory of floating-point numbers in ESBMC: an SMT-based context-bounded model checker that provides bit-precise verification of C and C++ programs. In particular, we exploit the availability of two different SMT solvers (MathSAT and Z3) to discharge and check the verification conditions produced by our encoding using the benchmarks from the International Competition on Software Verification (SV-COMP). The experimental results show that our encoding based on MathSAT is able to outperform not only Z3, but also other existing approaches that participated in the most recent edition of SV-COMP.

Keywords: Floating-point arithmetic · Satisfiability modulo theories · Software verification · Formal methods

1 Introduction

Over the years, computer manufacturers have experimented with different machine representations for real numbers [1]. The two basic ways to encode a real number are the fixed-point representation, usually found in embedded microprocessors and microcontrollers [2], and the floating-point representation, in particular, the IEEE floating-point standard (IEEE 754-2008), which has been adopted by many processors [3,4].

Each encoding can represent a range of real numbers depending on the word-length and how the bits are distributed. A fixed-point representation of a number consists of an integer component, a fractional component and a bit for the sign, while the floating-point representation consists of an exponent component, a mantissa component and a bit for the sign. Numbers represented using a floating-point encoding have a much higher dynamic range than the fixed-point one (e.g., a `float` in C has 24 bits of accuracy, but can have values up to 2^{127}), while numbers represented using a fixed-point representation can have a greater precision than floating-point, but less dynamic range [5]. Furthermore, the IEEE floating-point standard contains definition that have no direct equivalent in a

© Springer International Publishing AG 2017
S. Cavalheiro and J. Fiadeiro (Eds.): SBMF 2017, LNCS 10623, pp. 91–106, 2017.
https://doi.org/10.1007/978-3-319-70848-5_7

```
1  int main()
2  {
3     float x;
4     float y = x;
5     assert(x==y);
6     return 0;
7  }
```

Fig. 1. Simple floating-point program with a bug.

fixed-point encoding, e.g., two infinities ($+\infty$ and $-\infty$) and for signalling and quiet NaNs (**N**ot **a** **N**umber, used to represent an undefined or unrepresentable value), denormal numbers, rounding modes, etc.

In this paper, we present ESBMC, a bounded model checker that uses Satisfiability Modulo Theories (SMT) solvers to verify single- and multi-threaded C/C++ code [6,7]. The tool is able to encode the programs using either fixed-point arithmetics (using bitvectors) or floating-point arithmetic (using the SMT theory of floating-point numbers [8]). Initially, ESBMC was only able to encode `float`, `double` and `long double` using a fixed-point encoding (used in a wide range of applications in the verification of digital filters [9,10] and controllers [11,12]); the lack of a proper floating-point encoding, however, meant that ESBMC was not able to find an entire class of bugs, such as the one shown in Fig. 1.

The program shown in Fig. 1 will never fail if verified with a fixed-point encoding. However, when using a floating-point encoding, x can be NaN and comparing NaNs, even with themselves, is always false [3]. In this scenario, the assertion in line 5 does not hold.

Support for verifying programs that rely on floating-point arithmetic is an important contribution to the software verification community, as it helps demonstrate the applicability of SMT-based verification to real-world systems.

The main original contributions of this paper are:

- We describe the verification process in ESBMC from the C program to the SMT formula encoding, including the solvers that support floating-point arithmetic, special cases when encoding the program, unused operators from the SMT standard and an illustrative example (Sect. 3).
- We demonstrate that our floating-point encoding based on MathSAT is able to outperform not only ESBMC with Z3, but also all the other approaches that participated in the most recent round of SV-COMP [13]. In particular, ESBMC/MathSAT is able to verify 169 benchmarks in 9977.4 s, while ESBMC/Z3 verifies 127 in 44992.7 s. ESBMC was the most efficient verifier for the floating-point subcategory in SV-COMP 2017, with 308 scores, followed by Ceagle [14] (298 scores), and CBMC [15] (264 scores) (Sect. 4).

2 The Efficient SMT-Based Context-Bounded Model Checker (ESBMC)

In this section, we present ESBMC, an open source, permissively licensed (Apache 2), cross platform bounded model checker for C and C++ programs. ESBMC was developed to perform bounded model checks on both sequential and concurrent programs using a range of SMT solvers, and has a proven track of bug finding in real-world applications [6,7,16]. The tool also implements a technique to prove the correctness of (some) unbounded programs: the k-induction algorithm; this approach has been applied to a large number of benchmarks and has produced more correct results than similar competing tools [17]. Figure 2 shows the tool architecture. Rounded white rectangles represent input and output; squared gray rectangles represent the verification steps.

ESBMC has two alternative front-ends to parse the input program and generate an Abstract Syntax Tree (AST). There is the legacy CBMC-based front-end that supports both C and C++, and a new clang-based front-end that currently only supports C. The data types are created in the front-end when parsing the code, setting variable types to either fixed-point or floating-point for `float`, `double` and `long double`, depending on the options set by the user. Bitvector representations of constants are also created by the frontend, according to the fixed-point or floating-point semantics. The bitvector representation [7] of other data types (e.g., `int`, `char`) were not changed by the work described in this paper.

Regardless of the chosen front-end, the output is an AST that will be used by the GOTO converter to generate a GOTO program, which has simplified control flow and is suitable for bounded unwinding. The next step is the symbolic execution, when the GOTO program is executed (unrolling loops up to the bound k) and converted to Static Single Assignments (SSA) [18] form. During the symbolic execution, ESBMC aggressively tries to simplify the program; it propagates all constants and solves any assertions that can be statically determined. This is an important step for the verification; ESBMC can fully verify programs without calling a solver, if the inputs are deterministic.

The SSA expressions are then encoded using the chosen SMT solver; ultimately we are attempting to determine whether a formula, which is the disjunction

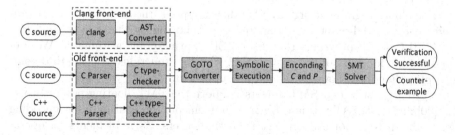

Fig. 2. ESBMC architecture for floating-point verification.

of all possible errors, can be satisfied. If the SMT formula is shown to be satisfiable, a counterexample is presented; if the formula is found to be unsatisfiable, there are no errors up to the unwinding bound k, and this result is presented. ESBMC supports 5 SMT solvers: Boolector (default) [19], Z3 [20], MathSAT [21], Yices [22] and CVC4 [23]. In order to support and maintain this number of solvers, an SMT layer was developed, in such way that the support for new solvers, or new features like the floating-point support, only requires the implementation of the specific API calls for each solver.

It is in this layer that most of our contribution is concentrated. We implemented the new floating-point API in the SMT layer and the corresponding function calls for Z3 and MathSAT. The remaining solvers do not support floating-point arithmetic so ESBMC aborts the verification if an user tries to use this functionality with them.

3 Floating-Point SMT Encoding

Here we describe our main contribution, the bit-precise encoding for ANSI-C programs using the SMT theory of floating-point. The SMT theory of floating-point covers almost all the operations performed at program level so the conversion is one-to-one and follows the encoding as described by Cordeiro et al. [7]. Given that, we focus on the limitations of the SMT theory of floating-point (casts to boolean types in Sect. 3.1 and the equality operator in Sect. 3.2) and how they were circumvented. In this section we also show operators from the SMT theory that are not being used in our implementation in Sect. 3.3 and an illustrative example of verification using the SMT theory of floating-point in Sect. 3.4; in this section we show the encoding and the counterexample generated by ESBMC, and the models generated by the solvers.

The SMT floating-point theory is an addition to the SMT standard, first proposed in 2010 by Rümmer and Wahl [8]. The current version of the theory largely follows the IEEE standard 754-2008 [3] and formalises the floating-point arithmetic, positive and negative infinities and zeroes, NaNs, comparison and arithmetic operators, and five rounding modes: round nearest with ties choosing the even value, round nearest with ties choosing away from zero, round towards positive infinity, round towards negative infinity and round towards zero. There are, however, some functionalities from the IEEE standard that are not yet supported by the SMT theory as described by Brain et al. [24].

Encoding programs using the SMT floating-point theory has several advantages over a fixed-point encoding, but the main one is the correct modeling of ANSI-C/C++ programs that use IEEE floating-point arithmetic. We created models for most of the current C11 standard functions [25]; floating-point exception handling, however, is not yet supported.

Currently, only two SMT solvers support the SMT floating-point theory: Z3 [20] and MathSAT [21] and ESBMC implements the floating-point encoding for both. In terms of the support from the solvers, Z3 implements all operators, while MathSAT implements all but two: `fp.rem` (remainder operator) and `fp.fma` (fused multiply-add).

Both solvers offer two (non-standard) functions to convert floating-point numbers to and from bitvectors: fp_as_ieeebv and fp_from_ieeebv, respectively. These functions can be used to circumvent any lack of operators, and only require the user to write the missing operators.

3.1 Casts to Boolean

The SMT standard defines conversion operations to and from signed and unsigned bitvectors, reals, integers and other floating-point types, but does not define a conversion operation for boolean types. ESBMC, however, generates these operations, as shown by the program in Fig. 3. The program in Fig. 3 forces ESBMC to generate two casts: one from boolean to double in line 5 and one from double to boolean in line 8. Figure 4a and b present the SMT formula generated by these lines, respectively. When casting from booleans to floating-point numbers (Fig. 4a), an ite operator is used, such that the result of the cast is 1.0 if the boolean is true; otherwise the result is 0.0. When casting from

```
1  int  main ( ) {
2     _Bool  c ;
3     double  b = 0.0 f ;
4
5     b = c ;
6     assert ( b != 0.0 f ) ;
7
8     c = b ;
9     assert ( c != 0 ) ;
10 }
```

Fig. 3. Program to demonstrate the casts to and from boolean generated by ESBMC.

```
(assert (= (ite |main::c|
        (fp #b0 #b01111111111 #x0000000000000)
        (fp #b0 #b00000000000 #x0000000000000))
    |main::b|))
```

(a) SMT generated when casting from boolean to floating-point.

```
(assert (= (not (fp.eq |main::b|
        (fp #b0 #b00000000000 #x0000000000000))))
    |main::c|))
```

(b) SMT generated when casting from floating-point to boolean.

Fig. 4. SMT formula generated by ESBMC to encode the casts to and from boolean types in Fig. 3.

floating-point numbers to booleans (Fig. 4b), we encode as a conditional assignment: the result of the cast is true when the floating is not 0.0; otherwise the result is false.

3.2   The fp.eq operator

Figure 4b also shows the second special cases when encoding ANSI-C programs. When encoding the program, both assignments and comparison operations are encoded using equalities. This must be changed, however, as the SMT standard defines a custom operator for floating-point equalities, fp.eq operator:

> :note
> "(fp.eq x y) evaluates to true if x evaluates to -zero and y to +zero, or vice versa. fp.eq and all the other comparison operators evaluate to false if one of their arguments is NaN."

In this case, the operator is defined to handle the special symbols from the IEEE floating-point standard, in particular, NaNs. It would not be correct to use the ordinary operator equality for comparison; it should only be used for assignments, while fp.eq is used for comparing floating-point numbers.

3.3   Unused Operators from the SMT Standard

When implementing the floating-point encoding, we did not use four operators defined by the SMT standard: fp.max, fp.min, fp.rem and fp.isSubnormal, instead we reimplemented them for enhanced perfomance:

1. fp.max: returns the larger of two floating-point numbers; equivalent to the fmax, fmaxf, fmaxl functions. Our model of the functions is shown in Fig. 5.
2. fp.min: returns the smaller of two floating-point numbers; equivalent to the fmin, fminf, fminl functions. Our model of the functions is shown in Fig. 6.
3. fp.rem: returns the floating-point remainder of the division operation x/y; equivalent to the fmod, fmodf, fmodl functions. Our model of the functions is shown in Fig. 7.

```
1  double fmax(double x, double y) {
2      // If both argument are NaN, NaN is returned
3      if(isnan(x) && isnan(y)) return NAN;
4
5      // If one arg is NaN, the other is returned
6      if(isnan(x)) return y;
7      if(isnan(y)) return x;
8
9      return (x > y ? x : y);
10 }
```

Fig. 5. Model for fmax.

```
1  double fmin(double x, double y) {
2    // If both argument are NaN, NaN is returned
3    if(isnan(x) && isnan(y)) return NAN;
4
5    // If one arg is NaN, the other is returned
6    if(isnan(x) || isnan(y)) {
7      if(isnan(x))
8        return y;
9      return x;
10   }
11
12   return (x < y ? x : y);
13 }
```

Fig. 6. Model for fmin.

```
1  double fmod(double x, double y) {
2    // If either argument is NaN, NaN is returned
3    if(isnan(x) || isnan(y)) return NAN;
4
5    // If x is +inf/-inf and y is not NaN, NaN is returned
6    if(isinf(x)) return NAN;
7
8    // If y is +0.0/-0.0 and x is not NaN, NaN is returned
9    if(y == 0.0) return NAN;
10
11   // If x is +0.0/-0.0 and y is not zero, returns +0.0/-0.0
12   if((x == 0.0) && (y != 0.0))
13     return signbit(x) ? -0.0 : +0.0;
14
15   // If y is +inf/-inf and x is finite, x is returned.
16   if(isinf(y) && isfinite(x)) return x;
17
18   return x - (y * (int)(x/y));
19 }
```

Fig. 7. Model for fmod.

4. `fp.isSubnormal`: checks if a number is subnormal, i.e., a non-zero floating-point number with magnitude less than the magnitude of that format's smallest normal number. A subnormal number does not use the full precision available to normal numbers of the same format [3]. We could not find any user case for it when modelling C11 standard functions.

3.4 Illustrative Example

As an illustrative example of the SMT encoding using the floating-point arithmetic, Fig. 8 shows the full SMT formula generated by ESBMC[1] for the program in Fig. 1, as printed by Z3.

```
; declaration of x and y
(declare-fun |main::x| () (_ FloatingPoint 8 24))
(declare-fun |main::y| () (_ FloatingPoint 8 24))

; symbol created to represent a nondeteministic number
(declare-fun |nondet_symex::nondet0| () (_ FloatingPoint 8 24))

; Global guard, used for checking properties
(declare-fun |execution_statet::\\guard_exec| () Bool)

; assign the nondeterministic symbol to x
(assert (= |nondet_symex::nondet0| |main::x|))

; assign x to y
(assert (= |main::x| |main::y|))

; assert x == y
(assert (let ((a!1 (not (=> true
                    (=> |execution_statet::\\guard_exec|
                    (fp.eq |main::x| |main::y|))))))
  (or a!1)))
```

Fig. 8. SMT formula generated by ESBMC for the program shown in Fig. 1.

The SMT formula contains all the symbol declaration (main::x and main::y), nondeteministic symbols (nondetsymex::nondet0) and a boolean variable (execution_statet::\\guard_exec), that evaluates to true if there is a property violation in the program. The pervasive occurrence of FloatingPoint 8 24 derives from the exponent and mantissa lengths of single precision floats.

---

[1] ESBMC actually generates a slightly different SMT formula, which includes all the symbols used for the memory model. The variable names are also more elaborate as the generated SSA has to reflect different valuations of the variable: the variable storage in memory, the thread to which the variable is associated, the specific thread interleaving the variable is related to, and the valuation of the variable at different points in the program. Each valuation is represented by a symbol (@, !, & and #) and an index. They were omitted to make the formula easier to read.

Both SMT solvers correctly find a failure model for the program; Z3 produces:

```
sat
(model
  (define-fun |main::x| () (_ FloatingPoint 8 24)
    (_ NaN 8 24))
  (define-fun |main::y| () (_ FloatingPoint 8 24)
    (_ NaN 8 24))
  (define-fun |nondet_symex::nondet0| () (_ FloatingPoint 8 24)
    (_ NaN 8 24))
  (define-fun |execution_statet::\\\\guard_exec| () Bool
    true)
)
```

and MathSAT produces:

```
          sat
          ( (|main::x| (_ NaN 8 24))
            (|main::y| (_ NaN 8 24))
            (|nondet_symex::nondet0| (_ NaN 8 24))
            (|execution_statet::\\guard_exec| true) )
```

```
Counterexample:

State 1 file main3.c line 3 function main thread 0
main
----------------------------------------------------
  main3::main::1::x=-NaN (11111111100000000000000000000001)

State 2 file main3.c line 4 function main thread 0
main
----------------------------------------------------
  main3::main::2::y=-NaN (11111111100000000000000000000001)

State 3 file main3.c line 5 function main thread 0
main
----------------------------------------------------
Violated property:
  file main3.c line 5 function main
  assertion
  (_Bool)(x == y)

VERIFICATION FAILED
```

Fig. 9. Counterexample generated by ESBMC when verifying the program in Fig. 1.

This is the expected result from the verification of the program in Fig. 1; the program violates the assertion if x (and consequently y) is NaN. This happens because x is left uninitialized.

The model generated by both solvers is converted back to SSA by ESBMC, that prints the assignments that lead to a property violation[2]. Figure 9 shows the counterexample presented by ESBMC when verifying the program in Fig. 1, using the floating-point arithmetic to encode the program. This is the counterexample generated when verifying the program with MathSAT; the counterexample generated by Z3 presents a positive NaN, but it is otherwise the same (both solvers are correct and either a positive or a negative NaN will lead to a property violation in the program). ESBMC also presents the IEEE bitvector representation of the values assigned to the variables, whenever possible.

4   Experimental Evaluation

This section is split into three parts. The description of benchmarks and setup is described in Sect. 4.1, while Sect. 4.2 describes the experimental objectives. In Sect. 4.3, we evaluate our encoding using two state-of-the-art SMT solvers (MathSAT and Z3) and compare our best approach to other verifiers that support floating-point arithmetic in Sect. 4.4.

4.1   Description of Benchmarks and Setup

We evaluate our approach using a set of verification tasks in the *ReachSafety-Floats* sub-category of SV-COMP, which contains programs using floating-point arithmetic [13]. As defined by the competition rules, we assume a 32-bit architecture and, for all benchmarks, we check the following property as specified by the SV-COMP rules:

```
CHECK( init(main()), LTL(G, !call(__VERIFIER_error())) )
```

which means that from the main() function, we check the reachability of the function __VERIFIER_error() through any possible program execution. If there is a path from the program start to __VERIFIER_error(), the program contains a bug.

All experiments were conducted on a computer with an Intel Core i7-2600 running at 3.40 GHz and 24 GB of RAM under Fedora 25 64-bit. For each benchmark, we set time and memory limits of 900 s (15 min) and 16 GB respectively. We provide a package with the latest version of ESBMC, all the benchmarks and the scripts to run the experiments at http://esbmc.org/benchmarks/pack-sbmf2017.tar.gz.

---

[2] In comparison, no model is generated by the solver when verified using the fixed-point arithmetic.

4.2   Objectives

Using the SV-COMP floating-point benchmarks given in Sect. 4.1, our experimental evaluation aims to answer two research questions:

RQ1 **(performance)** does our encoding generate verifications conditions that can be checked by state-of-the-art SMT solvers in a reasonable amount of time?

RQ2 **(sanity)** are the verification results sound and can their reproducibility be confirmed outside of our verifier?

4.3   Solver Performance Comparisons

Table 1 compares the results of ESBMC using both solvers on 172 benchmarks from SV-COMP'17, using a fixed unwind approach. Here, *Correct true* is the number of correct positive results (i.e., the tool reports SAFE correctly), *Correct false* is the number of correct negative results (i.e., the tool reports UNSAFE correctly), *Timeout* represents the number of time-outs (i.e., the tool was aborted after 900 s) and *Total time* is the total verification time, in seconds. Bold numbers represent better results. There is no case where ESBMC reports an incorrect result or exhausts the memory, so we are omitting them from the table.

When verifying the programs, ESBMC is able to statically verify 76 out of the 172 benchmarks (44.18%). This is due to the fact that the these programs are deterministic and, as described in Sect. 2, ESBMC is able to verify the program without calling a solver.

For the programs that ESBMC requires a solver for the verification, the verification time for both solvers is considerably longer when arrays are present, in comparison to array-free programs. Given the set of benchmarks, ESBMC/MathSAT is able to solve all but three (within the time limit), while ESBMC/Z3 times-out for most array programs with an increased verification time for the others.

ESBMC/Z3 also fails to verify the same 3 benchmarks as ESBMC/MathSAT. The 3 programs[3] were created by Delmas et al. [26] and try to calculate a sine

Table 1. Comparative results of ESBMC using MathSAT v5.3.14 and Z3 v4.5.0.

	ESBMC (MathSAT v5.3.14)	ESBMC (Z3 v4.5.0)
Correct true	**139**	111
Correct false	**30**	16
Timeout	**3**	45
Total time (s)	**9977.40**	44992.76

---

[3] `sin_interpolated_index_true-unreach-call.c`,
`sin_interpolated_bigrange_loose_true-unreach-call.c`
and `sin_interpolated_bigrange_tight_true-unreach-call.c`.

over a range of nondeteministic values, using an interpolation table. These programs assume a range of nondeterministic input and contains arrays, requiring a great deal of time to find the solution.

We provide a table that includes the number of variables, the number of clauses as well as the number of conflicts on the package previously mentioned in Sect. 4.1. However, we are unable to draw conclusions based on the provided numbers since we do not identify any pattern. For instance, one of the benchmarks that cannot be solved by MathSAT, `sin_interpolated_bigrange_tight_true-unreach-call.c` generates 545667 variables and 2240257 clauses, while 794852 variables and 3263282 clauses are generated when verifying `sin_interpolated_negation_true-unreach-call.c` and the latter can be verified in 61.3 s.

We can, however, compare these numbers, generated by both solvers. It is clear that MathSAT is more aggressively simplifying the program before bit-blasting. The total numbers are: Z3 generates 1.4×10^{10} variables and 1.4×10^{10} clauses in 44992.76 s (12.5 h), while MathSAT generated 1.21×10^7 variables 4.73×10^7 clauses in 9977.40 s (2.8 h). In terms of total numbers of conflicts, MathSAT generates 1.7 $\times$ more conflicts than Z3. However, Z3 was not able to finish the verification of 26.1% of the benchmarks, so this number is at best an approximation of the real value (this is not true for the number of variables and clauses, since they do not change during the execution of the DPLL algorithm [27]).

4.4 Comparison to Other Software Verifiers

ESBMC with MathSAT greatly outperforms Z3 when verifying the competition's benchmarks and was the solver we used for the competition. Figure 10 shows the results of all verifiers on the *ReachSafety-Floats* sub-category of SV-COMP'17.

Figure 10 relates each tool score (y-axis) to the time spent during verification, in seconds (x-axis). Note that verifiers which actually give incorrect results can accumulate negative scores [13]. Using the fixed unwind approach, ESBMC was able to verify all but the 3 benchmarks previously mentioned, with a final score of 308 out of 316, in 5200 s, followed by Ceagle [14], with final score of 298 int 15000 s, and CBMC [15], with a final score of 264 in 3000 s. ESBMC also competed with other approaches in the competition, *ESBMC-falsi*, an incremental approach focused on finding bugs, *ESBMC-incr*, an incremental approach that provides a successful answer when it unrolled all loops, and *ESBMC-kind*, that tries to find bugs and prove correctness using induction [17]; these 3 approaches use Z3 as it performs better in other categories. The results from SV-COMP'17 are on par with the results presented in Sect. 4.3, where MathSAT outperforms Z3 when verifying programs with floating-point arithmetic.

These results allow us to answer both the research questions proposed in Sect. 4.2. The first inquires after the performance of our solver. Under the limits imposed by SV-COMP'17 (15 min and 16 GB of RAM), ESBMC with Math-SAT or Z3 is able to verify 98.2% and 73.8% of the benchmarks, respectively.

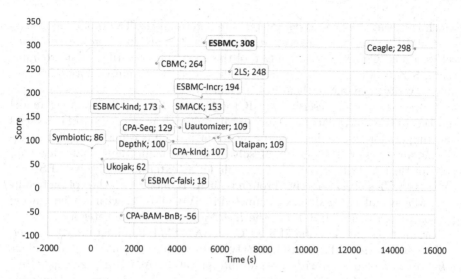

Fig. 10. Tool score versus time spent during verification over the ReachSafety-Floats sub-category of SV-COMP'17.

The verification time is almost half of the presented in our results, due to the fact that SV-COMP has faster processors [13].

The second research question enquiries about the soundness and reproducibility of the results. The benchmarks from SV-COMP are thoroughly tested by all the verifiers, months before the actual competition, to ensure that all the verdicts are correct. ESBMC was able to encode all benchmarks and no wrong result was provided by our tool. However, SV-COMP still lacks the ability to automatically reproduce the counterexamples produced by verifiers in the *ReachSafety-Floats* sub-category, mainly because of the availability of witness checkers; these currently do not handle floating-point arithmetic [13].

5 Related Work

SMT solvers are an improving technology, being able to reason about ever growing formulas. These constant improvements feed the creation of a number of SMT-based software verification tools to the extent that they are already being applied in industry (e.g., Static Driver Verifier [28]). Here, we present other tools that bridge the gap between a C/C++ program and the SMT solver.

Wang et al. [14] describe Ceagle, an automated verification tool for C programs. The tool applies 4 different approaches when verifying a program: (1) a bounded model checker with a fixed unwind approach that uses SMT to check for satisfiability; (2) a predicate lazy abstraction engine which verifies the program with a predicate-based abstract model and uses CEGAR to refine spurious counterexamples; (3) a structural abstraction engine which tries to reason about the program behaviour based on the program structure; and (4) an execution engine, which is executed when all parameters are deterministic. The tool competed in SV-COMP'17 and was ranked 2nd, if we consider only the *ReachSafety-Floats* sub-category. Ceagle was the only tool that was able to verify the 3 programs that ESBMC/MathSAT could not handle under the 15 min constraint; it was able to verify each one of them in less than 10 s.

Clarke et al. [15] describe CBMC, a C/C++ SAT/SMT bounded model checker. ESBMC originated as a fork of this tool with an improved SMT backend and support for the verification of concurrent programs using an explicit interleaving approach. CBMC uses SAT solvers as their main engine, but offers support for the generation of an SMT formula for an external SMT solver. ESBMC supports SMT solvers directly, through their APIs, along with the option to output SMT formulae. CBMC also competed in SV-COMP'17 with a fixed unwind approach, and was ranked 3rd in the *ReachSafety-Floats* sub-category.

Brain et al. [29] describe 2LS, C/C++ SAT/SMT bounded model checker. 2LS is a tool developed using the CPROVER framework [15] and aims to combine a k-induction algorithm with abstract interpretation. As CBMC, 2LS uses SAT solvers but instead of a fixed unwind approach, 2LS uses an incremental bounded model checking approach, where it first checks for property violations for a given bound, then tries to generate (and refine) invariants using abstract interpretation and then builds a proof using the k-induction algorithm. 2LS competed in SV-COMP'17 and was ranked 4th in the *ReachSafety-Floats* sub-category.

Compared to these tools, ESBMC is able to verify a program either using a fixed unwind approach (as Ceagle and CBMC) or an incremental BMC (as 2LS). Similar to Ceagle, ESBMC directly uses the solver API to encode the SMT formula, but ESBMC supports more SMT solvers than Ceagle (in particular, Ceagle only supports Z3).

Regarding the SMT solvers, after MathSAT and Z3, we expect the SMT solver CVC4 to support the floating-point theory shortly, as the code appears to be ready and waiting to be merged on its public repository. XSAT [30] is another solver that claims to be a "fast floating-point satisfiability solver": up to 700x faster than MathSAT and Z3 on the benchmarks from the International SMT competition. We were, however, unable to find the solver online to experiment with it.

6   Conclusions and Future Work

This paper presents a BMC approach to encoding C programs using SMT floating-point theory, evaluates the encoding using the SMT solvers that support this theory, and compares our approach with other existing floating-point verification tools.

The encoding was implemented in ESBMC, an SMT-based bounded model checker for C and C++ programs. ESBMC supports most of the current C11 standard functions and part of the floating-point environment behaviour; we currently support changing rounding modes, but floating-point exception handling is not yet supported.

We evaluated the results using two state-of-art SMT solvers, MathSAT and Z3, over a set of public benchmarks from the International Competition on Software Verification (SV-COMP) and the results show that, when using MathSAT, ESBMC is not only able to produce better results than Z3, but it is also able to produce better results than all other verifiers in SV-COMP.

For future work, we intend to create our own floating-point backend, so we are able to encode all the floating-point operations defined by the standard using bitvectors; this will allow us to use all available SMT solvers that support QF_BV when verifying programs with floating-point numbers.

Regarding the benchmarks, although we have reported a favourable assessment of ESBMC over a diverse set of floating-point benchmarks, this set of benchmarks is still of limited scope and ESBMC's performance needs to be assessed on a larger benchmark set in future.

References

1. Gerrity, G.W.: Computer representation of real numbers. IEEE Trans. Comput. **C–31**(8), 709–714 (1982)
2. Frantz, G., Simar, R.: Comparing fixed- and floating-point DSPs. SPRY061, Texas Instruments (2004)
3. IEEE: IEEE standard for floating-point arithmetic. Technical report, August 2008
4. Goldberg, D.: What every computer scientist should know about floating point arithmetic. ACM Comput. Surv. **23**(1), 5–48 (1991)
5. Nikolić, Z., Nguyen, H.T., Frantz, G.: Design and implementation of numerical linear algebra algorithms on fixed point DSPs. EURASIP J. Adv. Sig. Proc. **2007**(1) (2007)
6. Cordeiro, L.C., Fischer, B.: Verifying multi-threaded software using SMT-based context-bounded model checking. In: ICSE, pp. 331–340 (2011)
7. Cordeiro, L.C., Fischer, B., Marques-Silva, J.: SMT-based bounded model checking for embedded ANSI-C software. IEEE Trans. Softw. Eng. **38**(4), 957–974 (2012)
8. Rümmer, P., Wahl, T.: An SMT-lib theory of binary floating-point arithmetic. In: SMT Workshop (2010)
9. Ismail, H.I., Bessa, I.V., Cordeiro, L.C., Lima Filho, E.B., Chaves Filho, J.E.: DSVerifier: a bounded model checking tool for digital systems. In: Fischer, B., Geldenhuys, J. (eds.) SPIN 2015. LNCS, vol. 9232, pp. 126–131. Springer, Cham (2015). https://doi.org/10.1007/978-3-319-23404-5_9
10. Abreu, R.B., Gadelha, M.Y.R., Cordeiro, L.C., Filho, E.B.D.L., de Silva Jr., W.S.: Bounded model checking for fixed-point digital filters. J. Braz. Comput. Soc. **22**(1), 1:1–1:20 (2016)
11. Bessa, I., Ismail, H., Cordeiro, L.C., Filho, J.E.C.: Verification of fixed-point digital controllers using direct and delta forms realizations. Des. Autom. Embed. Syst. **20**(2), 95–126 (2016)
12. Bessa, I., Ismail, H., Palhares, R., Cordeiro, L.C., Filho, J.E.C.: Formal non-fragile stability verification of digital control systems with uncertainty. IEEE Trans. Comput. **66**(3), 545–552 (2017)
13. Beyer, D.: Software verification with validation of results. In: Legay, A., Margaria, T. (eds.) TACAS 2017. LNCS, vol. 10206, pp. 331–349. Springer, Heidelberg (2017). https://doi.org/10.1007/978-3-662-54580-5_20

14. Wang, D., Zhang, C., Chen, G., Gu, M., Sun, J.G.: C code verification based on the extended labeled transition system model. In: D&P@MoDELS, pp. 48–55 (2016)

15. Clarke, E., Kroening, D., Lerda, F.: A tool for checking ANSI-C programs. In: Jensen, K., Podelski, A. (eds.) TACAS 2004. LNCS, vol. 2988, pp. 168–176. Springer, Heidelberg (2004). https://doi.org/10.1007/978-3-540-24730-2_15

16. Ramalho, M., Freitas, M., Sousa, F., Marques, H., Cordeiro, L.C., Fischer, B.: SMT-based bounded model checking of C++ programs. In: ECBS, pp. 147–156 (2013)

17. Gadelha, M.Y.R., Ismail, H.I., Cordeiro, L.C.: Handling loops in bounded model checking of C programs via k-induction. STTT **19**(1), 97–114 (2017)

18. Cytron, R., Ferrante, J., Rosen, B.K., Wegman, M.N., Zadeck, F.K.: An efficient method of computing static single assignment form. In: POPL, pp. 25–35 (1989)

19. Brummayer, R., Biere, A.: Boolector: an efficient SMT solver for bit-vectors and arrays. In: Kowalewski, S., Philippou, A. (eds.) TACAS 2009. LNCS, vol. 5505, pp. 174–177. Springer, Heidelberg (2009). https://doi.org/10.1007/978-3-642-00768-2_16

20. de Moura, L., Bjørner, N.: Z3: an efficient SMT solver. In: Ramakrishnan, C.R., Rehof, J. (eds.) TACAS 2008. LNCS, vol. 4963, pp. 337–340. Springer, Heidelberg (2008). https://doi.org/10.1007/978-3-540-78800-3_24

21. Cimatti, A., Griggio, A., Schaafsma, B.J., Sebastiani, R.: The MathSAT5 SMT solver. In: Piterman, N., Smolka, S.A. (eds.) TACAS 2013. LNCS, vol. 7795, pp. 93–107. Springer, Heidelberg (2013). https://doi.org/10.1007/978-3-642-36742-7_7

22. Dutertre, B.: Yices 2.2. In: Biere, A., Bloem, R. (eds.) CAV 2014. LNCS, vol. 8559, pp. 737–744. Springer, Cham (2014). https://doi.org/10.1007/978-3-319-08867-9_49

23. Barrett, C., Conway, C.L., Deters, M., Hadarean, L., Jovanović, D., King, T., Reynolds, A., Tinelli, C.: CVC4. In: Gopalakrishnan, G., Qadeer, S. (eds.) CAV 2011. LNCS, vol. 6806, pp. 171–177. Springer, Heidelberg (2011). https://doi.org/10.1007/978-3-642-22110-1_14

24. Brain, M., Tinelli, C., Ruemmer, P., Wahl, T.: An automatable formal semantics for IEEE-754 floating-point arithmetic. In: ARITH, pp. 160–167 (2015)

25. Smith, R.: Working Draft, Standard for Programming Language C++ (2016). Accessed Jan 2017

26. Delmas, D., Goubault, E., Putot, S., Souyris, J., Tekkal, K., Védrine, F.: Towards an industrial use of FLUCTUAT on safety-critical avionics software. In: Alpuente, M., Cook, B., Joubert, C. (eds.) FMICS 2009. LNCS, vol. 5825, pp. 53–69. Springer, Heidelberg (2009). https://doi.org/10.1007/978-3-642-04570-7_6

27. Davis, M., Logemann, G., Loveland, D.: A machine program for theorem-proving. Commun. ACM **5**(7), 394–397 (1962)

28. Ball, T., Bounimova, E., Levin, V., Kumar, R., Lichtenberg, J.: The static driver verifier research platform. In: Touili, T., Cook, B., Jackson, P. (eds.) CAV 2010. LNCS, vol. 6174, pp. 119–122. Springer, Heidelberg (2010). https://doi.org/10.1007/978-3-642-14295-6_11

29. Brain, M., Joshi, S., Kroening, D., Schrammel, P.: Safety verification and refutation by k-invariants and k-induction. In: Blazy, S., Jensen, T. (eds.) SAS 2015. LNCS, vol. 9291, pp. 145–161. Springer, Heidelberg (2015). https://doi.org/10.1007/978-3-662-48288-9_9

30. Fu, Z., Su, Z.: XSat: a fast floating-point satisfiability solver. In: Chaudhuri, S., Farzan, A. (eds.) CAV 2016. LNCS, vol. 9780, pp. 187–209. Springer, Cham (2016). https://doi.org/10.1007/978-3-319-41540-6_11

Local Analysis of Determinism for CSP

Rodrigo Otoni[1(✉)], Ana Cavalcanti[2], and Augusto Sampaio[1]

[1] Centro de Informática, Universidade Federal de Pernambuco, Recife, Brazil
{rbo2,acas}@cin.ufpe.br
[2] Department of Computer Science, University of York, York, UK
ana.cavalcanti@york.ac.uk

Abstract. Nondeterminism is an inevitable constituent of any theory that describes concurrency. For the validation and verification of concurrent systems, it is essential to investigate the presence or absence of nondeterminism, just as much as deadlock or livelock. CSP is a well established process algebra; the main tool for practical use of CSP, the model checker FDR, checks determinism using a global analysis. We propose a local analysis, in order to improve performance and scalability. Our strategy is to use a compositional approach where we start from basic deterministic processes and check whether any of the composition operators introduce nondeterminism. We present the algorithms used in our strategy and experiments that show the efficiency of our approach.

Keywords: Model checking · FDR · Performance · Experiments

1 Introduction

Deadlock, livelock, and nondeterminism analyses are crucial in the specification and design of concurrent systems. Nondeterminism is expected in abstract models, but may indicate problems in concrete designs. Verification techniques to investigate the presence or absence of all these properties in a model are essential for validation and verification of concurrent systems.

Deadlock and livelock have been investigated in depth, and there are very efficient tools available [1–5,8]. Determinism has been less studied. It is, however, specially important in notations for refinement, where nondeterminism is used for abstraction. It is an inevitable constituent of any theory that describes concurrency where some form of arbitration is present [9].

CSP is a well established process algebra that is accompanied by a set of robust tools that allow its practical use both in academia and in industry. In particular, CSP is capable of modelling both explicit and implicit nondeterminism, such as the ones that can be introduced by parallelism, internal communications, or renaming. Its versatility in modelling nondeterminism together with its tool support makes CSP ideal for the analysis of determinism.

FDR [5] is the main tool for practical use of CSP; it is a model checker that takes as input specifications in CSP_M, a machine readable version of CSP. Other tools for CSP (or CSP dialects) like ProB [7] and PAT [11] also implement

S. Cavalheiro and J. Fiadeiro (Eds.): SBMF 2017, LNCS 10623, pp. 107–124, 2017.
https://doi.org/10.1007/978-3-319-70848-5_8

analysis strategies for these classical properties. The approach taken by all these tools for checking determinism is, however, based on global analysis, where the entire model is expanded and exhaustively checked. Here, we propose a local analysis strategy for determinism, to improve performance and scalability.

Local analysis has been adopted in verification of deadlock [1–3] and livelock [4]. Here, we present a local strategy for the verification of determinism in models written using a subset of CSP that includes most of its basic operators, with some restrictions on how they can be used in compositions. As far as we know, this is the first approach to local analysis of determinism, not only in the context of CSP, but also of any other formal or semi-formal modelling notation (such as UML), as well as concurrent programming languages.

Next we present CSP and how it defines determinism. In Sect. 3 we present our strategy. Our experiments and their results are discussed in Sect. 4. Finally we present our final remarks and future work in Sect. 5.

2   Background

We present here the background material to our work: CSP in Sect. 2.1 and its notion of determinism in Sect. 2.2.

2.1   CSP

CSP is a process algebra that can be used to describe systems as interacting components. These components, called processes, are independent entities that interact among themselves and with the environment. The interactions, called events, are atomic, instantaneous, and synchronous messages. The main CSP constructs are presented below; further information can be found in [6,9].

CSP has two basic processes, $SKIP$ and $STOP$; the former does nothing and terminates, and the latter deadlocks. A prefixing $a \rightarrow P$ is initially capable of performing the event a and then behaves like the process P. Events can be compound to communicate data. For instance, $c.5$ is the event that represents the transmission of the value 5 through the channel c.

Guards and conditionals are used in processes g & P and if b then P else Q. The former behaves as P if g is true, and as $STOP$ otherwise. The latter behaves as P if b is true, and as Q otherwise. Sequential composition is written as $P\,;Q$, which behaves as P, until it finishes, and then behaves as Q.

The process $P \;\square\; Q$ is the external choice between P and Q, resolved in favour of either of them when the environment agrees on their initials, the sets of events that they initially offers. In the internal choice, $P \;\sqcap\; Q$, the environment has no control over how the choice is resolved, which is nondeterministic. To make events internal to the process P we can write $P \setminus X$, which hides the events in the set X from the environment.

To model parallelism in CSP we have various options. The process $P \;\mvert\mvert\mvert\; Q$ is the interleaving of P and Q; in this composition P and Q behave independently. Another composition is the generalised parallelism, $P[\![X]\!]Q$, in which P and Q

synchronise on the events in the set X, but allow the events outside of X to occur independently; if X is the empty set, the operator behaves as interleaving.

As an example, we present a specification of a railway network from [10]. It is composed by a series of segments of tracks, with a signal between every two adjacent segments used to control the flow of trains. The segments are organised in overlapping pairs, as shown in Fig. 1(a), with segment pairs P_1, P_2 and P_3. In its initial state the railway can have a number of trains in specific segments. A safety requirement is that no two trains should be in adjacent segments.

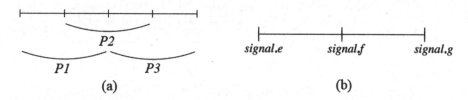

Fig. 1. Three overlapping pairs of segments (a), and signals of a pair of segments (b); modified from [10].

Each pair of segments has three signals: e, which indicates a train entering the pair; f, which indicates the train moving from the first to the second segment; and g, which indicates the train leaving the pair. A pair of segments is modelled as a process that can communicate three events, $signal.e$, $signal.f$, and $signal.g$, corresponding to the signals e, f, and g. A graphical representation of a pair of segments can be seen in Fig. 1(b). To deal with all possible initial states of a pair, three processes are defined. *Pair_Empty* specifies a pair that is initially empty, *Pair_First*, a pair in which a train is initially in its first segment, and *Pair_Second*, a pair in which a train is initially in its second segment.

$$Pair\_Empty = signal.e \rightarrow signal.f \rightarrow signal.g \rightarrow Pair\_Empty$$
$$Pair\_First = signal.f \rightarrow signal.g \rightarrow signal.e \rightarrow Pair\_First$$
$$Pair\_Second = signal.g \rightarrow signal.e \rightarrow signal.f \rightarrow Pair\_Second$$

To model a network we compose a number of instances of pairs of segments in parallel, with each instance having its own signals defined according to its position in the network. In Fig. 2 we present an example of a cyclic network that has four pairs and four segments, with the last and the first segments being adjacent to each other. Figure 2(a) gives an overview of the complete network, in which there is initially a single train in the segment demarcated by signal.0 and signal.1. Figure 2(b) shows the four segment pairs (from *Pair0* to *Pair3*).

The CSP processes that describe the four segment pairs are presented in Fig. 3. Note that these processes define the initial state of each segment pair. Therefore, although the *Pair0* segment pair is formed of the two segments demarcated by $signal.0$ and $signal.1$, and $signal.1$ and $signal.2$, the process is written as $Pair0 = signal.1 \rightarrow signal.2 \rightarrow signal.0 \rightarrow Pair0$, because the train is in

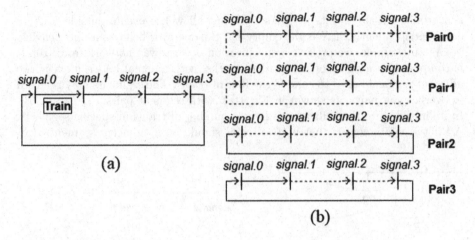

Fig. 2. Graphical representation of a network (a), and its pairs (b).

the first segment of this pair, and the next relevant event it must communicate is *signal*.1, indicating the train moving from the first to the second segment of *Pair*0. So *Pair*0 follows the form of *Pair_First*, previously explained. Similarly, *Pair*1 and *Pair*2 are modelled as *Pair_Empty*, since the train is not in any of their segments. Finally, *Pair*3 is modelled as *Pair_Second*, as the train is in the second segment of this pair. The composition of the pairs is made using the generalised parallel operator, since the signals of a pair need to synchronise with the signals of its adjacent pairs.

$Pair0 = signal.1 \rightarrow signal.2 \rightarrow signal.0 \rightarrow Pair0$
$Pair1 = signal.1 \rightarrow signal.2 \rightarrow signal.3 \rightarrow Pair1$
$Pair2 = signal.2 \rightarrow signal.3 \rightarrow signal.0 \rightarrow Pair2$
$Pair3 = signal.1 \rightarrow signal.3 \rightarrow signal.0 \rightarrow Pair3$
$SyncSet1 = \{signal.1, signal.2\}$
$SyncSet2 = \{signal.0, signal.2, signal.3\}$
$SyncSet3 = \{signal.0, signal.1, signal.3\}$
$RailwayNetwork = ((Pair0[\![SyncSet1]\!]Pair1)[\![SyncSet2]\!]Pair2)[\![SyncSet3]\!]Pair3$

Fig. 3. CSP model of the network in Fig. 2

The process *RailwayNetwork* can initially communicate *signal*.1, and afterwards *signal*.2, *signal*.3, *signal*.0, *signal*.1, *signal*.2 and so on. Each pair synchronises its first two signals with the pair on its left and its last two signals with the pair on its right, so when the network communicates *signal*.1, it means that a train is, simultaneously: moving from segment 1 to segment 2 of *Pair*0, entering segment 1 of Pair 1, and leaving *Pair*3.

2.2 Semantic Models and Determinism

A deterministic system can be thought of as one that always produces the same output, given a fixed input. CSP has different definitions for this property, depending on the semantic model being used. There are three well established semantic models for CSP: traces, failures, and failures-divergences.

In the traces model, a process P is represented by $traces(P)$, which is the set that contains all sequences of events that P can engage. This model does not allow us to determine if the process is deterministic or not.

In the failures model, a process P is represented by the pair $(traces(P), failures(P))$, with $failures(P)$ being a set of pairs (s, X), where s is a trace of P and X is a set of events that P can refuse after performing s. This model captures not only how a process can behave, but also how it cannot behave. The definition of determinism in the failures model is presented below.

Definition 1 (Determinism in the failures model). *Process P is determin-istic if, $\forall\, tr : traces(P), a : \Sigma \bullet \neg (tr ^\frown \langle a \rangle \in traces(P) \wedge (tr, \{a\}) \in failures(P))$*

This definition captures the essence of determinism: a process cannot have the possibility of both accepting and refusing an event at any given state, which can lead to different observable behaviours given the same input.

Example 1. The process $Ex1a = Pair1 \,\square\, Pair2$ is deterministic, since $Pair1$ and $Pair2$ are deterministic and the intersection of their initials is empty. Without initial events in common, the environment has a clear choice between $Pair1$ and $Pair2$, which, with their traces and failures, do not violate Definition 1.

The process $Ex1b = Pair1 \,\square\, Pair3$, on the other hand, is nondeterministic, because $signal.1$ is in the initials of both $Pair1$ and $Pair3$, so, by perform-ing $signal.1$, the environment has no control over how the external choice is resolved, allowing $Ex1b$ to both accept or refuse $signal.2$ afterwards, depending on whether $Pair1$ or $Pair3$ is chosen; the trace $\langle signal.1, signal.2 \rangle$ and the failure $(\langle signal.1 \rangle, \{signal.2\})$, for instance, break the condition of Definition 1.   □

Example 2. The composition in $Ex2 = Pair1 \,|||\, Pair2$ is nondeterminitic because we have an event, $signal.3$, after which $Pair1$ and $Pair2$ behave differ-ently. In terms of Definition 1, we note that $\langle signal.1, signal.2, signal.3, signal.1 \rangle$ is a trace of $Ex2$ and $(\langle signal.1, signal.2, signal.3 \rangle, \{signal.1\})$ is a failure of $Ex2$.   □

Nondeterminism can also arise from divergence, that is captured by the failures-divergences model [6,9]. Since there are tools that verify divergence in a compo-sitional way [4], our strategy is based on determinism in the failures model.

3 Strategy for Local Analysis of Determinism

Our analysis of a process is compositional. If the possibility of nondeterminism is found, the analysis stops and indicates the nondeterministic component.

Our strategy is sound for the verification of determinism, but not complete. When nondeterminism is indicated, we may have found a source of nondeterminism or it may be an inconclusive result. Local approaches to the analysis of classical concurrency properties tend to give up completeness in favour of efficiency gains; see [1–3], for deadlock analysis, and [4], for livelock analysis.

Example 3. We consider the following processes.

$$Ex3a = a \rightarrow b \rightarrow Ex3a \qquad\qquad Ex3c = Ex3a \sqcap Ex3b$$
$$Ex3b = c \rightarrow d \rightarrow SKIP \qquad\qquad Ex3d = Ex3a[\![\{a\}]\!]Ex3c$$

The process $Ex3c$ is nondeterministic, due to its internal choice. The process $Ex3d$, on the other hand, is deterministic. When analysing $Ex3d$, however, our strategy indicates the nondeterminism in $Ex3c$ and stops.   □

In Sect. 3.1 we present the subset of CSP that our strategy can currently handle, and the metadata gathered for the component processes. In Sect. 3.2, the rules to check for determinism are presented.

3.1   Process Structure and Metadata

In our strategy we deal with two categories of processes, Basic Processes and Composite Processes, defined in Fig. 4. Event, Condition, ProcessName, and SetOfEvents are the syntactic categories of the possible events, logical conditions, names of processes, and sets of events of CSP. We assume that all processes are divergence free and do not have parameters.

Due to the nature of the set of operators that can be used to create Basic Processes, they are deterministic by definition. A Composite Process is the result of a composition of Basic Processes or other Composite Processes.

Process ::= BasicProcess | CompositeProcess

BasicProcess ::= Event " → " BasicProcess
  | Condition " & " BasicProcess
  | "if" Condition " then " BasicProcess " else " BasicProcess
  | BasicProcess " ; " BasicProcess
  | "*SKIP*" | "*STOP*" | ProcessName

CompositeProcess ::=
  ProcessName " □ " ProcessName | ProcessName " ⊓ " ProcessName
  | ProcessName " ||| " ProcessName | ProcessName "⟦" SetOfEvents "⟧" ProcessName
  | ProcessName " \ " SetOfEvents

Fig. 4. BNF of the subset of CSP considered.

The subset of CSP that we deal with, as can be seen in Fig. 4, includes most of the basic operators of CSP. They are, however, restricted on their use.

Prefixing, guards, conditionals, and sequential composition can only be used in the definition of Basic Processes, while external and internal choice, interleaving, generalized parallel, and hiding are restricted to Composite Processes.

Each process in our strategy, upon being verified to be deterministic, is associated with a Set of Possible Behaviours (SPB). This is a set of sets of pairs, with each set of pairs in an SPB representing an alternative behaviour of the process, and each pair in a set representing a parallel behaviour. The first component of each pair in the set is a sequence that represents part of the syntactic structure of the process, and its second component is a set, which stores data relative to synchronisations among components of the process.

Example 4. The processes $Ex3a$ and $Ex3b$, from Example 3, have the SPBs: $SPB(Ex3a) = \{\{(\langle a, b, Ex3a \rangle, \varnothing)\}\}$, and $SPB(Ex3b) = \{\{(\langle c, d, SKIP \rangle, \varnothing)\}\}$. Each one has one set, because they do not have choices, with one pair, which holds the structure of the process, since there is no parallelism; the second element of the pairs is the empty set, also because we do not have any synchronisations between processes. For the process $Ex4 = Ex3a \,\square\, Ex3b$ we have that $SPB(Ex4) = \{\{(\langle a, b, Ex3a \rangle, \varnothing)\}, \{(\langle c, d, SKIP \rangle, \varnothing)\}\}$, which captures its two alternative behaviours, that depend on how the choice is resolved. □

Each element of a synchronisation set is itself a pair, with an integer value as the first component, and a set of events as the second component; the events in the set are the ones being synchronised. The integer values identify the sets that match in a synchronisation.

Example 5. We consider the following processes.

$$Ex5a \triangleq a \to STOP \qquad\qquad Ex5c = b \to Ex5c$$
$$Ex5b = Ex5a[\![\{a\}]\!] Ex3a \qquad\qquad Ex5d = Ex5b[\![\{b\}]\!] Ex5c$$

With the generalised parallel operator we add the synchronisation set to all pairs of the SPB of the composition, so, for the process $Ex5b$, we have that $SPB(Ex5b) = \{\{(\langle a, STOP \rangle, \{(1, \{a\})\}), (\langle a, b, Ex3a \rangle, \{(-1, \{a\})\})\}\}$; the module of the integer value uniquely identifies the synchronisation and its signal is used to differentiate between the two argument processes of the parallelism.

If $Ex5b$ is used in a composition with generalised parallel, we add the new synchronisation set to its pairs. For $Ex5d$, we have the set shown below.

$$SPB(Ex5d) = \left\{ \left\{ \begin{array}{l} (\langle a, STOP \rangle, \{(1, \{a\}), (2, \{b\})\}), \\ (\langle a, b, Ex3a \rangle, \{(-1, \{a\}), (2, \{b\})\}), \\ (\langle b, Ex5c \rangle, \{(-2, \{b\})\}) \end{array} \right\} \right\}$$

When more than one pair has a synchronisation set with the same integer, in this case 2, only one of those pairs need to synchronise with a counterpart with the opposite integer, in this case -2. □

Now we present the formal definition of SPB. It is important to record whether a sequence leads to a recursion or not. To this end, we add the name of the process that represents the final behaviour of the sequence as its last element. We call the set that contains these new sequences Valid Sequences (VS). With VS it is possible to know if a Basic Process, which can only have one sequence, is cyclic or not just by checking if the last element of its sequence is a process name (indicating a recursion), or if it is $SKIP$ or $STOP$.

Definition 2 (Valid Sequences (VS)).

$$VS = \{a : \Sigma^*, b : N \cup \{SKIP, STOP\} \bullet a ^\frown \langle b \rangle\}$$

where N is the set that contains all the valid names of processes.

To record a trace of behaviour in a parallel process with synchronisations, we use Synchronisation Sets, which is the set that contains integers associated with all possible sets of events on which a process can synchronise.

Definition 3 (Syncronisation Sets (SyncSets)). $SyncSets = \mathbb{P}(\mathbb{Z} \times \mathbb{P}(\Sigma))$

Finally we define the *eTraces* (a shorthand for Enhanced Traces) of a given process P. Its elements are pairs whose first element is a VS sequence and the second one is a set of $SyncSets$.

Definition 4 (Enhanced Traces of P (eTraces(P))).

$$eTraces(P) = \left\{ \begin{array}{l} et : VS \times SyncSets \mid front(first(et)) \in traces(P) \wedge \\ \left(\begin{array}{l} \quad\quad\quad\quad\quad P/front(first(et)) \equiv_F n \\ \exists n \in N \cup \{SKIP, STOP\} \bullet \wedge \\ \quad\quad\quad\quad last(first(et)) = n \end{array} \right) \end{array} \right\}$$

where P/t represents the behaviour of P after it has performed the trace t, and $\equiv_F$ indicates equivalence in the failures model [9].

An element of *eTraces* represents a possible Basic Process. The restrictions in Definition 4 ensure that each sequence leads the process to a recursive behaviour, or to $SKIP$ or $STOP$. For a process P, the set $SPB(P)$ is a subset of $\mathbb{P}(eTraces(P))$. The *eTraces* pairs in a set of an SPB represent Basic Processes in parallel, and pairs in different sets represent choices.

Now we present how SPB is calculated. For the Basic Processes, we calculate SPB as shown below; P and Q are processes, and n is a process name.

- $SPB(n) = \{\{(\langle n \rangle, \varnothing)\}\}$
- $SPB(a \rightarrow P) = \{setP : SPB(P) \bullet prefixing (\!| \{a\} \times setP |\!)\}$
- $SPB(g \;\&\; P) = SPB(P)$
- $SPB(\text{if } g \text{ then } P \text{ else } Q) = SPB(P)$
- $SPB(P \,;\, Q) = \{setP : SPB(P) \,;\, setQ : SPB(Q) \bullet seqComp (\!| setP \times setQ |\!)\}$

- $prefixing(event, eTrace) = (\langle event \rangle ^\frown first(eTrace), \varnothing)$
- $seqComp(eTrace1, eTrace2) = \text{if } last(first(eTrace1)) = SKIP$
$$\quad\quad\quad\quad\quad \text{then } (front(first(eTrace1)) ^\frown first(eTrace2), \varnothing)$$
$$\quad\quad\quad\quad\quad \text{else } eTrace1$$

For a process call, we create a sequence with the call. For a prefixing, $a \to P$, we apply *prefixing* to all pairs formed of the event a and a sequence in a set of the SPB of P; $(\![...]\!)$ is the relational image operator. The function *prefixing* yields the original sequence with the new event as its head.

We assume that the predicates in guards and conditionals are always true; in those cases we simply keep the SPB of P. In the conditional, if the processes P and Q are not equivalent, the strategy returns the possibility of nondeterminism. With this approach, we record behaviours for the processes that may not be actually possible. The addition of behaviours, however, can only lead to nondeterminism, never remove it. So, as already explained, it is possible that we indicate a nondeterminism that does not exist, but a process defined to be deterministic is guaranteed to be so.

For sequential composition we apply *seqComp* to all pairs of SPB(P) and SPB(Q), using relational image. This function returns the front of the first sequence appended with the second sequence, if the first one ends in $SKIP$, or the first sequence unmodified otherwise.

Example 6. The calculation of SPB($Ex3a$) is shown below.

$SPB(Ex3a) = \{\{(\langle Ex3a\rangle, \varnothing)\}\}$
$SPB(b \to Ex3a) = \{\{(\langle b, Ex3a\rangle, \varnothing)\}\}$
$SPB(a \to b \to Ex3a) = \{\{(\langle a, b, Ex3a\rangle, \varnothing)\}\}$
$SPB(Ex3a) = SPB(a \to b \to Ex3a)$

We differentiate between the process $Ex3a$ and its recursive call. For sequential composition, $SPB(Ex3a\,;Ex3b) = SPB(Ex3a)$, since the sequence of $Ex3a$ ends in a recursion, and $SPB(Ex3b\,;Ex3a) = \{\{(\langle c, d, a, b, Ex3a\rangle, \varnothing)\}\}$, because the sequence of $Ex3b$ ends in $SKIP$. □

We now present the SPB for the Composite Processes; X is a set of events, and i is a fresh integer, different from zero.

- $SPB(P \;\square\; Q) = SPB(P) \cup SPB(Q)$
- $SPB(P \;\sqcap\; Q) = SPB(P)$
- $SPB(P \;|||\; Q) = \{setP : SPB(P)\,;\,setQ : SPB(Q) \bullet setP \cup setQ\}$
- $SPB(P[\![X]\!]Q) = \left\{ \begin{array}{l} setP : SPB(P)\,;\,setQ : SPB(Q)\bullet \\ addSync\,(\!|\,setP \times \{X\} \times \{i\}\,|\!) \\ \cup \\ addSync\,(\!|\,setQ \times \{X\} \times \{-i\}\,|\!) \end{array} \right\}$
- $SPB(P \setminus X) = \{setP : SPB(P) \bullet remove\,(\!|\,setP \times \{X\}\,|\!)\}$

- $addSync(eTrace, X, id) = (first(eTrace), second(eTrace) \cup \{(id, X)\})$
- $remove((T, S), X) = (removeT(T, X), removeS(S, X))$
- $removeT(\langle\rangle, X) = \langle\rangle$
  $removeT(\langle a\rangle \frown t, X) = $ if $a \in X$ then $remove(t, X)$ else $\langle a\rangle \frown remove(t, X)$
- $removeS(\varnothing, X) = \varnothing$
  $removeS(\{(id, evSet)\} \cup s, X) = \{(id, evSet \setminus X)\} \cup removeS(s, X)$

For external choice, we get the union of the sets of the operands. For internal choice, since the composition is only deterministic if both operands are equivalent, we simply keep the SPB of one of them. For interleaving, for every pair of sets of SPB(P) and SPB(Q), we record their union. The calculation for a generalised parallel is similar to that of an interleaving, but we also add the new synchronisation to the elements of the sets, using the function *addSync*. For hiding we remove the elements in X from SPB(P), with the function *remove*.

Example 7. Considering the processes $Ex7a = a \rightarrow b \rightarrow c \rightarrow Ex7a$, and $Ex7b = Ex7a[\![\{b\}]\!]Ex7a$, we calculate SPB($Ex7b \setminus \{b\}$).

SPB($Ex7b$) = {{(($\langle a, b, c, Ex7a \rangle$,{(1,{b})}), ($\langle a, b, c, Ex7a \rangle$,{(-1,{b})}))}}
SPB($Ex7b \setminus \{b\}$) = {{(($\langle a, c, Ex7a \rangle$,{(1,{})}), ($\langle a, c, Ex7a \rangle$,{(-1,{})}))}}

$\square$

If a synchronisation introduces deadlock or if a synchronisation channel is hidden, there is the possibility that our strategy considers invalid behaviours of the process. This, however, can only introduce nondeterminism, never remove it.

Example 8. We consider the following processes.

$$Ex8a = b \rightarrow a \rightarrow c \rightarrow d \rightarrow Ex8a \qquad Ex8b = Ex7a[\![\{a, b\}]\!]Ex8a$$

The process $Ex8b$ is deterministic, because it is deadlocked from the start. Our strategy, however, predicts a nondeterministic behaviour when both $Ex7a$ and $Ex8a$ offer event c to the environment, which never happens. $\square$

Pairs of a set of a SPB are equivalent, $\equiv$, if the front of their sequences are equal, both either recurse or end in $SKIP$ or $STOP$, and they have the same meaningful synchronisations with equivalent pairs. A synchronisation is meaningful if it involves at least one of the events in the sequence of the pair.

Definition 5 (Meaningful Synchronisations). *Given a pair (Seq, SetOf Syncs), a synchronisation set sync $\in$ SetOfSyncs is meaningful if sync $\cap$ ran(Seq) $\neq \varnothing$.*

Example 9. We consider the following SPBs.

SPB($Ex9a$) = {{(($\langle a, b, c, P \rangle$,{(1,{r})}), ($\langle x, y, SKIP \rangle$,{(-1,{r})}))}}
SPB($Ex9b$) = {{(($\langle a, b, c, P \rangle$,{(2,{r})}), ($\langle x, y, SKIP \rangle$,{(-2,{r})}))}}
SPB($Ex9c$) = {{(($\langle a, b, c, Q \rangle$, $\varnothing$), ($\langle x, y, SKIP \rangle$, $\varnothing$))}}

They are all equivalent, since the only difference between them is their synchronisation sets, with the synchronisations of $Ex9a$ and $Ex9b$ not being meaningful, as they do not affect the sequences, and $Ex9c$ not having synchronisations. $\square$

In the next section, we present the algorithms that use the SPB of component processes to check determinism of a composite process.

3.2   Composition Rules

The algorithms that verify if the compositions are deterministic return true if the given composition is deterministic, and false otherwise. We present here the algorithms for external choice, and parallelism. The algorithms for internal choice and hiding can be found in the extended version of this paper[1].

External Choice

The external choice, with our restrictions, can only introduce nondeterminism if its two operands have at least one common initial event, since these are their only points of interaction. In this scenario the composition is deterministic only if the two processes have the same behaviour after every common initial event. The algorithm for this operator can be seen in Fig. 5. It checks for all pairs of sets of SPB(P) and SPB(Q) if they have sequences that start with the same event. If they do, those sets need to be equivalent not to introduce nondeterminism.

Algorithm 1 External Choice (P,Q)

1: **for** *each setP $\in$ SPB(P), setQ $\in$ SPB(Q)* **do**
2:   **for** *each elemP $\in$ setP, elemQ $\in$ setQ* **do**
3:   **if** *head(first(elemP)) == head(first(elemQ)) $\land \neg$(setP $\equiv$ setQ)* **then**
4:   **return** *false*
5: **return** *true*

Fig. 5. Algorithm to check if external choice introduces nondeterminism.

Internal Choice

An internal choice only results in a deterministic process if its operands have the same behaviour. The algorithm for this operator simply checks if the SPBs of both operands are equivalent, that is, if the SPBs have equivalent sets.

Parallelism

We deal with parallelism in two forms: interleaving and generalised parallel. We first discuss how interleaving can introduce nondeterminism. Afterwards, we present our considerations about generalised parallel. Finally, we show the algorithm for the verification of parallel compositions.

Differently from external and internal choice, with interleaving, as well as with the other parallel operators, both operands execute at the same time, so we

---

[1] http://www.cin.ufpe.br/~rbo2/SBMF2017.zip.

must take into account all of their events, not only the initials. With interleaving, we need to consider that when one of its operands is offering a specific event to the environment, the other operand can be offering any of its events.

The condition for a composition using interleaving to be deterministic is that, after each event in common to both processes, the composition needs to offer the same events to the environment, no matter which process performs the event, so the environment does not observe any different behaviour.

Example 10. We consider the following processes.

$$Ex10a = a \rightarrow b \rightarrow Ex10a \qquad Ex10d = Ex10a \,|||\, Ex10b$$
$$Ex10b = a \rightarrow Ex10b \qquad\qquad Ex10e = Ex10b \,|||\, Ex10c$$
$$Ex10c = b \rightarrow Ex10c \qquad\qquad Ex10f = Ex10a \,|||\, Ex10e$$

The process $Ex10d$ is nondeterministic, because after performing event a, the environment can synchronise on either a again or on a and b, depending if a was performed by $Ex10a$ or $Ex10b$. The process $Ex10e$ is deterministic, because the alphabets of its components are disjoint, so there are no events in common. The composition in $Ex10f$ is deterministic, because, although there is an intersection of the alphabets, events a and b are always available to the environment.   □

Generalised parallel allows us to have parallelism with synchronisations. The events that are not in the synchronisation set are analysed in a similar way to what is done with interleaving, and the events in the synchronisation set cannot introduce nondeterminism on their own, because each synchronised event happens only once and both operands engage in this event.

Example 11. The process $Ex11 = Ex10a [\![\{a\}]\!] Ex10b$, differently from $Ex10d$, is deterministic, because the event a is in the synchronisation set, so, after it occurs, the only possibility for the parallel composition is to offer event b.   □

We use the same algorithm for the two forms of parallelism discussed. It receives the processes being composed and the synchronisation set. For interleaving, the synchronisation set is empty. The algorithm is presented Fig. 6.

Algorithm 2 iterates over all pairs of behaviours of P and Q, evaluating all scenarios. In each iteration, it initially defines $avEvents$ (line 2), the set of events that is always available to the environment, in the given pair of behaviours.

To calculate $avEvents$ we use $setOfAvailableEvents$, which yields a set of events that must belong to an Enhanced Trace that has only one event in its sequence and is recursive. These sequences stand out because they do not lead to a change in the state of the composition. Another requirement is that these events need to be able to occur freely, which can be denied by synchronisations.

Example 12. We consider the following SPBs.

$$\mathrm{SPB}(Ex12a) = \{\{(\langle a, b, P\rangle, \varnothing), (\langle c, Q\rangle, \varnothing), (\langle d, SKIP\rangle, \varnothing), (\langle e, R\rangle, \varnothing)\}\}$$
$$\mathrm{SPB}(Ex12b) = \{\{(\langle x, S\rangle, \{(1, \{x\})\}), (\langle x, y, T\rangle, \{(-1, \{x\})\}), (\langle e, f, U\rangle, \varnothing)\}\}$$

Algorithm 2 Parallelism (P,Q,X)

1: **for** each setP ∈ SPB(P), setQ ∈ SPB(Q) **do**
2:    avEvents = setOfAvailableEvents(setP,setQ,X)
3:    **for** each elemP ∈ setP, elemQ ∈ setQ **do**
4:        **if** head(first(elemP)) == head(first(elemQ)) ∧ head(first(elemP)) ∉ X ∧
          (¬allSetsEquiv(SPB(P)) ∨ ¬allSetsEquiv(SPB(Q))) **then**
5:            **return** false
6:        **for** each evP ∈ front(first(elemP)), evQ ∈ front(first(elemQ)) **do**
7:            **if** evP == evQ ∧ evP ∉ X **then**
8:                eventsP = avEvents ∪ nextEvents(elemP,evP,setP) ∪ {evQ}
9:                eventsQ = avEvents ∪ nextEvents(elemQ,evQ,setQ) ∪ {evP}
10:               **if** eventsP ≠ eventsQ **then**
11:                   **return** false
12: **return** true

Fig. 6. Algorithm to check if parallelism introduces nondeterminism.

If we execute Parallelism($Ex12a$, $Ex12b$,{e}), we have one iteration of the algorithm with $avEvents = \{c\}$. The pairs with the sequences $\langle a, b, P\rangle$, $\langle x, y, T\rangle$, and $\langle e, f, U\rangle$ are discarded for having more than one event. The pair with $\langle d, SKIP\rangle$ is discarded for not being recursive. The pairs with sequences $\langle x, S\rangle$, and $\langle e, R\rangle$ are discarded due to their synchronisations, the former with the pair $(\langle x, y, T\rangle, \{(-1, \{x\})\}$, and the latter with the synchronisation being introduced in this composition, through the synchronisation set {e}. □

With $avEvents$ calculated, Algorithm 2 starts checking each pair of elements of the behaviour of P and Q. If we have two elements with the same initial events (line 4), then, for each operand, all the sets in its SPB need to be equivalent, which is checked by $allSetsEquiv$.

Example 13. We consider the following processes.

$$Ex13a = Ex10a \ \Box \ Ex10c \qquad\qquad Ex13b = Ex13a \ ||| \ Ex10c$$

The composition $Ex13b$ is nondeterministic, because, after performing b, the environment does not know if a is still available, since b can be performed by $Ex13a$ or $Ex9c$, so it is possible to accept or refuse a, given the circumstances. Algorithm 2 returns false because the conditional in line 4 returns true, having $allSetsEquiv(SPB(Ex13a)) = false$. □

Requiring that the SPB of each process have all sets equal is, however, not enough to ensure determinism, as we can see in the next example.

Example 14. We consider the following processes.

$$Ex14a = a \rightarrow b \rightarrow a \rightarrow Ex14a \qquad Ex14b = Ex14a \ ||| \ Ex14a$$

The process $Ex14b$ is nondeterministic, because after the environment performs the trace $\langle a, b, a \rangle$ it is possible to accept or refuse b. During the evaluation, the conditional in line 4 returns true, $allSetsEquiv(SPB(Ex14a)) = true$, so nondeterminism is not identified by Algorithm 2 at this point.   □

We then have the core of Algorithm 2 (line 6). The algorithm checks, for each event e that is in the intersection of the alphabets, if the events available to the environment, after e in P is performed, is equal to the events available after e in Q is performed. If they are not, then a source of nondeterminism has been found. This verification is only carried out if e is not in the synchronisation set.

We assume that the two sequences that we are analysing at a given moment are offering specific events, but we do not assume anything of the other sequences. The events available to the environment after the execution of the event in each process are given by the union of three sets: $avEvents$; the set of events that are available in the process that performed the event, after its execution; and the set that contains the event in question, that is still available in the other process.

The function $nextEvents$ (lines 8 and 9) returns the set of events that a process offers to the environment after one of its events, e, has occurred; in Algorithm 2, e can be evP or evQ. First it adds the event that comes after e, if any, to the return set. Afterwards it checks if the pair that contains e synchronises with other pairs, and if e is present in those pairs, which leads to a change in their states as well. If e is indeed present, then the events after it in these events will also be included in the return set.

Example 15. For process $Ex14b$, we have $avEvents = \varnothing$. The conditional in line 7 returns true for the first events in both $Ex14a$ operands, with $eventsP$ and $eventsQ$ being both the result of $\varnothing \cup \{b\} \cup \{a\}$, so $eventsP == eventsQ$ (line 10). For the first event of the first operand, a, and the second event of the second operand, b, the conditional in line 7 returns false. For the first event of the first operand, a, and the third event of the second operand, a, the conditional in line 7 returns true, but $eventsP = \varnothing \cup \{b\} \cup \{a\}$, and $eventsQ = \varnothing \cup \{a\} \cup \{a\}$, so Algorithm 2 returns false in line 11.   □

Example 16. We consider the following processes.

$$Ex16a = a \rightarrow b \rightarrow c \rightarrow Ex16a \qquad Ex16d = Ex16a \,|||\, Ex16b$$
$$Ex16b = d \rightarrow e \rightarrow f \rightarrow Ex16b \qquad Ex16e = Ex16c[\![\{d\}]\!]Ex16d$$
$$Ex16c = d \rightarrow e \rightarrow g \rightarrow Ex16c$$

To check if $Ex16e$ is deterministic we use $SPB(Ex16c) = \{\{((\langle d, e, g, Ex16c \rangle, \varnothing)\}\}$, and $SPB(Ex16d) = \{\{((\langle a, b, c, Ex16a \rangle, \varnothing), (\langle d, e, f, Ex16b \rangle, \varnothing)\}\}$. There is one set in $SPB(Ex16a)$ and in $SPB(Ex16b)$, so Algorithm 2 performs one iteration, with $avEvents = \varnothing$, since there is no sequence with a freely occurring event.

We check every pair being analysed (line 3). For the pairs $(\langle d, e, g, Ex16c \rangle, \varnothing)$ and $(\langle a, b, c, Ex16a \rangle, \varnothing)$, the conditional in line 4 returns false, since the head of the sequences is different, and so does all six occurrences of the conditional in line

7, inside the loop in line 6, because the two sequences have no event in common. For $(\langle d, e, g, Ex16c \rangle, \varnothing)$ and $(\langle d, e, f, Ex16b \rangle, \varnothing)$, the conditional in line 4 also returns false, this time because $d \in X$, but when the loop in line 6 executes for the second event of each sequence, the conditional in line 7 returns true. In this case we have that $eventsP = \varnothing \cup \{g\} \cup \{e\}$ and $eventsQ = \varnothing \cup \{f\} \cup \{e\}$, so Algorithm 2 returns false.   □

Example 17. We consider the following processes.

$$Ex17a = Ex16a \mathbin{\square} Ex16b \qquad\qquad Ex17b = Ex17a[\![\{e\}]\!]Ex16c$$

We have $\mathrm{SPB}(Ex17a) = \{\{(\langle a, b, c, Ex16a \rangle, \varnothing)\}, \{(\langle d, e, f, Ex16b \rangle, \varnothing)\}\}$. The application of Algorithm 2 to $Ex17b$ occurs similarly to that of $Ex16e$, but two iterations occur. The first iteration, with the sets $\{(\langle a, b, c, Ex16a \rangle, \varnothing)\}$, and $\{(\langle d, e, g, Ex16c \rangle, \varnothing)\}$ occurs without problems. The second iteration, with the sets $\{(\langle d, e, f, Ex16b \rangle, \varnothing)\}$ and $\{(\langle d, e, g, Ex16c \rangle, \varnothing)\}$, however, leads the conditional in line 4 to return true when analysing the only two pairs, because $allSetsEquiv(\mathrm{Ex17a}) = $ false, leading Algorithm 2 to return false.   □

The way we calculate the available events after an event occurs is the main source of efficiency gain when we deal with parallelism. A global analysis would consider all possible states of the other sequences to carry out the verification. Our strategy, with the use of $avEvents$, considers only a small part of the state space. The sequences that perform various events before a recursion, $SKIP$, or $STOP$, can offer different events, depending of their state, but, more importantly, can refuse to offer them. Since we cannot rely on the events of these sequences to ensure determinism we discard them altogether. For $Ex16d$, for instance, FDR4 visits 54 states, while our strategy only considers 9 states.

We have implemented all the algorithms presented in this section, plus the algorithm to check hiding, to construct a prototype determinism checker. In the next section, we show the results of experiments carried out using this prototype.

4   Experimental Results

We performed a number of experiments to compare FDR4 with our prototype. The railway network described in Sect. 2.1 is our main case study. To evaluate every algorithm, we also considered processes involving external and internal choice, interleaving, and hiding. The prototype and the files used in the experiments are available online, on the link referenced in footnote 1.

We used two models of the railway network: the original, deterministic, model, and a modified nondeterministic model, with an error in the last two pairs of tracks. For each model we consider three scenarios, consisting of one, six, and eleven trains, respectively. For each scenario, eight instances are evaluated, with an increasing number of pairs of tracks. The instance number indicates the number of pairs of tracks in it. The results of the experiments with the railway network can be seen in Tables 1, 2, 3, 4, 5 and 6; the * indicates an out-of-memory error.

Table 1. Deterministic instances with one train in the railway.

Instance	FDR4	Prototype
25	0.12 s	0.35 s
50	0.22 s	0.46 s
75	0.32 s	0.50 s
100	0.37 s	0.56 s
500	2.94 s	1.38 s
1000	8.67 s	2.19 s
5000	4 m 20.06 s	20.13 s
10000	*	1 m 29.63 s

Table 2. Nondeterministic instances with one train in the railway.

Instance	FDR4	Prototype
25	0.13 s	0.38 s
50	0.23 s	0.43 s
75	0.30 s	0.53 s
100	0.48 s	0.61 s
500	3.65 s	1.38 s
1000	12.76 s	2.21 s
5000	10 m 33.92 s	19.74 s
10000	*	1 m 26.83 s

Table 3. Deterministic instances with six trains in the railway.

Instance	FDR4	Prototype
25	0.52 s	0.35 s
50	3 m 6.67 s	0.44 s
75	*	0.50 s
100	*	0.60 s
500	*	1.37 s
1000	*	2.18 s
5000	*	19.55 s
10000	*	1 m 24.65 s

Table 4. Nondeterministic instances with six trains in the railway.

Instance	FDR4	Prototype
25	0.17 s	0.35 s
50	2.16 s	0.45 s
75	22.56 s	0.50 s
100	2 m 11.05 s	0.55 s
500	*	1.36 s
1000	*	2.07 s
5000	*	19.88 s
10000	*	1 m 24.16 s

Table 5. Deterministic instances with eleven trains in the railway.

Instance	FDR4	Prototype
25	0.18 s	0.34 s
50	*	0.43 s
75	*	0.51 s
100	*	0.58 s
500	*	1.37 s
1000	*	2.20 s
5000	*	19.97 s
10000	*	1 m 22.75 s

Table 6. Nondeterministic instances with eleven trains in the railway.

Instance	FDR4	Prototype
25	0.13 s	0.37 s
50	12.77 s	0.43 s
75	8 m 25.50 s	0.51 s
100	*	0.58 s
500	*	1.45 s
1000	*	2.13 s
5000	*	19.98 s
10000	*	1 m 23.92 s

The experiments were run in a server with an Intel Core i7-2600k, 16 GB of RAM, 160 GB of SSD, and Ubunto 17.94 64-bit. We used FDR 4.2.0. The results show that while for smaller examples FDR has a better performance, due to the overhead of calculation of metadata in our approach, it struggles to analyse large parallel systems. Our prototye was able to analyse the largest instance in less than two minutes, a very promising result.

To analyse the impact of external choice, our experiments consist of a number of processes in the form $Basici = a.i \rightarrow b.i \rightarrow c.i \rightarrow Basici$, all composed with this operator. Nondeterministic instances were created by modifying the last process to $Basici = a.(i - 1) \rightarrow b.i \rightarrow c.i \rightarrow Basici$. For the evaluation of the hiding operator, we modified the instances of the external choice experiments by hiding event $b.i$ after each composition, with the nondeterministic instances hiding $a.i$, instead of $b.i$, after the last composition.

The experiments with internal choice consist of compositions of processes of the form $Basici = a.0 \rightarrow b.0 \rightarrow c.0 \rightarrow Basici$, with the nondeterministic instances having $b.1$, instead of $b.0$, in the last process. For interleaving, we compose processes with the same structure of the processes used in the external choice experiments, with the nondeterministic instances having their last two processes ending with new events, $... \rightarrow c.(i - 1) \rightarrow d \rightarrow e \rightarrow f \rightarrow Basic(i - 1)$ and $... \rightarrow c.i \rightarrow d \rightarrow e \rightarrow g \rightarrow Basici$.

The results of our additional experiments are in the extended version of this paper. With them we identified that FDR4 does not scale well, specially with interleaving. For all problems considered, except the 10000 instance of our hiding experiment, the prototype completed its analysis in less than two minutes. It is fair to remember that, while FDR4 would correctly identify processes like $Ex3d$ as deterministic, our prototype would indicate the possibility of nondeterminism.

5   Conclusion

In this paper we propose a local analysis for the verification of determinism, considering a subset of CSP. We analyse each composition that is part of the process being verified, gathering metadata about them. With the metadata we gather, we are able to guarantee determinism by only checking conditions on the argument processes of the composition. We performed some experiments and the results show that our approach scales better than that of FDR4, the main tool for verification of CSP models, specially when dealing with interleaving.

Local analysis has been used for the verification of properties of concurrency. For livelock, a compositional strategy that handles a subset of CSP similar to our own is presented in [4]. For deadlock, there are works aimed at CSP that involve adherence to deadlock-free patters [2,3], with a focus on the analysis of cyclic networks of processes. Recent improvements on local deadlock analysis for CSP are reported in [1], but this work also presents an incomplete strategy. As already mentioned, we are not aware of any other approach to compositional analysis of determinism, so our work is an original contribution in this direction.

The composition of techniques that verify deadlock, livelock, and determinism locally is possible. By identifying a subset of CSP shared by all of them, an integrated approach to analyse all the three classical properties is viable.

Our strategy can be improved. We will widen the considered subset of CSP, removing some of the restrictions, to allow non-tail recursion and parameters. We will also prove the correctness of the algorithms and perform more case studies.

Acknowledgements. This work was partially supported by INES (grants CNPq/465614/2014-0, and FACEPE/APQ/0388-1.03/14) and FACEPE (grant IBPG-0074-1.03/16). We thank Madiel Conserva Filho and Joabe Jesus Júnior for the helpful discussions.

References

1. Antonino, P., Gibson-Robinson, T., Roscoe, A.W.: Tighter reachability criteria for deadlock-freedom analysis. In: Fitzgerald, J., Heitmeyer, C., Gnesi, S., Philippou, A. (eds.) FM 2016. LNCS, vol. 9995, pp. 43–59. Springer, Cham (2016). https://doi.org/10.1007/978-3-319-48989-6_3
2. Antonino, P.R.G., Oliveira, M.M., Sampaio, A.C.A., Kristensen, K.E., Bryans, J.W.: Leadership election: an industrial SoS application of compositional deadlock verification. In: Badger, J.M., Rozier, K.Y. (eds.) NFM 2014. LNCS, vol. 8430, pp. 31–45. Springer, Cham (2014). https://doi.org/10.1007/978-3-319-06200-6_3
3. Antonino, P., Sampaio, A., Woodcock, J.: A refinement based strategy for local deadlock analysis of networks of CSP processes. In: Jones, C., Pihlajasaari, P., Sun, J. (eds.) FM 2014. LNCS, vol. 8442, pp. 62–77. Springer, Cham (2014). https://doi.org/10.1007/978-3-319-06410-9_5
4. Filho, M.S.C., Oliveira, M.V.M., Sampaio, A., Cavalcanti, A.: Local livelock analysis of component-based models. In: Ogata, K., Lawford, M., Liu, S. (eds.) ICFEM 2016. LNCS, vol. 10009, pp. 279–295. Springer, Cham (2016). https://doi.org/10.1007/978-3-319-47846-3_18
5. Gibson-Robinson, T., Armstrong, P., Boulgakov, A., Roscoe, A.W.: FDR3 — a modern refinement checker for CSP. In: Ábrahám, E., Havelund, K. (eds.) TACAS 2014. LNCS, vol. 8413, pp. 187–201. Springer, Heidelberg (2014). https://doi.org/10.1007/978-3-642-54862-8_13
6. Hoare, C.A.R.: Communicating Sequential Processes. Prentice-Hall Inc, Upper Saddle River (1985)
7. Leuschel, M., Butler, M.: ProB: a model checker for B. In: Araki, K., Gnesi, S., Mandrioli, D. (eds.) FME 2003. LNCS, vol. 2805, pp. 855–874. Springer, Heidelberg (2003). https://doi.org/10.1007/978-3-540-45236-2_46
8. Ramos, R., Sampaio, A., Mota, A.: Systematic development of trustworthy component systems. In: Cavalcanti, A., Dams, D.R. (eds.) FM 2009. LNCS, vol. 5850, pp. 140–156. Springer, Heidelberg (2009). https://doi.org/10.1007/978-3-642-05089-3_10
9. Roscoe, A.: Understanding Concurrent Systems, 1st edn. Springer, New York (2010)
10. Schneider, S.: Concurrent and Real Time Systems: The CSP Approach, 1st edn. Wiley, New York (1999)
11. Sun, J., Liu, Y., Dong, J.S., Pang, J.: PAT: towards flexible verification under fairness. In: Bouajjani, A., Maler, O. (eds.) CAV 2009. LNCS, vol. 5643, pp. 709–714. Springer, Heidelberg (2009). https://doi.org/10.1007/978-3-642-02658-4_59

OptCE: A Counterexample-Guided Inductive Optimization Solver

Higo F. Albuquerque[1], Rodrigo F. Araújo[2], Iury V. Bessa[1],
Lucas C. Cordeiro[1,3(✉)], and Eddie B. de Lima Filho[1,4]

[1] Federal University of Amazonas, Manaus, Brazil
[2] Federal Institute of Amazonas, Manaus, Brazil
[3] University of Oxford, Oxford, UK
lucas.cordeiro@cs.ox.ac.uk
[4] Samsung Electronics, Manaus, Brazil

Abstract. This paper presents optimization through counterexamples (OptCE), which is a verification tool developed for optimizing target functions. In particular, OptCE employs bounded model checking techniques based on boolean satisfiability and satisfiability modulo theories, which are able to obtain global minima of convex and non-convex functions. OptCE is implemented in C/C++, performs all optimization steps automatically, and iteratively analyzes counterexamples, in order to inductively achieve global optimization based on a verification oracle. Experimental results show that OptCE can effectively find optimal solutions for all evaluated benchmarks, while traditional techniques are usually trapped by local minima.

1 Introduction

Optimization is a tool employed in several research fields, such as biology (*e.g.*, biomolecular modeling energy functions) [1], computer science (*e.g.*, complexity reduction) [2], engineering (*e.g.*, filter design for digital signal processing) [3], and business (*e.g.*, profit increase) [4], with the goal of obtaining maximum system performance. Although there are several available optimization techniques (*e.g.*, simulated annealing [5], particle swarm [6], and genetic algorithms [7]), their main difficulty lies on locating the global minima of functions. As a consequence, they often present suboptimal solutions, *i.e.*, they are trapped by local minima, which commonly lead to low performance [8].

The present work introduces a tool based on the counterexample-guided inductive optimization (CEGIO) algorithms proposed by Araújo *et al.* [9,10], which is named as Optimization through Counter-Examples (OptCE). Indeed, OptCE is a tool instantiation of the approach developed by Araújo *et al.* [9], which now presents further evaluation regarding other function classes (broader applicability) and verifiers. OptCE is inspired by syntax-guided synthesis (SyGuS) and performs *inductive generalization* based on counterexamples provided by a verification oracle [11]. In particular, OptCE employs nondeterministic representation of decision variables and then iteratively constrains

© Springer International Publishing AG 2017
S. Cavalheiro and J. Fiadeiro (Eds.): SBMF 2017, LNCS 10623, pp. 125–141, 2017.
https://doi.org/10.1007/978-3-319-70848-5_9

the state-space search based on counterexamples produced by boolean satisfiability (SAT) or satisfiability modulo theories (SMT) solvers via inductive generalization, *i.e.*, OptCE exploits the counterexample provided by the solver to achieve complete global optimization [3] about an objective function.

The mentioned techniques (CEGIO) do employ model checking based verification procedures to guide the global convergence and extract information from counterexamples. Unlike meta-heuristic optimization techniques (*e.g.*, genetic algorithms and simulated annealing), CEGIO always finds the global minima for all evaluated benchmarks, which is also true for the benchmarks evaluated by Araújo *et al.* [9,10]. In addition, OptCE requires only one file with the specification and constraints for a given objective function.

Although the resulting optimization times associated to the approach employed here are often higher than what is obtained with other traditional techniques [10], the present inductive optimization technique based on the counterexamples guarantees global coverage and is capable of handling convex and non-convex functions, since it performs inductive generalization based on the counterexamples provided by a verification oracle [12]. Our main novel contributions are:

- Development of the first CEGIO-based tool that is able to perform global optimization of several function classes (*e.g.*, convex, discontinuous, nonlinear, and non-convex);
- Extensive experimental evaluation of the CEGIO algorithms;
- Comparison regarding optimization performances provided by different verifiers (CBMC [13] and ESBMC [14]) and SAT/SMT solvers (MathSAT [15], Z3 [16], Boolector [17], and MiniSAT [18]).

Our experiments are based on a set of publicly available benchmarks and all related tools, scripts, benchmarks, and results can be obtained online through this link http://esbmc.org/benchmarks/optce.zip.

2   Inductive Optimization Based on Counterexamples

OptCE is an optimization tool based on CEGIO, which processes a function through three basic steps: modeling, specification, and verification. In order to illustrate the OptCE's optimization process, we consider the *adjiman* test objective function in Eq. (1) and its minimization process.

$$f(x_1, x_2) = cos(x_1)sin(x_2) - \frac{x_1}{x_2^2 + 1}. \tag{1}$$

In particular, the *adjiman* function is a non-convex, non-separable, and differentiable function; it is defined on 2-dimensional space [19].

(i) **Modeling.** In the modeling step, the optimization problem is defined for a cost function (*e.g.*, Eq. (1)) and then its constraints are introduced, in order to avoid the state-space explosion in model checking [20]. Regarding the Eq. (1), the optimization problem with its associated restrictions is described in Eq. (2).

$$
\begin{aligned}
\min \quad & f(x_1, x_2) \\
\text{s.t.} \quad & -1 \le x_1 \le 2 \\
& -1 \le x_2 \le 1.
\end{aligned}
\tag{2}
$$

In particular, the optimization problems are modeled through the CEGIO approach and using ANSI-C code, with the directive *ASSUME*, which represents the associated constraints and search space. The use of such directive (*e.g.*, `__ESBMC_assume()`) is illustrated in the code fragment as shown in Fig. 1.

(ii) **Specification.** This step consists in describing system behavior and properties to be checked, which results in a file according to the method proposed by Araújo *et al.* [9,10]. Indeed, the property specification is stated with *ASSERT* directives, which are used to check satisfiability and to control the verification procedure, *i.e.*, to search for violations of a given property, which, in the present case, consists of finding a function value that is smaller than the previous one. In summary, they represent calls to specific functions provided by the verification engine and also entry points for the proposed optimization. The mentioned resulting file contains the modeling and properties to be checked, as shown in Fig. 1 for the function *adjiman*. In this example, ESBMC is used as verification engine, where `__ESBMC_assume()` restricts the state-space, according to the performed modeling, and `__ESBMC_assert()` checks properties.

(iii) **Verification.** Finally, the C code generated in step 2 is checked by the underlying verifier, which can return "verification successful" or "verification failed". When "verification successful" is obtained, it means that the code is correct and no property has been violated; otherwise, "verification failed" indicates that the verification engine has found a violation, *i.e.*, a value smaller than the previous one, for a particular target function. It is worth noticing that when a violation is found, the associated counterexample, which is usually provided by such tools, already indicates a smaller value. As a consequence, this new limit can then be used for updating the respective variable (*i.e.*, f_i in the example shown in Fig. 1), which might iteratively lead to a minimum.

Araújo *et al.* [10] proposed three algorithms for the specification stage, which are suitable for different situations: the Generalized Algorithm (CEGIO-G), the Simplified Algorithm (CEGIO-S), and the Fast Algorithm (CEGIO-F). Figure 1 shows the specification for the function *adjiman* in CEGIO-G format, which can also be applied to any function class (*i.e.*, convex and non-convex ones). CEGIO-S is suitable for functions about which we have some prior knowledge (*e.g.*, semi- and positive-definite functions) and uses that to generate several properties in the specification step, which will be checked by the underlying verifier, with potentially increased chance of violation and reduced optimization times. Finally, CEGIO-F can be applied to convex functions and uses their properties to restrict

```
#define p 1
#include "math2.h"
int nondet_int();
float nondet_float();
int main() {
    float f_i = 69;
    int x[2], i;
    float X[2];
    float fobj;
    int lim[4] = {-1*p, 2*p, -1*p, 1*p};
    for (i = 0; i<2; i++){
        x[i] = nondet_int();
        X[i] = nondet_float();
    }
    for (i = 0; i<2; i++){
        __ESBMC_assume((x[i]>=lim[2*i])&&(x[i]<=lim[2*i+1]));
        __ESBMC_assume( X[i] == (float) x[i]/p );
    }
    fobj = cos2(X[0])*sin2(X[1]) - (X[0]/(X[1]*X[1]+1));
    __ESBMC_assume(fobj<f_i);
    assert(fobj>f_i);
    return 0;
}
```

Fig. 1. C code after the specification step for the function *adjiman*.

the associated state-space, according to the results presented by Araújo *et al.* [10], which show considerable improvement regarding optimization times. Each algorithm follows a fixed structure, which changes regarding only variable values.

3   OptCE: A Counterexample-Guided Inductive Optimization Solver

OptCE can be regarded as a front-end for model checkers that process C programs through CEGIO, where decision variables, which are in charge of generating the smallest value of a function, are checked. Such a tool can be called from a shell, via command line, and is able to optimize convex and non-convex functions, where users only need to describe, in a file, the specification and constraints regarding them, through a few code lines. In summary, OptCE is based on the CEGIO technique, which allows the discovery of global minima, while other techniques are usually trapped by local ones.

3.1   OptCE Architecture

As shown in Fig. 2, users need to provide an input *.func* file (*cf.* Sect. 3.2) containing a function's specification and constraints: this is the modeling phase. Indeed, such a task reveals that some knowledge about the target problem is necessary, in order to provide a correct basis.

The first step is the specification, which receives an input file and the desired settings for optimization, such as *verifier*, *solver*, *algorithm type*, and *precision*. In Fig. 2, α represents the number of decimal places of a solution, which is indicated

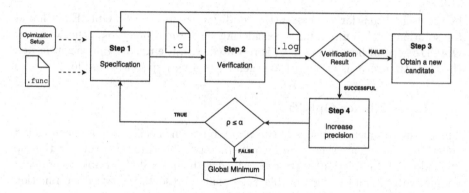

Fig. 2. An overview of the proposed OptCE architecture.

by the user. Based on the provided inputs, OptCE generates a specification file in ANSI-C (*cf.* Fig. 1), named as `min_<function>.c`.

During the first execution of Step 1, ρ, which is used to establish the solution accuracy throughout the optimization process, is initialized with zero, which indicates an optimization with integer precision solutions only (*i.e.*, no decimal digits are considered). In addition, an arbitrary minimum candidate is also considered, which is actually the algorithm's initialization value and can be provided by the user with the flag `--start-value`; otherwise, it is randomly generated, which is performed during the specification step.

During Step 2, the verification task occurs, *i.e.*, the ANSI-C file with a function's specification is checked by a verification engine, whose main output is a log file with the respective verification result. If "verification failed" is obtained, that means the underlying verification engine detected a property violation through the inserted assertions and consequently generated a counterexample. In the CEGIO context, a property violation indicates that the minimum candidate is not the global minimum for that value of ρ and then the tool flow proceeds to Step 3.

In Step 3, a `.log` file with the respective counterexample is used to obtain new decision variables, which provide a new global minimum candidate lower than the previous one, *i.e.*, the initialization value or the minimum candidate of the last OptCE iteration. Then, the new minimum candidate value is obtained (*i.e.*, extracted and computed from the counterexample), and used to perform Step 1 again, starting a new iteration and generating a new specification file. Such a procedure is iteratively performed until the verification step (Step 2) returns a `.log` file with "verification successful", which means that there are no decision variables capable of finding a minimum value smaller than the current one, considering the current value of the precision variable (ρ). When the verification result is "verification successful", OptCE proceeds to Step 4.

In Step 4, ρ is increased by one, *i.e.*, the precision associated to the optimal solution is increased by one decimal place, which is followed by a check that evaluates whether it is smaller than or equal to the desired accuracy (indicated by the user). If ρ is larger than α (the condition $\rho \leq \alpha$ is false), OptCE has found the solution (global minimum), considering the desired precision; otherwise, the OptCE's general flow (Steps 1–3) is repeated with the updated precision ρ, *i.e.*, the algorithm returns to Step 1 and generates a new specification file.

3.2   Input File for OptCE

The present input file consists of two parts: function specification and associated constraints, which are separated by a character "$\#$" isolated in a row. At the top of an input file, a function must be described with an ANSI-C variable assignment ending with "$;$" and using variable `fobj` that represents the objective function (see Fig. 3). We summarize the OptCE input language in Fig. 3.

$$
\begin{aligned}
Fml &::= Var \mid true \mid false \mid Fml \wedge Fml \mid \ldots \mid Exp = Exp \mid \ldots \\
Exp &::= Var \mid Const \mid Var[Exp] \mid Var[Exp][Exp] \mid Exp + Exp \mid \ldots \\
Cmd &::= Var = Exp \mid Var = * \mid Fml \mid sin2(Var) \mid cos2(Var) \\
&\quad \mid floor2(Var) \mid sqrt2(Var) \mid abs2(Var) \\
Prog &::= Cmd; \ldots; \#Cmd;
\end{aligned}
$$

Fig. 3. OptCE input program language.

Equation 3 presents the format adopted for constraint matrices, where the associated number of lines indicates the amount of decision variables and columns 1 and 2 represent the lower and upper bounds, respectively.

$$
\begin{bmatrix}
x_{11} & x_{12} \\
x_{21} & x_{22} \\
& \ldots \\
x_{n1} & x_{n2}
\end{bmatrix}
\tag{3}
$$

The constraints of the considered optimization problem (Eq. (2)) can be represented by $A = [-1\,2\,; -1\,1]$ and an input file containing the entire optimization problem (related to Eq. (2)) is illustrated in Fig. 4.

```
fobj = cos2(x1)*sin2(x2) - (x1/(x2*x2+1));
#
A = [-1  2;  -1  1];
```

Fig. 4. Input file for function *adjiman*.

3.3 OptCE Features

The current OptCE version allows us to define different configurations regarding the optimization process (*i.e.*, optimization algorithm and verification engine), which is used to reduce optimization times. Thus, users have to add suitable flags during a call via command-line. The following configurations are supported:

- **BMC configuration:** chooses between model checkers CBMC (--cbmc) and ESBMC (--esbmc);
- **Solver configuration:** chooses between solvers Boolector (--boolector), Z3 (--z3), MathSAT (--mathsat), and MiniSAT (--minisat);
- **Algorithm configuration:** chooses between the proposed algorithms, where the flag --generalized implements the CEGIO-G algorithm (*cf.* Sect. 2), which is used when there is no prior knowledge about the objective function, the flag --positive implements the CEGIO-S algorithm (*cf.* Sect. 2), which is used when a function is semi- and positive-definite, and the flag --convex implements the CEGIO-F algorithm (*cf.* Sect. 2), which is used for convex functions.
- **Initialization:** assigns an initial minimum candidate value (--start-value =*value*), which is random by default;
- **Insert library:** users can include their own library containing implementations of operators and functions used in the objective function's description (--library=*name-library*);
- **Timeout:** configures the time limit, in seconds (--timeout=*value*).
- **Precision:** sets the desired precision, *i.e.*, the number of decimal places of a solution (--precision=*value*).

3.4 Optimizing via OptCE

The user must create a description input file to find the global minimum of a function using the OptCE tool, as explained in Subsect. 3.2. Figure 5 shows all possible OptCE calls with input file and set of properties. Here, we employ the function *adjiman* to illustrate the use of OptCE, considering the input file shown in Fig. 4.

Call	Set Properties						
Binary + Function	**BMC**	**Solver**	**Algorithm**	**Initialization**	**Library**	**Timeout**	**Precision**
./optCE name.funct	--esbmc	--mathsat --boolector --z3	--generalized --positive --convex	--start-value=?	--library=name	--timeout=?	--precision=?
	--cbmc	--minisat					

Fig. 5. OptCE configuration options.

Currently, OptCE supports two verifiers: CBMC [13] and ESBMC [21]. Optimization employing CBMC as model checker (-cbmc) uses MiniSAT as default solver, while ESBMC (`--esbmc`) uses MathSAT. In our evaluation, we also tried to use the SMT solvers available in CBMC, but it failed to check all benchmarks reported in Table 1 due to problems in the SMT back-end. Regarding ESBMC, the user can choose between solvers Z3 (`--z3`) or Boolector (`--boolector`); however, we did not further evaluate other SMT solvers (*e.g.*, CVC4 and Yices). Indeed, verification times vary according to the selected verifier and solver and, as already mentioned, the user has the possibility to choose different configurations. If a given user is unsure about which verifier and solver to select, then a default choice would be to employ ESBMC with MathSAT or CBMC with MiniSAT, given that they normally present the shortest execution times; however, our experimental evaluation does not conclusively show that they are the best possible configurations (given the small benchmark set). As future work, we intend to automatically select the verifier and solver pair, using machine learning techniques that take into account objective functions, with a large set of benchmarks. Indeed, such an approach is similar to the work done by Hutter *et al.* [22], who apply a parameter optimization tool to improve SAT solvers for large, real-world bounded model-checking instances, via automatic tuning of decision procedures.

Another important parameter is the algorithm type, which can be `--convex`, for convex functions, `--positive`, for semi- and definite-positive functions, and `--generalized`, for functions about which we do not have any prior knowledge. Since Eq. (1) is not convex and it is not possible to ensure that it is nonnegative, the suggested setup uses flag `--generalized` (*./optCE adjiman.func* `--generalized`).

Following the execution flow illustrated in Fig. 5, the flag `--start-value` is used to specify the proposed algorithm's initialization (*./optCE<name> .func* `--start-value=20`) and, when it is not adopted, such a value is assigned in a random way. We noticed that variations regarding initialization values do not significantly influence convergence times, since OptCE evaluates only the integer part of the solutions, at the beginning of the optimization tasks. In addition, checking with integer values is fast, it is normal to get "verification failed" in the first round, and a "verification failed" result is generally faster than a "verification successful" one, as also experimentally observed by Araújo *et al.* [9, 10].

If the input function consists of arithmetic operators, then it is not mandatory to use the flag `--library`; however, when mathematical functions are present, it is necessary to implement them in ANSI-C. Such implementations considerably influence the verification results and the simpler they are, *i.e.*, the smaller their number of operations and loops is, the easier it is for the proposed approach to conclude the verification tasks. In the case of the *adjiman* function, which uses mathematical functions such as *sin()* and *cos()*, the library *math2.h* was created, with our own implementation, which was included using the flag `--library` (*./optCE adjiman.func* `--library=math2.h`). This library contains an improved implementation of the original *math.h*, which includes pre- and post-conditions to ensure that a (given) predicate holds before and after the execution of a (given) math function, respectively.

Our mathematical functions in *math2.h* have the same name of the corresponding elements in the ANSI-C library, except that we appended the character 2 (*e.g.*, *cos2()*, *sin2()*, *abs2()*).

The `--timeout` flag is used to interrupt optimization processes, if they reach the indicated time limit (*./optCE<name_function>.func* `--timeout=3600`). Finally, the user has the option to define the OptCE's solution accuracy, *i.e.*, the `--precision` flag indicates the number of decimal places of a solution. When a reference value is not provided, OptCE finds a global minimum with 3 decimal places, by default.

4 Experimental Evaluation

This section reports the performed experiments configuration and execution, along with an analysis of the results obtained with OptCE.

4.1 Experimental Objectives

Our experiments have been carried out seeking answers to the following questions:

RQ1 **(correctness)** Is OptCE able to find the global minima of functions?

RQ2 **(sanity check)** Does the settings choice between BMC tools and solvers influence optimization results?

RQ3 **(performance)** What are the advantages and disadvantages of OptCE, in comparison with traditional optimization techniques?

4.2 Description of the Benchmarks

In order to evaluate the proposed tool and answer those research questions presented in Sect. 4.1, a benchmark suite with 10 convex and nonconvex functions was created, with functions related to optimization problems extracted from the available literature [19]. They have different characteristics: continuous, differentiable, separable, non-separable, scalable, non-scalable, uni-modal, and multi-modal, including sine, cosine, polynomials, floor, sum, and square root. The chosen benchmarks are shown in Table 1, as follows: benchmark name, optimization domain, and global minimum.

All functions were used to evaluate the flag `--generalized`, which implements the CEGIO-G algorithm (*cf.* Sect. 2). In order to evaluate the flag `--positive`, which implements the CEGIO-S algorithm (*cf.* Sect. 2), semidefinite positive functions *Booth*, *Himmelblau*, and *Leon* were used. Lastly, functions *Zettl*, *Rotated Ellipse*, and *Sum Square* were used to evaluate the flag `--convex`, which implements the CEGIO-F algorithm (*cf.* Sect. 2).

The results of the proposed approach were compared with the ones presented by other techniques (*i.e.*, genetic algorithm, particle swarm, pattern search, simulated annealing, and nonlinear programming), where all benchmarks were executed with the MATLAB's optimization toolbox (2016b) [23].

Table 1. Benchmark suite.

#	Benchmark	Domain	Global minimum
1	Alpine 1	$-10 \le x_i \le 10$	$f(0,0) = 0$
2	Cosine	$-1 \le x_i \le 1$	$f(0,0) = -0.2$
3	Styblinski Tang	$-5 \le x_i \le 5$	$f(2.903, 2.903) = -78.332$
4	Zirilli	$-10 \le x_i \le 10$	$f(1.046, 0) \approx -0.3523$
5	Booth	$-10 \le x_i \le 10$	$f(1,3) = 0$
6	Himmeblau	$-5 \le x_i \le 5$	$f(3,2) = 0$
7	Leon	$-2 \le x_i \le 2$	$f(1,1) = 0$
8	Zettl	$-5 \le x_i \le 10$	$f(0.029, 0) = -0.0037$
9	Sum Square	$-10 \le x_i \le 10$	$f(0,0) = 0$
10	Rotated Ellipse	$-500 \le x_i \le 500$	$f(0,0) = 0$

Similarly to the experiments performed by Araújo *et al.* [9,10], the elapsed times presented in the following tables are related to the average CPU time measured with the *times* system call (POSIX system) of 20 consecutive executions for each benchmark, where the measurement unit is always in seconds. Finally, our experiments were set for obtaining the global minima with 3 decimal places and were conducted on an otherwise idle computer equipped with Intel Core i7-4790 CPU 3.60 GHz, 16 GB of RAM, and Linux OS Ubuntu 14.10.

4.3 Experimental Results

The experimental results are presented in four tables. Tables 2, 3, and 4 refer to the benchmarks with the flags `--generalized`, `--positive`, and `--convex`, respectively. Table 5 refers to a comparison between OptCE v1.0 and other traditional techniques. Each column of Table 2 is described as follows: column 1 is related to functions of the reference benchmark suite, columns 2, 3 and 4 are related to the ESBMC v3.1.0 configuration with MathSAT v.5.3.13, Z3 v4.5.0, and Boolector v2.2.0 solvers, respectively, and column 5 is related to the CBMC v4.5 configuration with MiniSat v2.2.0.

The overall minimum was found in all benchmarks, considering all combinations between BMC tools and solvers. As presented by Araújo *et al.* [10], those algorithms ensure the global minimum, considering the desired accuracy, which was described in previous section; their proofs of convergence are provided in [10], which confirm the experimental results. The optimization times varied significantly in Table 2, which makes it difficult to reason about the best configuration; however, according to Fig. 6, the total optimization time with the configuration ESBMC + MathSAT (the best one) was 2.8 times faster than the one presented by CBMC + MiniSAT, while the configuration ESBMC + Z3 presented the longest execution time, being 40 times longer than the best case.

Table 2. Execution times for the generic algorithm (CEGIO-G [10]), in seconds.

#	ESBMC			CBMC
	MathSAT	Z3	Boolector	MiniSAT
1	**1068**	105192	3387	5344
2	**4130**	80481	5003	8509
3	**443**	37778	2027	2438
4	468	387	**190**	1143
5	7	1244	4016	**2**
6	12	14205	6217	**4**
7	5	2443	212	**2**
8	13	753	389	**9**
9	18	4171	4438	**13**
10	3	72	39	**2**

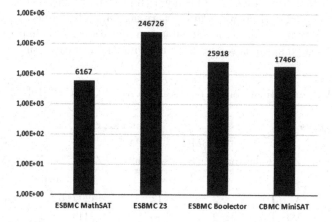

Fig. 6. Histogram of the total optimization time for the adopted benchmark suite, in logarithmic scale.

Another interesting observation regarding Table 2 is that although CBMC + MiniSAT provided the second best performance, considering the entire benchmark suite, such a configuration was the best in 60% of the benchmarks, *i.e.*, a few cases required long run times, but they were exceedingly time consuming. Benchmarks #1 − 4 are non-convex and presented long times when searching for the global minima, considering all possible settings. Benchmarks #5 − 7 are semi- and positive-definite functions, while #8 − 10 are convex ones. Regarding them, OptCE was able to find solutions using the algorithms CEGIO-S and CEGIO-F, by providing, respectively, the flags --positive and --convex.

Nonetheless, in order to evaluate the implementation of CEGIO-G, all benchmarks were optimized with the flag --generalized. The experiments were repeated for different combinations of model checkers and SAT/SMT solvers, *i.e.*, ESBMC was combined with three solvers (MathSAT, Z3, and Boolector) and CBMC with MiniSAT only. Particularly, the combinations ESBMC + MathSAT and CBMC + MiniSAT presented results significantly better than the ones provided by other configurations of OptCE, given that Boolector does not support floating-point arithmetic [17]. In particular, MathSAT (the one that obtained the best results) supports both fixed- and floating-point arithmetic and, surprisingly, the performance for floating-point optimization is significantly better if compared to the fixed-point one. As a consequence, when using the flag --generalized, the configurations ESBMC + MathSAT and CBMC + MiniSAT are recommended.

Table 3 presents the results for the flag --positive, which is suitable for semi- and positive-definite functions. As a consequence, we used only benchmarks #5 − 7, in this experiment. Those functions make use of modules with high even powers, *i.e.*, by mathematical inspection we can ensure that such functions can not reach one global negative minimum. Table 3 compares the use of the flags --generalized and --positive, for this class of problems. One may notice that the implementation of the CEGIO-S algorithm with the flag --positive does indeed work, since optimization times were significantly reduced, if compared to the flag --generalized, in all possible configurations. This happens because the solution search space is reduced, by ignoring the negative part.

Table 3. Execution times for the positive algorithm (CEGIO-S [10]), in seconds.

#	--positive				--generalized			
	ESBMC			CBMC	ESBMC			CBMC
	MathSAT	Z3	Boolector	MiniSAT	MathSAT	Z3	Boolector	MiniSAT
5	3	<1	1	3	7	1244	4016	2
6	4	1	1	2	12	14205	6217	4
7	3	<1	1	2	5	2443	212	2

The CEGIO-F algorithm implementation is assigned with the flag --convex. In order to evaluate its performance, benchmarks #8 − 10 were used, because they are convex functions, and their results are presented in Table 4. The optimization times using a specific algorithm for this function class were considerably lower than the times presented by the generalized algorithm. That happens because, in this algorithm and with each performed check, the search space is reduced according to the found global minimum candidate, which then decreases verification and, consequently, optimization times.

The best results using the proposed tool, for each benchmark, are presented in Table 5, along with results for other techniques. The *configuration* column shows the combinations regarding algorithm types (by the initials of flags "G" for --generalized, "P" for --positive, and "C" for --convex), BMC tools, and solvers. The comparison is performed with traditional optimization techniques:

Table 4. Execution times for the convex algorithm (CEGIO-F [10]), in seconds.

#	--convex				--generalized			
	ESBMC			CBMC	ESBMC			CBMC
	MathSAT	Z3	Boolector	MiniSAT	MathSAT	Z3	Boolector	MiniSAT
8	15	6	21	5	13	753	389	9
9	14	3	19	5	18	4171	4438	13
10	3	1	2	2	3		72	39	2

genetic algorithm (GA), particle swarm (ParSwarm), pattern search (PatSearch), simulated annealing (SA), and nonlinear programming (NLP). All evaluated benchmarks were executed 1000 times with the traditional techniques, using MATLAB, and 20 times with CEGIO, using OptCE. The number of repetitions was selected to ensure the convergence of hit rate for all algorithms.

Table 5. Experimental results for traditional techniques and the best proposed CEGIO algorithms, in seconds.

#	OptCE			GA		ParSwarm		PatSearch		SA		NLP	
	Configuration	R%	T	R%	T	R%	T	R%	T	R%	T	R%	T
1	G + ESBMC + MathSAT	100	1068	29.1	1	22.2	3	16	4	0.4	1	4.8	9
2	G + ESBMC + MathSAT	100	4130	100	9	9.8	1	96.7	3	88.5	2	28.4	2
3	G + ESBMC + MathSAT	100	443	68.1	9	47.8	1	51.8	3	99.5	1	35.8	2
4	G + ESBMC + Boolector	100	190	95.7	9	53.9	1	98.8	3	74.4	1	62.5	2
5	P + ESBMC + Z3	100	< 1	100	10	100	2	100	6	93.5	1	100	2
6	P + ESBMC + Z3	100	1	42.4	9	43.9	1	26	3	21	1	35	2
7	P + ESBMC + Z3	100	< 1	84.4	1	80.3	2	1	7	24.3	1	100	4
8	C + CBMC + MiniSAT	100	5	100	9	48.1	1	99.8	4	26.4	1	100	3
9	C + ESBMC + Z3	100	3	100	9	71.5	1	100	4	96.9	1	100	2
10	C + ESBMC + Z3	100	1	100	9	100	2	100	7	99.8	1	100	2

OptCE's hit rate is 100% for this benchmark suite, considering the domain established in Table 1, for each benchmark. The present experiments show that OptCE generally takes longer than other techniques, in order to locate the global minima; however, its hit rate is always higher. In particular, the time results with the flags --positive (CEGIO-S) and --convex (CEGIO-F) are similar to what is provided by the other techniques, but with superior hit rates. The chosen traditional optimization techniques, in many cases, failed to obtain solutions for the adopted benchmarks, considering the established precision of 3 decimal places. That happened because they are sensitive to non-convexity and, in many cases, they get trapped by local minima, which resulted in sub-optimal solutions. If only benchmarks 8, 9, and 10, in Table 1, are evaluated, which are convex functions, the rate obtained by existing methods is 100%, since those functions do not have local minima that can compromise their results.

In summary, the proposed technique can be used in any optimization problem, but there are always restrictions regarding the time and number of variables. Usually, cost functions in practical problems are distance or power functions, *i.e.*, they are semi- and positive-definite. Therefore, as OptCE has the CEGIO-S algorithm implemented in its structure, which is specific to this function class, it implies that OptCE is able to solve those particular optimization problems.

OptCE presents good performance with non-convex functions, if compared to the traditional techniques, because the global minima are found in all benchmarks. Traditional techniques, in turn, are lost at local minimum and return sub-optimal solutions, which then reduces their hit rate.

The performance of OptCE using specific flags for convex and positive-definite functions proved to be competitive, once the obtained execution times were very close to the ones from other techniques, given that global minima were found in all cases. Depending on the problem type, the number of solution decimal places might be lower than the amount used in this experimental evaluation. For those cases, execution times regarding the location of optimal solutions are reduced, once there are fewer decimal places to check, which then implies fewer verifications and fewer states to be considered.

5   Related Work

Since the earliest research with SMT application to solve optimization problems, which was presented by Nieuwenhuis and Oliveras [24], several satisfiability-theory based tools have emerged, with the purpose of solving optimization problems. Conversely, various SAT/SMT specialized solvers have been developed, which employ optimization techniques in their engines to improve solving performance (*e.g.*, ABsolver [25], and CalCs [26]). Shoukry *et al.* [27] proposed the Satisfiability Modulo Convex (SMC) Optimization [28] to solve satisfiability problems over SMC formulas, which generalizes several formulas over Boolean and nonlinear real arithmetic.

Recently, νZ [29] extended the SMT solver Z3 [16] for linear optimization problems and Li *et al.* proposed the SYMBA algorithm [30], which is an SMT-based symbolic optimization algorithm that uses linear real arithmetic theory and SMT solvers, as black boxes. Similarly, OptiMathSat presented by Sebastiani and Trentin [31] is also an optimization tool that extends MathSAT5 SMT solver to allow solving linear functions in the boolean, rational, and integer domains, or a combination of them. Although the OptCE tool presented in this study is based on satisfiability theories, it does not employ SAT/SMT solvers directly, in contrast to other techniques [29–31]. OptCE incorporates the model checking approach and employs SAT- and SMT-based model checkers to model, specify, and verify ANSI-C representations of optimization problems by exploiting the counterexample provided by them.

Model-checking has already been employed to model and solve optimization problems, in some previous studies. Trindade *et al.* [32,33] used the ESBMC tool to solve optimization problems over booleans decision variables related to hardware/software partition, in embedded systems. Araújo *et al.* [9,10] proposed the CEGIO algorithms to globally optimize non-convex functions on the rational domain, with adjustable precision.

Most previous studies related to SMT-based optimization can only solve linear problems over integer, rational, and Boolean domains, in specific cases. Indeed, only a few studies [27] are able to solve non-linear problems, but they are also constrained to convex functions. In contrast, this paper proposes a new tool that implements the CEGIO algorithms [9,10] and is able to globally minimize a wide variety of functions: linear or non-linear, convex or non-convex, and continuous or discontinuous.

6   Conclusion

OptCE is a novel optimization tool that models a wide range of constrained optimization problems (convex, nonlinear, and nonconvex) as a model checking problem and inductively analyzes counterexamples, in order to achieve global optimization of functions, by employing SAT- or SMT-based verification. In particular, this tool is based on a class of optimization algorithms, named CEGIO, and it is able to ensure the global optimal convergence with a given precision. OptCE supports the following features: three different CEGIO algorithms (CEGIO-G, CEGIO-S, and CEGIO-F), two state-of-art BMC tools (CBMC and ESBMC), and four SAT/SMT solvers (MiniSAT, Boolector, Z3, and MathSAT).

Our experiments showed that OptCE achieved 100% of hit rate, being able to ensure the global optimization. In contrast, other traditional techniques (GA, PatSearch, ParSwarm, NLP, and SA) employed for comparison were usually trapped by local minima. In addition, the experimental results indicated that the most flexible CEGIO algorithm (CEGIO-G), which is suitable for every function class supported by OptCE, presented times significantly longer than the others from the CEGIO algorithms and traditional techniques, despite ensuring the global optimization. Nonetheless, the other two CEGIO algorithms (CEGIO-S and CEGIO-F), which are suitable for nonnegative and convex optimization problems, respectively, were able to solve global optimization problems with times similar to the ones provided by the traditional techniques, but with superior hit rate.

OptCE is available for free download (Linux x86 version)[1], including documentation, benchmarks, results, publications, and source code. Although the OptCE's time performance is slow, it has been and will be continuously improved, given that verifiers and SAT/SMT solvers evolve, even with the inclusion of new and adaptive techniques, such as machine learning [22]. Future work includes parallelization and state space partitioning, thus linearly reducing checking times. We also intend to enhance our model-checking procedure for reducing the verification time by means of automatic invariant generation [34,35].

---

[1] Available at http://esbmc.org/benchmarks/optce.zip.

Acknowledgements. This research was supported by FAPEAM and CNPq. Higo Albuquerque was also supported by a CAPES studentship.

References

1. Park, H., Bradley, P., Greisen Jr., P., Liu, Y., Mulligan, V.K., Kim, D.E., Baker, D., DiMaio, F.: Simultaneous optimization of biomolecular energy functions on features from small molecules and macromolecules. J. Chem. Theory Comput. **12**(12), 6201–6212 (2016)
2. Cooper, K.D., Torczon, L.: Engineering a Compiler. Morgan Kaufmann, San Francisco (2004)
3. Deb, K.: Optimization for Engineering Design: Algorithms and Examples. Prentice-Hall of India, New Delhi (2004)
4. Vergidis, K., Tiwari, A., Majeed, B.: Business process analysis and optimization: beyond reengineering. IEEE Trans. Syst. Man Cybern. C Appl. Rev. **38**(1), 69–82 (2008)
5. Laarhoven, P.J.M., Aarts, E.H.L. (eds.): Simulated Annealing: Theory and Applications. Kluwer Academic Publishers, Norwell (1987)
6. Olsson, A.: Particle Swarm Optimization: Theory, Techniques and Applications, Engineering tools, Techniques and Tables. Nova Science Publishers, USA (2011)
7. Goldberg, D.: Genetic Algorithms in Search, Optimization, and Machine Learning, Artificial Intelligence. Addison-Wesley Publishing Company, Boston (1989)
8. Floudas, C.: Deterministic Global Optimization. Nonconvex Optimization and Its Applications. Springer, Berlin (2000). https://doi.org/10.1007/978-1-4757-4949-6
9. Araújo, R., Bessa, I., Cordeiro, L., Filho, J.E.C.: SMT-based verification applied to non-convex optimization problems. In: SBESC, pp. 1–8 (2016)
10. Araújo, R., Bessa, I., Cordeiro, L., Filho, J.E.C.: Counterexample guided inductive optimization, pp. 1–32 (2017). arXiv:1704.03738 [cs.AI]
11. Alur, R., Bodik, R., Juniwal, G., Martin, M.M.K., Raghothaman, M., Seshia, S.A., Singh, R., Solar-Lezama, A., Torlak, E., Udupa, A.: Syntax-guided synthesis. In: FMCAD, pp. 1–8 (2013)
12. Solar-Lezama, A.: The sketching approach to program synthesis. In: Hu, Z. (ed.) APLAS 2009. LNCS, vol. 5904, pp. 4–13. Springer, Heidelberg (2009). https://doi.org/10.1007/978-3-642-10672-9_3
13. Kroening, D., Tautschnig, M.: CBMC – C bounded model checker. In: Ábrahám, E., Havelund, K. (eds.) TACAS 2014. LNCS, vol. 8413, pp. 389–391. Springer, Heidelberg (2014). https://doi.org/10.1007/978-3-642-54862-8_26
14. Cordeiro, L., Fischer, B., Marques-Silva, J.: SMT-based bounded model checking for embedded ANSI-C software. IEEE TSE **38**(4), 957–974 (2012)
15. Cimatti, A., Griggio, A., Schaafsma, B.J., Sebastiani, R.: The MathSAT5 SMT solver. In: Piterman, N., Smolka, S.A. (eds.) TACAS 2013. LNCS, vol. 7795, pp. 93–107. Springer, Heidelberg (2013). https://doi.org/10.1007/978-3-642-36742-7_7
16. de Moura, L., Bjørner, N.: Z3: an efficient SMT solver. In: Ramakrishnan, C.R., Rehof, J. (eds.) TACAS 2008. LNCS, vol. 4963, pp. 337–340. Springer, Heidelberg (2008). https://doi.org/10.1007/978-3-540-78800-3_24
17. Brummayer, R., Biere, A.: Boolector: an efficient SMT solver for bit-vectors and arrays. In: Kowalewski, S., Philippou, A. (eds.) TACAS 2009. LNCS, vol. 5505, pp. 174–177. Springer, Heidelberg (2009). https://doi.org/10.1007/978-3-642-00768-2_16

18. Eén, N., Sörensson, N.: An extensible SAT-solver. In: Giunchiglia, E., Tacchella, A. (eds.) SAT 2003. LNCS, vol. 2919, pp. 502–518. Springer, Heidelberg (2004). https://doi.org/10.1007/978-3-540-24605-3_37
19. Jamil, M., Yang, X.: A literature survey of benchmark functions for global optimization problems, CoRR abs/1308.4008. http://arxiv.org/abs/1308.4008
20. Baier, C., Katoen, J.-P.: Principles of Model Checking (Representation and Mind Series). The MIT Press, Cambridge (2008)
21. Morse, J., Ramalho, M., Cordeiro, L., Nicole, D., Fischer, B.: ESBMC 1.22. In: Ábrahám, E., Havelund, K. (eds.) TACAS 2014. LNCS, vol. 8413, pp. 405–407. Springer, Heidelberg (2014). https://doi.org/10.1007/978-3-642-54862-8_31
22. Hutter, F., Babic, D., Hoos, H.H., Hu, A.J.: Boosting verification by automatic tuning of decision procedures. In: FMCAD, pp. 27–34 (2007)
23. The Mathworks Inc, Matlab Optimization Toolbox User's Guide (2016)
24. Nieuwenhuis, R., Oliveras, A.: On SAT modulo theories and optimization problems. In: Biere, A., Gomes, C.P. (eds.) SAT 2006. LNCS, vol. 4121, pp. 156–169. Springer, Heidelberg (2006). https://doi.org/10.1007/11814948_18
25. Bauer, A., Pister, M., Tautschnig, M.: Tool-support for the analysis of hybrid systems and models. In: DATE, pp. 924–929 (2007)
26. Nuzzo, P., Puggelli, A.A.A., Seshia, S.A., Sangiovanni-Vincentelli, A.L.: CalCS: SMT solving for non-linear convex constraints, Technical report UCB/EECS-2010-100, EECS Department, University of California, Berkeley, Jun 2010
27. Shoukry, Y., Nuzzo, P., Saha, I., Sangiovanni-Vincentelli, A.L., Seshia, S.A., Pappas, G.J., Tabuada, P.: Scalable lazy smt-based motion planning. In: CDC, pp. 6683–6688 (2016)
28. Shoukry, Y., Nuzzo, P., Sangiovanni-Vincentelli, A.L., Seshia, S.A., Pappas, G.J., Tabuada, P.: SMC: satisfiability modulo convex optimization. In: HSCC, pp. 19–28 (2017)
29. Bjørner, N., Phan, A.-D., Fleckenstein, L.: VZ - an optimizing SMT solver. In: Baier, C., Tinelli, C. (eds.) TACAS 2015. LNCS, vol. 9035, pp. 194–199. Springer, Heidelberg (2015). https://doi.org/10.1007/978-3-662-46681-0_14
30. Li, Y., Albarghouthi, A., Kincaid, Z., Gurfinkel, A., Chechik, M.: Symbolic optimization with SMT Solvers. In: POPL, pp. 607–618 (2014)
31. Sebastiani, R., Trentin, P.: OptiMathSAT: a tool for optimization modulo theories. In: Kroening, D., Păsăreanu, C.S. (eds.) CAV 2015. LNCS, vol. 9206, pp. 447–454. Springer, Cham (2015). https://doi.org/10.1007/978-3-319-21690-4_27
32. Trindade, A., Ismail, H., Cordeiro, L.: Applying multi-core model checking to hardware-software partitioning in embedded systems. In: SBESC, pp. 102–105 (2015)
33. Trindade, A., Cordeiro, L.: Applying SMT-based verification to hardware/software partitioning in embedded systems. Des. Autom. Embed. Syst. 20(1), 1–19 (2016)
34. Rocha, H., Ismail, H., Cordeiro, L., Barreto, R.: Model checking embedded C software using k-induction and invariants. In: SBESC, pp. 90–95 (2015)
35. Gadelha, M.Y.R., Ismail, H.I., Cordeiro, L.C.: Handling loops in bounded model checking of C programs via k-induction. STTT 19(1), 97–114 (2017)

Formal Analysis of the Information Leakage of the DC-Nets and Crowds Anonymity Protocols

Arthur Américo[1(✉)], Artur Vaz[1], Mário S. Alvim[1], Sérgio V.A. Campos[1], and Annabelle McIver[2]

[1] Universidade Federal de Minas Gerais, Belo Horizonte, Brazil
aamerico@dcc.ufmg.br
[2] Macquarie University, Sydney, Australia

Abstract. A crucial goal in computer security is to protect sensitive information from unwanted disclosure. However, some leakage is often unavoidable, be it by design of the system or by technological limitations. The field of *Quantitative Information Flow* (QIF) is concerned with the quantification, and limitation, of information leakage in systems.

The QIF framework models systems as information-theoretic *channels* taking *(secret) inputs* and producing *(observable) outputs*, thereby increasing the adversary's knowledge about the secret value, as measured by some *information metric*.

In this paper we use probabilistic model checking to obtain channels modeling two popular anonymity protocols, the *Dining Cryptographers* (a.k.a. *DC-Nets*) and *Crowds*, in two versions each. We then derive the systems' *capacities* w.r.t. the g-leakage framework, which are robust upper bounds on information leakage that hold irrespectively of the probability distribution on secret values, or of the interests and goals of the adversary. To the best of our knowledge, this is the most general QIF analyses of such protocols.

Keywords: Quantitative Information Flow · Formal methods · Model checking · Dining Cryptographers · Crowds · g-leakage

1 Introduction

Protecting sensitive information is a crucial goal of computational security, and the more dependent human affairs are on computational systems, the more pressing becomes the matter. Ideally, we would like to prevent *all* leakage of sensitive information, but this might not be achievable in practice. For example, a password checker on an ATM will always leak some information—either by accepting the user's input (which completely reveals the password value), or by rejecting it (which rules out one possible value).

Nevertheless we use ATMs regularly, and many other systems suffering from similar issues. We are comfortable in doing so not because they do not leak

© Springer International Publishing AG 2017
S. Cavalheiro and J. Fiadeiro (Eds.): SBMF 2017, LNCS 10623, pp. 142–158, 2017.
https://doi.org/10.1007/978-3-319-70848-5_10

sensitive information, but because we consider the *amount* of information they leak to be "acceptable". In fact, most systems, either by technical limitation or by design, leak some information, and developing ways to measure *how much* information is leaked is essential in order to analyze the security of such systems. However, quantifying leakage or guaranteeing that it is limited is a difficult task.

Quantitative Information Flow (QIF) is the branch of security that studies the amount of information leaked by a system. It has seen growing interest over the past decade, including foundational works [4,8,11,15,22,27,35], verification of information flow properties [6,10,13,14,16,24,36], detection of real system vulnerabilities [20,23], and, of course, methods to réduce information leakage.

In QIF, security systems are modeled as information-theoretical *channels*, from which various properties of interest can be deduced. One crucial, and in general non-trivial task, however, is to compute the channel corresponding to the behavior of a given computational system—even for small but intricate protocols.

In this paper we describe a general procedure to derive such channels using *probabilistic model checking*. Using this procedure we model the *Dining Cryptographers* (a.k.a. *DC-Nets*) [12], and *Crowds* [33], two well-known anonymity protocols, in two variations each: (i) the standard DC-Nets, in which nodes are organized in a ring; (ii) a version of DC-Nets in which nodes are all connected to each other; (iii) the standard Crowds protocols; and (iv) a version of Crowds in which nodes are organized in a grid and each node can only communicate with its immediate neighbors. We then analyze them using the state of art in QIF metrics: the *g-vulnerability* framework [5]. More precisely, we derive *g-capacities* [3] of such channels, which are robust upper bounds on the information leakage they may present in any possible context of execution. This means that the bounds computed hold irrespectively of the probability distribution on secret values, or of the interests and goals of an adversary. To the best of our knowledge, this is the most general information-flow analyses of such protocols.

The main contributions of this paper are:

1. Allowing anonymity protocols to be expressed in a precise modeling language which closely reflects their implementation.
2. A direct computation of the relevant channels.
3. The first characterization of the *g*-capacities of the Dining Cryptographers and the Crowds anonymity protocols, which are state-of-the-art robust measures of information flow.
4. A detailed comparison of the superiority of one variant of each protocol over the other in terms of information leakage guarantees.

Future work could lead to a general purpose tool support to allow the computation of critical information flow properties.

This remaining of this paper is organized as follows. Section 2 reviews necessary background on QIF and on probabilistic model checking, including the PRISM tool. Section 3 describes the Dining Cryptographers and the Crowds anonymity protocols, in two variations each. Section 4 describes the general procedure using probabilistic model checking to derive channels from protocols, and presents the channels produced for the protocols we study. Section 5 analyzes the channels obtained the in light of QIF metrics. Finally, Sect. 6 discusses related work, and Sect. 7 discusses future work, and concludes.

2 Preliminaries

In this section we review basic concepts from quantitative information flow, and from probabilistic model checking.

2.1 Quantitative Information Flow

Secrets and Vulnerability. A *secret* is some piece of sensitive information the defender wants to protect, such as a user's password, social security number, or current location. The attacker usually only has some partial knowledge about the value of a secret, represented as a probability distribution on secrets called a *prior*. We denote by $\mathcal{X}$ the set of possible secrets, and we typically use π to denote a prior belonging to the set $\mathbb{D}\mathcal{X}$ of probability distributions over $\mathcal{X}$.

The *vulnerability* of a secret is a measure of the utility of the attacker's knowledge about the secret. Several notions of vulnerability (or their dual concept, *entropy*) have been proposed in the literature, including Shannon entropy [34], guessing entropy [25], and Bayes vulnerability/risk [11,35].

Recently, the *g-vulnerability* framework [5] has been proposed, consisting of a family of vulnerability measures that capture various adversarial models. It has been shown that these functions coincide with the set of continuous and convex functions on $\mathbb{D}\mathcal{X}$, and are, in a precise sense, the most general information measures w.r.t. a set of basic axioms.[1] In this paper we shall adopt g-vulnerabilities as our measures of information.

The operational scenario captured by g-vulnerabilities is parameterized by a set $\mathcal{W}$ of *guesses* (possibly infinite) that the attacker can take w.r.t. a secret, and a *gain function* $g : \mathcal{W} \times \mathcal{X} \to \mathbb{R}$. The gain $g(w, x)$ expresses the attacker's benefit for making guess w when the actual secret is x. Given a distribution π, *(prior) g-vulnerability* measures the attacker's success as the expected gain of an optimal guess, being defined as

$$V_g\left[\pi\right] \stackrel{\text{def}}{=} \max_{w \in \mathcal{W}} \sum_{x \in \mathcal{X}} \pi(x) g(w, x).$$

Channels, Posterior Vulnerability, and Leakage. Systems can be modeled as information theoretic channels. A *channel matrix*, or simply a *channel*, $C : \mathcal{X} \times \mathcal{Y} \to \mathbb{R}$ is a function in which $\mathcal{X}$ is a set of *input values*, $\mathcal{Y}$ is a set of *output values*, and $C(x, y)$ represents the conditional probability of the channel producing output $y \in \mathcal{Y}$ when input $x \in \mathcal{X}$ is provided. Every channel C satisfies $0 \leq C(x, y) \leq 1$ for all $x \in \mathcal{X}$ and $y \in \mathcal{Y}$, and $\sum_{y \in \mathcal{Y}} C(x, y) = 1$ for all $x \in \mathcal{X}$.

---

[1] More precisely, if posterior vulnerability is defined as the expectation of the vulnerability of posterior distributions, the measure respects the data-processing inequality and yields non-negative leakage iff vulnerability is convex.

A distribution $\pi \in \mathbb{D}\mathcal{X}$ and a channel C with inputs $\mathcal{X}$ and outputs $\mathcal{Y}$ induce a joint distribution $p(x, y) = \pi(x)C(x, y)$ on $\mathcal{X} \times \mathcal{Y}$, producing joint random variables X, Y with marginal probabilities $p(x) = \sum_y p(x, y)$ and $p(y) = \sum_x p(x, y)$, and conditional probabilities $p(x|y) = p(x,y)/p(y)$ if $p(y) \neq 0$. For a given y (s.t. $p(y) \neq 0$), the conditional probabilities $p(x|y)$ for each $x \in \mathcal{X}$ form the *posterior distribution* $p_{X|y}$.[2]

A channel C in which $\mathcal{X}$ is a set of secret values and $\mathcal{Y}$ is a set of observable values produced by a system can be used to model computations on secrets. Assuming the attacker has prior knowledge π about the secret value, knows how a channel C works, and can observe the channel's outputs, the effect of the channel is to update the attacker's knowledge from a prior π to a collection of posteriors $p_{X|y}$, each occurring with probability $p(y)$.[3]

Example 1. Given $\mathcal{X} = \{x_1, x_2, x_3\}$ and $\mathcal{Y} = \{y_1, y_2, y_3, y_4\}$, and the channel matrix C below, the (uniform) prior $\pi = (1/3, 1/3, 1/3)$ combined with C leads to the joint matrix J as follows.

C	y_1	y_2	y_3	y_4
x_1	1	0	0	0
x_2	0	$1/2$	$1/4$	$1/4$
x_3	$1/2$	$1/3$	$1/6$	0

$\xrightarrow{\pi}$

J	y_1	y_2	y_3	y_4
x_1	$1/3$	0	0	0
x_2	0	$1/6$	$1/12$	$1/12$
x_3	$1/6$	$1/9$	$1/18$	0

Summing the columns of J gives the marginal distribution $p_Y = (1/2, 5/18, 5/36, 1/12)$, and normalizing gives the posterior distributions $p_{X|y_1} = (2/3, 0, 1/3)$, $p_{X|y_2} = (0, 3/5, 2/5)$, $p_{X|y_3} = (0, 3/5, 2/5)$, and $p_{X|y_4} = (0, 1, 0)$. □

The *posterior vulnerability* is the vulnerability of the secret after the attacker observed the output of the channel. Formally, given a g-vulnerability V_g, the *posterior g-vulnerability* w.r.t. a prior π and a channel C is defined as

$$V_g[\pi, C] \stackrel{\text{def}}{=} \sum_{y \in \mathcal{Y}} p(y) V_g(p(X|y))$$

$$= \sum_{y \in \mathcal{Y}} \max_{w \in W} \sum_{x \in \mathcal{X}} \pi(x) C(x, y) g(w, x).$$

The *information leakage* of a channel C under a prior π is a comparison between the vulnerability of the secret before the system was run—called *prior vulnerability*—and the posterior vulnerability of the secret. Leakage, then, reflects by how much the observation of the system's outputs increases the utility of the attacker's knowledge about the secret. It can be defined either

multiplicatively: $\mathcal{L}_g[\pi, C] = \dfrac{V_g[\pi, C]}{V_g[\pi]}$,

---

[2] To avoid ambiguity, we may write probabilities with subscripts, e.g., p_{XY} or p_Y.
[3] This collection of posterior distributions is, in fact, a distribution on (posterior) distributions, and is called a *hyper-distribution* on secrets [27].

which measures the relative increase in the adversary's information about the secret; or

$$additively: \qquad \mathcal{L}_g^+[\pi, C] = V_g[\pi, C] - V_g[\pi],$$

which measures the absolute increase in the adversary's information.

Multiplicative and additive versions of leakage provide complimentary information about the behavior of a channel. Depending on the system itself, on the nature of the secret inputs, and even on the interests of the adversary, one definition of leakage may be more suitable than the other to express information leakage on a certain scenario, but in general a proper assessment of leakage may have to take both versions into consideration [3].

Capacities. Although both multiplicative and additive g-leakages represent useful quantities, to properly compute them one needs to know not only the channel C representing the system, but also the prior π and the gain-function g, and both can vary depending on the adversary's knowledge and interests. For robustness, we can consider *capacities*, which are leakage measures that universally quantify over the prior π, over the gain function g, or over both, making the measurements less dependent on the particular context in which the system will run.

Quantifying over the prior π acknowledges that, in many situations, it is unknown and the assumption that it is uniform is not reasonable. Quantifying over the gain function g acknowledges that we might not know the value to the adversary of different sorts of partial information about the secret, neither now nor even in the future. Combining all ways of quantifying over π and g (one, other, or both), and the two versions of leakage (multiplicative and additive), we arrive at a total of six types of capacities, which are depicted in Table 1.

Table 1. Types of capacities.

Types of capacities	Multiplicative leakage	Additive leakage
For all π, fixed g	$\mathcal{L}_g[\forall, C] = \max\limits_{\pi} \mathcal{L}_g[\pi, C]$	$\mathcal{L}_g^+[\forall, C] = \max\limits_{\pi} \mathcal{L}_g^+[\pi, C]$
Fixed π, for all g	$\mathcal{L}_\forall[\pi, C] = \max\limits_{g} \mathcal{L}_g[\pi, C]$	$\mathcal{L}_\forall^+[\pi, C] = \max\limits_{g} \mathcal{L}_g^+[\pi, C]$
For all π, for all g	$\mathcal{L}_\forall[\forall, C] = \max\limits_{\pi, g} \mathcal{L}_g[\pi, C]$	$\mathcal{L}_\forall^+[\forall, C] = \max\limits_{\pi, g} \mathcal{L}_g^+[\pi, C]$

Although finding a way to compute the capacities $\mathcal{L}_g[\forall, C]$ and $\mathcal{L}_\forall^+[\forall, C]$ is still an open problem, there are known algorithms for computing the other four capacities [3]. More precisely, $\mathcal{L}_\forall[\pi, C]$, $\mathcal{L}_\forall[\forall, C]$, and $\mathcal{L}_\forall^+[\pi, C]$ can be computed in time linear on the size of the channel C. $\mathcal{L}_g^+[\forall, C]$, however, is NP-hard. We will use these capacities to compare our protocols in Sect. 5.

Capacities are upper bounds on the information leakage of a protocol over a variety of combinations of adversarial prior knowledge about the secret (captured by different priors), and of adversarial intentions and interests (captured by different gain functions). For this reason, they are particularly useful bounds on the leakage of channels that will execute in possibly unknown contexts.

2.2   Probabilistic Model Checking

Here we briefly review key concepts from probabilistic model checking, and some of the basic features of the model checker we use, PRISM [1]. Our formalism and notation are similar to that used by C. Baier and J.-P. Katoen [7], and D. Parker [31].

Discrete Time Markov Chains. Probabilistic model checking works by modeling the system of interest as a probabilistic automaton. All protocols in this paper are modeled as discrete-time Markov chains (DTMC).

A *discrete-time Markov chain* M is a tuple $M = (S, P, i, AP, L)$ such that S is a (finite and nonempty) set of *states*, $P : S \times S \to [0,1]$ is the *probabilistic transition function*, $i \in S$ is the initial state, AP is the set of atomic propositions, and $L : S \to 2^{AP}$ is a labeling function. We also require that, for all $s \in S$, $\sum_{s' \in S} P(s, s') = 1$.

A *path* ω in a DTMC is a infinite sequence of states $s_0 s_1 ...$ such that, for all $k \geq 0$, $P(s_k, s_{k+1}) > 0$. Any execution of a DTMC corresponds to a path. Therefore, in order to reason about probabilities over executions of a DTMC, we must first associate a probability to each path. For each $s \in S$, we define $Path_s$ to be the set of all paths that start on s. A probability distribution $Prob_s$ over $Path_s$ is defined as follows. Let $\omega_f = s\, s_1 ... s_n$ be any finite path starting in s, and $Cyl(\omega_f)$ be the set of (infinite) paths that have ω_f as a prefix. Let Σ_s be the smallest σ-algebra on $Path_s$ that contains $Cyl(\omega_f)$ for all ω_f starting in s. We define $Prob_s$ as the unique probability distribution on Σ_s such that $Prob_s(Cyl(\omega_f)) = P(s, s_1)...P(s_{n-1}, s_n)$ for all finite paths ω_f starting in s.

PCTL [18]. The temporal logic used by PRISM to verify properties of DTMCs is the PCTL (Probabilistic Computational Tree Logic), whose syntax is given by:

$$\phi ::= true \mid a \mid \phi_1 \wedge \phi_2 \mid \neg\phi \mid \mathcal{P}_{\bowtie p}(\psi)$$
$$\psi ::= \mathcal{X}\phi \mid \phi_1 \mathcal{U}^{\leq k} \phi_2 \mid \phi_1 \mathcal{U} \phi_2$$

Here ϕ represents state formulas and ψ path formulas, a is an atomic proposition, $p \in [0,1]$, and $\bowtie$ is a symbol to represent either $\leq, <, >$ or $\geq$. The semantics of the *probabilistic path operators* $\mathcal{P}_{\bowtie p}$ is $s \models \mathcal{P}_{\bowtie p}(\psi) \Leftrightarrow Prob_s(\{\omega \in Path_s \mid \omega \models \psi\}) \bowtie p$, for all $s \in S$. The operators *next* ($\mathcal{X}$), *bounded until* ($\mathcal{U}^{\leq k}$) and *until* ($\mathcal{U}$) are defined as usual.

Intuitively, $\mathcal{P}_{\bowtie p}(\psi)$ is satisfied by a state s if the probability of taking a path starting at s which satisfies ψ is in the interval determined by $\bowtie p$. This operator allows PRISM to calculate probabilities of certain event occurring, a feature that is extremely useful in calculating channels, as we discuss in Sect. 4.

3   The Dining Cryptographers and the Crowds Anonymity Protocols

In this section we describe two well-known anonymity protocols from the literature, and their variations, the leakage analyses of which we performed.

3.1   The Dining Cryptographers Protocol

The *Dining Cryptographers (DC)* anonymity protocol was proposed by David Chaum [12]. It is usually described within the following setting. Three cryptographers are invited by the NSA (The U.S. National Security Agency) to have dinner at a restaurant. Along with the invitation, one of them might have been secretly told by the NSA to pay the bill. Otherwise, the NSA itself would pay. The cryptographers wish to know whether one of them was asked to pay the bill (as opposed to the NSA paying the bill), without revealing, however, which one of them is the payer. In order to do so, they execute the following protocol.

Sitting in a round table, each cryptographer flips a coin, and shares the result with the cryptographer to their right. In this way each cryptographer sees the results of only two of the coins: the one he himself flipped, and the one flipped by the cryptographer sitting to his left. Each cryptographer then makes a public announcement. If he is not paying the bill, he announces 0 if the results of the two coins he sees are the same (i.e., both heads or both tails), and announces 1 if they are different. However, if the cryptographer is the payer, he announces 1 if the results of the two coins coincide, and announces 0 otherwise.

The cryptographers now can learn whether the NSA is paying: if the sum of all three announcements (modulo 2) equals 0, the NSA is paying. If the sum equals 1, then one of them is paying. This can be easily seen from the fact that the announcement of each cryptographer not paying the bill is the number of heads he has seen (modulo 2). If no one is paying, then the final result is equal to twice the number of coins that landed heads up to modulo 2, which is certainly 0. If one of them is paying, however, the final result will be 1.

If the coins are fair, the identity of the cryptographer who pays the bill is totally preserved, both in relation to the other two cryptographers and to any external observer. If the coins are biased, however, the announcements made by the cryptographers might make one of them more likely to be the payer than the others. For example, if the coin tosses are very likely to yield tails, and only one cryptographer announces 1, then he is probably paying the bill.

We are specially interested in scenarios with a biased coin, for some information is leaked by the protocol. We can use QIF to precisely quantify this leakage and we can determine by how much the attacker can improve his guessing strategy. In this paper we study two different generalizations of the DC protocol, which expand the number of cryptographers involved.

The Cycle-DC Variation. Our first variation of the DC protocol is akin to the original, but the number of cryptographers can be any integer greater than 2.

Similarly to the original protocol, the cryptographers are arranged in a circular table, each tosses a coin and shares the result to the cryptographer at his right. The announcements are made in the same manner as before. Also in this scenario, one of the cryptographers is the payer if, and only if, the sum of the announcements (modulo 2) equals 1.

The Complete-DC Variation. In our second variation of the DC protocol, all pairs of cryptographers share a coin toss result (i.e., they form a clique). If there are N cryptographers, each one has access to $N - 1$ coin-toss results. After all the coin tosses are made, each cryptographer computes the number of heads he has seen (modulo 2). If he is not paying for the bill, this is the number that he announces. If he is paying, however, he inverts the announcement. Since each heads is counted twice, we also have that one of the cryptographers is paying if, and only if, the sum of the announcements (modulo 2) equals 1.

3.2   The Crowds Protocol

The *Crowds* protocol was first devised to protect anonymity on web transactions. Suppose there is a group of users who wish to make requests to a server, without revealing their identities to that server.

The users agree to cooperate on the protocol, and take the following steps. (1) If a user wants to send a request (we call such user an *initiator*), he chooses at random a user in the group (including himself), and forwards the request to this user. (2) If a user receives a request, he forwards it to a random user with probability p_f, and forwards it directly to the server with probability $1 - p_f$. The second step is repeated until the request reaches the server.

The protocol protects the initiator's identity because, after being forwarded for the first time, the request has an equal probability of landing at any user of the system. Therefore, the server does not acquire any information by observing which user sent the request to him at the end of the process.

The analysis of the protocol becomes more interesting when there are some *corrupt* users in the group. These corrupt users are in collusion with the server, and reveal to it the identity of any regular user that sent them a request—in this case, we say that the regular user in question was *detected*. Because the initiator must be in any path of the message on its way to the server, whenever a user is detected, he is the most likely to be the initiator. As expected, the level of anonymity provided by the protocol in this scenario depends on the number of users, on the number of corrupt users, and on the probability p_f.

In this paper we consider two variants of the Crowds protocol.

The (original) Crowds Variation. In this variation, each user can communicate with any other user (they form a clique), and there is no restriction on who can forward a message to whom.

The Grid-Crowds Variation. A common variation of this protocol occurs when a user is able to forward a request only to a subset of the remaining users. One particular instance of this scenario is when users are placed on a grid, as illustrated in Fig. 1. Edges represent users who can communicate, and we consider the edges going off the grid to connect users at opposite sides, e.g., user 1 is connected to users 2, 3, 4 and 7. We consider that every user can also communicate directly with the server.

Other than this limitation, the protocol works as the original: upon receiving a request, each user forwards to a user with whom he can communicate (including himself) with probability p_f, or sends it directly to the server with probability $1-p_f$. In this scenario, even if there are no corrupt users, the server can infer some information about the originator of the request. For example, if the server receives a request from user 2 in Fig. 1, there is a greater chance that it was originated by user 1 than by user 6.

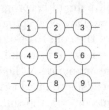

Fig. 1. 3×3 instance of grid-Crowds.

On this grid variation, the information leakage of the protocol depends not only on the number of corrupt users and on p_f, but also on where the corrupt users are located in the grid. One of our goals is to study the effects these topological variations have on QIF measures.

4 Deriving the Channels Corresponding to the Protocols

In this section we show how to use the PRISM model checker [1] to derive the channels representing the behavior of the protocols we analyze.

The general procedure to compute the channel corresponding to a protocol is the following. (1) We identify the sets $\mathcal{X}$ and $\mathcal{Y}$ representing, respectively, the secret and observable values of the protocol. (2) We implement the protocol in PRISM, creating variables that can uniquely identify each element on the sets $\mathcal{X}$ and $\mathcal{Y}$. A variable that signals the end of the protocol's execution is used. (3) We set the variables accordingly for each value $x \in \mathcal{X}$, and use PRISM to calculate the conditional probability $p(y \mid x)$ for each $y \in \mathcal{Y}$.

The third step can easily be accomplished by observing the first step, with the aid of an operator present in PRISM. Given a model, it is possible to verify the probability of taking a path from the initial state that respects a property `pathprop` with the operator `P =? [pathprop]`. If the second step is correctly observed, there is, for any $y \in \mathcal{Y}$, a way to make `pathprop` equivalent to the path formula $\mathcal{F}y$, where $\mathcal{F}$ is the finally operator. This path formula holds if and only if the system's output equals y. By setting the variables of the system to make the secret value $x \in \mathcal{X}$ for all x, we can use this operator to systematically calculate $p(y|x)$ for every pair x, y, which defines our channel.

Next we illustrate how our general procedure can be applied to derive the channels corresponding to all variations of the protocols we consider.

4.1   Modeling the Dining Cryptographers

We now discuss how to derive the channel for both variations of the DC protocol: cycle-DC, and complete-DC. The first task is to characterize $\mathcal{X}$ and $\mathcal{Y}$, and to devise a suitable representation of them to implement in our code.

Let N denote the number of cryptographers in an instance of the Dining Cryptographers protocol. In both variations of the protocol, the secret value is the identity of who pays the bill. We have, then, $\mathcal{X} = \{c_1, c_2, ..., c_N, n\}$ where each c_i represents the case in which cryptographer c_i is the payer, and n represents in which the case the NSA pays.

The observable values of the protocol, in both variations, are the public announcements made by all cryptographers. We can represent these announcements by a string of N bits, where the value of the bit at position i corresponds to the announcement of the cryptographer c_i. To illustrate, consider a protocol with four cryptographers. If c_1 and c_2 announced 1, and c_3 and c_4 announced 0, this would be represented by the string 1100. Hence, we can represent all possible outputs by taking $\mathcal{Y} = \{0,1\}^N$.

Having established $\mathcal{X}$ and $\mathcal{Y}$, as well as how to translate their elements into variables in the code, we can write the protocol in PRISM language. Our implementation is available online [2]. Table 2 depicts the channels (omitting the NSA output) computed by PRISM for cycle- and complete-DC, with the probability of heads equal to 0.7.

Table 2. Channels for both variations of the *Dining Cryptographers* protocol, with the probability of heads equal to 0.7

$C_{cycle\text{-}DC}$	1000	1100	0010	1110	0001	1101	1011	0111
c_1	0.2482	0.1218	0.0882	0.1218	0.1218	0.0882	0.1218	0.0882
c_2	0.1218	0.2482	0.1218	0.0882	0.0882	0.1218	0.0882	0.1218
c_3	0.0882	0.1218	0.2482	0.1218	0.1218	0.0882	0.1218	0.0882
c_4	0.1218	0.0882	0.1218	0.0882	0.2482	0.1218	0.0882	0.1218

(a) Channel $C_{cycle\text{-}DC}$ for the cycle-DC protocol.

$C_{comp\text{-}DC}$	1000	1100	0010	1110	0001	1101	1011	0111
c_1	0.1666	0.1218	0.1218	0.1218	0.1218	0.1218	0.1218	0.1026
c_2	0.1218	0.1666	0.1218	0.1218	0.1218	0.1218	0.1026	0.1218
c_3	0.1218	0.1218	0.1666	0.1218	0.1218	0.1026	0.1218	0.1218
c_4	0.1218	0.1218	0.1218	0.1026	0.1666	0.1218	0.1218	0.1218

(b) Channel $C_{comp\text{-}DC}$ for the complete-DC protocol.

4.2   Modeling Crowds

We now discuss how to derive the channel for both variations of the Crowds protocol: original Crowds, and grid-Crowds. The first step is to identify what the sets $\mathcal{X}$ and $\mathcal{Y}$ shall represent, and to find a suitable implementation of them.

In both variations of the protocol, the secret value is the identity of the initiator of the request. There is no need to represent corrupt users, as we assume they do not initiate requests. Therefore, we can represent the secret values set of Crowds with N honest users by $\mathcal{X} = \{u_1, u_2, ..., u_N\}$.

The observable values are different in the two variations. In original Crowds, the server does not gain any information by identifying the user who forwarded the request to him, therefore we must have one output value d_i representing the scenario in which each honest user u_i was detected by a corrupt one, and another case s representing the scenario where the server receives the request. Therefore, we have $\mathcal{Y} = \{d_1, ..., d_N, s\}$. In grid-Crowds, however, the identity of a user that forwards a request to the server is relevant. We need, therefore, to break the output s into multiple ones, indicating which user forwarded the request to the server. Thus, in this second variation, we must have $\mathcal{Y} = \{d_1, ..., d_N, s_1, ..., s_N\}$.

Having determined $\mathcal{X}$ and $\mathcal{Y}$, it is possible to implement the protocols in the PRISM language. Our implementation of all protocols are available online [2].

5   QIF Analyses of the Protocols

We now analyze the information-leakage of the channels corresponding to the protocols. Recall that the smaller the capacity of a channel (c.f.r. Sect. 2.1), the less information an adversary will obtain about the secret by observing the output of that channel, and the safer, hence, the channel is considered.

5.1   Analyses of the Dining Cryptographers

We implemented both variations of the Dining cryptographers for 5, 6, 7, 8, and 9 cryptographers. Our results suggest the complete-DC variation is safer than the cycle-DC variation, yielding smaller values for all capacities measured.

Results for Multiplicative Capacities. It has been proven [3] that the multiplicative capacity $\mathcal{L}_\forall[\pi, C]$ (which quantifies over all gain-functions g for a fixed prior π) collapses into the multiplicative capacity $\mathcal{L}_\forall[\forall, C]$ (which quantifies over all priors and gain-functions) when the prior π has full-support. Since we consider any cryptographer can be the payer, the prior has full support, and we can focus only on the latter capacity, which can be computed as follows.

Theorem 1 ([9]).   *Given channel* $C{:}\mathcal{X}\times\mathcal{Y}{\to}\mathbb{R}$, $\mathcal{L}_\forall[\forall, C] = \log\sum_{y\in\mathcal{Y}} \max_{x\in\mathcal{X}} C(x,y)$.

Figure 2 shows the values of this capacity for both variants of the DC protocol, and varying values of the probability p of heads. Note that the graph of capacity must be symmetric w.r.t. $p = 0.5$, for a coin with probability of heads $1-p$ is nothing more than a coin with probability of tails p.

Note also that in all instances of both variations, the minimum capacity is 1, and occurs at $p = 0.5$. This reflects the fact that, if the coins are fair, the only information leaked is whether the NSA is paying the bill. When $p = 1$, however,

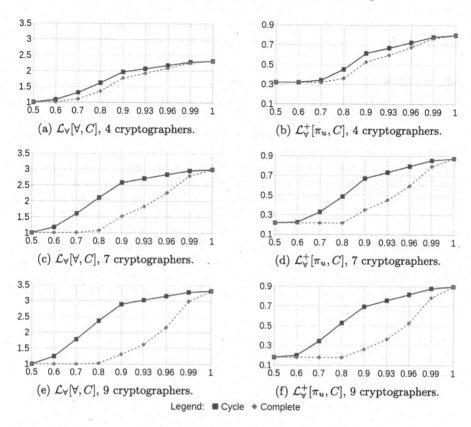

(a) $\mathcal{L}_\forall[\forall, C]$, 4 cryptographers.

(b) $\mathcal{L}_\forall^+[\pi_u, C]$, 4 cryptographers.

(c) $\mathcal{L}_\forall[\forall, C]$, 7 cryptographers.

(d) $\mathcal{L}_\forall^+[\pi_u, C]$, 7 cryptographers.

(e) $\mathcal{L}_\forall[\forall, C]$, 9 cryptographers.

(f) $\mathcal{L}_\forall^+[\pi_u, C]$, 9 cryptographers.

Legend: ■ Cycle ◆ Complete

Fig. 2. Capacities for both variations of the Dining Cryptographers, and different probabilities of heads. The x-axis, for the value of probability, is *not* in scale.

all coin tosses yield heads, and any observer can deduce with certainty who is paying the bill from the announcements of the cryptographers. In this case the capacity reaches its maximum, being $\log(n + 1)$ for n cryptographers, for the outputs of the protocol always reveal the payer's identity.

It is clear from the graph that the complete variation leaks less than the cycle one. Also, while the capacity of the cycle variation increases rapidly even when p approaches 0.5, the complete variation is less susceptible to these small changes, maintaining information leakage close to 0.

Results for Additive Capacity. The additive capacity $\mathcal{L}_\forall^+[\pi, C]$ (quantifying over all gain functions g, for a given prior π) can be computed by $\mathcal{L}_\forall^+[\pi, C] = \sum_{x,y} \pi(x)|C(x,y) - \sum_{x'} \pi(x')C(x',y)|$ [3]. Note that, unlike its multiplicative counterpart, this capacity actually depends on the prior π.

Figure 2 shows the values for this capacity for an uniform prior π_u, and varying probabilities p of heads. The graphs confirm that the minimum and maximum values of information leakages occur, respectively, for $p = 0.5$ and

$p = 1$. We can see that complete-DC is always more secure than cycle-DC, and its capacity keeps almost unaltered until p deviates substantially from 0.5.

5.2   Analyses of Crowds

We implemented both variants of the Crowds protocol for 9 users, and from 1 up to 3 corrupted users.

In particular, in grid-Crowds, we need to consider another variable: the position of the corrupt users makes a great difference in the channels' capacities. Figure 3 shows all possible positions for three corrupt users on a 3×3 grid, up to symmetry. (Recall that the edges going off the grid connect at opposite sides—e.g., user 1 can communicate with user 3 and with user 7.) If, for instance, the corrupt users are 1, 2 and 3, each honest user would be connected to only one corrupt user. If the corrupt were 1, 5 and 9, however, each honest user would be connected to two corrupt ones. Therefore, the chance that the initiator will forward a message directly to a corrupt user is 20% on the first scenario, and 40% on the second one (please recall that the initiator may send the message to itself). Thus, it is natural to expect that the capacities for the former will be smaller than for the latter.

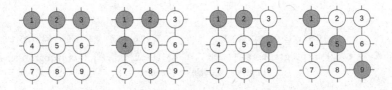

Fig. 3. All positions (up to symmetry) for three corrupted users (colored in dark) on a 3×3 grid.

Results for Multiplicative Capacities. We compute $\mathcal{L}_\forall[\forall, C]$ using Theorem 1. Figure 4 shows the corresponding values for 9 users, both in original DC and in grid-DC. Note that the probability p_f of forwarding does not influence multiplicative capacity in the original DC, which confirms a known result from the literature [17]. However, we can see that it does for the grid variation. To understand this, notice that even if the originator does not forward the message to a corrupt user at first, his immediate neighbors are more likely to receive the message than the users he cannot communicate with. For example, if user 8 is detected in the 3×3 grid, it is more probable that the originator was user 7 than user 4. Therefore, as the expected number of interactions between users decreases with p_f, the more likely it is that a message is detected by a corrupt user or forwarded to the server near its originator.

As we can verify, the capacities of the channels on the grid variation varies considerably according to the position of the corrupt users. The results also reiterate our intuition that, for the 3×3 grid with three corrupt users, the protocol where 1, 2 and 3 are the corrupt users would be the safer one.

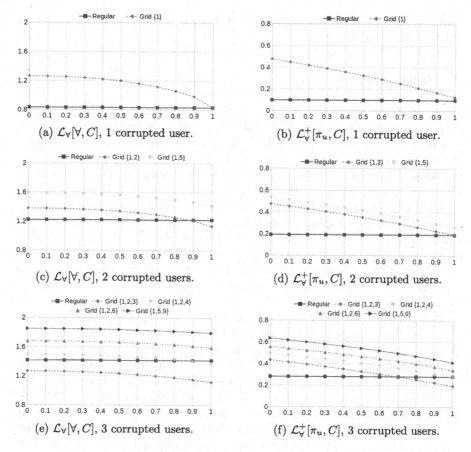

Fig. 4. Capacities for both variations of Crowds, and varying number of corrupt users. The brackets in the captions indicate positions of corrupt users.

It is also interesting to notice that some choice of corrupt users in grid-DC actually yield smaller capacities than the original variation. For 9 users with 3 corrupt ones, for instance, the odds of the initiator being detected are 33%. As we have seen, when the corrupt users are 1, 2 and 3 in the 3×3 grid, this chance is 20%, and our data suggest that this difference is sufficient to compensate the extra leakage usually caused by the grid structure.

Results for Additive Capacity. To calculate this capacity, we again use the equation on Sect. 5.1 and consider a uniform prior π_u. The results are shown on Fig. 4. We can verify that the additive capacities for the original Crowds protocol also do not vary with p_f. Also, they behave quite differently from their multiplicative counterparts. For example, consider again the protocol with 3 corrupt users in positions 1, 2 and 3 in the 3×3 grid. The multiplicative capacity of this scenario is always smaller that of the regular protocol, but this is not true at all for the additive capacity.

6   Related Work

In this paper we have explored the use of model checking to compute bounds on quantitative information flow. Our approach is to express protocols as transition systems and then to use probabilistic model checking to compute a channel abstraction. The benefits of this approach are that protocols can be expressed in a direct way, and their abstraction as a channel can be easily computed. By computing the whole channel, rather than say a specific leakage or capacity measure, we make it available for use with any appropriate gain function.

Other work on computing information flow [28] gives a semantics of programs as hidden Markov models, of which channels are a special case. This allows hyper-distributions—a compact form of posterior joint distributions—to be computed directly. With this generality the monadic features of functional programming languages can be exploited to compute leakage w.r.t. arbitrary gain functions [29].

Other approaches to computing information flow typically use alternative measures. For example, McCamant and Ernst [26] provide estimates for the quantity of bits flowing from input to output (of programs) using network flow capacity. Novakovic [30] uses a model based on mutual information (Shannon) and min-entropy; the starting point for the analysis is a program expressed in a probabilistic imperative language, with an interpretation based on DTMCs. High Order Logic theorem provers were used by Hölz and Nipkow [21] to study properties of the Crowds protocol and its behavior regarding Shannon entropy, and by Helali et al. [19] to derive general results regarding min-entropy and belief min-entropy. Finally, Phan et al. [32] use reliability analysis to quantify leaks, also based on Shannon- and min-entropy.

7   Conclusions and Future Work

In this work we presented a systematic way of deriving channels representing the behavior of security protocols, and used these channels to derive robust information-flow guarantees about these protocols. More precisely, we provided the first analyses of additive and multiplicative g-capacities of two versions of the Dining Cryptographers and the Crowds anonymity protocols. The bounds provided hold irrespectively of the probability distribution on secret values, or of the interests and goals of an adversary, constituting, to the best of our knowledge, the most general information-flow analyses of such protocols ever performed.

Future work could lead to a general purpose tool support to allow the computation of critical information flow properties. Moreover, we want to explore algorithms for computing capacities for systems whose possible contexts of execution are limited in a more restricted set of priors and gain-functions.

Acknowledgments. Arthur Américo, Artur Vaz, Mário S. Alvim, and Sérgio V. A. Campos were supported by CNPq, CAPES, and FAPEMIG.

References

1. PRISM: A Probabilistic Symbolic Model Checker. www.prismmodelchecker.org/
2. http://homepages.dcc.ufmg.br/~arturvaz/sbmf/
3. Alvim, M.S., Chatzikokolakis, K., McIver, A., Morgan, C., Palamidessi, C., Smith, G.: Additive and multiplicative notions of leakage, and their capacities. In: Proceedings of CSF, pp. 308–322. IEEE (2014)
4. Alvim, M.S., Chatzikokolakis, K., McIver, A., Morgan, C., Palamidessi, C., Smith, G.: Axioms for information leakage. In: Proceedings of CSF, pp. 77–92 (2016)
5. Alvim, M.S., Chatzikokolakis, K., Palamidessi, C., Smith, G.: Measuring information leakage using generalized gain functions. In: Proceedings of CSF, pp. 265–279 (2012)
6. Andrés, M.E., Palamidessi, C., Rossum, P., Smith, G.: Computing the leakage of information-hiding systems. In: Esparza, J., Majumdar, R. (eds.) TACAS 2010. LNCS, vol. 6015, pp. 373–389. Springer, Heidelberg (2010). https://doi.org/10.1007/978-3-642-12002-2_32
7. Baier, C., Katoen, J.-P.: Principles of Model Checking. The MIT Press (2008)
8. Boreale, M., Pampaloni, F.: Quantitative information flow under generic leakage functions and adaptive adversaries. Logical Methods Comput. Sci. **11**(4:5), 1–31 (2015)
9. Braun, C., Chatzikokolakis, K., Palamidessi, C.: Quantitative notions of leakage for one-try attacks. Electron. Theoret. Comput. Sci. **249**, 75–91 (2009)
10. Chatzikokolakis, K., Chothia, T., Guha, A.: Statistical measurement of information leakage. In: Esparza, J., Majumdar, R. (eds.) TACAS 2010. LNCS, vol. 6015, pp. 390–404. Springer, Heidelberg (2010). https://doi.org/10.1007/978-3-642-12002-2_33
11. Chatzikokolakis, K., Palamidessi, C., Panangaden, P.: On the Bayes risk in information-hiding protocols. J. Comp. Security **16**(5), 531–571 (2008)
12. Chaum, D.: The dining cryptographers problem: Unconditional sender and recipient untraceability. J. Cryptology **1**(1), 65–75 (1988)
13. Chothia, T., Kawamoto, Y., Novakovic, C.: LeakWatch: estimating information leakage from Java Programs. In: Kutyłowski, M., Vaidya, J. (eds.) ESORICS 2014. LNCS, vol. 8713, pp. 219–236. Springer, Cham (2014). https://doi.org/10.1007/978-3-319-11212-1_13
14. Chothia, T., Kawamoto, Y., Novakovic, C., Parker, D.: Probabilistic point-to-point information leakage. In: Proceedings of CSF, pp. 193–205. IEEE Computer Society (2013)
15. Clark, D., Hunt, S., Malacaria, P.: Quantitative information flow, relations and polymorphic types. J. Logic Comput. **18**(2), 181–199 (2005)
16. Clark, D., Hunt, S., Malacaria, P.: A static analysis for quantifying information flow in a simple imperative language. J. Comp. Security **15**(3), 321–371 (2007)
17. Espinoza, B., Smith, G.: Min-entropy as a resource. Inf. Comp. **226**, 57–75 (2013)
18. Hansson, H., Jonsson, B.: A logic for reasoning about time and reliability. Formal Aspects Comput. **6**(5), 512–535 (1994)

19. Helali, G., Hasan, O., Tahar, S.: Formal analysis of information flow using min-entropy and belief min-entropy. In: Iyoda, J., de Leonardo, M. (eds.) SBMF 2013. LNCS, vol. 8195, pp. 131–146. Springer, Heidelberg (2013). https://doi.org/10.1007/978-3-642-41071-0_10
20. Heusser, J., Malacaria, P.: Quantifying information leaks in software. In: Proceedings of ACSAC, pp. 261–269. ACM (2010)
21. Hölzl, J., Nipkow, T:: Interactive verification of Markov Chains: two distributed protocol case studies, p. 103 (2012)
22. Köpf, B., Basin, D.A.: An information-theoretic model for adaptive side-channel attacks. In: Proceedings of CCS, pp. 286–296. ACM (2007)
23. Köpf, B., Mauborgne, L., Ochoa, M.: Automatic quantification of cache side-channels. In: Madhusudan, P., Seshia, S.A. (eds.) CAV 2012. LNCS, vol. 7358, pp. 564–580. Springer, Heidelberg (2012). https://doi.org/10.1007/978-3-642-31424-7_40
24. Köpf, B., Rybalchenko, A.: Approximation and randomization for quantitative information-flow analysis. In: Proceedings of CSF, pp. 3–14. IEEE (2010)
25. Massey, J.L.: Guessing and entropy. In: Proceedings of the IEEE International Symposium on Information Theory, p. 204. IEEE (1994)
26. McCamant, S., Ernst, M.D.: Quantitative information flow as network flow capacity. In: Proceedings of SIGPLAN, Tucson, AZ, USA, 9–11 June 2008, pp. 193–205 (2008)
27. McIver, A., Meinicke, L., Morgan, C.: Compositional closure for Bayes risk in probabilistic noninterference. In: Abramsky, S., Gavoille, C., Kirchner, C., Meyer auf der Heide, F., Spirakis, P.G. (eds.) ICALP 2010. LNCS, vol. 6199, pp. 223–235. Springer, Heidelberg (2010). https://doi.org/10.1007/978-3-642-14162-1_19
28. McIver, A., Morgan, C., Rabehaja, T.M.: Abstract hidden Markov Models: a monadic account of quantitative information flow. In: Proceedings of LICS, pp. 597–608 (2015)
29. Morgan, C.: A Haskell program to compute hyper distributions for measuring information leakage (2017). http://www.cse.unsw.edu.au/~carrollm/Hypers170731.zip
30. Novakovic, C.: Computing and estimating information leakage with a quantitative point-to-point information flow model. PhD thesis, Birmingham University, UK (2014)
31. Parker, D.: Implementation of symbolic model checking for probabilistic systems. PhD thesis, University of Birmingham (2002)
32. Phan, Q., Malacaria, P., Pasareanu, C.S., d'Amorim, M.: Quantifying information leaks using reliability analysis. In: Proceedings of SPIN, pp. 105–108 (2014)
33. Reiter, M.K., Rubin, A.D.: Crowds: anonymity for Web transactions. ACM Trans. Inform. Syst. Secur. 1(1), 66–92 (1998)
34. Shannon, C.E.: A mathematical theory of communication. Bell Syst. Tech. J. 27(379–423), 625–56 (1948)
35. Smith, G.: On the foundations of quantitative information flow. In: Alfaro, L. (ed.) FoSSaCS 2009. LNCS, vol. 5504, pp. 288–302. Springer, Heidelberg (2009). https://doi.org/10.1007/978-3-642-00596-1_21
36. Yasuoka, H., Terauchi, T.: Quantitative information flow as safety and liveness hyperproperties. Theor. Comp. Sci. 538, 167–182 (2014)

Refinement and Verification

A Refinement Relation for Families of Timed Automata

Guillermina Cledou[(✉)], José Proença, and Luís S. Barbosa

HASLab INESC TEC, University of Minho, Braga, Portugal
mgc@inesctec.pt, {jose.proenca,lsb}@di.uminho.pt

Abstract. Software Product Lines (SPLs) are families of systems that share a high number of common assets while differing in others. In component-based systems, components themselves can be SPLs, i.e., each component can be seen as a family of variations, with different interfaces and functionalities, typically parameterized by a set of *features* and a *feature model* that specifies the valid combinations of features. This paper explores how to safely replace such families of components with more refined ones. We propose a notion of refinement for Interface Featured Timed Automata (IFTA), a formalism to model families of timed automata with support for multi-action transitions. We separate the notion of IFTA refinement into *behavioral* and *variability* refinement, i.e., the refinement of the underlying timed automata and feature model. Furthermore, we define behavioral refinement for the semantic level, i.e., transition systems, as an alternating simulation between systems, and lift this definition to IFTA refinement. We illustrate this notion with examples throughout the text and show that refinement is a pre-order and compositional.

Keywords: Software product lines · Refinement · Timed automata

1 Introduction

A Software Product Line (SPL) is a set of software systems that share a high number of *features* while differing in others, where concrete configurations are derived from a core of common assets in a prescribed way. A feature is referred as a characteristic of the system visible to the user. A concrete configuration of the SPL results in a particular product and is given by a selection of features. The set of all valid feature selections, i.e., the products that can be derived from the SPL, is determined by a *feature model*.

As in the development of any complex system, common and variable assets of an SPL, such as software components, can be designed and developed by different engineers agreeing on a common specification of what their interfaces should be. In this sense, being able to reason about how standalone components, and in this case *families* of components, *implemented* separately satisfy a given *specification* becomes crucial. In this paper, we propose a notion of *refinement* for real timed

© Springer International Publishing AG 2017
S. Cavalheiro and J. Fiadeiro (Eds.): SBMF 2017, LNCS 10623, pp. 161–178, 2017.
https://doi.org/10.1007/978-3-319-70848-5_11

software product lines that are modeled as *Interface Featured Timed Automata* (IFTA), a formalism to model families of timed automata. We introduced IFTA in [7] as an extension to Featured Timed Automata, in turn introduced by Cordy et al. [8], which incorporates interfaces in order to reason about variability during composition and prepare the way to reason about refinement. Figure 1 shows an example of an IFTA representing a family of coffee machines (left), and its corresponding projections into its concrete products (right), a coffee machine that serves coffee and cappuccino (top right) and a coffee machines that serves only coffee (bottom right), both represented as Timed Automata (TA). Projections are obtained by selecting a valid feature selection. The necessary background on (Interface Featured) Timed Automata is introduced in Sect. 2. Briefly, an IFTA is a TA with: logic guards over transitions, restricting the set of products where the transitions are present; a logic guard associated to the automaton representing the feature model; interface actions representing communication points with other automata; and inferred logic guards associated to interfaces, indicating the set of products where the interface action was designed to be present in.

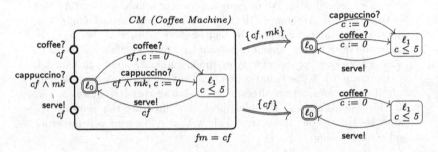

Fig. 1. Example of an IFTA representing a family of coffee machines (left), and its two projections into concrete products, represented as Timed Automata (right).

Refinement allows us to compare two models of the same system presented at different levels of abstraction. The most abstract one is referred to as the *specification*, while the most detailed one is referred to as an *implementation* of the system. If an implementation refines the specification, it agrees with the requirements of the specification in the sense that one may replace the implementation in any context where the specification is used, and still obtain an equivalent system. However, since we are dealing with families of components, we need to reason about how a *set of implementations* refine a *set of specifications*. Figure 2 exemplifies this problem. The figure shows two composed systems (top): one (top left), composed by an IFTA C, representing a context (here left undefined), and an IFTA CM corresponding to the coffee machine in Fig. 1; and the other (top right), which is a refinement of the system on the left, is composed by the same context C, and a new family of coffee machines CM' (defined in Fig. 4). Because refinement is compositional (up to some pre-conditions), as will be discussed in Sect. 3, it suffices to verify if CM' refines CM (in addition to

such pre-conditions). However, both IFTA, CM and CM', are actually families
of components which model different concrete automata, as depicted in Fig. 2
(bottom). Thus, we need to consider if each of the new automaton CM'_i, for
$i = 1, \ldots, 4$ refines an automaton CM_j, for $j = 1, 2$.

   In order to simplify this reasoning and allow greater flexibility we separate
the notion of refinement into *variability refinement* – which deals with feature
model refinement, i.e., when is a set of features considered a refinement of another
one; and *behavioral refinement* – which captures timed automata refinement,
i.e., when a specific system refines another one. Refinement of timed automata
is defined in terms of refinement of timed transition systems, their semantic
representation.

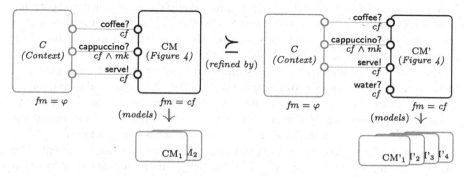

Fig. 2. Example scenario when reasoning about refinement of families of components.
A system composed by two IFTA, C and CM (left), is refined by a more detailed system
composed by the same IFTA C and a new IFTA CM' (right).

   There are not many publications in the literature that explore the notion of a
refinement relation between two feature models. In [10] the authors reason about
four kinds of relations between feature models. However, we believe neither of
these aligns with the notion of refinement. Intuitively, a feature model refines
another one if it preserves its variability, i.e., allows the same set of products,
and such that new variability can only be defined in terms of new features.

   There exist various notions of automata refinement in the literature, differing
on requirements made over the set of actions of the systems being compared,
properties inherent to the models used to specify the systems, and properties
that the relation should preserve, among others. Commonly, when dealing with
closed systems, i.e., systems that do not interact with the environment through
inputs or outputs, refinement is defined as a simulation relation [4]. The advantage is that it preserves all safety properties from the specification. However,
when dealing with open systems, as in our case, simulation is a too strict relation, since it requires the implementation to have the same or less inputs than
the specification. On the one hand, this means that a refinement can not incorporate new behavior in terms of new inputs, which would not be a problem since
it would imply no behavioral changes in the resulting system, provided that we

can guarantee that the new inputs are not used. On the other hand, it allows the refinement to have less inputs than the specification. But, in the case of reactive systems, we can not replace a system for another that reacts to less inputs than the original one. This would limit the behavior of the system, since there will be output actions that are now not capture by the system, but are left unattended. Then, when dealing with open systems it is common to define refinement in terms of an *alternating simulation* relation [1–3,9], in which the implementation must simulate all input behavior of the specification, while the latter must simulate all output behavior from the implementation. For example, de Alfaro et al. [2] introduce Interface Automata, without time, and define the notion of refinement in terms of alternating simulation, extended to support internal steps, i.e., internal actions from both automata which are independent from each other. In [9] David et al. provide a complete specification theory for Timed I/O Automata where they define refinement, logical conjunction, structural composition, and a quotient operator. However, their theory is based on input enabled automata.

Our notion of refinement can be seen as an adaptation of [2] for families of timed systems with support for multi-action transitions. We as well define refinement as an alternating simulation, however, we relax some of the requirements as discussed in Sect. 3.2. We show that refinement is a pre-order and congruent with respect to IFTA operations, meaning refinement is compositional.

The rest of this document is structured as follows. Section 2 presents the required theory to understand IFTA. Section 3 proposes a refinement relation for IFTA. Finally, Sect. 4 concludes and hints on future work.

2   Interface Featured Timed Automata

Interface Featured Timed Automata is a mechanism introduced in [7] to enrich Featured Timed Automata (FTA) [8] with (1) interfaces that restrict the way multiple automata interact, and (2) transitions labelled with multiple actions that simplify the design of synchronous coordination. Interfaces are input-output synchronisation actions that can be linked to interfaces of other automata when composing automata in parallel.

First, we recall some basic notions of timed automata and variability, and the definition of IFTA. Then, we deconstruct IFTA into another formalisms, namely, Interface Transition Systems (ITS), and Interface Featured Transition Systems (IFTS), upon which we base the definition of refinement proposed here. Finally, we explain IFTA operations and their properties.

2.1   IFTA Preliminaries

Informally, an IFTA is an automaton whose *edges* are enriched with *clocks*, *clock constraints* (CC), *feature expressions* (FE), and *multiple synchronisation actions*. A *clock* $c \in C$ is a logical entity that captures the (continuous and dense) time that has passed since it was last reset. When a timed automaton evolves over time, all clocks are incremented simultaneously. A *clock constraint* is a logic condition over the value of a clock. A *feature expression* (FE) is a logical constraint over a set of *features* F. Each feature denotes a unit of variability; by selecting a desired combination of features one can map an IFTA into an (Interface) Timed Automaton. The *synchronization actions* can be *input* or *output* actions, and represent the *interface* of the automaton, i.e., the actions through which an automaton can communicate with other automata. Each *synchronization action* has associated an inferred feature expression that expresses the valid set of products in which such action was designed to be present. Finally, an IFTA has a special feature expression representing its *feature model*, which imposes restrictions over possible combinations of features.

For example, consider the IFTA CM from Fig. 1 (left). It has two locations, ℓ_0 and ℓ_1, with a clock c and two features cf and mk, standing for the support for brewing *coffee* and for including *milk* in the coffee. There are two input actions, coffee?, and cappuccino?, and one output action, serve!, standing, respectively, for the selection of coffee, cappuccino, and the action of serving the beverage. Initially the automaton is in location ℓ_0, indicated by a double-edge node (following UPPAAL[1] real time model checker notation), and it can evolve either by waiting for time to pass (incrementing the clock c) or by taking one of its two transitions to ℓ_1. The top transition, for example, is labelled by the action coffee? and is only active when the feature cf is present. Taking this transition triggers the reset of the clock c back to 0, evolving to the state ℓ_1. Here it can again wait for the time to pass, but for at most 5 time units, determined by the invariant $c \leq 5$ in ℓ_1. The synchronization actions are lifted to the interface of the automaton, depicted with and associated to the corresponding inferred feature expression. Finally, the lower expression $fm = cf$ defines the *feature model*, i.e., how the features relate to each other. We model this as restrictions, thus, in this case cf is a mandatory feature, however nothing is expressed about mk, meaning it can either be present or absent.

Formally, clock constraints, feature expressions, and IFTA can be defined as follows.

Definition 1 (Clock Constraints (CC), valuation, and satisfaction). *A clock constraint over a set of clocks C, written $g \in CC(C)$ is defined by*

$$g ::= c < n \mid c \leq n \mid c = n \mid c > n \mid c \geq n \mid g \wedge g \mid \top \qquad \text{(clock constraint)}$$

where $c \in C$, and $n \in \mathbb{N}$.

A clock valuation η for a set of clocks C is a function $\eta \colon C \to \mathbb{R}_{\geq 0}$ that assigns each clock $c \in C$ to its current value $\eta(c)$. We use $\mathbb{R}^C$ to refer to the set of all clock valuations over a set of clocks C. Let $\eta_0(c) = 0$ for all $c \in C$ be the initial clock valuation that sets to 0 all clocks in C. We use $\eta + d$, $d \in \mathbb{R}_{\geq 0}$, to denote the clock assignment that maps all $c \in C$ to $\eta(c) + d$, and let $[r \mapsto 0]\eta$, $r \subseteq C$, be the clock assignment that maps all clocks in r to 0 and agrees with η for all other clocks in $C \setminus r$.

---

[1] http://www.uppaal.org.

The satisfaction *of a clock constraint g by a clock valuation η, written $\eta \models g$, is defined as follows*

$$
\begin{array}{lll}
\eta \models \top & always \\
\eta \models c \,\square\, n & if\ \eta(c) \,\square\, n & \text{(clock satisfaction)} \\
\eta \models g_1 \wedge g_2 & if\ \eta \models g_1 \wedge \eta \models g_2 &
\end{array}
$$

where $\square \in \{<, \leq, =, >, \geq\}$.

Definition 2 (Feature Expressions (FE), satisfaction, and semantics).
A feature expression φ over a set of features F, written $\varphi \in FE(F)$, is defined by

$$\varphi ::= f \mid \varphi \wedge \varphi \mid \varphi \vee \varphi \mid \neg\varphi \mid \top \qquad \text{(feature expression)}$$

where $f \in F$ is a feature. The other logical connectives can be encoded as usual: $\bot = \neg\top$; $\varphi_1 \to \varphi_2 = \neg\varphi_1 \vee \varphi_2$; and $\varphi_1 \leftrightarrow \varphi_2 = (\varphi_1 \to \varphi_2) \wedge (\varphi_2 \to \varphi_1)$.

Given a feature selection $FS \subseteq F$ over a set of features F, and a feature expression $\varphi \in FE(F)$, FS satisfies φ, noted $FS \models \varphi$, if

$$
\begin{array}{lll}
FS \models \top & always \\
FS \models f & \Leftrightarrow f \in FS \\
FS \models \varphi_1 \wedge \varphi_2 & \Leftrightarrow FS \models \varphi_1\ and\ FS \models \varphi_2 & \text{(FE satisfaction)} \\
FS \models \varphi_1 \vee \varphi_2 & \Leftrightarrow FS \models \varphi_1\ or\ FS \models \varphi_2 \\
FS \models \neg\varphi & \Leftrightarrow FS \not\models \varphi
\end{array}
$$

The semantics of a feature expression φ with respect to a set of features F, denoted $[\![\varphi]\!]^F$, is the set of valid feature selections over F that satisfy φ, formally,

$$[\![\varphi]\!]^F = \{FS \subseteq F \mid FS \models \varphi\} \qquad \text{(FE semantics)}$$

Definition 3 (Interface Featured Timed Automata). *An IFTA is a tuple $\mathcal{A} = (L, l_0, A, C, E, Inv, F, fm, \gamma)$ where L is a finite set of locations, l_0 is the initial location, $A = I \uplus O \uplus H$ is a finite set of actions, where I is a set of input ports, O is a set of output ports, and H is a set of hidden (internal) actions, C is a finite set of clocks, $E \subseteq L \times CC(C) \times 2^A \times 2^C \times L$ is the set of edges, $Inv : L \to CC(C)$ is the invariant, a total function that assigns clock constraints to locations, F is a finite set of features, $fm \in FE(F)$ is a feature model defined as a Boolean formula over features in F, and $\gamma : E \to FE(F)$ is a total function that assigns feature expressions to edges.*

Notation: When not clear from the context, we will use $L_{\mathcal{A}}, l_{0_{\mathcal{A}}}, A_{\mathcal{A}}, \dots$ to refer to the elements of an IFTA $\mathcal{A}$, and when using automata names with subscripts such as $\mathcal{A}_1, \mathcal{A}_2, \dots$, we will simply use $L_1, L_2, l_{0_1}, l_{0_2}, \dots$. For simplicity, sometimes we write $l \xrightarrow{g,\omega,r}_{\mathcal{A}} l'$ instead of $(l, g, \omega, r, l') \in E_{\mathcal{A}}$, and use $l \xrightarrow[\varphi]{g,\omega,r}_{\mathcal{A}} l'$ to express that $(l, g, \omega, r, l') \in E_{\mathcal{A}}$ and $\gamma_{\mathcal{A}}(l, g, \omega, r, l') = \varphi$.

The *interface* of an IFTA $\mathcal{A}$ is the set $\mathbb{P}_{\mathcal{A}} = I_{\mathcal{A}} \uplus O_{\mathcal{A}}$ of all input and output ports of $\mathcal{A}$. Given a port $\mathsf{p} \in \mathbb{P}_{\mathcal{A}}$ we write p? and p! to denote that p is an input or output port, respectively, and write p instead of $\{\mathsf{p}\}$ when clear from context.

Notice that at this point, the definition of IFTA only incorporates the notion of feature expressions associated to transitions through function γ, but does not incorporate the notion of feature expressions associated to interfaces. Before doing this, we define the notion of feature expression of an action. Given an IFTA $\mathcal{A}$, it is possible to infer for each action $a \in A_{\mathcal{A}}$ a feature expression based on the feature expressions of the edges in which a appears. Intuitively, this feature expression determines the set of products requiring a. The formal definition follows.

Definition 4 (Feature Expression of an Action). *Given an IFTA $\mathcal{A}$, the inferred feature expression of any action a is the disjunction of the feature expressions of all of its associated edges, defined as*

$$\widehat{\Gamma}_{\mathcal{A}}(a) = \bigvee \{\gamma_{\mathcal{A}}(l \xrightarrow{g,\omega,r}_{\mathcal{A}} l') \mid a \in \omega\} \qquad \text{(FE of an action)}$$

Now we can associate feature expressions to the actions of an IFTA. In order to do this, we incorporate a new function Γ to the definition of an IFTA $\mathcal{A}$, and we say that $\mathcal{A}$ is *grounded*. Thus, given an IFTA $\mathcal{A}$ we can construct a *grounded* $\mathcal{A} = (L_{\mathcal{A}}, l_{0_{\mathcal{A}}}, A_{\mathcal{A}}, C_{\mathcal{A}}, E_{\mathcal{A}}, Inv_{\mathcal{A}}, F_{\mathcal{A}}, fm_{\mathcal{A}}, \gamma_{\mathcal{A}}, \Gamma)$, where $\Gamma : A_{\mathcal{A}} \to FE(F_{\mathcal{A}})$ is a total function that assigns a feature expression to each action of $\mathcal{A}$, and is constructed based on $\widehat{\Gamma}_{\mathcal{A}}$. By doing this association only once, we are *fixing* the feature expressions associated to each action, such that it represents the set of products where each action was originally design to be present in.

The need for this function and for fixing it instead of using directly $\widehat{\Gamma}$ has to do with the way we define the composition of IFTA and the properties that we expect from it. We discuss this in Sect. 2.3.

2.2 Semantics

The above definition of IFTA, introduced in [7], is built on top of Featured Transition Systems [5] extended with multi-action transitions. This section discusses the decomposition of an IFTA into *Interface Featured Transition Systems* (IFTS) and *Interface Transition Systems* (ITS). These two formalisms can be seen as an infinite transition system semantics for IFTA, and as an IFTS without variability, respectively. The notion of refinement will be presented in Sect. 3 based on the semantics of IFTA as an IFTS.

We define an ITS as a regular transition system with multi-action transitions and with an interface, i.e., we distinguish between input, output and internal actions. An IFTS is then defined by extending ITS with variability, by incorporating features and a feature model.

Definition 5 (Interface Transition System). *An ITS is a tuple $S = (St, s_0, A, T)$, where St is the set of states, s_0 is the initial state, $A = I \uplus O \uplus H$ is the set of actions where I, O, and H are the set of input, output, and hidden actions, respectively, and $T \subseteq St \times (2^A \cup \mathbb{R}_{\geq 0}) \times St$ is the transition relation.*

Definition 6 (Interface Featured Transition System). *An IFTS is a tuple* $S = (St, s_0, A, T, F, fm, \gamma, \Gamma)$, *where* St, s_0, A, T *are defined as in ITS, F is a set of features, fm is the feature model,* $\gamma : T \to FE(F)$, *is a total function that assigns feature expressions to transitions, and* $\Gamma : A \to FE(F)$, *is a total function that assigns feature expressions to actions.*

Notation: As before, when not clear from the context, we will use St_S, s_{0_S}, $A_S, \ldots$ to refer to the elements of an I(F)TS S.

We may now present the formal definition of semantics of a *grounded* IFTA in terms of an IFTS.

Definition 7 (Semantics of an IFTA as an IFTS). *The semantics of a grounded IFTA* $\mathcal{A} = (L, l_0, A, C, E, Inv, F, fm, \gamma, \Gamma)$ *written* $[\![\mathcal{A}]\!]$, *is an IFTS* $S = (St, s_0, A, T, F, fm, \gamma', \Gamma)$, *where* $St \subseteq L \times \mathbb{R}^C$ *is the set of states,* $s_0 = \langle l_0, \eta_0 \rangle$ *is the initial state,* $T \subseteq St \times (2^A \cup \mathbb{R}_{\geq 0}) \times St$ *is the transition relation, and* $\gamma' : T \to FE(F)$ *is the total function that assigns feature expressions to transitions in T, both defined as follows.*

$$\langle \ell, \eta \rangle \xrightarrow[\top]{d} \langle \ell, \eta + d \rangle \ \text{if} \ \eta \models Inv(\ell) \ \text{and} \ (\eta + d) \models Inv(\ell), \tag{1}$$

$$\text{for} \ d \in \mathbb{R}_{\geq 0}$$

$$\langle \ell, \eta \rangle \xrightarrow[\varphi]{\omega} \langle \ell', \eta' \rangle \ \text{if} \ \exists \, \ell \xrightarrow[\varphi]{g, \omega, r} \ell' \in E \ \text{s.t.} \ \eta \models g, \tag{2}$$

$$\eta \models Inv(l), \ \eta' = [r \mapsto 0]\eta, \ \text{and} \ \eta' \models Inv(\ell')$$

Given a feature selection FS it is possible to *project* an IFTS into an ITS. Only transitions and actions satisfied by FS are preserved by the projection.

Definition 8 (IFTS Projection). *The projection of an IFTS S over a set of features FS is an ITS* $S \downarrow_{FS} = (St_S, s_{0_S}, A, T)$, *where A and T are defined as*

$$T = \{t \in T_S \mid FS \models \gamma_S(t)\}$$
$$A = \{a \in A_S \mid FS \models \Gamma_S(a)\}$$

2.3   Operations on IFTA

Two IFTA can be composed by combining their feature models and linking interfaces, imposing new restrictions over them. The composition is built on top of two operations: *product* and *synchronisation*. The *product* operation for IFTA, unlike the classical product of timed automata, is defined over grounded IFTA with disjoint sets of actions, clocks and features, performing their transitions in an interleaving or synchronous-step fashion.

Definition 9 (Product of IFTA). *Let* $\mathcal{A}_1$ *and* $\mathcal{A}_2$, *be two different grounded IFTA with disjoint actions, clocks and features; then, the product of* $\mathcal{A}_1$ *and* $\mathcal{A}_2$, *denoted* $\mathcal{A}_1 \times \mathcal{A}_2$, *is*

$$\mathcal{A} = (L_1 \times L_2, l_{0_1} \times l_{0_2}, A, C_1 \cup C_2, F_1 \cup F_2, E, Inv, fm_1 \wedge fm_2, \gamma, \Gamma)$$

where A, E, Inv, γ and Γ are defined as follows

- $A = I \uplus O \uplus H$, where $I = I_1 \cup I_2$, $O = O_1 \cup O_2$, and $H = H_1 \cup H_2$.
- E and γ are defined by the rules below, for any $\omega_1 \subseteq A_1$, $\omega_2 \subseteq A_2$.

$$\frac{\ell_1 \xrightarrow[\varphi_1]{g_1,\omega_1,r_1}_1 \ell_1'}{\langle \ell_1, \ell_2 \rangle \xrightarrow[\varphi_1]{g_1,\omega_1,r_1} \langle \ell_1', \ell_2 \rangle} \qquad \frac{\ell_2 \xrightarrow[\varphi_2]{g_2,\omega_2,r_2}_2 \ell_2'}{\langle \ell_1, \ell_2 \rangle \xrightarrow[\varphi_2]{g_2,\omega_2,r_2} \langle \ell_1, \ell_2' \rangle}$$

$$\frac{\ell_1 \xrightarrow[\varphi_1]{g_1,\omega_1,r_1}_1 \ell_1' \quad \ell_2 \xrightarrow[\varphi_2]{g_2,\omega_2,r_2}_2 \ell_2'}{\langle \ell_1, \ell_2 \rangle \xrightarrow[\varphi_1 \wedge \varphi_2]{g_1 \wedge g_2, \omega_1 \cup \omega_2, r_1 \cup r_2} \langle \ell_1', \ell_2' \rangle}$$

- $Inv(\ell_1, \ell_2) = Inv_1(\ell_1) \wedge Inv_2(\ell_2)$.
- $\forall_{a \in \mathbb{P}_A} \cdot \Gamma(a) = \Gamma_i(a)$ if $a \in A_i$, for $i = 1, 2$.

Both top transitions represent the interleaving of both automata. The bottom transition represents the synchronous execution of transitions from $\mathcal{A}_1$ and $\mathcal{A}_2$, for every combination of outgoing transitions from a state $\ell_1 \in L_1$ and $\ell_2 \in L_2$.

The *synchronisation* operation over an IFTA $\mathcal{A}$ connects and synchronises two actions a and b in $A_{\mathcal{A}}$. The resulting automaton has transitions without neither a and b, nor both a and b. The latter become internal transitions.

Definition 10 (Synchronisation). *Given a grounded IFTA* $\mathcal{A} = (L, \ell_0, A,$ $C, F, E, Inv, fm, \gamma, \Gamma)$ *and two actions* $a, b \in A$, *the synchronisation of* a *and* b *is given by* $\Delta_{a,b}(\mathcal{A}) = (L, \ell_0, A', C, F, E', Inv, fm', \gamma, \Gamma)$ *where* A', E' *and* fm' *are defined as follows*

- $A' = I' \uplus O' \uplus H'$, where $I' = I \setminus \{a, b\}$, $O' = O \setminus \{a, b\}$, and $H' = H \cup \{a, b\}$.
- $E' = \{\ell \xrightarrow{g,\omega,r} \ell' \in E \mid a \notin \omega \text{ and } b \notin \omega\} \cup$
  $\{\ell \xrightarrow{g,\omega \setminus \{a,b\},r} \ell' \mid \ell \xrightarrow{g,\omega,r} \ell' \in E \text{ and } a \in \omega \text{ and } b \in \omega\}$
- $fm' = fm \wedge (\Gamma_{\mathcal{A}}(a) \leftrightarrow \Gamma_{\mathcal{A}}(b))$.

The resulting feature model imposes new restrictions over the set of features based on the actions being synchronised. Intuitively, if two actions a and b are synchronised, they depend on each other. Thus, we require that they should both be present or both absent in any valid set of features. This is done based on Γ which gives us the original set of products in which a and b where design to be present in.

Together, the product and the synchronisation can be used to obtain in a *compositional* way, a complex IFTA built out of primitive ones. The composition of IFTA is made by linking ports and by combining their variability models. Thus, we define the composition of two IFTA as their product, followed by the explicit binding of actions through synchronization. The composition is defined for interface actions synchronized on an input-output fashion only.

Definition 11 (Composition of IFTA). *Given two grounded IFTA,* $\mathcal{A}_1$ *and* $\mathcal{A}_2$, *with disjoint set of actions, features and clocks; and a possible empty set of* bindings $\{(a_1, b_1), \ldots, (a_n, b_n)\}$, *such that for each pair a_i and b_i, for $1 \leq i \leq n$, we have that*

$$(a_i, b_i) \in I_1 \times O_2 \text{ or } (a_i, b_i) \in O_1 \times I_2 \qquad\qquad (\text{io-only})$$

then, their composition is a new grounded IFTA defined as follows

$$\mathcal{A}_1 \bowtie_{(a_1,b_1),\ldots,(a_n,b_n)} \mathcal{A}_2 = \Delta_{a_1,b_1} \ldots \Delta_{a_n,b_n} (\mathcal{A}_1 \times \mathcal{A}_2)$$

Figure 3 exemplifies the composition of the coffee machine CM (top right) from Fig. 1, and a new IFTA R, representing a *router* (top left), which receives an input i?, and executes simultaneously one of its outputs, if they are present, or receives i? and does nothing if neither output are present. The composition is done by linking the ports o_1! with coffee?, and o_2! with cappuccino?. The resulting IFTA combines the feature models of both IFTA, imposing additional restrictions given by the binded ports, e.g., the binding $(o_1!, \text{coffee}?)$ imposes that o_1! will be present, if and only if, coffee? is present, which depends on the feature expressions of each port, i.e., $(f_i \wedge f_{o1}) \leftrightarrow cf$. In the composed IFTA, transitions with binded actions transition together, while transitions with non-binded actions (i? and serve!) can transition independently or together.

Notice that because we define composition as the product followed by the synchronization, the product will produce many transitions that are later *cut* by the synchronization when linking actions. Then, the order in which actions are

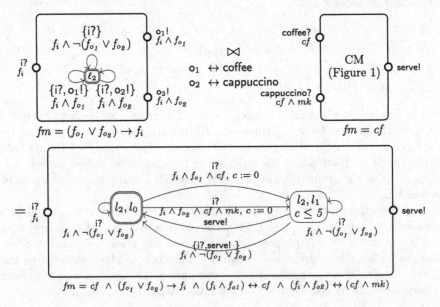

Fig. 3. Composition of an IFTA R (top left), representing a router coordination component, with the IFTA CM (top right), defined in Fig. 1, by binding ports (o_1, coffee) and $(o_2, \text{cappuccino})$, yielding the IFTA at the bottom.

linked, and therefore, the order in which transitions are cut by the synchronization operation affects the inferred feature expression of actions. Thus, if we were to use $\widehat{\Gamma}$ instead of Γ, synchronization would not be commutative. By *fixing* the feature expression of an action before doing the product, we avoid this issue and the synchronization remains commutative.

By allowing each IFTA to have its own feature model and taking into account variability during composition, we can reason about how composing families of timed automata in parallel affects the presence of interfaces and the variability of the composed system.

Operations over IFTA satisfy the usual properties up to *strong bisimulation* ($\sim$) and are discussed in [7]. We recall them in the following theorem.

Theorem 1. *Given any IFTA $\mathcal{A}_1, \mathcal{A}_2$ and $\mathcal{A}_3$, and actions $a, b, c, d \in A_{\mathcal{A}_1}$, such that a, b, c, d are different actions, the following properties hold.*

$$\mathcal{A}_1 \times \mathcal{A}_2 \sim \mathcal{A}_2 \times \mathcal{A}_1 \qquad (\times\text{-commutativity})$$
$$\mathcal{A}_1 \times (\mathcal{A}_2 \times \mathcal{A}_3) \sim (\mathcal{A}_1 \times \mathcal{A}_2) \times \mathcal{A}_3 \qquad (\times\text{-associativity})$$
$$\Delta_{a,b}\Delta_{c,d}\mathcal{A}_1 \sim \Delta_{c,d}\Delta_{a,b}\mathcal{A}_1 \qquad (\Delta\text{-commutativity})$$
$$(\Delta_{a,b}\mathcal{A}_1) \times \mathcal{A}_2 \sim \Delta_{a,b}(\mathcal{A}_1 \times \mathcal{A}_2) \qquad (\Delta \text{ interacts well with } \times)$$

3 Refinement

As mentioned in the introduction, there are two different aspects to be taken into account when discussing a notion of refinement for IFTA. The first concerns refinement of the feature model, which we call *variability refinement*. The second one is refinement of timed automata obtained by projection onto a feature selection, which we call *behavioural refinement*. Thus, refinement of an IFTA will be defined as a refinement of both its feature model and its projections.

3.1 Variability Refinement

Thum et al. [10] recognize four type of relations between two feature models fm_1 and fm_2, based on their set of products, even when their set of features, may not coincide: fm_1 *refactors or is equivalent* to fm_2 if they model the same set of products; fm_1 *specializes* fm_2 if the set of products of fm_1 is a subset of the products of fm_2; fm_1 *generalizes* fm_2 if the set of products of fm_1 is a superset of the products of fm_2; and fm_1 and fm_2 are *arbitrarily* related otherwise.

However, in order to reason about refinement of families of timed automata we also would like to relate feature models in terms of a refinement relation. Intuitively, a feature model fm_1 refines a feature model fm_2 if, when considering the set of features of fm_2, fm_1 expresses exactly the same set of products as expressed by fm_2. Thus, fm_1 can add new variability or details only in terms of new features. Formally, if we consider feature models with only terminal features [10], i.e., no abstract features, we define feature model refinement as follows.

Definition 12 (Feature model refinement). *Given two feature models* $fm_i \in FE(F_i)$ *over a set of features* F_i, $i = 1, 2$, fm_1 *refines* fm_2, *denoted* $fm_1 \sqsubseteq fm_2$, *if and only if,*

$$F_1 \supseteq F_2 \qquad \text{(preserves features)}$$

$$[\![fm_1]\!]^{F_1}\big|_{F_2} = [\![fm_2]\!]^{F_2} \qquad (fm_1 \text{ refines } fm_2)$$

where $[\![fm]\!]^F\big|_{F'} = \{FS \cap F' \mid FS \in [\![fm]\!]^F\}$.

For example, if we consider the coffee machines CM and CM' from Fig. 4, we have that $[\![fm_{CM}]\!] = \{\{cf\}, \{cf, mk\}\}$ and $[\![fm_{CM'}]\!] = \{\{cf\}, \{cf, wt\}, \{cf, mk\}, \{cf, mk, wt\}\}$. When we restrict $fm_{CM'}$ to only features in F_{CM}, we have $[\![fm_{CM'}]\!]\big|_{F_{CM}} = \{\{cf\}, \{cf, \not{wt}\}, \{cf, mk\}, \{cf, mk, \not{wt}\}\} = [\![fm_{CM}]\!]$, where $\not{wt}$ means that feature wt is removed from the set. Thus, $fm_{CM'} \sqsubseteq fm_{CM}$. However, let us assume that the feature model of CM' is $fm_{CM'} = cf \wedge mk$ instead of just cf, then we have $[\![fm_{CM'}]\!]\big|_{F_{CM'}} = \{\{cf, mk\}, \{cf, mk, \not{wt}\}\}$. In this case $fm_{CM'} \not\sqsubseteq fm_{CM}$, since it does not preserves variability by not allowing a coffee machine that only serves coffee.

Theorem 2 ($\sqsubseteq$ **is a partial order**). *For any feature model* fm_i, *for* $i = 1, 2, 3$, $fm_1 \sqsubseteq fm_1$; *if* $fm_1 \sqsubseteq fm_2$ *and* $fm_2 \sqsubseteq fm_3$, *then* $fm_1 \sqsubseteq fm_3$; *and if* $fm_1 \sqsubseteq fm_2$ *and* $fm_2 \sqsubseteq fm_1$, *then* $fm_1 \equiv fm_2$.

Proof. Immediate by unfolding definitions and set-theoretic properties.

3.2 Behavioral Refinement

Intuitively, an automata $\mathcal{A}$ that refines an automata $\mathcal{B}$ should be able to replace $\mathcal{B}$ in every environment that $\mathcal{B}$ appears in, yielding an equivalent system. Refinement allows to check if a given *implementation* agrees with a *specification*. We consider implementations as automata that are more detailed specifications. Our notion of refinement is similar to the one in [2], where there is an alternating simulation between both automata: $\mathcal{A}$ must simulate all input behavior of $\mathcal{B}$, while $\mathcal{B}$ must simulate all output behavior from $\mathcal{A}$. Thus, $\mathcal{A}$ can allow more legal inputs, and fewer outputs, than $\mathcal{B}$.

Similarly to [9] we define refinement at the semantic level, i.e., IFTS, and then we define refinement of IFTA in terms of IFTS refinement. However, first we define the notion of refinement for Interface Transition Systems, separating the notion of behavioral refinement from variability refinement.

Our notion of refinement can be seen as an extension of [2] for timed systems and multi-action transitions. Here as well, the definition of refinement must consider the fact that both automata have internal actions which are independent from each other. Since we are dealing with timed transition systems, the definition of refinement must consider that internal steps can incorporate delays. Thus, we define a transition relation that captures all transition steps that can be done from a state s to a state s', by any combination of internal and delay steps.

Definition 13. *Given an ITS S and states $s, s' \in St_S$, we write $s \overset{d}{\Rightarrow}_S s'$ if there is a sequence of transition steps from T_S, such that*

$$\exists\ s \xrightarrow{d_0 \cup \tau}_S s_1 \ldots s_n \xrightarrow{d_n \cup \tau}_S s' \text{ and } d = \sum_{i=0}^{n} d_i$$

where $d_i \in \mathbb{R}_{\geq 0}$, and τ represents any internal action. For simplicity, we write $s \overset{\omega}{\Rightarrow}_S^d s'$ if there is a sequence of transition steps from T_S, such that

$$\exists\ s \overset{d}{\Rightarrow}_S s_n \overset{\omega}{\longrightarrow}_S s'$$

In this context, ITS refinement is defined as follows.

Definition 14 (Refinement of ITS). *Given two ITS, S and T, such that $I_T \subseteq I_S$ and $O_S \subseteq O_T$, S refines T, denoted $S \preceq T$, if and only if, $\exists\ \mathcal{R} \subseteq St_S \times St_T$, such that $(s_0, t_0) \in \mathcal{R}$ and for each $(s, t) \in \mathcal{R}$, we have*

1. $s \overset{d}{\Rightarrow}_S s', d \in \mathbb{R}_{\geq 0}$ *then* $t \overset{d}{\Rightarrow}_T t'$ *and* $(s', t') \in \mathcal{R}$, *for some* $t' \in St_T$
2. $s \xrightarrow{OI_s}_S^d s', d \in \mathbb{R}_{\geq 0}, O \neq \emptyset$ *then* $t \xrightarrow{OI_s}_T^d t'$ *and* $(s', t') \in \mathcal{R}$ *for some* $t' \in St_T$
3. $t \xrightarrow{IO}_T^d t', d \in \mathbb{R}_{\geq 0}, I \neq \emptyset$ *then* $s \xrightarrow{IO}_S^d s'$ *and* $(s', t') \in \mathcal{R}$ *for some* $s' \in St_S$

where I_s is either $\emptyset$, or has only inputs shared by both automata, $I_s \subseteq I_T$.

Condition 1 expresses that any delay d allowed by s, possibly through internal steps, must be a delay allowed from t, possibly through internal steps. Condition 2 expresses that any transition with output O, with a possible empty set of inputs $I_s \subseteq I_T$ that are *shared* by both systems, which can be taken from s after a delay d, possibly through internal steps, must simulate a (sequence of) transition(s) from t. In case there is a multi-action transition with outputs and inputs, such that the inputs include new inputs in I_S, is considered as new behavior incorporated by the new inputs, and as such, it is ignored. Condition 3 expresses that any transition with inputs I, with a possible empty set of outputs O, which can be taken from t after a delay d, possibly through internal steps, must be simulated by a (sequence of) transition(s) from s.

In comparison with de Alfaro et al., we relax some of the requirements made over the states being compared, s and t. In particular, when considering input labeled transitions (Condition 3), de Alfaro et al. defines that s and t are in a refinement relationship, only if, whenever in t is possible to receive and input, s may receive the same input. Here, we require that whenever in t is possible to receive an input within certain time, possibly through a sequence of internal steps, s may receive the same input within the same time, possibly through a series of internal steps.

3.3   IFTA Refinement

Before considering refinement for families of timed automata, let us consider refinement for IFTS. Informally, given two IFTS, S and T, S refines T if for each product in S, the projection of S onto such product refines the projection of T onto the same product. However, depending on the relation existing between the set of products of S and T, this can lead to different notions of refinement. Ideally, S should preserve the variability of T, i.e., S should allow exactly the products in T, although it may also increase the set of features and allow more products when considering the new features. Formally, the refinement of IFTS and IFTA are defined as follows.

Definition 15 (Refinement of IFTS). *Given two IFTS, S and T, S refines T, denoted $S \preceq T$, if and only if,*

$$fm_S \sqsubseteq fm_T \qquad \text{(variability refinement)}$$

$$\forall\, FS \in [\![fm_S]\!]^{Fs} \cdot S \!\downarrow_{FS}\ \preceq\ T \!\downarrow_{FS} \qquad \text{(behaviour refinement)}$$

Definition 16 (Refinement of IFTA). *Given two grounded IFTA $\mathcal{A}$ and $\mathcal{B}$, $\mathcal{A}$ refines $\mathcal{B}$, denoted $\mathcal{A} \preceq \mathcal{B}$, if and only if, $[\![\mathcal{A}]\!] \preceq [\![\mathcal{B}]\!]$.*

Figure 4 shows an implementation of a family of coffee machines, CM' (right), which refines the IFTA CM (left). The new automaton introduces a new input, water? that depends on a new feature wt which represents the support for serving water. In addition, CM' ensures that coffee is served faster than in *CM*, as indicated by the invariant $c \leq 3$.

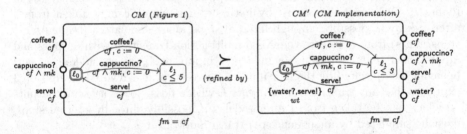

Fig. 4. Example of a family of coffee machines CM' with new variability, interfaces and time restrictions, refining the family CM introduced in Fig. 1.

Figure 5 shows a more complex example of refinement incorporating internal actions. The IFTA on the left, P_1, specifies a payment system using PayPal, and is part of a larger system composed of various automata, which models a family of licensing services introduced in [7]. The IFTA on the right, P_2, represents a more detailed implementation of P_1. The specification requires that whenever the user makes a payment through PayPal, the system will issue an error or a success signal in less than ten units of time. The implementation deals with

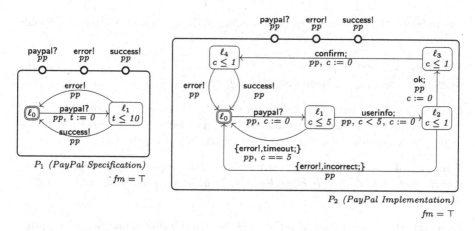

Fig. 5. An example of IFTA refinement with internal actions, where $P_2 \preceq P_1$.

the actual login into PayPal and confirmation of the payment. In P_2, after the user requests to issue a payment through PayPal, the user must login within 5 units of time, or an error is issued. The log in can be successful or it can issue an error in less than one unit of time. In case the user logs in successfully, a confirmation of the payment must be issued in less than one unit of time after which the system issues a signal of error or success. Both, P_1 and P_2, share the same feature model. In addition, P_2 guarantees that whenever a payment is made through PayPal, the system will issue an error or success signal in less than seven units of time, satisfying the requirements of P_1. Thus, $P_2 \preceq P_1$.

Refinement of IFTA is a pre-order and it is compositional. The latter allows decomposition of refinement proofs, improving efficiency in refinement checking. In order to be compositional, refinement must be congruent with respect to IFTA operations, product and synchronization. The former is straightforward, however stronger pre-conditions are required to ensure congruence with respect to synchronization.

The problem arises with feature model refinement. Intuitively, by definition of refinement, in the implementation an input can be present in more products and an output can be present in less products, than in the specification. Thus, it is natural that the feature expressions associated to the input and output that we want to synchronize in the implementation differ from the feature expressions in the specification. Thus, if an implementation refines a specification, after synchronization, the feature model of the implementation does not necessarily refine the feature model of the specification.

Intuitively, a possible solution is to require that an implementation can only replace the specification if it does not add new interface bindings and maintains all bindings already in the specification. This means that, for each valid product in the implementation, the corresponding automata in the implementation can be synchronized over a given set of input and outputs, if and only if, the corresponding automata in the specification can be synchronized over the same inputs and outputs. The following theorems capture the pre-order and compositional properties of IFTA refinement.

Theorem 3 ($\preceq$ is a pre-order). *For any grounded IFTA $\mathcal{A}_1$, $\mathcal{A}_2$ and $\mathcal{A}_3$, $\mathcal{A}_1 \preceq \mathcal{A}_1$, and if $\mathcal{A}_1 \preceq \mathcal{A}_2$ and $\mathcal{A}_2 \preceq \mathcal{A}_3$, then $\mathcal{A}_1 \preceq \mathcal{A}_3$.*

Proof. $\mathcal{A}_1 \preceq \mathcal{A}_1$ is trivial by definition of $\preceq$. In the case of transitivity, feature model refinement follows immediately from Theorem 2. Behavioral refinement follows by induction on the structure of IFTA for each case of Definition 14.

Theorem 4 ($\preceq$ is congruent w.r.t. $\times$). *For any grounded IFTA $\mathcal{A}_1$, $\mathcal{A}_2$, and $\mathcal{B}$, such that $\mathcal{A}_i$ and $\mathcal{B}$ have disjoint set of actions and features, $i = 1, 2$, if $\mathcal{A}_1 \preceq \mathcal{A}_2$, then $\mathcal{A}_1 \times \mathcal{B} \preceq \mathcal{A}_2 \times \mathcal{B}$.*

Proof. Feature model refinement follows by definition of semantics of a feature expression. Behavioral refinement follows by induction on the structure of IFTA for each case of Definition 14.

Theorem 5 ($\preceq$ is congruent w.r.t. Δ). *For any grounded IFTA $\mathcal{A}_1$, $\mathcal{A}_2$, and actions i, o such that $(i, o) \in I_i \times O_i$ for $i = 1, 2$, if $\mathcal{A}_1 \preceq \mathcal{A}_2$, then $\Delta_{i,o}\mathcal{A}_1 \preceq \Delta_{i,o}\mathcal{A}_2$, only if, $fm_1 \rightarrow ((\Gamma_1(i) \leftrightarrow \Gamma_1(o)) \leftrightarrow (\Gamma_2(i) \leftrightarrow \Gamma_2(o)))$.*

Proof. Feature model refinement follows by definition of semantics of a feature expression, and by the precondition on Γ_i for $i \in \{1, 2\}$. Behavioral refinement follows by induction on the structure of IFTA for each case of Definition 14.

To meet strict space limitations, detailed proofs of all results are omitted in the paper, but will appear in [6].

Let us consider again the IFTA CM composed with the router R (Fig. 3). If we want to check if we can replace CM by CM' (Fig. 4) in the system composed by CM and R, because refinement is compositional, instead of checking $CM' \bowtie_{(\text{coffee},o_1),(\text{cappuccino},o_2)} R \preceq CM \bowtie_{(\text{coffee},o_1),(\text{cappuccino},o_2)} R$ it suffices to check the following conditions:

1. $fm_1 \rightarrow ((\Gamma_{CM'}(\text{coffee}) \leftrightarrow \Gamma_{CM'}(o_1)) \leftrightarrow (\Gamma_{CM}(\text{coffee}) \leftrightarrow \Gamma_{CM}(o_1)))$
2. $fm_1 \rightarrow ((\Gamma_{CM'}(\text{cappuccino}) \leftrightarrow \Gamma_{CM'}(o_2)) \leftrightarrow (\Gamma_{CM}(\text{cappuccino}) \leftrightarrow \Gamma_{CM}(o_2)))$
3. CM' $\preceq$ CM

Conditions 1 and 2 correspond to the precondition for Δ congruence. In our example, both conditions are satisfied. However, let us assume now that we have an IFTA CM" which differs from CM only by changing the feature expression associated to the transition labeled with cappuccino!, from $cf \wedge mk$ to $(cf \wedge mk) \vee instc$, where $instc$ represents the support for instant cappuccino. In this case, when we try to replace CM by CM", condition 2 does not hold. This is because in CM, cappuccino appears only when cf and mk are both present, however in CM" cappuccino can appear when cf and $instc$ are present but not mk. Thus, the resulting composed system with CM" and R, models a concrete automaton that enables a synchronization between o_2! and cappuccino? that was not possible before.

4   Conclusions

We proposed a refinement relation for families of timed automata which are modeled as Interface Featured Timed Automata. Since each IFTA can be seen as: (1) a feature model, which determines a set of valid feature combinations; and (2) a set of concrete automata, where each of the concrete automata is determined by a valid set of features; we separated the notion of IFTA refinement into *variability refinement* and *behavioral refinement*. Furthermore, we decompose IFTA into other formalisms on which we based such notions of refinement, namely Interface Featured Transition System (IFTS) and Interface Transition Systems (ITS).

The refinement relation proposed here is a pre-order and congruent with respect to IFTA product and synchronization, meaning refinement is compositional. However, in order to be congruent with respect to synchronization, stronger conditions must be made over the synchronization actions used in the composition. In particular, the implementation can only replace the specification in a composed environment, if it does not add new interface connections and maintains all connections of the specification. Although the requirement of not allowing new connections and maintain existed ones is reasonable, it can be too strict. For example, in alignment with the notion of ITS refinement, which allows to incorporate new behavior through new inputs, it will be desirable to incorporate new behavior in terms of new features, in a way that the example of CM", introduced in Sect. 3.3, can be considered a refinement of CM. In fact, in [2], de Alfaro et al. only require that no new connections with the environment are made, while some connections can be lost, however, this is not sufficient to ensure that IFTA refinement is compositional. In this sense, as a future work we would like to explore and formalize other notions of refinement and how these can affect the properties that we can expect from the relation. For example, in the case of behavioral refinement, we could have defined that $\mathcal{A}$ refines $\mathcal{B}$, if and only if, for every feature selection FS in $fm_{\mathcal{B}}$ (instead of $fm_{\mathcal{A}}$), $[\![\mathcal{A}]\!] \downarrow_{FS} \preceq [\![\mathcal{B}]\!] \downarrow_{FS}$. The advantage is that we can now incorporate behavior in terms of new features, aligning better with the notion of refinement. However, on the one hand, this requires that $fm_{\mathcal{A}}$ contains at least all feature selections allowed by $fm_{\mathcal{B}}$, meaning $fm_{\mathcal{A}}$ can not incorporate mandatory features; and on the other hand, it can be too flexible, since we can not account for how the system will behave for new variability.

Currently, we are working on defining a notion of refinement over IFTS that takes advantage of the variability to perform a refinement checking on the entire family instead of a product by product approach. In addition, previously we developed a prototype tool[2] to specify IFTA, compose them and translate them to other formalisms, including UPPAAL Timed Automata to verify properties, and we plan to extend it to support refinement checking.

---

[2] https://github.com/haslab/ifta.

Acknowledgements. The first author is supported by the European Regional Development Fund (ERDF) through the Operational Programme for Competitiveness and Internationalisation (COMPETE 2020), and by National Funds through the Portuguese funding agency, FCT, within project TRUST, POCI-01-0145- FEDER-016826. In addition the first and second author are supported by FCT grants PD/BD/52238/2013 and SFRH/BPD/91908/2012, respectively.

References

1. de Alfaro, L., Henzinger, T.A.: Interface automata. SIGSOFT Softw. Eng. Notes **26**(5), 109–120 (2001). http://doi.acm.org/10.1145/503271.503226
2. de Alfaro, L., Henzinger, T.A.: Interface-based design. In: Broy, M., Grünbauer, J., Harel, D., Hoare, T. (eds.) Engineering Theories of Software Intensive Systems. NATO Science Series (Series II: Mathematics, Physics and Chemistry), vol. 195. Springer, Dordrecht (2005)
3. Alur, R., Henzinger, T.A., Kupferman, O., Vardi, M.Y.: Alternating refinement relations. In: Sangiorgi, D., Simone, R. (eds.) CONCUR 1998. LNCS, vol. 1466, pp. 163–178. Springer, Heidelberg (1998). https://doi.org/10.1007/BFb0055622
4. Baier, C., Katoen, J.P., Larsen, K.G.: Principles of model checking (2008)
5. Classen, A., Heymans, P., Schobbens, P.Y., Legay, A.: Symbolic model checking of software product lines. In: International Conference on Software Engineering (ICSE), pp. 321–330 (2011). http://dl.acm.org/citation.cfm?id=1985838
6. Cledou, G.: A Virtual Factory for Smart City Service Integration (forthcoming). Ph.D. thesis, Universidades do Minho, Aveiro and Porto (Joint MAP-i Doctoral Programme) (2018, to appear)
7. Cledou, G., Proença, J., Barbosa, L.: Composing families of timed automata. FSEN 2017. LNCS, vol. 10522. Springer, Cham (2017). https://doi.org/10.1007/978-3-319-68972-2_4
8. Cordy, M., Schobbens, P.Y., Heymans, P., Legay, A.: Behavioural modelling and verification of real-time software product lines. In: Proceedings of the 16th International Software Product Line Conference, vol. 1, pp. 66–75. ACM (2012)
9. David, A., Larsen, K.G., Legay, A., Nyman, U., Wasowski, A.: Timed I/O automata: a complete specification theory for real-time systems. In: Proceedings of the 13th ACM International Conference on Hybrid Systems: Computation and Control (HSCC 2010), pp. 91–100. ACM, New York (2010). http://doi.acm.org/10.1145/1755952.1755967
10. Thum, T., Batory, D., Kastner, C.: Reasoning about edits to feature models. In: Proceedings of the 31st International Conference on Software Engineering (ICSE 2009), pp. 254–264. IEEE Computer Society, Washington (2009). http://dx.doi.org/10.1109/ICSE.2009.5070526

Rapidly Adjustable Non-intrusive Online Monitoring for Multi-core Systems

Normann Decker[1(✉)], Philip Gottschling[2(✉)], Christian Hochberger[2(✉)],
Martin Leucker[1(✉)], Torben Scheffel[1(✉)], Malte Schmitz[1(✉)],
and Alexander Weiss[3(✉)]

[1] Institute for Software Engineering and Programming Languages,
Universität zu Lübeck, Lübeck, Germany
{decker,leucker,scheffel,schmitz}@isp.uni-luebeck.de
[2] Rechnersysteme, Technische Universität Darmstadt, Darmstadt, Germany
{gottschling,hochberger}@rs.tu-darmstadt.de
[3] Accemic Technologies GmbH, Kiefersfelden, Germany
aweiss@accemic.com

Abstract. This paper presents an approach for rapidly adjustable embedded trace online monitoring of multi-core systems, called RETOM. Today, most commercial multi-core SoCs provide accurate runtime information through an embedded trace unit without affecting program execution. Available debugging solutions can use it to reconstruct the run offline, but usually for up to a few seconds only. RETOM employs a novel online reconstruction technique that makes the program run available outside the SoC and allows for evaluating a specification formulated in the stream-based specification language TeSSLa in real time. The necessary computing performance is provided by an FPGA-based event processing system. In contrast to other hardware-based runtime verification techniques, changing the specification requires no circuit synthesis and thus seconds rather than minutes or hours. Therefore, iterated testing and property adjustment during development and debugging becomes feasible while preserving the option of arbitrarily extending observation time, which may be necessary to detect rarely occurring errors. Experiments show the feasibility of the approach.

1 Introduction

Software for resource-constrained environments demands for an application-specific and highly optimised implementation. Testing and debugging is challenging in this setting because of strong limitations regarding the acquisition and analysis of execution information. On one hand, comprehensive logging output provided by the software decreases the performance significantly and requires to anticipate the information needed in the debugging and testing process. On

This work is supported in part by the European Cooperation in Science and Technology (COST Action ARVI), the BMBF projects ARAMIS II with funding ID 01 IS 16025 and CONIRAS with funding ID 01 IS 13029, and the European Horizon 2020 project COEMS under number 732016.

S. Cavalheiro and J. Fiadeiro (Eds.): SBMF 2017, LNCS 10623, pp. 179–196, 2017.
https://doi.org/10.1007/978-3-319-70848-5_12

the other hand, runtime information can be observed dynamically using automatic code instrumentation, producing suitable program output, or standard breakpoint-based debugging features of the processor. The latter methods, however, are highly intrusive as they modify the software temporarily for the analysis or interrupt the execution. This is especially problematic for concurrent programs running on multi-core processors or real-time applications. Errors due to race conditions or inappropriate timing may be introduced or hidden.

To allow for a non-intrusive observation of the program trace, many modern microprocessors feature an *embedded trace unit (ETU)* [2,12,14,28]. An ETU delivers runtime information to a debug port of the processor in a highly compressed format. State-of-the-art debugging solutions, such as ARM DSTREAM [3], allow the user to record this information for offline reconstruction and analysis. The essential disadvantage of this technology is, however, that traces can be recorded for at most a few seconds because high-performance memory with very fast write access is required to store the delivered information. For example, the ARM DSTREAM solution offers a trace buffer of 4 GB for a recording speed of 10 Gbit/s or more which means that the buffer can only hold data of less than four seconds. While the majority of errors can be found immediately within a short program trace, some of them may only be observable on long-running executions or under specific, rarely occurring (logical or physical) conditions. It is therefore desirable for the developer and maintainer to be able to monitor the program execution for an arbitrary amount of time during development and testing and even in the field after deployment.

Contribution. To overcome the limitations of current technology we propose a novel runtime verification methodology for evaluating long-term program executions that is suitable for development and debugging, testing, and in-field monitoring. Based on the runtime information provided by the ETU, we perform a real-time reconstruction of the program trace. The latter is evaluated with respect to a specification formulated by the user in the stream-based specification language TeSSLa [18]. To deliver sufficient performance for online analysis, both reconstruction and monitoring system are implemented using FPGA hardware.

FPGAs have become a very popular technology to implement digital systems. Designing digital circuits with FPGAs typically starts from hardware description languages like VHDL or Verilog. Synthesis software is responsible to map such designs to the elements available in an FPGA and then these elements must be positioned and routed on the FPGA fabric. Even for moderately large designs, this process can take hours. In case the design should run at high clock speed, this time is dramatically increased. Our monitoring system is therefore designed to not only evaluate a specific property specification. Instead, it builds on a flexibly and quickly configurable FPGA-based event processing platform described in [13]. We provide a tool chain for mapping TeSSLa specifications to the platform automatically within seconds. Formulating hypotheses, adapting property specification and checking them on the target system can be iterated quickly without time-intensive synthesis.

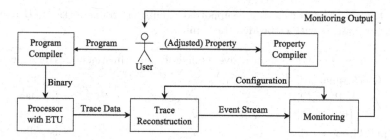

Fig. 1. General overview of the RETOM workflow cycle.

Figure 1 provides an overview of the proposed workflow based on our app-roach to *rapidly adjustable embedded trace online monitoring (RETOM)*. The user, e.g. the developer, tester, or maintainer, specifies the correct behaviour of the program under test based on program events such as a function call or vari-able access. The program is compiled and the binary is uploaded to the processor as usual. The property compiler automatically generates a corresponding config-uration for the monitoring and trace reconstruction units that is then uploaded to the platform. When running the program on the processor, the monitoring platform reports the computed output stream to the user who can then use the information to adjust the program or the property.

We show the feasibility of RETOM in terms of a prototype implementation using the ARM CoreSight technology as specific but widely available variant of an ETU. A concurrent scenario is used to demonstrate the characteristics of parallel and time-critical applications and how corresponding runtime properties can be specified in TeSSLa and evaluated using our monitoring system.

Related Work. This paper focuses on runtime monitoring techniques which analyzes one particular program execution. For a general introduction into the field of runtime verification especially in comparison with static verification tech-niques such as model checking see [16,17]. Non-intrusive observation of pro-gram executions is a long-standing issue [23] that becomes increasingly chal-lenging with high circuit integration. On the other hand, integrated hardware extensions were described, e.g., in [29] and today many standard ("commercial off-the-shelf") products feature advanced observation facilities [28]. Alternative approaches that aim at more powerful and flexible evaluation were developed based on programmable logic. Systems with on-chip programmable logic (SoPC) allow for direct observation and property evaluation by using specifically syn-thesised designs [26]. While this is appealing from a technical point of view, it introduces significant additional costs per unit. In [19] the authors propose similarly a partial reconfiguration of a (soft-core) processor. An external alter-native based on a side channel is discussed in [22]. However, a lot of training is required in order to identify specific system behaviour. Extending the system by an external FPGA-based device using peripheral buses [25] seems more realistic, although it comes with the restriction that only the external communication on

Table 1. Comparison of hardware-supported monitoring frameworks. ETU refers to standard processors with embedded trace unit.

Framework	Non-intrusive	Online	Rapid adjustment	Trace source
QSTL mon. [15]	n/a	✓	–	n/a
P2V [19]	✓	✓	–	cust.
HidICE [5]	✓	✓	–	cust.
ptMTL mon. [24]	(✓)	✓	✓	cust./dbg. port
BusMOP [25]	✓	✓	–	periph. bus
SoPC monitoring [27]	–	✓	–	SoPC
ARM DSTREAM [3]	✓	–	✓	ETU
RETOM	✓	✓	✓	ETU

the used bus can be observed. A custom high-bandwidth trace interface is used in [5] to obtain trace data but the practical drawback is again, that this is not available in any standard product.

While many of these approaches have the merit of unbounded online evaluation, they are inconvenient in an iterative development or testing process because the properties to be evaluated are synthesised directly to programmable logic which is extremely time-consuming. The same applies to the monitor construction presented in [15]. A solution that allows for a rapidly adjustable evaluation of past-time MTL properties is given in [24]. Compared to ETU-based solutions, however, the used interfaces are not available on commonly available hardware or provide less runtime information, operate at low speeds and are, like JTAG, possibly intrusive. Table 1 provides an overview of related approaches.

This paper is organized as follows: In Sect. 2 we explain the online trace reconstruction on the FPGA. Section 3 describes TeSSLa, the language used to specify the monitors. How data flow graphs are constructed out of the specification and how monitors are synthesized on the FPGA is discussed in Sect. 4. Finally we present a case study in Sect. 5.

2   Trace Reconstruction

Figure 2 shows an overview of the RETOM setup: The cores of the multi-core processor are communicating with periphery, such as the memory, through the system bus. Every core is observed by its own tracer. The trace data is sent through the trace bus to the trace port without affecting the core. The trace bus is separated from the system bus and does not interfere with it. The trace port of the processor is connected to the FPGA on which the trace reconstruction and interpretation and the actual monitoring are located. The final monitoring output is displayed and reported on a standard PC connected via USB.

In this paper we use the ARM CoreSight [2] debugging technology as a widely available example of an ETU, which is included in every current ARM processor (Cortex M, R and A). In particular, we use the Program Flow Trace (PFT) [1] to acquire trace data of the operations executed by the ARM processors.

As stated in the PFT manual [1] the "PFT identifies certain instructions in the program, and certain events, as waypoints. A waypoint is a point where instruction execution by the processor might involve a change in the program flow." With PFT we only observe as waypoints conditional and unconditional direct branches as well as all indirect branches and all other events, e.g. interrupts and other exceptions, that affect the program counter other than incrementing it. In order to save bandwidth on the trace bus, the Program Flow Trace Protocol (PFTP) does not report the current program counter address for every cycle. Especially for direct branches, the target address is not provided but only the information whether a (conditional) jump was executed or not. The full program counter address is sent irregularly for synchronization (I-Sync message). In case of an indirect branch those address bits that have changed since the last indirect branch or the last I-Sync message are outputted.

For RETOM we employ an online (real time) trace-reconstruction method implemented on the FPGA hardware [30, 31]: From a static analysis of the binary running on the CPU we know all the jump targets of conditional direct jumps and can store those in a lookup table in the memory of the FPGA. Due to the high parallelism of the FPGA, we can split the trace data stream and reconstruct the program trace using the lookup table. The trace data stream can be split at the synchronization points that contain the full program counter address. A FIFO buffer stores the trace data stream until we reach the next synchronization point. The buffer must be able to store at least the trace data between two synchronization points. For further processing we then immediately filter the reconstructed trace by comparing the reconstructed addresses to a list of addresses, called *tracepoints*, that correspond to the input events used in the TeSSLa specification to be evaluated. This comparison is realized by adding an additional tracepoint flag to the lookup table. After putting the slices back

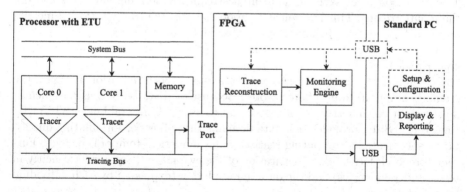

Fig. 2. Overview of the RETOM setup. Operations of the cores are traced by the ETU, the trace is then reconstructed, filtered and monitored on the FPGA.

together in the right order we end up with a stream of tracepoints. Every tracepoint contains an ID and a timestamp. The timestamp is either assigned by the ARM processor if cycle accurate tracing is enabled or during the reconstruction on the FPGA otherwise. Cycle accurate tracing is only available for certain processor architectures, because it requires high bandwidth on the trace port in order to attach timing information to every message. This trace-reconstruction approach can also be used for execution time measurement [9, 10].

Note that PFT traces logical addresses used in the CPU before the memory management unit (MMU) translates them to physical addresses, which are used to address certain cells in the memory. Because logical addresses are used in the program binary and by the CPU, RETOM does not need to handle physical addresses.

In a typical multithreaded application, we have multiple threads running on different cores and multiple threads running on the same core using any kind of scheduling. While we can distinguish instructions traced from the different CPUs, we have to consider the actual thread ID in order to distinguish different threads running on the same core. This information is provided by a so-called context ID message [2], sent every time when the operation system changes the context ID register of the CPU. The logical addresses for different threads might be exactly the same, because the MMU is reconfigured in the context switch to point to another physical memory region. If we see a context switch to another process, we have to change the lookup table for the program flow reconstruction information.

3   Specification of Trace Properties

In order to specify correctness properties as well as to describe the computation of statistical and numerical metrics based on the trace data, we use TeSSLa[1]. This temporal stream-based specification language is described and analyzed in detail in [18] and was specifically designed for program traces derived from ETUs. TeSSLa reasons over asynchronous input streams by deriving new streams from the input streams. This key concept supports both, the computation of metrics and specifying desired behavior of the observed program trace.

TeSSLa can be seen as an asynchronous extension of the stream based language LOLA [8]. LOLA is based on synchronous streams, but as we want to observe multi-core systems, we can not assume synchronization between the streams coming in from different cores. Because of that, TeSSLa uses asynchronous streams as underlaying model, similar to Signal Temporal Logic (STL) [20]. However, TeSSLa provides rich data domains that allow for formulating quantitative specifications computing statistics and numerical temporal metrics. Furthermore, STL lacks a clean separation of the evaluation (expressed explicitly in terms of dependencies) and the data manipulation (expressed by each individual operation).

---

[1] For more information on TeSSLa see http://www.isp.uni-luebeck.de/tessla.

3.1   Syntax and Semantics of TeSSLa

TeSSLa supports signals and event streams, a concept which has already been used for example for the definition of Timed Regular Expressions [4]. Let in the following $\mathbb{T}$ be a suitable time domain, e.g. $\mathbb{Q}$. An *event stream* is a partial function $\eta : \mathbb{T} \rightarrow D$ where D is a data domain. This partial function is only allowed to be defined for finitely many timestamps in a finite interval. We call the set of time points at which an event stream η is defined $E(\eta)$. The set of all event streams over D is denoted by $\mathcal{E}_D$.

In addition to the definition in terms of partial functions, an event stream $\eta \in \mathcal{E}_D$ can be naturally represented as a timed word with a sequence $s_\eta = (t_0, \eta(t_0))(t_1, \eta(t_1)) \cdots \in (E(\eta) \times D)^\infty$ ordered by time $(t_i < t_{i+1})$ and containing all event points, i.e. $\{t \mid (t, v) \text{ occurs on } s_\eta\} = E(\eta)$.

In contrast to event streams, a *signal* defines a value for every point in time. It is a piece-wise constant function $\sigma : \mathbb{T} \rightarrow D$ that can be represented as an event stream of value update events and can thus only change its value a finite number of times within a finite time interval. We denote the set of time points at which the value of a signal changes by $\Delta(\sigma)$. The set of all signals over a data domain D is denoted by $\mathcal{S}_D$. Section 5 provides some practical examples of signals and event streams.

Structure of TeSSLa Specifications. The syntax of TeSSLa is inspired by existing stream-based specification languages like LOLA [8] and the underlying concept of functional reactive programming [11]. TeSSLa is built around the basic concept of deriving internal or output streams by applying functions to input streams or already derived internal streams. Because it is designed to be readable with prior knowledge of C-style programming languages, the derived streams are defined in an imperative manner. Consider the following example of a TeSSLa specification where we assume two input streams, an event stream e whose events are counted and an event stream *trigg* which is used as trigger.

```
define numberOfEvents := eventCount(e)
define triggerInLast2Sec := inPast(trigg, 2s)
define error :=
  filter(e, triggerInLast2Sec && numberOfEvents < 5)
out error
```

It defines the signal *numberOfEvents* as the result of applying the function $eventCount : \mathcal{E}_D \rightarrow \mathcal{S}_\mathbb{N}$ to the input stream e. At every time point $t \in \mathbb{T}$ the signal provides the number of events that occurred on e up to t. Also, the signal *triggerInLast2Sec* is true as long as *trigg* had an event at most two seconds ago. Further, an event occurs on the event stream *error* whenever an event occurs on e while during the past two seconds an event occurred on *trigg* and the number of events on e has not reached the limit of five, i.e. the event on e is not filtered out by the *filter* function. For readability, type annotations can be omitted and are inferred at compile time. The semantics of a TeSSLa specification is a mapping from a set of input streams to a set of output streams and the keyword **out** defines *error* to be one of the latter. These are visible outside of the monitor and can be used for further processing or be presented to the user.

TeSSLa does not allow for recursive definitions of streams in any way. This leads to a large library of built in functions which incorporate specific recursive functionality. The big advantage of this approach is that the dependency graph of a TeSSLa specification is a directed acyclic graph. In combination with restricting real-time operators to refer only to the current and past events, this enables us to use more effective algorithms for synthesizing a specification onto an FPGA which leads to greater flexibility. The concrete process of doing so is described in Sect. 4.

By providing a set of built-in functions we can use an optimized translation for FPGA synthesis. Consider the idea of summing up the values of the events of an event stream. If the user would define this in a recursive fashion, the evaluation on the FPGA would typically consist of an adder and a delay unit storing the result of the adder such that it is used with the next input event of the stream to be summed up. By using a specialized function called *sum*, just one operation unit needs to be synthesized onto the FPGA that internally stores the last output in a register and adds it to the next value of the event stream.

Next, a selection of important functions available in TeSSLa is provided. An in-depth discussion of the TeSSLa design and an exhaustive list of available functions can be found in [18].

Available Functions. There are five different types of functions in TeSSLa: simple arithmetic functions, aggregations, stream manipulators, timing functions and temporal property functions.

Simple arithmetic functions combine multiple input signals with an arithmetic operation into one output signal. All operations available in common programming languages can also be used in TeSSLa, for example a function *add* for point-wise summation of the value of two signals or a function *mul* for multiplication. More complex calculation functions in TeSSLa are *aggregations*. These generally take event streams as input and produce a signal. For example the function $sum : \mathcal{E}_\mathbb{N} \to \mathcal{S}_\mathbb{N}$ computes the sum of the data of all events on an event stream and always outputs the current sum. Variants for other additive types, like rational numbers $\mathbb{Q}$ or time points $\mathbb{T}$, are also available; polymorphism is resolved at compile time. The function *eventCount* counts the events on an event stream that occurred until a certain point in time, ignoring the values carried by events. Another important function in this category is $mrv : \mathcal{E}_D \times D \to \mathcal{S}_D$ that computes the *most recent value* of an event stream. It returns the value of the last event that happened or the default value given as second parameter as long as no event occurred, yet. With *mrv* one can transform event streams into signals and then apply arithmetic functions on them.

Conversely, *sampling functions* convert signals into event streams. The function $changeOf : \mathcal{S}_D \to \mathcal{E}_D$ returns an event stream with an event at those points in time where the value of the input signal changes. The function $sample : \mathcal{S}_D \times \mathcal{E}_D \to \mathcal{E}_D$ samples a signal clocked by an event stream and thus returns for every input event an event containing the values of the signal at the respective point in time.

With *stream manipulators* one can split and combine streams. Typical functions are *filter*, that works like a mask and deletes events by a certain criteria, and *merge*, that combines two event streams into one. Constructs like if-then-else are also stream manipulators essentially combining filter and merge functionality.

With *timing functions* one can refer to the past or future given a (real) time offset. The functions *delay* and *shift* are delaying a signal for a certain amount of time or shifting the values of the events of an event stream by a certain number of events, respectively. The two functions *inPast* and *inFuture* let us describe if an event happened on an event stream a certain amount of time in the past or future, respectively.

Finally there is the generic *monitor* function. This function provides a closed scope for specifying properties in different propositional temporal logics. For example, LTL or SALT [7] can be used with classical (finitary) semantics or more informative ones like LTL_3 [6]. Especially for the last one, this closed scope is needed because the LTL formula has to be processed in a complex way to build the monitor. Hence it has to be known what exactly belongs to the formula. The input consists of a set of boolean signals as propositions and an arbitrary event stream as clock for stepping the monitor. The type of the output stream depends on the output type of the used semantics.

3.2 Observation Specification

With the observation specification we can define in the TeSSLa specification certain streams based on the tracepoints generated by the online trace reconstruction. Such an observation can be defined on three different levels: (1) On the level of the C code, (2) on the level of the binary and (3) on the level of the processor. Because in the end we need to define the tracepoints for the trace reconstruction in terms of logical addresses in the binary, we need to translate the code level and the processor level to the binary level. On the binary level we can simply define streams with an event each time a given logical address is executed. On the code level we can define streams with an event each time a function is entered or left or each time a certain line of code gets executed. This information can be translated to the execution of logical addresses in the binary using the debug information in the binary. On the processor level we can for example specify streams with an event each time a floating point instruction is executed. This could be translated to the execution of logical addresses in the binary by simply analysing the binary for all floating point operations and listing all their addresses. In this paper we will use the following TeSSLa functions to define streams on the code level:

- `functionCalls("`$\langle file \rangle$`:`$\langle function \rangle$`")` creates an event each time the function with the specified name in the given five file is entered,
- `functionReturns("`$\langle file \rangle$`:`$\langle function \rangle$`")` creates an event for leaving the function and
- `codeLine("`$\langle file \rangle$`:`$\langle line \rangle$`")` creates an event each time the given line in the given file is executed.

4   Monitor Synthesis and FPGA Implementation

The observation specification is compiled into tracepoint declarations as already sketched in the previous section. Unique IDs are assigned to every tracepoint. The first stage of the trace evaluation is a filter that creates the logical streams based on the tracepoint IDs attached to the events generated by the trace recon‑ struction unit. As depicted in Fig. 2 on page 5 in order to monitor a certain property the generated tracepoints for that property must be configured in the reconstruction engine on the FPGA using the PC interface.

In our setup the FPGA fulfills three major functions. First, it realizes the reconstruction explained in Sect. 2. Second, it implements the monitor system that evaluates the reconstructed trace stream as described in the next sections. Third, it provides a softcore processor as a communication interface to the host system for configuration and monitor evaluation.

4.1   Merging Data Flow Graphs

Each TeSSLa specification (monitor) produces a new control and dataflow graph (CDFG) that can be transformed into a datapath (DP), i.e. the hardware imple‑ mentation that executes the operations given by its CDFG on the FPGA. To be able to check all specifications in parallel one would assemble all specified mon‑ itors into a directly synthesized monitor system consisting of different DPs, one for each specification. This approach has a major drawback: As soon as only one monitor specification changes the whole system has to be resynthesized. Long FPGA-synthesis time, however, would render the interactive RETOM workflow impossible in which TeSSLA specifications are adapted frequently. To overcome this problem, we follow [13] by merging several CDFGs into one super CDFG with reconfiguration capabilities. Now the monitoring system consists of multi‑ ple instances of the same reconfigurable DP, which can implement at least all of the previously specified monitors. This is even more flexible: It is no longer nec‑ essary to know how many monitors of a certain type are required in the monitor system as now all DPs can be reconfigured to implement the desired monitor.

Consider the two CDFGs CDFG$_A$ and CDFG$_B$ given in Fig. 3a and b. We want to merge those CDFGs into a new CDFG that can implement both of them. It can be seen that the CDFGs contain identical operations among each other. These operations can be shared instead of adding every operation from both graphs into the new one. Finding a preferably large amount of sharable opera‑ tions is essential for merging two CDFGs. A higher amount of shared operations reduces the resulting CDFG size and thereby, reduces the resulting hardware resources required for the DP.

Therefore, we have to create a matching in which every operation of CDFG$_A$ matches to either exactly one or no other node in CDFG$_B$. We use a generated compatibility graph (CG) as described in a formal way by Moreano et al. in [21]. Here, compatible matches are represented as edges between them. We search for a preferably large fully connected subgraph in the CG, also known as a maximal clique. This clique only contains matchings that can be applied simultaneously and do not conflict. The resulting merged CDFG (CDFG$_M$) is given in Fig. 3c. Operations that are used by both input CDFGs are filled.

4.2   Implementing Datapaths

A CDFG can be translated into a hardware description language – more precisely, a Verilog module to implement the configurable datapath. The CDFG has to be preprocessed, as there are some premises. In Fig. 3c it is clear, that the output of the CDFG can only have one input, either the "less than" or the finite state machine (FSM). Therefore, multiplexers are inserted at every operand input that has more than one predecessor. These allow later configuration at runtime to select the desired functionality. To further increase the degree of freedom, constants are never hardcoded into the module. As they change most often, they are replaced by configurable registers, so that their value can be changed quickly during runtime. The FSM is implemented as a microprogrammable state machine whose behavior only depends on the context of a memory. This context can be exchanged during runtime as well and thereby, offers a huge amount of flexibility.

The resulting DP copes without any kind of control logic. It works like a pipeline that can accept new data at its input in every clock cycle. Hence, the amount of time to calculate a result is constant and determined by the number of pipeline stages in the DP. At last, a configuration interface that connects all configurable elements is added.

4.3   Programming Monitors

After loading the monitor system onto the FPGA, the context for programming one of the monitors has to be created. During the preprocessing phase for

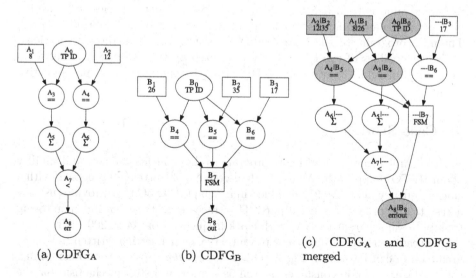

(a) CDFG$_A$ (b) CDFG$_B$ (c)   CDFG$_A$ and   CDFG$_B$ merged

Fig. 3. Example of two CDFGs (a, b) merged into one (c)

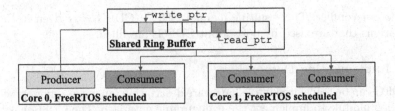

Fig. 4. Overview of the ring buffer scenario. The producer and consumer threads are distributed over two cores. On core 0 the producer and one consumer is located, on core 1 two consumers are located. The ring buffer is located in a memory section shared between the two cores.

generating the Verilog module, additional information about configurable operations is stored. From that information and the CDFG to program, it can be calculated which operation is executed on which resource on the DP. Another matching is constructed for the edges. The input CDFG does not necessarily need to be a CDFG of the merging set. As shown in [13] disjoint problems can be matched on already synthesized datapaths when the required resources are available.

As each edge match automatically implies two node matches, it is sufficient to find a complete matching for the edges. The matching is said to be complete when every edge in the input CDFG is matched to an edge in the implemented DP. It is automatically constrained by the node matchings. When an edge match matches operation A_i onto resource R_j, no other operation may be matched on this resource. If one complete matching is found, the search can be stopped, as all complete solutions are of equivalent quality. Neither resources nor processing time can be reduced at this point as the DPs are already synthesized.

From a complete matching the context for the elements can be extracted: a register's value is then determined by the constant that matches to it. Multiplexers use the incoming edge to determine if their control signal must be 0 or 1. The microprogram for the FSM can be generated from the states, transitions, and output values of the FSM that was created by the TeSSLa compiler for a monitor function. Programming a DP with this context turns it into an active monitor.

5   Case Study

We have implemented a multi-core program to show the feasibility and flexibility of our RETOM approach. We used a dual-core ARM Cortex-A9 processor with a clock frequency of 866 MHz embedded in a Zynq-7000 SoC that provides us easy access to the processor's trace port. The trace reconstruction and monitoring took place on separate FPGAs with clock frequencies of about 200 MHz.

Our case study is a concurrent producer/consumer setting written in C. The architecture can be seen in Fig. 4. The C-file *core0.c* runs on core 0 containing the producer and one consumer as well as a start and stop mechanism for the

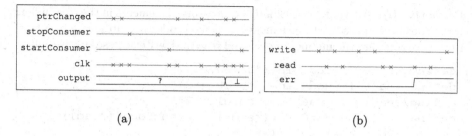

(a)   (b)

Fig. 5. Evaluation of the TeSSLa streams on an example run.

consumers on both cores. The C-file *core1.c* runs on core 1 containing two identical consumer threads. We use the FreeRTOS scheduler independently on both physical cores to run multiple threads per core. The producer writes elements into a ring buffer and the three consumers read these elements from the buffer. After an element is read, the read pointer (read_ptr) is moved to the next element by the consumer that reads it. Each time the producer writes an element to the buffer it increments the write pointer (write_ptr).

We introduced a bug in *core1.c* such that the section where the ring buffer is read and the read pointer is moved is no longer thread exclusive. This leads to a data race which we want to detect using RETOM.

Property (a). We want to check if the start and stop mechanism for the consumers works. Therefore, we use TeSSLa to specify a monitor which checks that when all consumers are stopped, the read pointer must not be changed anymore until they are started again:

```
define ptrChanged := merge(codeLine("core0.c:27"),
                           codeLine("core1.c:27"))
define stop := functionCalls("core0.c:stopConsumers")
define start := functionCalls("core0.c:startConsumers")
define clk := merge(stop, ptrChanged, start)
define output :=
  monitor("always(stop implies
    (not(ptrChanged) until start))",
      step := clk)
out output
```

The two *codeLine* streams reference the code line in which the read pointer is moved on. *stop* and *start* reference a call to the respective function. All these streams have an event whenever the piece of code referenced by them is executed. The clock stream *clk* is defined to be used to step the monitor. An example run for this property can be found in Fig. 5a. Here, the LTL_3 semantics is used and therefore the monitor outputs ? as long as the property can still be fulfilled and violated, while $\bot$ or $\top$ occurs as soon as the property is certainly violated or fulfilled, respectively.

Property (b). We want to check multi-processing of elements in the ring buffer: If the consumers process more elements then the producer writes we spot a bug. Hence, we compare the number of observed read and write accesses to the buffer:

```
define write := codeLine("core0.c:37")
define read0 := codeLine("core0.c:24")
define read1 := codeLine("core1.c:24")
define err := eventCount(read0) + eventCount(read1)
            > eventCount(write)
out err
```

The input streams contain an event if an element is written or read, respectively. Then *err* is defined by counting the number of written elements and the number of read elements. If more elements are read from than written to the buffer, some elements have been processed twice. The diagram in Fig. 5b shows an example evaluation of the streams.

For both properties (a) and (b) it is necessary to observe the system for an arbitrary amount of time because errors can occur randomly due to scheduling and timing differences on the cores. This means that the time when the error may occur also varies per execution. Because of that it is not feasible to just log data and evaluate that to find a possible bug. Also, a non-intrusive observation method is crucial for this property, because intrusiveness would change the timing of the code execution.

If we synthesize the monitors for property (a) and (b) on the FPGA, connect the FPGA to the processor running the ring buffer example and execute the program, we detect a violation of the property (b). The time needed to detect this violation differs for every execution due to scheduling reasons. Property (a) always produces ? which means that no error occurred yet. Property (b) states that some elements in the ring buffer are processed multiple times. To investigate this issue further we write another property to check if a data race already happens locally on one of the cores.

Property (c). We observe the accesses to the memory and to the read pointer to see if, after one consumer thread accessed the memory, another one accesses the memory before the read pointer is moved. This property can be expressed as follows in TeSSLa:

```
out doubleRead(
  read := codeLine("core0:24"),
  ptrChanged := codeLine("core0:27"))
```

where `doubleRead` is a macro defined as follows:

```
macro doubleRead(read, ptrChanged) := {
  define clk := merge(read, ptrChanged)
  monitor("always(read implies
    next(not(read) until ptrChanged))",
    step := clk)
}
```

Fig. 6. Evaluation of the TeSSLa streams of Property (c) on an example run.

Using this macro the property can be expressed for core 1 by changing *core0* to *core1*. All macros are fully expanded by the TeSSLa compiler before the monitor synthesis. The diagram in Fig. 6 shows an example run.

With RETOM we can now adjust the monitor system on the FPGA to check property (c) without the need to re-synthesize the FPGA.

As shown in Fig. 4, there is only one consumer thread on core 0, so on that core we only check if this consumer does not read an element twice. But on core 1, we found the data race because one of the consumer threads sometimes read the ring buffer before the other one increments the read pointer.

In the properties (a), (b) and (c) tracepoints happen rather seldomly during the program execution with an average event rate of about 1 kHz, because the main filtering happens already in the tracepoint matching during the trace reconstruction. Nevertheless with the RETOM approach one can also monitor high-frequency events like quantitative analysis on how many certain CPU instructions are performed. The synthesized monitoring pipeline on the FPGA can process a new external event with every clock cycle. With a clock frequency of 200 MHz the monitors are capable of processing up to 200 million events per second. For the properties described above we needed 196 lookup tables (LUTs) and 414 flip-flops (FFs). As a comparison, the Virtex 7 xc7vx485t that we used has 303600 LUTs and 607200 FFs available. Hence, one could synthesize on one FPGA about 1400 monitors of the size we used in this case study, all checking possibly different properties in parallel.

6   Conclusion

In this paper we proposed non-intrusive online monitoring for multi-core systems. Our approach RETOM utilises the embedded trace unit (ETU) of the system under test, which allows non-intrusive observation not only for collaborative software with debug statements, but for arbitrary software. With online monitoring one can react almost immediately to events of interest without having any limits regarding the execution length of the system under test. Using the stream-based specification language TeSSLa we can express correctness properties as well as statistics and numeric metrics, both with support for real-time operations. The control and data flow graph (CDFG) created from a TeSSLa specification contains no cyclic dependencies which simplifies its realization on FPGA hardware. By using merged CDFGs on the FPGA we can change the currently evaluated TeSSLa specification without the need of re-synthesizing the FPGA. This rapid adjustment is suitable for a debugging workflow where the user incrementally updates the specification based on the last monitoring output in order to understand the system under test. We have shown the feasibility of RETOM in a case study involving three properties spotting a race condition in a multi-core system by detecting a bug due to a long time observation of the system. With the possibility to interactively adjust the specification, one can have iterative debugging sessions in order to find more specific causes based on previous results. The next step to show the feasibility in a broader scale would be an industry case study which we are planning for the future.

Acknowledgements. We thank Jannis Harder and Sebastian Hungerecker for their work on TeSSLa, its compiler and the case study.

References

1. ARM Limited: ARM IHI 0035B: CoreSight Program Flow Trace: PFTv1.0 and PFTv1.1 - Architecture Specification, Issue B, March 2011
2. ARM Limited: ARM IHI 0029B: CoreSightTM Architecture Specification v2.0, Issue D (2013)
3. ARM Limited: DS-5 ARM DSTREAM User Guide Version 5.27 (2017)
4. Asarin, E., Caspi, P., Maler, O.: Timed regular expressions. J. ACM **49**(2), 172–206 (2002)
5. Backasch, R., Hochberger, C., Weiss, A., Leucker, M., Lasslop, R.: Runtime verification for multicore SoC with high-quality trace data. ACM Trans. Des. Autom. Electr. Syst. **18**(2), 18:1–18:26 (2013)
6. Bauer, A., Leucker, M., Schallhart, C.: Runtime verification for LTL and TLTL. ACM Trans. Softw. Eng. Methodol. **20**(4), 14:1–14:64 (2011)
7. Bauer, A., Leucker, M., Streit, J.: SALT—structured assertion language for temporal logic. In: Liu, Z., He, J. (eds.) ICFEM 2006. LNCS, vol. 4260, pp. 757–775. Springer, Heidelberg (2006). https://doi.org/10.1007/11901433_41
8. D'Angelo, B., Sankaranarayanan, S., Sánchez, C., Robinson, W., Finkbeiner, B., Sipma, H.B., Mehrotra, S., Manna, Z.: LOLA: runtime monitoring of synchronous systems. In: TIME, pp. 166–174. IEEE (2005)
9. Dreyer, B., Hochberger, C., Lange, A., Wegener, S., Weiss, A.: Continuous non-intrusive hybrid WCET estimation using waypoint graphs. In: WCET. OASICS, vol. 55, pp. 4:1–4:11. Schloss Dagstuhl - Leibniz-Zentrum fuer Informatik (2016)
10. Dreyer, B., Hochberger, C., Wegener, S., Weiss, A.: Precise continuous non-intrusive measurement-based execution time estimation. In: WCET. OASICS, vol. 47, pp. 45–54. Schloss Dagstuhl - Leibniz-Zentrum fuer Informatik (2015)
11. Eliot, C., Hudak, P.: Functional reactive animation. In: Proceedings of ICFP 2007, pp. 163–173. ACM (1997)
12. Freescale Semiconductor, Inc.: P4080 Advanced QorIQ Debug and Performance Monitoring Reference Manual, Rev. F (2012)
13. Gottschling, P., Hochberger, C.: ReEP: a toolset for generation and programming of reconfigurable datapaths for event processing. In: 2017 IEEE International Parallel and Distributed Processing Symposium Workshops (IPDPSW), pp. 141–149 (2017)
14. Intel Corporation: Intel(R) 64 and IA-32 Architectures Software Developer's Manual (2016)

15. Jakšić, S., Bartocci, E., Grosu, R., Ničković, D.: Quantitative monitoring of STL with edit distance. In: Falcone, Y., Sánchez, C. (eds.) RV 2016. LNCS, vol. 10012, pp. 201–218. Springer, Cham (2016). https://doi.org/10.1007/978-3-319-46982-9_13

16. Leucker, M.: Teaching runtime verification. In: Khurshid, S., Sen, K. (eds.) RV 2011. LNCS, vol. 7186, pp. 34–48. Springer, Heidelberg (2012). https://doi.org/10.1007/978-3-642-29860-8_4

17. Leucker, M., Schallhart, C.: A brief account of runtime verification. J. Log. Algebraic Program. **78**(5), 293–303 (2009)

18. Leucker, M., Sánchez, C., Scheffel, T., Schmitz, M., Schramm, A.: TeSSLa: runtime verification of non-synchronized real-time streams (2017). unpublished

19. Lu, H., Forin, A.: Automatic processor customization for zero-overhead online software verification. IEEE Trans. VLSI Syst. **16**(10), 1346–1357 (2008)

20. Maler, O., Nickovic, D.: Monitoring temporal properties of continuous signals. In: Lakhnech, Y., Yovine, S. (eds.) FORMATS/FTRTFT -2004. LNCS, vol. 3253, pp. 152–166. Springer, Heidelberg (2004). https://doi.org/10.1007/978-3-540-30206-3_12

21. Moreano, N., Borin, E., de Souza, C., Araujo, G.: Efficient datapath merging for partially reconfigurable architectures. IEEE Trans. Comput. Aided Des. Integr. Circuits Syst. **24**(7), 969–980 (2005)

22. Moreno, C., Fischmeister, S.: Non-intrusive runtime monitoring through power consumption: a signals and system analysis approach to reconstruct the trace. In: Falcone, Y., Sánchez, C. (eds.) RV 2016. LNCS, vol. 10012, pp. 268–284. Springer, Cham (2016). https://doi.org/10.1007/978-3-319-46982-9_17

23. Nutt, G.J.: Tutorial: computer system monitors. SIGMETRICS Perform. Eval. Rev. **5**(1), 41–51 (1976)

24. Reinbacher, T., Függer, M., Brauer, J.: Runtime verification of embedded real-time systems. Form. Methods Syst. Des. **44**(3), 203–239 (2014)

25. Roşu, G., Chen, F., Ball, T.: Synthesizing monitors for safety properties: this time with calls and returns. In: Leucker, M. (ed.) RV 2008. LNCS, vol. 5289, pp. 51–68. Springer, Heidelberg (2008). https://doi.org/10.1007/978-3-540-89247-2_4

26. Shobaki, M.E., Lindh, L.: A hardware and software monitor for high-level system-on-chip verification. In: ISQED, pp. 56–61. IEEE Computer Society (2001)

27. Solet, D., Béchennec, J., Briday, M., Faucou, S., Pillement, S.: Hardware runtime verification of embedded software in SoPC. In: SIES, pp. 171–176. IEEE (2016)

28. Stollon, N.: On-Chip Instrumentation: Design and Debug for Systems on Chip, 1st edn. Springer, London (2010). https://doi.org/10.1007/978-1-4419-7563-8

29. Tsai, J.J.P., Fang, K., Chen, H., Bi, Y.: A noninterference monitoring and replay mechanism for real-time software testing and debugging. IEEE Trans. Softw. Eng. **16**(8), 897–916 (1990)

30. Weiss, A., Lange, A.: Trace-data processing and profiling device. EP Patent EP 2873983 A1, May 2015

31. Weiss, A., Lange, A.: Trace-data processing and profiling device. US Patent 9286186 B2, March 2016

Sound Transpilation from Binary to Machine-Independent Code

Roberto Metere[1]([⊠]), Andreas Lindner[2]([⊠]), and Roberto Guanciale[2]([⊠])

[1] Newcastle University, Newcastle upon Tyne, UK
r.metere2@ncl.ac.uk
[2] KTH Royal Institute of Technology, Stockholm, Sweden
{andili,robertog}@kth.se

Abstract. In order to handle the complexity and heterogeneity of modern instruction set architectures, analysis platforms share a common design, the adoption of hardware-independent intermediate representations. The usage of these platforms to verify systems down to binary-level is appealing due to the high degree of automation they provide. However, it introduces the need for trusting the correctness of the translation from binary code to intermediate language. Achieving a high degree of trust is challenging since this transpilation must handle (i) all the side effects of the instructions, (ii) multiple instruction encoding (e.g. ARM Thumb), and (iii) variable instruction length (e.g. Intel). We overcome these problems by formally modeling one of such intermediate languages in the interactive theorem prover HOL4 and by implementing a proof-producing transpiler. This tool translates ARMv8 programs to the intermediate language and generates a HOL4 proof that demonstrates the correctness of the translation in the form of a simulation theorem. We also show how the transpiler theorems can be used to transfer properties verified on the intermediate language to the binary code.

Keywords: Binary analysis · Formal verification · Proof producing analysis · Theorem proving

1 Introduction

Despite the existence of formally verified compilers, the verification of binary code is a critical task to guarantee trustworthiness of critical systems. This is particularly necessary for software mixing high-level language with assembly (system software), using ad-hoc languages and compilers (specialized software), in presence of instruction set extensions (like encryption and decryption), and when the source code is not available (binary blobs). This necessity is not only limited to the general-purpose computing scenario but also applies to connected embedded systems, where software bugs can enable a remote attacker to tamper with the security of automobiles, payment services, and smart IoT devices.

© Springer International Publishing AG 2017
S. Cavalheiro and J. Fiadeiro (Eds.): SBMF 2017, LNCS 10623, pp. 197–214, 2017.
https://doi.org/10.1007/978-3-319-70848-5_13

The need of semi-automatic analysis techniques for binary code has lead to the development of several tools [7, 24, 25]. To handle the complexity and heterogeneity of modern instruction set architectures (ISAs), all these tools followed a common design: They have introduced a platform independent intermediate representation that allows to implement analysis independently of (i) names and number of registers, (ii) instruction decoding, (iii) endianness of memory access, and (iv) instruction side-effects (like updating conditional flags or the stack pointer). This intermediate representation is often a dialect of the Valgrind's IR [21]. Soundness of the transpiler (i.e. the tool translating from machine code to intermediate language) should not be foregone: It may have to handle multiple instruction encoding (e.g. ARM Thumb), variable instruction length (e.g. Intel), and complex side effects of instructions (e.g. ARM branch with link and conditional executions). Clearly, a transpiler bug jeopardizes the soundness of all analyses done on the intermediate representation.

Our strategy to handle this issue is to use formal models of the ISA and of the intermediate language of the analyses platform, and to formally demonstrate that the transpilation is correct. We chose ARMv8 [17] as demonstrating ISA, reusing the model for the HOL4 theorem prover that was previously developed in [9, 10]. For the target language, we implemented a deep-embedding of the Intermediate Language of the Binary Analysis Platform [7] (BIL) in the HOL4 logic and implemented its small-step semantics. Verification of the transpilation is done via a HOL4 proof producing transpiler, which translates ARMv8 programs to BIL programs, and yields the HOL4 proof that demonstrates its correctness. The theorem establishes a simulation between the input binary program and the generated BIL program, showing that the two programs have the same behavior. Our contribution enables a verifier to prove properties of the generated BIL program (i.e. by directly using the theorem prover or proof-producing analysis techniques) and to transfer them to the original ARMv8 program using the generated simulation theorems.

Outline. We present the state of the art and the previous works relating to our contribution in Sect. 2. Section 3 introduces the HOL4 formal models of the ARMv8 ISA and the BIL language. Section 4 presents the certifying transpiler. We demonstrate that the theorems produced by the transpiler can be used to transfer verification conditions in Sect. 5, where we test and evaluate our development too. We give concluding remarks in Sect. 6.

2   Related Work

Recent works have shown that formal techniques are ready to achieve detailed verification of real software, making it possible to provide low-level platforms with unprecedented security guarantees [1, 8, 13]. For such system software, limiting the verification to the source code level is undesirable. A modern compiler (e.g. GCC) consists of several millions of lines of code, in contrast to micro-kernels that consist of few thousand lines of code, making it difficult to trust the compiler output even when optimization is disabled[1].

To overcome this limitation, formally verified compilers [6,14,15] and proof/producing compilers [16] have been developed. Similarly to our work, these compilers use detailed models of the underlying ISA to show the correctness of their output. This usually involves a simulation theorem, which demonstrates that the behavior of the produced binary code resembles the one specified by the semantics of the high level language (e.g. C or ML). These theorems permit properties verified at the source-level to be automatically transferred to the binary-level. For instance, CompCert has been used in [3] to verify security of OpenSSL HMAC by transferring functional correctness of the source code to the produced binary.

Even if formally verified compilers obviate the need for trusting their output, they do not fulfill all the needs of verified system software. Some of these compilers target languages that are unsuitable for developing system software (e.g. ML cannot be used to develop a microkernel due to its garbage collector). Also, they do not support mixing the high-level language with assembly code, which is necessary for storing and restoring the CPU context or for managing the page table. Some of the effects of these operations can break the assumptions made to define a precise semantics of the high level language (e.g. a memory write can alter the page table which in turn affects the virtual memory layout). Also, some properties (e.g. absence of side channels due to non-secure accesses to the caches) cannot be verified at the source code level; the analysis must be aware of the exact sequence of memory accesses performed by the software. Finally, binary blob analysis is imperative for verifying memory safety of binary code whose source code is not available (e.g. the power management of ARM trusted firmware).

Unfortunately, detailed formal specifications of machine languages (e.g. the ones used to verify compiler correctness [11]) consist of thousands of lines of definitions. The complexity of these models makes them unusable to directly verify any binary code that is not a toy example. Moreover, the target verification tools, usually interactive theorem provers, provide little or no support for either automatic reasoning or reuse of algorithms among different hardware models. To make machine-code verification proofs reusable by different architectures, Myreen et al. [20] developed a proof-producing decompilation procedure. Those tools have been implemented in the HOL4 system and have been used by the seL4 project to check that the binary code produced by the compiler is correct, permitting to transfer properties verified at the source code level to the actual binary code executed by the CPU [22]. The same framework has been used to verify a bignum integer library [19]. However, the automatism provided by this framework is still far from what is provided by today's binary analysis platforms (e.g. [7,24,25]). These provide tools to compute and analyze control-flow graphs, to perform abstract interpretation and symbolic execution, to verify

---

[1] An example of a very recent bug found in GCC: https://gcc.gnu.org/bugzilla/show_bug.cgi?id=80180.

contracts, and to verify information flow properties [2]. On the other hand, their usage requires to trust the used transpiler. Due to the complexity of writing a transpiler for each architecture, recent work has been done to synthesize the transpiler from compiler backends [12]. However, this requires to trust both: the synthesis procedure and the compiler backend.

In this paper, we address this issue by providing sound transpilation of ARMv8 binary code to the intermediate language of BAP. BAP is an analysis platform that provides utilities to compute and analyze control-flow graphs, to transform programs (e.g. by unrolling cycles), to verify contracts via generation of weakest preconditions and their export to SMT solvers. The platform has also been externally extended with tools for information flow security based on relational analysis. We developed a HOL4 formal model of the BAP intermediate language, which can be used to provide precise semantics of programs expressed in BIL and to verify soundness of analysis tools. This allows us to implement a proof-producing transpiler, which can translate an ARMv8 program to a BIL program while generating a HOL4 proof that demonstrates its correctness.

3   Formal HOL4 Models

3.1   The ARMv8 Model

In our work, we use the ARMv8 model developed by Fox [10], which is constructed from the pseudocode described in the ARM specification [17] and provides a detailed HOL4 formalization of the effects of the instructions, taking into account the different execution modes, flags, and other characteristics of the processor behavior.

The system state is modeled as a tuple $s = \langle r, sr, p, c, m \rangle$. Here, r represents a sequence of 64-bit general purpose registers. We identify the i-th register with $r(i)$. The tuple $sr = \langle pc, sp, lr \rangle$ contains the special registers representing the program counter, the stack pointer, and the link register respectively. The tuple p representing the current processor state and contains the arithmetical flags, the execution mode, and the interrupt disabling. The tuple c encodes the system and coprocessor registers, it also contains the current endianness and the configuration of the Memory Management Unit. The 64-bit addressable memory is modeled as the function $m : \mathbb{B}^{64} \to \mathbb{B}^8$. Finally, the system behavior is represented by the deterministic transition relation $s \to s'$, describing how the ARM state s reaches the state s' by executing a single instruction. Hereafter, we use . to access tuple fields; for example $s.sr.pc$ states for the program counter of the state s.

The HOL4 model consists of hundreds of definitions and its complexity makes it difficult to analyze large programs. To simplify the analyses, the model is equipped with a mechanism to statically compute the effects of a single instruction via the *arm_step* function. Let i be the binary encoding of an instruction and ad be the address where the instruction is stored, then the function

$arm\_step(i, ad)$ returns a list of step theorems $[st_1, \ldots, st_n]$. Each theorem st_j has the following structure:

$$\forall s.\, \text{read}_{32}(s.m, s.sr.pc) = i \wedge s.sr.pc = ad \wedge c_j(s) \Rightarrow s \rightarrow t_j(s)$$

where read_{32} is a function that reads 32 bits from the memory. Intuitively, each step theorem describes one of the possible behaviors of the instruction and consists of the guard condition c_j that enables the transition and the function t_j that transforms the starting state into the next state. We use three examples to illustrate this mechanism.

Let the instruction stored at the address 0x1000000c be the addition of the registers $x0$ and $x1$ into the register $x0$ (whose encoding is 0x8b000020), the step function produces the following step theorem:

$$\forall s.\, \text{read}_{32}(s.m, s.sr.pc) = \text{0x8b000020} \wedge s.sr.pc = \text{0x1000000c} \Rightarrow$$
$$s \rightarrow \big(\lambda s'.s' \text{ with } r(0) = s'.r(0) + s'.r(1) \text{ with } sr.pc = s'.sr.pc + 4\big)\, s$$

(where s' with $r(0) = v$ updates the register zero of the state s' with v). In this case, only one theorem is generated, and there is no guard condition (i.e. c_1 is a tautology).

Some ARMv8 instructions (i.e. conditional branches) can have different behavior according to the value of some state components. In these cases, the step function produces as many theorems as the number of possible execution cases. For example, the output of the step function for the Signed Greater Than (GT) branch consists of the following two theorems:

$$\forall s.\, \text{read}_{32}(s.m, s.sr.pc) = \text{0x54fffe8c} \wedge s.sr.pc = \text{0x1000000c}$$
$$\wedge\, s.p.Z = 0 \wedge s.p.N = s.p.V \Rightarrow$$
$$s \rightarrow (\lambda s'.s' \text{ with } sr.pc = s'.sr.pc - \text{0x30})s$$

$$\forall s.\, \text{read}_{32}(s.m, s.sr.pc) = \text{0x54fffe8c} \wedge s.sr.pc = \text{0x1000000c}$$
$$\wedge \neg\, (s.p.Z = 0 \wedge s.p.N = s.p.V) \Rightarrow$$
$$s \rightarrow (\lambda s'.s' \text{ with } sr.pc = s'.sr.pc + 4)s$$

That is, if the test succeeds (i.e. $c_1 = s.p.Z = 0 \wedge s.p.N = s.p.V$ holds) then the jump is taken (in this case jumping back in a loop to the address $pc - \text{0x30}$), otherwise (i.e. $c_2 = \neg(s.p.Z = 0 \wedge s.p.N = s.p.V)$) holds) the jump is not taken (the program counter is updated to point to the next instruction). Notice that for every state s the condition $c_1 \vee c_2$ hold.

Finally, some ARMv8 instructions (i.e. memory stores) can have unsound behavior if some conditions are not met. In these cases, the step function generates the step theorems only for the correct behaviors; for a given instruction, let $st_1, \ldots, st_n$ be the generated theorems and $c_1, \ldots, c_n$ the corresponding guards, the behavior of the instruction is soundly deduced by the step function for every state s such that $\bigvee_j c_j(s)$ holds and can not be deduced otherwise. For example, the output of the step function for a memory store consists of the theorem:

$$\forall s.\ \text{read}_{32}(s.m, s.sr.pc) = \texttt{0xf90007e0} \wedge s.sr.pc = \texttt{0x1000000c}$$
$$\wedge\ aligned(s.sr.sp + 8) \Rightarrow$$
$$s \rightarrow \left(\begin{array}{l} \lambda s'.s' \text{ with } m = write_{64}(s'.m, s'.sr.sp\ + 8, s'.r(0)) \\ \text{with } sr.pc = s'.sr.pc + 4 \end{array} \right) s$$

Intuitively, the step function can predict the behavior only for states having the target address (i.e. $s.sr.sp + 8$) aligned.

3.2   The BIL Model

The target of our transpilation is BIL. In this language, a statement has only explicit state changes, i.e. there are no implicit side effects, and it can only affect one variable.

BIL's syntax is depicted in Table 1. A program is a list of blocks, each one consisting of a uniquely identifying label (i.e. a string or an integer) and a list of atomic statements. A statement can affect the state by (i) assigning the evaluation of an expression to a variable, (ii) (conditionally or unconditionally) modifying the control flow, (iii) halting the system in a successful state, and (iv) terminating the system in a failure state if an assertion does not hold. As usual, labels are used to refer to the specific locations in the program and can be the target of jump statements. BIL expressions are built using constants (i.e. strings and integers), conditionals (i.e. **ifthenelse**), standard binary and unary operators (ranged over by $\Diamond_b$ and $\Diamond_u$ respectively) for finite integer arithmetic, and accessing variables of the environment (i.e. **var**). Additionally, two types of expressions can operate on memories. The expression **load** $(exp_1, exp_2, \tau_{reg,n})$ reads n bytes from the memory exp_1 starting from the address exp_2. The expression **store** $(exp_1, exp_2, exp_3, \tau_{reg,n})$ returns a new memory in which all the locations have the same values as the initial memory exp_1 except the addresses $exp_2 + i$ where $i \in [0 \dots n-1]$ that contain the chunks of exp_3.

Hereafter we use Δ to represent the set of all possible strings. These can be used to identify both labels and variable names. We use τ to range over BIL data types; let $n \in \{1, 8, 16, 32, 64\}$, the type for words of n-bits is denoted by $\tau_{reg,n}$ and the type for memories addressed using n-bits is denoted by $\tau_{mem,n}$. We use T and V to represent the set of all BIL types and values respectively.

A program b is well-defined if it has no duplicate block labels and each block has at least one statement. In the following we assume that all programs are well defined. Notice that the program b is not part of the state, since it is not allowed to be changed dynamically.

A BIL environment σ maps variable names (given as strings) to pairs of type and value; $\sigma : \Delta \rightarrow (T \times V)$. Types of variables are immutable and any wrongly typed operation produces a run-time failure. The semantics of BIL expressions is modeled by the evaluation function *eval*: It takes an expression α and an environment σ and yields either a value having a type in T or $\bot$. The evaluation

Table 1. BIL's syntax

$$
\begin{aligned}
program \ &:= \ block^* \\
block \ &:= \ (string \mid integer, stmt^*) \\
stmt \ &:= \ \mathbf{assign}\,(string, exp) \mid \\
& \quad \mathbf{jmp}\,(exp) \mid \mathbf{cjmp}\,(exp, exp, exp) \mid \\
& \quad \mathbf{halt} \mid \mathbf{assert}\,(exp) \\
exp \ &:= \ string \mid integer \mid \\
& \quad \mathbf{ifthenelse}\,(exp, exp, exp) \mid \\
& \quad \Diamond_u \, exp \mid exp \, \Diamond_b \, exp \mid \mathbf{var} \; string \mid \\
& \quad \mathbf{load}\,(exp, exp, \tau) \mid \mathbf{store}\,(exp, exp, exp, \tau)
\end{aligned}
$$

intuitively follows the semantics of operations by recursively evaluating the sub-expressions given as operands. The value $\bot$ results when operators and types are incompatible, thus modeling a type error, which in turn is used by the statement semantics to cause the program counter to transition to the error state $\bot$.

A BIL state $\gamma = (\sigma, p) \in \Gamma$ is a pair of an environment σ and a program counter p. Let $L = \Delta \cup \mathbb{B}^{64}$ be the set of all labels, a program counter p is an element of the set $\Lambda = (L \times \mathbb{N}) \cup \{\bot, \top\}$. While executing a program, the program counter is $(l, n) \in L \times \mathbb{N}$, where l is the label of the executing block and n is the index for the executing statement within this block. A successfully halting program results in the program counter being $\top$. Failures (e.g. type mismatch or failing assertion) terminate the program and set the program counter to $\bot$.

The system behavior is modeled by the deterministic transition relation $b : \gamma \rightsquigarrow \gamma'$, which describes the execution of one BIL statement. In HOL4, this relation is modeled by the execution function exc, which defines the small step semantics of one statement.

The execution of $\mathbf{assign}(X, \alpha)$ assigns the evaluation of the expression α to the variable X. Let $v = eval\,(\alpha, \sigma)$ and t be the type of v, the value of the variable is updated in the context $(\sigma\,[X \leftarrow (t, v)])$ and the program counter is incremented. The statement fails in case of a type mismatch: $v = \bot$ or $\sigma(X) = (t', \_) \wedge t \neq t'$.

The statement $\mathbf{halt}$ sets the program counter to $\top$ and thereby terminates execution. The statement $\mathbf{assert}\,(\alpha)$ just increments the program counter if the expression evaluates to true (i.e. $(\tau_{reg,1}, 1) = eval\,(\alpha, \sigma)$) and terminates in an error state otherwise.

The execution of $\mathbf{jmp}\,(\alpha)$ jumps to the beginning of the referenced block, by setting the program counter to $(eval\,(\alpha, \sigma), 0)$. If the type of α is neither string nor integer then the statement fails. The statement $\mathbf{cjmp}\,(\alpha_c, \alpha_1, \alpha_2)$ changes the control flow based on the condition α_c. The statement fails if the type of the condition is not $\tau_{reg,1}$ or the the targets (i.e. $eval\,(\alpha_1, \sigma)$ or $eval\,(\alpha_2, \sigma)$) are not valid labels. Notice that the targets of the jump are evaluated using the current context, allowing BIL to express indirect jumps that are resolved at run-time.

4   The Transpiler

The translation procedure uses a mapping of HOL4 ARM states to BIL states. Every ARM state field is mapped to a BIL variable or to the program counter: For example, the variable $R0$ represents the register number zero, the variable MEM represents the system memory, and the BIL program counter reflects the ARM program counter. This mapping induces a simulation relation $\sim \subseteq \Gamma \times S$ that relates BIL states to ARM states.

To transform an ARM program to the corresponding BIL fragment we need to capture all the possible effects of the program execution in terms of affected registers, flags and memory locations. The generated BIL fragment should emulate the behaviour of the instructions executed on an ARM machine. This goal is accomplished by reusing the arm_step function and the following three HOL4 certifying procedures.

- A procedure to translate HOL4 word terms (i.e. those having type $\mathbb{B}^{64}$, $\mathbb{B}^8$, $\mathbb{B}$ etc.) to BIL expressions. This procedure is used to convert the guards of the step theorems and the expressions contained in the transformation functions.
- A procedure to translate a single instruction to the corresponding BIL fragment. This procedure computes the possible effects of an instruction using the transformation functions of the step theorems. It also symbolically executes the resulting BIL fragment to demonstrate that it emulates the effects of the translated instruction.
- A procedure that glues together the theorems produced for the instructions to translate the entire ARM program.

To phrase the theorem produced by the transpiler we introduce the following notations. An ARM program π is represented by a finite set of pairs (ad_j, i_j), where each pair represents that the instruction i_j is located at the address ad_j. The predicate $stored(s, \pi)$ states that the program π is stored in the memory of the state s (formally, $stored(s, \pi) \stackrel{\text{def}}{=} \forall (ad_j, i_j) \in \pi. \, \text{read}_{32}(s.m, ad_j) = i_j$). The predicate $start\text{-}block(p)$ holds if a BIL program counter p points to the first statement of a block. For readability, let $\gamma = (\sigma, p)$, we use $\gamma \neq \bot$ and $start\text{-}block(\gamma)$ to denote $p \neq \bot$ and $start\text{-}block(p)$ respectively. We denote n transitions of ARM states with $\to^n$, and n transitions of BIL states with $\leadsto^n$. The translation procedure produces a theorem that resembles compiler correctness[2]:

Theorem 1. Let ad_0 be the entry point of the ARM program π. For every ARM state s and BIL state γ, if $stored(s, \pi)$, $s.sr.pc = ad_0$, and $\gamma \sim s$, then

1. for every $n > 0$ if $s \to^n s'$ then
   $$\exists n' > 0. \, b : \gamma \leadsto^{n'} \gamma' \wedge (\gamma' = \bot \vee \gamma' \sim s'), \text{ and}$$
2. for every $n' > 0$ if $b : \gamma \leadsto^{n'} \gamma' \wedge start\text{-}block(\gamma') \wedge \gamma' \neq \bot$ then
   $$\exists n > 0. \, s \to^n s' \wedge \gamma' \sim s'.$$

---

[2] The ARM and BIL transition systems are deterministic and live, thus the transition relations are total functions. For this reason we omit quantifiers over the states on the right hand side of transitions, since they always exist and are unique.

The meaning of the transpiler theorem is depicted in Fig. 1a. Each ARM instruction is translated to a single BIL block consisting of multiple statements. Assuming that the program is stored in the ARM memory, the state is configured to start the execution from the entry point ad_0 of the program, and the initial HOL4 ARM state resembles the initial BIL states, then (1) for every state s' reachable by the ARM model, there is an execution of the BIL program b that results (after n' statements) in either an error state ($\gamma' = \bot$) or in a state γ' that resembles s', and (2) for every state γ' reachable by the BIL program after the competition of a block ($start\text{-}block(\gamma')$), there is an execution of the ARM program that re-establishes the simulation relation.

Error states permit to identify if an initial configuration can cause a program to reach a state that cannot be handled by the transpiler (e.g. self-modifying programs or programs containing instructions whose behavior can not be predicted by the step function). It is worth noticing that these cases can not be identified statically without knowing the program preconditions (e.g. misaligned memory accesses can be caused by the initial content of the stack where pointers are stored).

4.1 Translation of Expressions

In order to build the transpiler on top of the step function, the HOL4 expressions occurring in the guards and the transformation functions must be converted to BIL expressions. For example, while translating the binary instruction 0x54fffe8c of Sect. 3.1 to a conditional jump, the expressions $s.p.Z = 0 \wedge s.p.N = s.p.V$ and $s'.sr.pc - \text{0x30}$ must be expressed in BIL to generate the condition and the target of the jump respectively.

Let e be a HOL4 expression, the output of the transpiler is the theorem $\forall \sigma. A(\sigma) \Rightarrow (eval\,(\alpha, \sigma) = e)$, stating that, if the environment satisfies the assumption A, then the evaluation of α is e. These assumptions usually constrain the values of the variables in the environment to match the free variables of the HOL4 expressions. For instance, for the expression $s.p.N = s.p.V$ the transpiler generates the theorem $\forall \sigma, s.(\sigma(''N'') = (\tau_1, s.p.N) \wedge \sigma(''V'') = (\tau_1, V)) \Rightarrow (eval\,((\mathbf{var}\ ''N'' = \mathbf{var}\ ''V''), \sigma) = (N = V))$.

If a HOL4 operator has no direct correspondence in BIL, the transpiler uses a set of manually verified theorems to justify the emulation of the operator via a composition of the primitive BIL operators. This is the case for expressions that involve conversion of words to natural numbers and arithmetic operations with arbitrary precision. A relevant example is the computation of the *carry (overflow) flag* in 64-bit additions. Following the pseudocode of the ARMv8 reference manual [17], the step theorem contains the expression $[x] + [y] < 2^{64}$, where $x, y \in \mathbb{B}^{64}$ and $[\cdot] : \mathbb{B}^{64} \to \mathbb{N}$ is their interpretation as natural numbers. Both the inequality and the addition cannot be directly converted as BIL expression, because BIL can only handle numbers up to 64 bits. For the *carry flag* the transpiler uses the theorem $\forall n > 0.\ \forall x, y \in \mathbb{B}^n.\ ([x] + [y] < 2^n) \Leftrightarrow (x \gg 2 + y \gg 2 + (x\ \&\ 1) * (y\ \&\ 1) < 2^{n-1})$.

4.2   Translation of Single Instructions

The transpilation of a single instruction takes three arguments: the binary code i of the instruction, the address ad of the instruction in memory, and a HOL4 predicate $q_m : \mathbb{B}^{64} \to \mathbb{B}$. The latter argument identifies which memory addresses should not be modified by the instruction and is used to guarantee that the ARM program is not self-modifying. In fact, a self-modifying program cannot be transformed to equivalent BIL programs (due to BIL following the Harvard architecture). If an instruction modifies the program code then then the translated BIL program must terminate in an error state. The predicate q_m is used to instrument the instruction transpiler with the information about where the program code is stored.

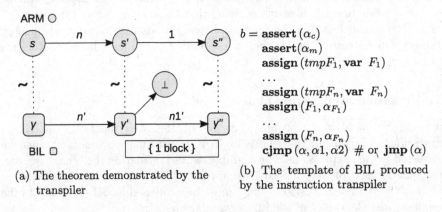

(a) The theorem demonstrated by the transpiler

(b) The template of BIL produced by the instruction transpiler

Fig. 1. Translating procedure

An ARM instruction is translated to a single BIL block, following the template of Fig. 1b. Hereafter we detail its generation and the verification of its correctness.

The transpiler uses the *arm_step* function to compute the behavior of the input instruction i and to generate the step theorems $[st_1, \ldots, st_n]$. These are used to demonstrate $\forall s.(\mathrm{read}_{32}(s.m, s.sr.pc) = i \wedge s.sr.pc = ad) \Rightarrow s \to t(s)$ where $t(s) = if\ c_1(s)\ then\ t_1(s)\ else\ if\ \ldots\ else\ if\ c_n(s)\ then\ t_n(s)$, and c_j and t_j are the guards and transformation functions of the step theorems respectively.

The behavior of the instruction can be soundly deduced by the step function only if one of the c_j predicate holds (see Sect. 3.1). The transpiler simplifies the disjunction of the guards demonstrating $\forall s. \bigvee_j c_j(s) = e_c$ (where e_c is a HOL4 predicate) and translates it to a BIL expression α_c (demonstrating $\forall \sigma, s.((\sigma, p) \sim s) \Rightarrow (eval\,(\alpha_c, \sigma) = e_c))$. The BIL statement **assert** (α_c) is generated as preamble of the instruction. Intuitively, if an ARM state s does not satisfy any guard, then any similar BIL state (σ, p) does not satisfy the assertion, causing the BIL program to terminate in a error state. On the other hand, if the

BIL state satisfies the assertion, then every similar ARM state satisfies at least one of the guards, thus the instruction's behavior can be deduced by the step function.

The second task is to translate the effects of the instruction on every field of the ARM state. Let f be one field of the ARM state (e.g. $f = r(0)$ is the register zero) and let F be the corresponding variable of BIL according to the relation $\sim$. The transpiler uses HOL4 rewriting to compute the new value e_F of the field (and demonstrating $\forall s.(t(s)).f = e_F$). If $e_F = s.f$ then the ARM field is not affected by the instruction and the corresponding variable F should not be modified by the generated BIL block, otherwise the variable F must be updated accordingly. The expression e_F is translated to obtain the theorem $\forall \sigma.eval\,(\alpha_F, \sigma) = e_F$ and the BIL statement $\mathbf{assign}\,(F, \alpha_F)$ is generated. A complication raises when there are instructions affecting several state variables, and whose resulting values depend on each other (i.e. imagine an instruction swapping registers zero and one, where $t(s) = s$ $with$ $\{r(0) = s.r(1)$ and $r(1) = s.r(0)\}$). To handle these cases, the translation procedure generates a statement $\mathbf{assign}\,(tmpF, \mathbf{var}\ F)$, which backups the value of the variable F into the temporary variable $tmpF$.

Special care is needed for memory updates (i.e. $f = m$). The BIL program should fail if it updates a memory location where q_m holds. The transpiler inspects the expression e_{MEM} to identify the addresses that can be changed by the instruction and extracts the corresponding set of $\mathbb{B}^{64}$ expressions $e_1, \ldots, e_n$ (in ARM a single instruction can store multiple registers). To ensure that this identification is complete, the transpiler proves $\forall s, a.(\bigwedge_i a \neq e_i) \Rightarrow (e_{MEM}(a) = s.m(a))$. The expression $\bigwedge_i \neg q_m(e_i)$ (which guarantees that no modified address belongs to the reserved memory region) is translated to obtain the theorem $\forall \sigma.eval\,(\alpha_m, \sigma) = \bigwedge_i \neg q_m(e_i)$. Finally the BIL statement $\mathbf{assert}(\alpha_m)$ is added as further preamble of the instruction. If the ARM instruction modifies an address in q_m, then the corresponding BIL state does not satisfy the assertion, causing the BIL program to terminate in an error state.

Symbolic evaluation of the program counter field is used to generate statements that update the control flow. If e_{pc} is syntactically equivalent to if c $then$ e_1 $else$ e_2, then the expressions c, e_1 and e_2 are translated to α_c, α_1 and α_2, and the statement $\mathbf{cjmp}(\alpha_c, \alpha_1, \alpha_2)$ is appended as last statement of the BIL fragment. Otherwise, e_{pc} is directly translated to α and $\mathbf{jmp}(\alpha)$ is appended to the BIL fragment. Whenever possible, e_1, e_2, or e_{pc} are first simplified to constants, thus reducing the number of indirect jumps in the BIL program.

To compute the effects of the generated BIL block, the transpiler uses a small symbolic execution engine. The transpiler uses the intermediate theorems generated during the process to discard the hypotheses of the symbolic execution and to instantiate the expression evaluations. Finally, it establishes the *instruction-theorem*.

Theorem 2. Let i be the binary encoding of the instruction, ad be its location in memory, and q_m the predicate identifying the memory region used to store the complete program. Also, let $block$ be the generated BIL block, n be the corresponding number of BIL statements, and $b[ad]$ be the BIL block of the

BIL program b having label ad. For every ARM state s, BIL state γ, and BIL program b if $\text{read}_{32}(s.m, s.sr.pc) = i$, $s.pc = ad$, $\gamma \sim s$, and $b[ad] = block$, then

1. if $s \to s'$ and $b : \gamma \leadsto^n \gamma'$ then
$$((\gamma' = \bot) \lor (\gamma' \sim s' \land \forall a.q_m(a) \Rightarrow s'.m(a) = s.m(a))), \text{ and}$$
2. for every $n' < n$, if $b : \gamma \leadsto^{n'} \gamma''$ then $\neg start\text{-}block(\gamma'')$.

The theorem shows (1) that if the complete execution of the block succeeds then it behaves equivalently to the ARM instruction and memory in q_m is not modified, and (2) that completing the block requires exactly n steps.

4.3 Transpiling Programs

The theorems generated for every instruction are composed to verify Theorem 1. Property (1) is verified by induction over n, using the predicate $q_{mem}(a) \triangleq a \in \{ad \mid (ad,i) \in \pi\}$. This ensures that the ARM program is in memory after the execution of each instruction, thus allowing to make the precondition of the translation theorem (i.e. $\forall(ad_j, i_j) \in \pi. \, \text{read}_{32}(s.m, ad_j) = i_j$) an invariant.

Property (2) is verified by induction over n'. We split the execution of n' steps (leading from the initial state to γ') in two parts: $n_0' < n'$ steps from the initial state to the last state γ_0 satisfying $start\text{-}block$ and $n_1' = n' - n_0'$ steps from γ_0 to γ'. By inductive hypothesis there must exists n_0 such that the ARM program reaches a state $\gamma_0 \sim s_0$ in n_0 steps. Since $\gamma_0 \sim s_0$ then the program counter of γ_0 points to one of the blocks produced by the transpiler. If γ' satisfies $start\text{-}block$ then we can use the corresponding instruction-theorem to show that n_1' is equal to the length of the block. This and the fact that the ARM transition relation is total enables part (1) of the instruction-theorem, showing that the ARM instruction behaves equivalently to the BIL block.

4.4 Support for More Architectures

In the following, we review the modifications of the certifying procedures needed to support other common computer architectures, like MIPS, x86 and ARMv7.

The transpiler has three main dependencies: A formal model of the architecture, a function producing step theorems, and the definitions of a simulation relation. There exist HOL4 models for x86, x64, ARMv7-M, and MIPS that are equipped with the corresponding step function. On the other hand, the simulation relation can differ for each architecture since it maps machine state fields to BIL variables. In fact, the name, the number, and the type of registers can be very different among unrelated architectures.

The expression translation has to handle the expressions of guard conditions and transformation functions that are present in the step theorems. Since these use HOL4 number and word theories, independently of the architecture, big parts of the translation of Sect. 4.1 can be reused. There are two exceptions: One is the possible usage different word lengths, and the other is the need of proving helper theorems to justify the emulation of operators that have no direct correspondence in BIL (e.g. for the computation of carry flag in ARM).

The transpilation of single instructions of Sect. 4.2 would produce BIL blocks with a similar structure. However, the changed simulation relation can affect the transpilation procedure. In fact, the BIL variables that have to be temporarily saved and the ones that must be modified can be different, matching the different registers. On the other hand, the expressions computing the state transformation are the result of the expression translation and do not require changes. Also, a jump instruction must terminate the instruction block to steer the control flow dependent on program counter changes.

The verification of Theorem 1 by the program transpilation of Sect. 4.3 involves only reasoning on BIL and the theorems generated for the individual instructions. This reasoning can be largely reused since the structure of these individual theorems is unchanged. Even though our proof procedure for this is fairly general, differences in the simulation relation might require slight changes.

5   Using the Transpiler to Verify Binary Programs

The output of the transpiler can be used to verify properties of the translated ARM program. The verification work flow consists of three tasks, (1) proving that the BIL program does not reach error states, (2) proving that the desired properties of the BIL program hold, and (3) using the refinement relation to transfer these properties to the original ARM program. Here, we show that the transpiler output fulfills this purpose for four common verification tasks: Control Flow Graph (CFG) analysis, contract-based verification, partial correctness refinement, and verification of termination.

Program's CFG is essential to many compiler optimizations and static analysis tools. Furthermore, proving control flow integrity ensures resiliency against return-oriented programming [23] and jump-oriented programming attacks [4]. In its simplest form, the CFG consists of a directed connected graph G, whose node set is $\mathbb{B}^{64}$, and a root node ad_0: The graph G contains (ad_1, ad_2) if the program can flow from the address ad_1 to the address ad_2 by executing a single instruction; The root node represents the entry point of the program.

Analyzing the CFG of a binary program requires to deal with indirect jumps. Even if the source program avoids using function pointers, indirect jumps are introduced by the compiler, e.g. to handle function exits and exceptions. For instance, the ARM link register is used to track the return address of functions and can be pushed to and popped from the stack. For this reason, the correctness of the control flow depends on the integrity of the stack itself. Thus, verifying the CFG (G, ad_0) of a program π requires assuming a precondition P, which constraints the content of the heap, stack and registers.

Definition (Control flow graph integrity). For every ARM state s such that $stored(s, \pi)$, $s.sr.pc = ad_0$, and $P(s)$, for every n, if $s \to^n s_1$ and $s_1 \to s_2$ then $(s_1.sr.pc, s_2.sr.pc) \in G$.

It is straightforward to show that CFG integrity can be verified using the transpiler theorem, by defining a BIL precondition P' that corresponds to P, and by proving the following verification conditions.

Condition (BIL control flow integrity). Let $lbl(\gamma) = pc$ be the label of the program counter of the state γ, which is undefined when $pc = \bot$. For every γ such that $P'(\gamma)$ and for every n_1 and n_2, if $b : \gamma \rightsquigarrow^{n_1} \gamma_1 \rightsquigarrow^{n_2} \gamma_2$, $start\text{-}block(\gamma_1)$ and $start\text{-}block(\gamma_2)$, and $(\forall n_3 < n_2.b : \gamma_1 \rightsquigarrow^{n_3} \gamma_3 \Rightarrow \neg start\text{-}block(\gamma_3))$ then $\gamma_1 \neq \bot$, $\gamma_2 \neq \bot$, and $(lbl(\gamma_1), lbl(\gamma_2)) \in G$.

Condition (Transfer of precondition). For every γ, s such that $\gamma \sim s$, if $P(s)$ then $P'(\gamma)$.

Contract based verification consists in verification of Hoare triples to establish partial correctness. Let $P(s)$ and $Q(s, s')$ be two predicates, representing the pre- and post-condition of a contract, verifying that a program π (starting from the entry point ad_0) meets the contract (P, Q) means establishing the following property.

Definition (Contract verification). For every s such that $stored(s, \pi)$, $s.sr.pc = ad_0$ and $P(s)$, for every n_1, if $s \rightarrow^{n_1} s_1$ then $Q(s, s_1)$.

Let PC_{end} be the set of exit points of the program and $End(s_1)$ be $s_1.sr.pc \in PC_{end}$. Usually Q has the form $End(s_1) \Rightarrow Q_1(s, s_1)$, meaning that if the program reached one of its exit points then the post-condition Q_1 is satisfied. This property can be verified using the theorem produced by the transpiler, by identifying a BIL contract (P', Q'), and by proving the following verification conditions:

Condition (BIL contract verification). For every γ such that $P'(\gamma)$ and for every n, if $b : \gamma \rightsquigarrow^n \gamma'$ then $\gamma' \neq \bot$ and $Q'(\gamma, \gamma')$.

Condition (Transfer of contracts). For every γ, γ', s, s' such that $\gamma \sim s$ and $\gamma' \sim s'$, if $P(s)$ then $P'(\gamma)$ and if $Q'(\gamma, \gamma')$ then $Q(s, s')$.

Partial correctness is proved as a refinement using an abstract specification and reusing contract verification. With composability of specifications in mind, we assume that the specification is phrased such that domain and codomain are the same. Let $a_{out} = f_{spec}(a_{in})$ be a functional specification with the signature $f_{spec} : A \rightarrow A$.

Definition (Partial correctness refinement). For every s, a such that $R(s, a)$, forall n_1 such that $s \rightarrow^{n_1} s_1$, if $End(s_1)$ then $R(s_1, f_{spec}(a))$.

Notice, that the refinement relation $R(s, a)$ implicitly contains the mapping from a to s and an invariant to enable establishing the refinement. By using the assumption $R(s, a)$, we can simply derive a verification condition in the shape of the definition for contract-based verification, which can be proved as described before. We call this the binary correctness condition in this context, where $P(s)$

resembles the invariant of the refinement relation, and $Q_1(s, s_1)$ incorporates the functional specification f_{spec} with respect to the mapping of R.

The assertion of total correctness (or functional correctness) additionally requires termination. Therefore, we consider the following definition, where the precondition P should be not stronger than the precondition we used for partial correctness (i.e. the invariant of the refinement relation).

Definition (Termination verification). For every s such that $stored(s, \pi)$, $s.sr.pc = ad_0$ and $P(s)$, exists an n_1 such that $s \rightarrow^{n_1} s_1$ and $End(s_1)$.

To prove this property, we use the theorem produced by the transpiler (i.e. the second clause of Theorem 1), identify an appropriate BIL precondition P', and prove the following conditions.

Condition (BIL termination verification). For every γ such that $P'(\gamma)$, exists an n such that $b : \gamma \leadsto^n \gamma'$ and $End'(\gamma)$.

Condition (Transfer of termination conditions). For every γ, s such that $\gamma \sim s$, if $P(s)$ then $P'(\gamma)$ and if $End'(\gamma)$ then $End(s)$.

5.1   Evaluation

Our contribution counts $\sim$4600 lines of HOL4 code: (1) $\sim$1000 lines for the syntax and the semantics of BIL, the most of which are for the (signed an unsigned) cast operators between bitvectors of different size; (2) $\sim$2000 for the expression transpiler, a fourth of which proves the theorems handling arithmetic conversions; (3) $\sim$1500 for the instruction transpiler, one third of which generates the BIL fragments, and the remaining two thirds generate the proofs of correctness; and (4) the remainder for merging the instruction theorems together and generate the translation of a complete ARM program.

The whole proof-producing transpilation of an instruction takes $\sim$9 s on a modern computer (Intel Core i7-6650U 2.2 GHz). We follow a backward-proof strategy; firstly, we generate the proof goal by invoking the step function, merging its output, translating the expressions and generating the supposedly corresponding BIL code. This first part takes $\sim$1 s. The second part symbolically evaluates the BIL statements. This takes $\sim$6.5 s, with each BIL statement requiring between $\sim$0.5 s and $\sim$1.5 s. In the third and last part, which takes $\sim$2 s, we prove that the simulation relation is established.

As described in Sect. 4.2, the translation of one instruction follows two steps: (i) it translates the ARM instruction to a BIL block, establishing several intermediate theorems (i.e. for translation of expressions), and setting up the goal of Theorem 2, (ii) it demonstrates Theorem 2 in a backward proof, by symbolically evaluating the BIL block and by using the intermediate theorems. The usage of a backward-proof for this procedure provides a naive strategy to speed up analyses: the user can rely on the goal produced in step (1) to translate the ARM program to BIL without generating the corresponding certification theorem. This certificate can be generated offline later. Step (2) can be optimized with additional engineering effort by using a forward-proof strategy. Furthermore, program independent helper theorems can be verified once and reused in this process.

We experimented with the transpiler using various unmodified binary programs produced by a standard GCC, including a bignum library and an implementation of AES encryption. The three C functions `internal_mul`, `newbn`, and `freebn` of the bignum library consist of 38 lines of C code, which are compiled to 141 instructions. After transpilation, we obtain 907 lines of BIL code for these functions. The encryption function of AES consists of 131 lines of C code (excluding the constant lookup tables used for the S-Boxes), which are compiled to 535 instructions. With this example, we obtain 3920 lines of BIL code. We observe that the average binary instruction consists of 6 to 7 BIL statements.

6   Concluding Remarks

We presented the HOL4 formal model of the intermediate language of BAP and the implementation of a transpiler for ARMv8 programs. This is the first work toward this approach, and its results overcome two of the main barriers in adopting binary analysis platforms to formally verifying binary code: the lack of a formal ground to prove analysis correctness and the need for trusting translation soundness.

The formal model of BIL can be used for verifying BAP tools, which are ISA independent and analyze BIL programs, e.g., Dijkstra's weakest precondition propagation, transformation to single static assignment, loop unrolling.

In this paper, we focus on the ARMv8 architecture. To handle other machine architectures (e.g. x86, x64, ARMv7-M, MIPS), new transpilers must be developed. Fortunately, the majority of the transpiler code does not depend on specific ARMv8 features, but on the theorems produced by the step function. There are several other HOL4 models for the main commodity architectures that are equipped with the same functionality [10]. We comment on the required transpiler modifications to support these architectures in Sect. 4.4.

Further research is needed to develop a complete trustworthy binary analysis platform. For example, a trustworthy semi-automatic verification tool based on pre/post conditions for binary code can be implemented by completing two additional tasks: (i) a trustworthy verification condition generator to compute the weakest precondition needed by the BIL program to meet the postcondition, and (ii) a sound satisfiability solver for bitvectors to check if the precondition entails the weakest precondition. For the first task, Vogels et al. [26] verified the soundness of an algorithm for weakest precondition generation in Coq. For the second task, Satisfiability Modulo Theory (SMT) solvers can be used. Böhme et al. [5] demonstrated HOL4 proof reconstruction for Z3 [18] capable of handling the theory of fixed-size bit-vectors.

Acknowledgments. Partially funded by framework grant "IT 2010" from the Swedish Foundation for Strategic Research, and by the KTH CERCES Center for Resilient Critical Infrastructures, which is supported by the Swedish Civil Contingencies Agency.

References

1. Alkassar, E., Hillebrand, M.A., Leinenbach, D., Schirmer, N.W., Starostin, A.: The verisoft approach to systems verification. In: Shankar, N., Woodcock, J. (eds.) VSTTE 2008. LNCS, vol. 5295, pp. 209–224. Springer, Heidelberg (2008). https://doi.org/10.1007/978-3-540-87873-5_18
2. Balliu, M., Dam, M., Guanciale, R.: Automating information flow analysis of low level code. In: SIGSAC Conference on Computer and Communications Security, pp. 1080–1091. ACM (2014)
3. Beringer, L., Petcher, A., Katherine, Q.Y., Appel, A.W.: Verified correctness and security of OpenSSL HMAC. In: USENIX Security Symposium, pp. 207–221 (2015)
4. Bletsch, T., Jiang, X., Freeh, V.W., Liang, Z.: Jump-oriented programming: a new class of code-reuse attack. In: Symposium on Information, Computer and Communications Security, pp. 30–40. ACM (2011)
5. Böhme, S., Fox, A.C.J., Sewell, T., Weber, T.: Reconstruction of Z3's bit-vector proofs in HOL4 and Isabelle/HOL. In: Jouannaud, J.-P., Shao, Z. (eds.) CPP 2011. LNCS, vol. 7086, pp. 183–198. Springer, Heidelberg (2011). https://doi.org/10.1007/978-3-642-25379-9_15
6. Boldo, S., Jourdan, J., Leroy, X., Melquiond, G.: A formally-verified C compiler supporting floating-point arithmetic. In: Symposium on Computer Arithmetic, pp. 107–115. IEEE (2013)
7. Brumley, D., Jager, I., Avgerinos, T., Schwartz, E.J.: BAP: a binary analysis platform. In: Gopalakrishnan, G., Qadeer, S. (eds.) CAV 2011. LNCS, vol. 6806, pp. 463–469. Springer, Heidelberg (2011). https://doi.org/10.1007/978-3-642-22110-1_37
8. Dam, M., Guanciale, R., Nemati, H.: Machine code verification of a tiny ARM hypervisor. In: Workshop on Trustworthy Embedded Devices, Co-located with CCS, pp. 3–12. ACM (2013)
9. Fox, A.: Directions in ISA specification. In: Beringer, L., Felty, A. (eds.) ITP 2012. LNCS, vol. 7406, pp. 338–344. Springer, Heidelberg (2012). https://doi.org/10.1007/978-3-642-32347-8_23
10. Fox, A.: L3: a specification language for instruction set architectures. http://www.cl.cam.ac.uk/~acjf3/l3/. Accessed 2015
11. Fox, A.C., Gordon, M.J., Myreen, M.O.: Specification and verification of ARM hardware and software. In: Hardin, D. (ed.) Design and Verification of Microprocessor Systems for High-Assurance Applications, pp. 221–247. Springer, Boston (2010). https://doi.org/10.1007/978-1-4419-1539-9_8
12. Hasabnis, N., Sekar, R.: Lifting assembly to intermediate representation: a novel approach leveraging compilers. ACM SIGOPS Oper. Syst. Rev. **50**(2), 311–324 (2016)
13. Klein, G., Elphinstone, K., Heiser, G., Andronick, J., Cock, D., Derrin, P., Elkaduwe, D., Engelhardt, K., Kolanski, R., Norrish, M., et al.: seL4: formal verification of an OS kernel. In: Operating systems principles, pp. 207–220. ACM (2009)

14. Kumar, R., Myreen, M.O., Norrish, M., Owens, S.: CakeML: a verified implementation of ML. SIGPLAN Not. **49**, 179–191 (2014). ACM
15. Leroy, X.: Formal verification of a realistic compiler. Commun. ACM **52**(7), 107–115 (2009)
16. Li, G., Owens, S., Slind, K.: Structure of a proof-producing compiler for a subset of higher order logic. In: De Nicola, R. (ed.) ESOP 2007. LNCS, vol. 4421, pp. 205–219. Springer, Heidelberg (2007). https://doi.org/10.1007/978-3-540-71316-6_15
17. Arm Limited: ARM Architecture Reference Manual (ARMv8, for ARMv8-A architecture profile) (2013). http://infocenter.arm.com/help/index.jsp?topic=/com.arm.doc.ddi0487a.h/index.html
18. Moura, L., Bjørner, N.: Z3: an efficient SMT solver. In: Ramakrishnan, C.R., Rehof, J. (eds.) TACAS 2008. LNCS, vol. 4963, pp. 337–340. Springer, Heidelberg (2008). https://doi.org/10.1007/978-3-540-78800-3_24
19. Myreen, M.O., Curello, G.: Proof pearl: a verified bignum implementation in x86-64 machine code. In: Gonthier, G., Norrish, M. (eds.) CPP 2013. LNCS, vol. 8307, pp. 66–81. Springer, Cham (2013). https://doi.org/10.1007/978-3-319-03545-1_5
20. Myreen, M.O., Gordon, M.J.C., Slind, K.: Machine-code verification for multiple architectures - an application of decompilation into logic. In: Formal Methods in Computer-Aided Design, pp. 1–8. IEEE Press (2008)
21. Nethercote, N., Seward, J.: Valgrind: a program supervision framework. Electron. Notes Theor. Comput. Sci. **89**(2), 44–66 (2003)
22. Sewell, T.A.L., Myreen, M.O., Klein, G.: Translation validation for a verified OS kernel. In: SIGPLAN Conference on Programming Language Design and Implementation, pp. 471–482. ACM (2013)
23. Shacham, H.: The geometry of innocent flesh on the bone: return-into-libc without function calls (on the x86). In: Conference on Computer and Communications Security, pp. 552–561. ACM (2007)
24. Shoshitaishvili, Y., Wang, R., Salls, C., Stephens, N., Polino, M., Dutcher, A., Grosen, J., Feng, S., Hauser, C., Krügel, C., Vigna, G.: SOK: (state of) the art of war: offensive techniques in binary analysis. In: Symposium on Security and Privacy, pp. 138–157. IEEE (2016)
25. Song, D., et al.: BitBlaze: a new approach to computer security via binary analysis. In: Sekar, R., Pujari, A.K. (eds.) ICISS 2008. LNCS, vol. 5352, pp. 1–25. Springer, Heidelberg (2008). https://doi.org/10.1007/978-3-540-89862-7_1
26. Vogels, F., Jacobs, B., Piessens, F.: A machine-checked soundness proof for an efficient verification condition generator. In: Symposium on Applied Computing, pp. 2517–2522. ACM (2010)

Using Linear Logic to Verify Requirement Scenarios in Composite Web Service

Kênia Santos de Oliveira$^{(\boxtimes)}$ and Stéphane Julia

Computing Faculty, Federal University of Uberlândia, Uberlândia, MG, Brazil
keniasoli@gmail.com, stephane@ufu.br

Abstract. This paper presents a method for requirements verification in Web service models based on workflow modules. In this approach, a requirement model (a service contract publication) only specify tasks which are of interest of all parties involved in the corresponding Web service. Architectural models (detailed Web service) contain the detailed tasks of all the individual workflow processes that interact through asynchronous communication mechanisms in order to produce the services specified in the requirement model. In the proposed approach, services correspond to scenarios of workflow modules. For each scenario of the requirement and architectural models, a proof tree of Linear Logic is produced and transformed into a precedence graph that specifies task sequence requirements. Precedence graphs of the requirement and architectural models are then compared in order to verify if all the existing scenarios of the requirement model also exist in the architectural model. The comparison of the models is based on the notion of branching bisimilarity that prove behavioral equivalence between distinct finite automatas.

Keywords: Web service · Service Oriented Architecture · Workflow module · Petri nets · Linear Logic · Bisimilarity

1 Introduction

In the context of distributed architecture, Service Oriented Computing (SOC) has been detached. SOC is a generic term representing a new generation of distributed computing platform [4]. This computing paradigm uses services as fundamental elements for applications/solutions development [10]. According to [10], to build the service model, SOC relies on the Service Oriented Architecture (SOA) which is a way of reorganizing software applications and infrastructure into a set of interacting services. SOA has been widely used in order to integrate systems through services that can be reusable by several systems. The architectural model establish by SOA aims to improve the efficiency, agility and the productivity of a business by positioning services as primary means [4].

A service is an organization's business capability that is implemented and available in a distributed environment, on the Internet (or intranet), for that other applications can access it [10]; it is also called a Web service. A service

© Springer International Publishing AG 2017
S. Cavalheiro and J. Fiadeiro (Eds.): SBMF 2017, LNCS 10623, pp. 215–232, 2017.
https://doi.org/10.1007/978-3-319-70848-5_14

performs functions that can be simple requisitions or complex business processes. A distinct functional context is assigned to each service and each service is composed by a set of capabilities related to this context. The capabilities suitable for invocation by external consumer programs are then usually expressed through a service contract publication [4].

One of the main characteristic of Web services is the weak coupling existing between services and the existence of interoperability standards that allows certain services to be grouped together. Service compositions can be implemented in several ways, like orchestration and choreography, for example [3]. In both cases, the composition mechanisms are based on synchronous and asynchronous interaction mechanisms.

For the specification and analysis of Web service compositions, many studies have already considered Petri nets as an appropriate model [7,8,13,18]. In [13], for example, a method was presented for the identification of deadlock-free scenarios in Web service compositions based on the analysis of Linear Logic proof trees. The approach presented by the authors detects specific safe scenarios which ensures that no deadlock situation will be reached during the execution of the composite system. In [8], the services, named modules, are classified as usable (modules that can be used in any composition) or not usable (modules that cannot be used in any composition). In the proposed approach, a framework for the modeling and analysis of Web services based on business processes by help of Petri nets was presented. In [7], the authors address the problem of abstracting and checking correctness of Web service compositions, taking into consideration four variants of Soundness property (Soundness, Weak Soundness, Relaxed Soundness and Easy Soundness).

An important issue in software projects is to ensure that the architectural models reproduce the behavior of the requirement analysis models. Such verification will minimize risks of failure in projects, increasing the guarantee of software quality and avoiding rework costs [6]. Therefore, in this paper, an approach based on a kind of comparative analysis between requirement and architectural models in the context of Web services is presented. The analysis will be based on Linear Logic proofs produced from workflow modules modeled by acyclic Petri nets. A definition of semantic equivalence in the context of Linear Logic will then be introduced, as it has already be performed, for example, in the context of process algebras with the notion of bisimulation [1]. The requirement and architectural models will be based on workflow modules. The approach will consider sound requirement models but the architectural models will not be necessarily sound and may lead the system to a deadlock situation. The proposed approach will accept in particular relaxed sound processes (when all the activities of the system appeared in at least one process that ended correctly).

The remainder of the paper is organized as follows. In Sect. 2, the definition of a workflow module is presented as well as an overview of Linear Logic and of the notion of Branching Bisimilarity. The approach to formally detect requirements present in architectural models based on Web services is proposed in Sect. 3. Finally, Sect. 4 concludes this work.

2   Theoretical Background

2.1   Workflow Module

In general, a Web service is seen as an application accessible to other applications over the Web [9]. The service has a published interface which allows access to the service and can be invoked across the Internet.

According to [8], a Web service can be modeled through the help of an acyclic Petri net called a workflow module. A Petri net, $N = (P, T, F)$, consists of a set of transitions T, a set of places P and a flow relation F. Therefore, a workflow module is defined as a Petri net $N = (P, T, F)$ such as [8]:

1. The set of places is divided into three disjoint sets: internal places P^N, input places P^I and output places P^O.
2. The flow relation is divided into internal flow $F^N \subseteq (P^N \times T) \cup (T \times P^N)$ and communication flow $F^C \subseteq (P^I \times T) \cup (T \times P^O)$.
3. The net $PN = (P^N, T, F^N)$ is a WorkFlow net (an acyclic Petri net that models a workflow process).
4. No transition of the model is connected at the same time to an input place and an output place.

To clarify the concepts defined above, the synthetic example presented in Fig. 1(a) can be considered, where two modules A and B exist. For example, considering the module A, the internal places are iA, $PA1$ and oA, the input places are $PC2$ and $PC3$, and the output places is $PC1$.

When two modules are composed, their common places are merged and the dangling input and output places become the new interface [8]. To achieve a syntactically correct workflow module, it is necessary to add new components

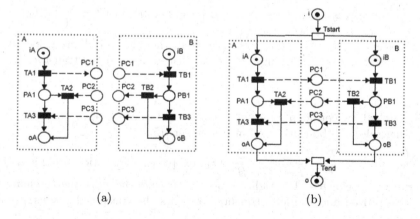

(a)   (b)

Fig. 1. (a) Workflow modules. (b) Composite workflow modules $(A \oplus B)$.

for initialization and termination. Therefore, a composite system is defined as follow [8]:

- Let $A = (P_a, T_a, F_a)$ and $B = (P_b, T_b, F_b)$ be two syntactically compatible modules (if both internal processes are disjoint and each common place is an output place of one module and an input place of the other).
- Let $i, o \notin (P_a \cup P_b)$ be two new places and $t_i, t_o \notin (T_a \cup T_b)$ two new transitions.
- The composite system $A \oplus B$ is given by (P_s, T_s, F_s), such that $P_s = P_a \cup P_b \cup \{i, o\}$, $T_s = T_a \cup T_b \cup \{t_i, t_o\}$ and $F_s = F_a \cup F_b \{(i, t_i), (t_i, \alpha_a), (t_i, a_b), (\omega_a, t_o), (\omega_b, t_o), (t_o, o)\}$.

Figure 1(b) shows the composite system $A \oplus B$ of the workflow modules shown in Fig. 1(a).

2.2 Linear Logic

Linear Logic [5] emphasizes the role of formulas as resources instead of emphasizing truth, as in classical logic, or proof, as in intuitionistic logic.

In the Linear Logic, there are several connectives, but in this paper only two connectives will be used [15]:

- The *times* connective, denoted by $\otimes$, represents simultaneous availability of resources. For instance, $A \otimes B$ represents the simultaneous availability of resources A and B.
- The *linear implies* connective, denoted by $\multimap$, represents a state change. For instance, $A \multimap B$ denotes that consuming A, B is produced; after the production of B, A will not be available anymore.

To translate a Petri net model into a Linear Logic formula, the following definition presented in [15] are used:

- A marking M is a monomial in $\otimes$ and is represented by $M = A_1 \otimes A_2 \otimes ... \otimes A_k$, where A_i are place names.
- A sequent $M, t_i \vdash M'$ represents a scenario, where M and M' are respectively the initial and final markings, and t_i is a list of non-ordered transitions.

To prove a sequent of the Linear Logic a proof tree is built applying rules. In this paper, only three Linear Logic rules are considered. To achieve this, F, G and H will be considered formulas, and Γ and Δ as blocks of formulas. The following rules will be those used in this paper [15]:

- The $\multimap_L$ rule, $\dfrac{\Gamma \vdash F \quad \Delta, G \vdash H}{\Gamma, \Delta, F \multimap G \vdash H} \multimap_L$, expresses a transition firing and generates two sequents. The right sequent represents the subsequent remaining to be proved and the left sequent represents the consumed tokens by this firing.

- The $\otimes_L$ rule, $\dfrac{\Gamma, F, G \vdash H}{\Gamma, F \otimes G \vdash H} \otimes_L$, is used to transform a marking in an atoms list.
- The $\otimes_R$ rule, $\dfrac{\Gamma \vdash F \quad \Delta \vdash G}{\Delta, \Gamma \vdash F \otimes G} \otimes_R$, transforms a sequent such as $A, B \vdash A \otimes B$ into two identity ones $A \vdash A$ and $B \vdash B$.

Linear Logic proof tree is read from the bottom-up. The proof stops when the identity sequent $o \vdash o$ ('o' correspond to a sink place) is produced, when there is not any rule that can be applied or when all the leaves of the proof tree are identity sequents.

The Linear Logic proof trees can be transformed into precedence graphs, as shown in [2], by labeling the corresponding proof trees. To label a proof tree, each time the $\multimap_L$ rule is applied, the corresponding transition t_i label the application of the rule, as well as the atoms produced and consumed. Furthermore, the initial event must be labeled by i_i and the final event must be labeled by f_i. Once the labeling is performed, each identity sequence represents the association of two views of the same atom: the left part of an identity sequent is labeled by the event that produced it and the right part of on identity sequent is labeled by the event that consumed it. The labels are shown in the proof tree above the atoms and below the rules $\multimap_L$. In a precedence graph, the vertices are events and the arcs are identity sequent, i.e. relation between the event that produced the atom and event that consumed the atom [2]. The Sect. 3 shows how proof trees and the corresponding labelings are built.

2.3   Branching Bisimilarity

In the bisimilarity equivalence relation [11], two processes are equivalent if and only if they can always copy or simulate the actions of each other. Bisimilarity is not a suitable equivalence concept for processes with internal behavior, because it does not make the distinction between external actions and internal actions. The distinction between external and internal behavior captures the idea that an environment observing two processes might not be able to see any differences in their behavior while internally the two processes perform different computations [1].

Branching bisimilarity [17] is a variant of bisimilarity; however, it distinguishes external behavior from internal behavior. In case we are interested in processes with the same observable behavior, but with eventually different internal behavior, branching bisimilarity corresponds then to an equivalence concept that can satisfy the kind of requirements (in term of equivalent behavior) that have to be verified in Web services.

To be able to make a distinction between external and internal behavior (hidden events), silent actions can be introduced. Silent actions are actions that cannot be observed. Usually, silent actions are denoted with the action label τ.

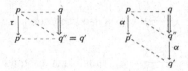

Fig. 2. The essence of branching bisimulation.

According to [1], to define branching bisimilarity, two auxiliary definitions are needed:

1. a relation expressing that a process can evolve into another process by executing a sequence of zero or more τ actions;
2. a predicate expressing that a process can terminate by performing zero or more τ actions.

The Fig. 2, presented in [1], shows the essence of a branching bisimulation. In this figure, τ represents a silent action, α represents an observable action, p, q, p', q', q'' represent processes and the relation '$\Longrightarrow$' represents that one processe can evolve into another process by executing a sequence of zero or more τ actions. The Fig. 2 shows, for example, that the process q can evolve into another process q'' by executing a sequence of zero or more τ actions.

On the left side of the Fig. 2, it is possible to observe that the process p has an equivalence relation with the processes q and q'' and the process p' has an equivalence relation with the process q''. These facts clearly state that two equivalent processes will continue equivalent after the introduction of some additional silent actions in one of the processes or even in both.

On the right side of the Fig. 2, it is possible to observe that the process p has an equivalence relation with the processes q and q'', and the process p' has an equivalence relation with the process q'. These facts clearly state that two equivalent processes will continue equivalent after the introduction of some additional observable actions in one of the processes only if the same observable actions also exists in the other process and respect the same sequence constraints in both processes.

3   Requirement Verification in Composite Web Services

The approach proposed in this paper considers that the requirement model is a Web service contract containing the capabilities suitable for invocation by external consumer. The Web service contract specifies the expected system requirements the parties involved will have to perform; therefore, it only contains the tasks which are of interest to all parties. Figure 3, shows an example of composite Web service contract modeled by workflow modules. This example involves two business partners: a contractor and a subcontractor. As it can be observed in Fig. 3, first the contractor sends an order to the subcontractor. Then, the contractor sends a detailed specification to the subcontractor and the subcontractor sends a cost statement to the contractor. Based on the cost statement,

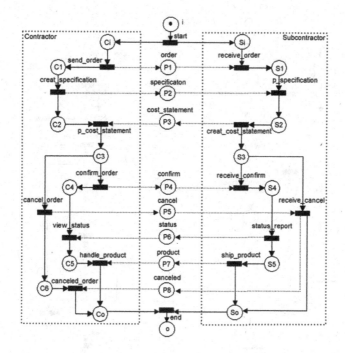

Fig. 3. Composite Web service contract (requirement model).

the contractor can confirm the order or cancel the order. If the order is canceled the process is finalized in both sides. If the order is confirmed, the subcontractor manufactures the desired product and, during this process, it sends a status report to the contractor. Finally, it sends the final product to the contractor.

Considering this composition, it is possible to identify the scenarios that the parties involved in the process will have to perform. In this context a scenario corresponds to a well defined route mapped into the corresponding workflow module and, if the workflow module has more than one route (places with two or more output arcs), more than one scenario will have to be considered then. The approach presented in this paper considers that the composite Web service contract is sound. Such a statement does not necessarily mean that the corresponding architectural model will be sound too, which may lead the system to a deadlock situation.

An architectural model typically contains several tasks which are only of local interest and which do not appear in the service contract. In this approach, the architectural model is also modeled by workflow modules; however, it contains the detailed tasks of the internal workflow processes. Therefore, the architectural model corresponds to a more detailed Web Service.

Figure 4 shows the detailed composition of the Web service, which in this approach, corresponds to the architectural model related to the Web service contract shown in Fig. 3.

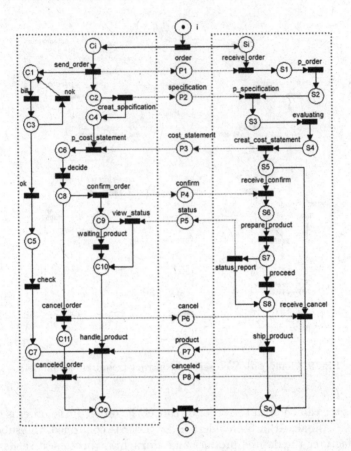

Fig. 4. Composite detailed Web service (architectural model).

To verify if the scenarios of the requirement model are present in the architectural model, the composite models of the Web service contract (Fig. 3) and of the detailed Web service (Fig. 4) are considered. We will call the detailed composite Web service of detailed composite Web Service architecture. Therefore, the proposed method in this work respects the following sequence of steps:

1. build the Linear Logic proof trees for each scenario of the composite Web service contract and transformed the obtained proof trees into the corresponding precedence graphs;
2. build the Linear Logic proof trees for each scenario of the detailed composite Web service architecture and transformed the obtained proof trees into the corresponding precedence graphs;
3. verify the equivalence between the precedence graphs of the composite Web service contract and the precedence graphs of the detailed composite Web service architecture.

Because the precedence graphs show in a formal way the sequencing constraints of a set of activities performed by a workflow module, they can be seen as a kind of operational semantic associated to a workflow process.

The equivalence between composite Web service contract and the detailed composite Web service architecture can consequently be verified using the branching bisimilarity concept presented in Sect. 2.3, whose purpose is to compare operational semantics of distinct formal behavioral models.

In our approach, the activities of the detailed composite Web service architecture that do not appear in the composite Web service contract are considered as silent actions. When removing the silent actions of the precedence graphs of the detailed composite Web service architecture, the obtained reduced graph has to be the same as the one of the composite Web service contract when the behavior of the architectural model reproduces the behavior of the requirement model.

To illustrate the approach, we consider the examples of Figs. 3 (composite Web service contract) and 4 (detailed composite Web service architecture). The transitions of the models are named according to the initial letters of the activities associates to them. For example, *send_order* and *receive_order* are represented by t_{so} and t_{ro}, respectively.

The transitions (activities) of the requirement model (composite Web service contract, Fig. 3) are represented by the following formulas of Linear Logic:

$$start = t_s = i \multimap C_i \otimes S_i, \quad send\_order = t_{so} = C_i \multimap C_1 \otimes P_1,$$
$$receive\_order = t_{ro} = S_i \otimes P_1 \multimap S_1, \quad p\_specification = t_{ps} = S_1 \otimes P_2 \multimap S_2,$$
$$creat\_specification = t_{cs} = C_1 \multimap C_2 \otimes P_2,$$
$$p\_cost\_statement = t_{pcs} = C_2 \otimes P_3 \multimap C_3,$$
$$creat\_cost\_statement = t_{ccs} = S_2 \multimap S_3 \otimes P_3,$$
$$confirm\_order = t_{cfo} = C_3 \multimap C_4 \otimes P_4,$$
$$receive\_confirm = t_{rcf} = S_3 \otimes P_4 \multimap S_4, \quad status\_report = t_{sr} = S_4 \multimap S_5 \otimes P_6,$$
$$view\_status = t_{vs} = C_4 \otimes P_6 \multimap C_5, \quad cancel\_order = t_{co} = C_3 \multimap C_6 \otimes P_5,$$
$$receive\_cancel = t_{rc} = S_3 \otimes P_5 \multimap S_o \otimes P_8,$$
$$ship\_product = t_{sp} = S_5 \multimap S_o \otimes P_7, \quad canceled\_order = t_{cdo} = C_6 \otimes P_8 \multimap C_o,$$
$$handle\_product = t_{hp} = C_5 \otimes P_7 \multimap C_o, \quad end = t_e = C_o \otimes S_o \multimap o.$$

The requirement model contains two scenarios called respectively Sr1 and Sr2. The first one corresponds to the situation that the order was canceled by the contractor and the second one corresponds to the situation that the order was confirmed by the contractor.

Before the construction of the precedence graph, it is necessary to prove that the sequent corresponding to a possible scenario is syntactically correct in accordance with the Linear Logic theory.

Considering the scenario Sr1 of the composite Web service contract of Fig. 3, the following sequent needs to be proven:

$$i, t_s, t_{so}, t_{ro}, t_{cs}, t_{ps}, t_{ccs}, t_{pcs}, t_{co}, t_{rc}, t_{cdo}, t_e \vdash o.$$

The corresponding proof tree for scenario Sr1 is the following:

$$
\cfrac{\cfrac{\cfrac{\cfrac{\cfrac{\cfrac{\cfrac{\cfrac{\cfrac{\cfrac{\cfrac{\cfrac{\cfrac{\cfrac{S_o \vdash S_o \quad C_o \vdash C_o}{S_o,C_o \vdash S_o \otimes C_o} \otimes R \quad \cfrac{o \vdash o}{} -\!\circ L}{}}{}}{}}{}}{}}{}}{}}{}}{}}{}}{}}{}}{}}{}
$$

$$\cfrac{S_o \vdash S_o \quad C_o \vdash C_o}{S_o,C_o \vdash S_o \otimes C_o} \otimes R \qquad o \vdash o \;\; -\!\circ L$$

$$\cfrac{\cfrac{C_6 \vdash C_6 \quad P_8 \vdash P_8}{C_6,P_8 \vdash C_6 \otimes P_8}\otimes R \qquad S_o,C_o,C_o \otimes S_o -\!\circ o \vdash o}{C_6,S_o,P_8,C_6 \otimes P_8 -\!\circ C_o,t_e \vdash o}\otimes L$$

$$\cfrac{\cfrac{S_3 \vdash S_3 \quad P_5 \vdash P_5}{S_3,P_5 \vdash S_3 \otimes P_5}\otimes R \qquad C_6,S_o \otimes P_8,C_6 \otimes P_8 -\!\circ C_o,t_e \vdash o}{S_3,C_6,P_5,S_3 \otimes P_5 -\!\circ S_o \otimes P_8,t_{cdo},t_e \vdash o}\otimes L$$

$$\cfrac{C_3 \vdash C_3 \qquad S_3,C_6 \otimes P_5,S_3 \otimes P_5 -\!\circ S_o \otimes P_8,t_{cdo},t_e \vdash o}{S_3,C_3,C_3 -\!\circ C_6 \otimes P_5,t_{rc},t_{cdo},t_e \vdash o}-\!\circ L$$

$$\cfrac{\cfrac{C_2 \vdash C_2 \quad P_3 \vdash P_3}{C_2,P_3 \vdash C_2 \otimes P_3}\otimes R \qquad S_3,C_3,C_3 -\!\circ C_6 \otimes P_5,t_{rc},t_{cdo},t_e \vdash o}{C_2,P_3,S_3,C_2 \otimes P_3 -\!\circ C_3,t_{co},t_{rc},t_{cdo},t_e \vdash o}\otimes L$$

$$\cfrac{S_2 \vdash S_2 \qquad C_2,S_3 \otimes P_3,C_2 \otimes P_3 -\!\circ C_3,t_{co},t_{rc},t_{cdo},t_e \vdash o}{S_2,C_2,S_2 -\!\circ S_3 \otimes P_3,t_{pcs},...,t_{cdo},t_e \vdash o}-\!\circ L$$

$$\cfrac{\cfrac{S_1 \vdash S_1 \quad P_2 \vdash P_2}{S_1,P_2 \vdash S_1 \otimes P_2}\otimes R \qquad C_2,S_2,S_2 -\!\circ S_3 \otimes P_3,t_{pcs},...,t_{cdo},t_e \vdash o}{S_1,P_2,C_2,S_1 \otimes P_2 -\!\circ S_2,t_{ccs},...,t_{cdo},t_e \vdash o}\otimes L$$

$$\cfrac{C_1 \vdash C_1 \qquad S_1,C_2 \otimes P_2,S_1 \otimes P_2 -\!\circ S_2,t_{ccs},...,t_{cdo},t_e \vdash o}{C_1,S_1,C_1 -\!\circ C_2 \otimes P_2,t_{ps},...,t_{cdo},t_e \vdash o}-\!\circ L$$

$$\cfrac{\cfrac{S_i \vdash S_i \quad P_1 \vdash P_1}{S_i,P_1 \vdash S_i \otimes P_1}\otimes R \qquad C_1,S_1,C_1 -\!\circ C_2 \otimes P_2,t_{ps},...,t_{cdo},t_e \vdash o}{S_i,C_1,P_1,S_i \otimes P_1 -\!\circ S_1,t_{cs},...,t_{cdo},t_e \vdash o}\otimes L$$

$$\cfrac{C_i \vdash C_i \qquad S_i,C_1 \otimes P_1,S_i \otimes P_1 -\!\circ S_1,t_{cs},...,t_{cdo},t_e \vdash o}{C_i,S_i,C_i -\!\circ C_1 \otimes P_1,t_{ro},t_{cs},...,t_{cdo},t_e \vdash o}-\!\circ L$$

$$\cfrac{i \vdash i \qquad C_i \otimes S_i,C_i -\!\circ C_1 \otimes P_1,t_{ro},t_{cs},...,t_{cdo},t_e \vdash o}{i,i -\!\circ C_i \otimes S_i,t_{so},t_{ro},t_{cs},t_{ps},t_{ccs},t_{pcs},t_{co},t_{rc},t_{cdo},t_e \vdash o}-\!\circ L$$

To generate the precedence graph, the proof tree must be labeled as explained in Subsect. 2.2. The simplified labeled proof tree of scenario Sr1 is the following:

$$\cfrac{\cfrac{\overset{t_{rc}}{S_o} \vdash \overset{t_{te}}{S_o} \quad \overset{t_{cdo}}{C_o} \vdash \overset{t_e}{C_o}}{\overset{t_{rc}}{S_o},\overset{t_{cdo}}{C_o} \vdash \overset{t_e}{S_o} \otimes \overset{t_e}{C_o}}\otimes R \qquad \overset{t_e}{o} \vdash \overset{f_i}{o}}{}-\!\circ \underset{t_e}{L}$$

$$\vdots$$

$$\cfrac{\overset{i_i}{i} \vdash \overset{t_s}{i} \qquad \overset{t_s}{C_i} \otimes \overset{t_s}{S_i},C_i -\!\circ C_1 \otimes P_1,t_{ro},t_{cs},...,t_{cdo},t_e \vdash o}{}-\!\circ \underset{t_s}{L}$$

$$\overset{i_i}{i},i -\!\circ C_i \otimes S_i,t_{so},t_{ro},t_{cs},t_{ps},t_{ccs},t_{pcs},t_{co},t_{rc},t_{cdo},t_e \vdash o$$

The complete precedence graph of scenario Sr1 for the requirement model is presented in Fig. 5. In this graph, the vertices represented the activities, and the arcs the conditions that activate the activities. Such a graph corresponds to the formal specification of the requirement in terms of behavior. It represents too a possible view of the operational semantic associated to the corresponding workflow process.

Considering the scenario Sr2 of the composite Web service contract (requirement model) of Fig. 3, the following sequent needs to be proven:

$$i,t_s,t_{so},t_{ro},t_{cs},t_{ps},t_{ccs},t_{pcs},t_{cfo},t_{rcf},t_{sr},t_{vs},t_{sp},t_{hp},t_e \vdash o$$

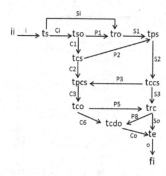

Fig. 5. Precedence graph for scenario Sr1.

For the next proof trees only the beginning and the end of the proof are presented. The simplified corresponding proof tree for scenario Sr2 is the following:

$$\cfrac{\cfrac{S_o \vdash S_o \qquad C_o \vdash C_o}{S_o, C_o \vdash S_o \otimes C_o} \otimes R \qquad o \vdash o}{\vdots} \multimap_L$$

$$i, t_s, t_{so}, t_{ro}, t_{cs}, t_{ps}, t_{ccs}, t_{pcs}, t_{cfo}, t_{rcf}, t_{sr}, t_{vs}, t_{sp}, t_{hp}, t_e \vdash o$$

The simplified labeled proof tree of scenario Sr2 is the following:

$$\cfrac{\cfrac{\overset{t_{ps}}{S_o} \overset{t_e}{\vdash} \overset{}{S_o} \qquad \overset{t_{hp}}{C_o} \overset{t_e}{\vdash} \overset{}{C_o}}{\overset{t_{ps}}{S_o}, \overset{t_{hp}}{C_o} \overset{t_e}{\vdash} \overset{t_e}{S_o \otimes C_o}} \otimes R \qquad \overset{t_e}{o} \overset{f_i}{\vdash} \overset{}{o}}{\vdots} \multimap_L$$

$$i, t_s, t_{so}, t_{ro}, t_{cs}, t_{ps}, t_{ccs}, t_{pcs}, t_{cfo}, t_{rcf}, t_{sr}, t_{vs}, t_{sp}, t_{hp}, t_e \vdash o$$

The precedence graph for scenario Sr2 of the composite Web service contract (requirement model) is presented in Fig. 6.

The detailed composite Web service architecture of Fig. 4 contain four scenarios called respectively Sa1, Sa2, Sa3 and Sa4. The scenario Sa1 corresponds to the situation that order was confirmed by the contractor but he did not request to see the product status. The scenario Sa2 corresponds to the situation that order was confirmed by the contractor and he requested to see the product status. The scenario Sa3 corresponds to the situation that the order was canceled by the contractor. The scenario Sa4 corresponds to the situation that order was confirmed by the contractor but he did not request to see the product status; however, even so the subcontractor sent the status report.

Iterative routes of workflow module will be replaced by simple global tasks, as it is generally the case of hierarchical approaches based on the notion of well formed blocks [16]. The iterative route constraint that exists in the detailed composite Web service architecture of Fig. 4 will be transformed into a global single task *bill'*, as shown in the Fig. 7, that corresponds to the many possible iterations of the activity *bill* each time the condition *nok* is valid.

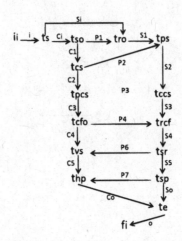

Fig. 6. Precedence graph for scenario Sr2.

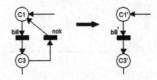

Fig. 7. Transformation of an iterative route constraint into a single task.

The transitions of the architectural model are represented by the following formulas of Linear Logic:

$start = t_s = i \multimap C_i \otimes S_i, \quad send\_order = t_{so} = C_i \multimap C'_1 \otimes C_2 \otimes P_1,$
$receive\_order = t_{ro} = S_i \otimes P_1 \multimap S_1, \quad p\_order = t_{po} = S_1 \multimap S_2,$
$bill' = t_b = C'_1 \multimap C'_3, \quad ok = t_{ok} = C'_3 \multimap C_5,$
$check = t_c = C_5 \multimap C_7, \quad creat\_specification = t_{cs} = C_2 \multimap C_4 \otimes P_2,$
$p\_specification = t_{ps} = P_2 \otimes S_2 \multimap S_3,$
$evaluating = t_{ev} = S_3 \multimap S_4, \quad p\_cost\_statement = t_{pcs} = C_4 \otimes P_3 \multimap C_6,$
$creat\_cost\_stament = t_{ccs} = S_4 \multimap P_3 \otimes S_5, \quad decide = t_d = C_6 \multimap C_8,$
$cancel\_order = t_{co} = C_8 \multimap C_{11} \otimes P_6,$
$receive\_confirm = t_{rc} = S_5 \otimes P_6 \multimap P_8 \otimes S_o,$
$canceled\_order = t_{cdo} = C_7 \otimes C_{11} \otimes P_8 \multimap C_o,$
$proceed = t_p = S_7 \multimap S_8, \quad confirm\_order = t_{cfo} = C_8 \multimap C_9 \otimes P_4,$
$receive\_confirm = t_{rcf} = P_4 \otimes S_5 \multimap S_6, \quad prepare\_product = t_{pp} = S_6 \multimap S_7,$
$view\_status = t_{vs} = C_9 \otimes P_5 \multimap C_{10},$
$status\_report = t_{sr} = S_7 \multimap P_5 \otimes S_8, \quad waiting\_product = t_{wp} = C_9 \multimap C_{10},$
$handle\_product = t_{hp} = C_7 \otimes C_{10} \otimes P_7 \multimap C_o,$
$ship\_product = t_{sp} = S_8 \multimap P_7 \otimes S_o, \quad end = t_e = C_o \otimes S_o \multimap o.$

Considering each scenario of the detailed composite Web Service architecture of Fig. 4, the following sequents needs to be proven:

- (scenario Sa1)
  $i, t_s, t_{so}, t_{ro}, t_b, t_{cs}, t_{ok}, t_c, t_{po}, t_{ps}, t_{ev}, t_{ccs}, t_{pcs}, t_d, t_{cfo}, t_{rcf}, t_{wp}, t_{pp}, t_p, t_{sp}, t_{hp},$
  $t_e \vdash o$
- (scenario Sa2)
  $i, t_s, t_{so}, t_{ro}, t_b, t_{cs}, t_{ok}, t_c, t_{po}, t_{ps}, t_{ev}, t_{ccs}, t_{pcs}, t_d, t_{cfo}, t_{rcf}, t_{vs}, t_{pp}, t_{sr}, t_{sp}, t_{hp},$
  $t_e \vdash o$
- (scenario Sa3)
  $i, t_s, t_{so}, t_{ro}, t_b, t_{cs}, t_{ok}, t_c, t_{po}, t_{ps}, t_{ev}, t_{ccs}, t_{pcs}, t_d, t_{co}, t_{rc}, t_{cdo}, t_e \vdash o$
- (scenario Sa4)
  $i, t_s, t_{so}, t_{ro}, t_b, t_{cs}, t_{ok}, t_c, t_{po}, t_{ps}, t_{ev}, t_{ccs}, t_{pcs}, t_d, t_{cfo}, t_{rcf}, t_{wp}, t_{pp}, t_{sr}, t_{sp}, t_{hp},$
  $t_e \vdash o$

The simplified corresponding proof tree for scenario Sa1 is the following:

$$\cfrac{\cfrac{S_o \vdash S_o \qquad C_o \vdash C_o}{S_o, C_o \vdash S_o \otimes C_o} \otimes R \qquad o \vdash o}{\vdots} \multimap L$$

$$\overline{i, t_s, t_{so}, ..., t_c, t_{po}, t_{ps}, t_{ev}, t_{ccs}, t_{pcs}, t_d, t_{cfo}, t_{rcf}, t_{wp}, t_{pp}, t_p, t_{sp}, t_{hp}, t_e \vdash o}$$

The labeled proof tree for the scenarios Sa1, Sa2, Sa3 and Sa4 will not be shown.

The precedence graph for scenario Sa1 is presented in Fig. 8(a). In this graph, all sequences of activities performed in the detailed composite Web service architecture are clearly specified. In this graph, dashed lines are used when an arc corresponds to a link to a silent activity (one of its vertices corresponds to a silent activity). As a matter of fact, these activities are of interest only to their respective local workflow module. By removing a silent action from a precedence graph, it is necessary to connect the precedent activity that is connected to the silent activity to the successor activity of the silent activity. For example, by removing the activity t_d in Fig. 8(a), a new directed arc is created between the activities t_{pcs} and t_{cfo}. By removing all the silent activities of the precedence graph in Fig. 8(a), the reduced precedence graph of Fig. 8(b) is obtained.

The simplified corresponding proof tree for scenario Sa2 is the following:

$$\cfrac{\cfrac{S_o \vdash S_o \qquad C_o \vdash C_o}{S_o, C_o \vdash S_o \otimes C_o} \otimes R \qquad o \vdash o}{\vdots} \multimap L$$

$$\overline{i, t_s, t_{so}, ..., t_c, t_{po}, t_{ps}, t_{ev}, t_{ccs}, t_{pcs}, t_d, t_{cfo}, t_{rcf}, t_{vs}, t_{pp}, t_{sr}, t_{sp}, t_{hp}, t_e \vdash o}$$

The precedence graph for scenario Sa2 is presented in Fig. 9(a). By removing all the silent activities from the precedence graph in Fig. 9(a), the reduced precedence graph of Fig. 9(b) is obtained.

The simplified corresponding proof tree for scenario Sa3 is the following:

$$\cfrac{\cfrac{S_o \vdash S_o \qquad C_o \vdash C_o}{S_o, C_o \vdash S_o \otimes C_o} \otimes R \qquad o \vdash o}{\vdots} \multimap L$$

$$\overline{i, t_s, t_{so}, ..., t_c, t_{po}, t_{ps}, t_{ev}, t_{ccs}, t_{pcs}, t_d, t_{co}, t_{rc}, t_{cdo}, t_e \vdash o}$$

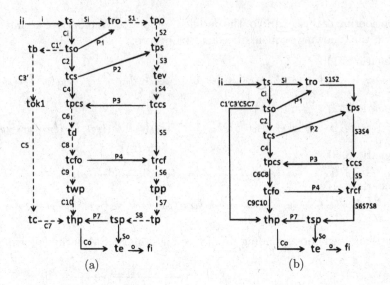

Fig. 8. (a) Precedence graph for scenario Sa1. (b) Reduced precedence graph for scenario Sa1.

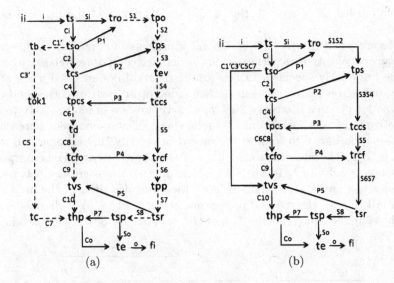

Fig. 9. (a) Precedence graph for scenario Sa2. (b) Reduced precedence graph for scenario Sa2.

The precedence graph for scenario Sa3 is presented in Fig. 10(a). By removing all the silent activities from the precedence graph in Fig. 10(a), the reduced precedence graph of Fig. 10(b) is obtained.

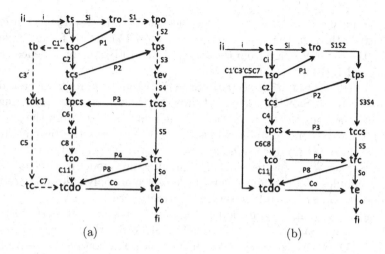

(a)   (b)

Fig. 10. (a) Precedence graph for scenario Sa3. (b) Reduced precedence graph for scenario Sa3.

The simplified proof tree corresponding to scenario Sa4 is the following one:

$$\cfrac{\cfrac{S_o\vdash S_o \quad C_o\vdash C_o}{S_o,C_o\vdash S_o\otimes C_o}\otimes_R \quad P_5,o\vdash o}{\vdots}\multimap_L$$

$$i,i\multimap\!\!\circ C_i\otimes S_i,t_{so},t_{ro},t_b,t_{cs},t_{po},t_{ps},\ldots,t_{sr},t_{sp},t_{hp},t_e\vdash o$$

The last line of the proof tree clearly shows that even with the last place 'o' of the detailed composite Web service architecture marked, another token is present in the process in place P_5. This means that scenario Sa4, in case it is executed, will produce a kind of information duplication; such a scenario does not correspond then to a sound behavior and will not be considered as part of the scenarios necessary to cover the business requirement of the composite Web service contract. As a direct consequence, the precedence graph for scenario Sa4 is not produced.

The last step of the approach is to compare the precedence graphs of the composite Web service contract with the precedence graphs of the detailed composite Web service architecture to verify if the requirements specified in term of behavior in the Web service contract are also present in the architectural proposal specified in the detailed composite Web service architecture. The precedence graphs obtained from scenarios Sr1 and Sr2 have then to be compared with precedence graphs obtained from scenarios Sa1, Sa2 and Sa3.

The precedence graph for scenario Sr1 (Fig. 5) and the reduced precedence graph for scenario Sa3 (Fig. 10(b)) execute the same activities respecting the same sequential constraints. The additional arc $C_1'C_3'C_5C_7$ that exist in the graph of Fig. 10(b), and that do not exist in the graph of Fig. 5, are simply redundant constraints that can be removed without modifying the requirement specification. As a matter of fact, the arc $C_1'C_3'C_5C_7$ of Fig. 10(b) simply states that the activity t_{so} has to happen before activity t_{cdo}. However, this statement already exists through the sequence of arcs C_2, C_4, C_6C_8, C_{11}, for example. By removing the redundant arc from the graph of Fig. 10(b), the precedence graphs of Figs. 5 and 10(b) are exactly the same.

The precedence graph for scenario Sr2 (Fig. 6) and the reduced precedence graph for scenario Sa2 (Fig. 9(b)) execute the same activities respecting the same sequential constraints. By removing the redundant arc from the graph in Fig. 9(b), the precedence graphs of Figs. 6 and 9(b) are exactly the same too.

The scenario Sa1 produces a behavior that was not specified in the contract model. This fact was expected since the architecture model is a set of private workflow modules that contains several tasks which are only of local interest and which do not appear in the Web service contract.

Although the architectural model (Fig. 4) is not sound (scenario Sa4), the scenarios Sa2 and Sa3 are correctly executed and verify the requirements specified in the Web service contract. According to the definition presented in [12], it can be verified that the model is relaxed sound, i.e. each transaction (activity) appears in, at least, one scenario that finishes correctly. Therefore, even though the detailed composite Web service architecture is not sound, which may lead the system to a deadlock situation, it is possible to verify that it possesses the scenarios that correctly satisfy the business needs defined in the contract model. For the example shown in this work, one concludes that the requirements defined in the analysis model are well defined in the architectural model. In particular, the scenarios Sr1 and Sr2 of the conctrat model are also present, through scenarios Sa3 and Sa2, in the architectural model.

4   Conclusion

This paper presented an approach for requirement verification in Web service models based on workflow modules and Linear Logic. Our purpose was to present an approach to verify that, in the context of Web services, all scenarios present in a requirement model (Web service contract) are also present in the corresponding architectural model (detailed composite Web service architecture).

This approach was based in particular on the construction of Linear Logic proof trees and of precedence graphs that show the operational semantic of distinct models. Building a precedence graph for each scenario of the requirement model and for each scenario of the architecture model, it was possible to compare and check the behavioral equivalence between a composite Web service contract and a detailed Web service architecture model, in particular when the obtained models simulate each other's behavior, respecting the notion of branching bisimilarity. In this approach, precedence graphs were in particular built for the sequents of Linear Logic syntactically correct, i.e. sound scenarios that ended correctly the modeled business process. The time complexity to prove a linear sequent of Linear Logic that represents a scenario of a WorkFlow net is O(n), where n is the number of transitions; besides that the additional complexity the parallel structure of a Petri net produced in the state oriented reachability graph will disappear in the proof tree of the sequent calculus of Linear Logic [14].

One of the main advantage of this approach is to propose, through the use of Linear Logic and precedence graphs, a kind of operational semantic associated to business processes that allows to verify in a formal way business requirements within the Web service context. The presented approach considers architectural models not necessarily sound. The organizations do not have then to be constrained by external actors to build their private workflow processes, as it is the case generally when considering existing enterprise systems. Therefore, the organizations involved can simply verify if the set of requirement scenarios of a contract model are also present in an available Web service model candidate for the implementation of the required service. In this sense, the impacts and deviations generated by collaboration between different organizations can be minimized.

In this article, only a kind of functional requirement was verified in the models. As a future work proposal, we will associate explicit time constraints in the models to evaluate the performance of the models and apply a kind of quantitative analysis in the context of Web services.

References

1. Basten, A.A.: In Terms of Nets: System Design with Petri Nets and Process Algebra. Eindhoven University of Technology (1998)
2. Diaz, M.: Petri Nets: Fundamental Models, Verification and Applications. Wiley-IEEE Press, Reading, Massachusetts (2009)
3. Erl, T.: Service-Oriented Architecture Concepts, Technology, and Design. Prentice Hall, Upper Saddle River (2005)
4. Erl, T.: SOA Principles of Service Design. Prentice Hall, Upper Saddle River (2009)
5. Girard, J.-Y.: Linear logic. Theor. Comput. Sci. **50**, 1–102 (1987). Elsevier Science Publishers Ltd
6. Goknil, A., Kurtev, I., Van Den Berg, K.: Generation and validation of traces between requirements and architecture based on formal trace semantics. J. Syst. Softw. **88**, 112–137 (2014). Elsevier
7. Klai, K., Ochi, H., Tata, S.: Formal abstraction and compatibility checking of web services. In: IEEE 20th International Conference on Web Services, pp. 163–170. IEEE (2013)
8. Martens, A.: Analyzing web service based business processes. In: Cerioli, M. (ed.) FASE 2005. LNCS, vol. 3442, pp. 19–33. Springer, Heidelberg (2005). https://doi.org/10.1007/978-3-540-31984-9_3
9. Nghiem, A.: IT Web Services: A Roadmap for the Enterprise. Prentice Hall Professional Technical Reference (2002)
10. Papazoglou, M.P.: Service-oriented computing: concepts, characteristics and directions. In: Fourth International Conference on Web Information Systems Engineering, pp. 03–12. IEEE Computer Society Press (2003)
11. Park, D.: Concurrency and automata on infinite sequences. In: Deussen, P. (ed.) GI-TCS 1981. LNCS, vol. 104, pp. 167–183. Springer, Heidelberg (1981). https://doi.org/10.1007/BFb0017309
12. Passos, L.M.S.: A Metodology based on Linear Logic for Interorganizational Workflow Processes Analysis. Ph.D. Dissertation, Federal Univerty of Uberlândia (2016)

13. Passos, L.M.S., Julia, S.: Deadlock-freeness scenarios detection in web service composition. In: 12th International Conference on Information Technology - New Generations, pp. 780–783. IEEE (2015)
14. Passos, L.M.S., Julia, S.: Linear Logic as a Tool for Qualitative and Quantitative Analysis of Work OW Processes. Int. J. Artif. Intell. Tools **25**, 1650008-01-25 (2016). World Scientifc Publishing Company
15. Riviere, N., Pradin-Chezalviel, B., Valette, R.: Reachability and temporal conflicts in t-time Petri nets. In: 9th International Workshop on Petri Nets and Performance Models, pp. 229–238. IEEE (2001)
16. Valette, R.: Analysis of Petri nets by stepwise refinements. J. Comput. Syst. Sci. **18**, 35–46 (1979). Elsevier
17. van Glabbeek, R.J., Weijland, W.P.: Branching time and abstraction in bisimulation semantics. J. ACM **43**, 555–600 (1996). ACM
18. Xiong, P., Fan, Y., Zhou, M.: A Petri net approach to analysis and composition of web services. IEEE Trans. Syst. Man Cybern. Part A: Syst. Humans **40**, 376–387 (2010). IEEE

Checking Static Properties Using Conservative SAT Approximations for Reachability

Pedro Antonino$^{(\boxtimes)}$, Thomas Gibson-Robinson, and A.W. Roscoe

Department of Computer Science, University of Oxford, Oxford, UK
{pedro.antonino,thomas.gibson-robinson,bill.roscoe}@cs.ox.ac.uk

Abstract. The use of specialised approximations for reachability, instead of exact reachability, has given rise to scalable methods to verify deadlock freedom in the context of distributed finite-state systems. In this work, we extend these approaches to check *static properties*. These properties capture the immediate/static behaviour of a system. The static nature of these properties make them a good match for the sort of over-approximations we use. Local-deadlock freedom and mutual exclusion are two commonly desired properties for distributed systems that naturally fit into our framework. Local-deadlock freedom, in particular, specifies that no subsystem can reach a permanently blocked state. We show by a series of experiments that our approximate framework can prove such properties for a number of interesting systems, and it can do so more efficiently compared to complete approaches.

1 Introduction

The main shortcoming of verification frameworks for concurrent and distributed systems is, arguably, their lack of scalability. Generally, the main driving force behind the inefficiency of such frameworks is the *state-space explosion problem*: the state space of these systems grows exponentially with the linear increase in the number of components. Approximative frameworks are an alternative to deal with the state space explosion; these methods give up precision to achieve scalability. In a series of papers, we have demonstrated the effectiveness of methods based on replacing exact reachability by approximations calculated by SAT solving for achieving scalable deadlock-freedom verification for finite-state distributed systems [1–3]. Due to the use of reachability over-approximations, when our framework finds a blocked state, it produces an inconclusive result: it does not know whether this state is reachable or not. If no blocked state is found, however, the system is deadlock free. Unlike complete frameworks, we are happy to precisely tackle only a class of systems as long as verification results are efficiently provided for most systems, be it inconclusive or not. We believe this incompleteness is a small price to pay to achieve better scalability. An inconclusive result can be understood as a quick alert to the user that our framework is unable to precisely tackle the input system.

These frameworks try to generate a candidate counter-example, i.e. a possible deadlock, by assigning to each component one of its states in a way they satisfy

S. Cavalheiro and J. Fiadeiro (Eds.): SBMF 2017, LNCS 10623, pp. 233–250, 2017.
https://doi.org/10.1007/978-3-319-70848-5_15

some overall SAT constraints; these constraints test whether a given assignment (i.e. system state) is in some reachability approximation and is blocked. Deadlock freedom is a natural target for such frameworks because a blocked system state can be easily recognised based on the analysis of the interactions available for this combination of component states, and such an analysis can be naturally encoded into the sort of overall constraints we use.

In this paper, we show how the same ideas work for further properties. We introduce a notation to capture properties that can be specified based on the *static* (i.e. immediate) behaviour available in a system state, i.e. the events the system can (or cannot) perform when in the given state. We call such properties *static properties*. One property that naturally fits into this notation is *local-deadlock freedom*, namely, the property that no subsystem can become irretrievably blocked. This is a naturally desirable property that is quite hard to specify and efficiently check using conventional techniques. Like deadlock freedom, this property can be characterised by the interactions available for a combination of component states. Mutual exclusion and safe invocation, namely, ensuring components only invoke services that are properly initialised, are other relevant properties that can be seamlessly specified and effectively checked in our framework.

This new framework generalises our frameworks for deadlock analysis; it tries to generate a candidate counter-example for a given static property by finding a system state that satisfy some similar overall SAT constraints. Instead of looking for blocked states, however, it generates a constraint to analyse whether a given system state constitutes a violation for the input static property. Furthermore, we combine all constraints that approximate reachability in [1–3] to enhance the precision of our framework. These reachability approximations are designed to capture some common interaction mechanisms used by systems to avoid undesired states. For instance, the technique in [1] captures token-based interactions: it can predict how tokens flow in a system and whether a given combination of component states is consistent with token invariants it discovers. Finally, we capture distributed systems using *supercombinator machines*. This notation describes a system by its components and the way these components interact. It is notably used to capture CSP systems [14, 22] within the FDR4 checker [12], but it should be able to capture systems in other formalisms as long as these systems can be expressed in terms of finite-state interacting components.

We implement our framework in a tool called *ApprOx*. The efficiency and precision of this tool is assessed by practical experiments where we test our implementation in some systems described in CSP. The core of our framework should be easily adaptable to similar formalisms. To the best of our knowledge, in the context of distributed systems, our framework is the first approximate approach to directly tackle such a general class of properties.

Outline. Section 2 briefly introduces CSP's operational semantics, which is the formalism upon which our strategy is based. Section 3 introduces some techniques to approximate reachability. In Sect. 4, we introduce a notation to capture static properties, whereas in Sect. 5, we propose an approximate framework to check static properties using SAT solving. Section 6 presents two experiments conducted to evaluate ApprOx. In Sect. 7, we present our concluding remarks.

2   Background

In the CSP notation, distributed systems are modelled as processes that exchange messages. Here, we describe some structures used by the refinement checker FDR4 in implementing CSP's operational semantics. As this work does not depend on the details of CSP, we do not describe the details of this notation. These can be found in [22]. FDR4 interprets CSP terms as a *labelled transition system* (LTS).

Definition 1. *A labelled transition system is a 4-tuple* $(S, \Sigma, \Delta, \hat{s})$ *where* S *is a set of states,* Σ *is the alphabet,* $\Delta \subseteq S \times \Sigma \times S$ *is a transition relation, and* $\hat{s} \in S$ *is the starting state.*

FDR4 represents distributed systems as *supercombinator machines*. A supercombinator machine consists of a set of component LTSs along with a set of rules that describe how components transitions should be combined. We restrict ourselves to systems with pairwise communication, as per [2]. Many systems are naturally, or can be easily made, triple-disjoint.

Definition 2. *A triple-disjoint supercombinator machine is a pair* $(\mathcal{L}, \mathcal{R})$ *where:*

- $\mathcal{L} = \langle L_1, \ldots, L_n \rangle$ *is a sequence of component LTSs;*
- $\mathcal{R}$ *is a set of rules of the form* (e, a) *where:*
  - $e \in (\Sigma^-)^n$ *specifies the event that each component must perform, where* $-$ *indicates that the component performs no event. e must also be triple-disjoint: at most two components must be involved in a rule.*
    - $triple\_disjoint(e) \triangleq \forall i, j, k : \{1 \ldots n\} \mid i \neq j \wedge j \neq k \wedge i \neq k \bullet$
      $$e_i = - \vee e_j = - \vee e_k = -$$
  - $a \in \Sigma$ *is the event the supercombinator machine performs.*

Given a supercombinator machine, a corresponding LTS describing the system's behaviour can be constructed.

Definition 3. *Let* $\mathcal{S} = (\langle L_1, \ldots, L_n \rangle, \mathcal{R})$ *be a supercombinator machine where* $L_i = (S_i, \Sigma_i, \Delta_i, \hat{s}_i)$. *The LTS induced by* $\mathcal{S}$ *is the tuple* $(S, \Sigma, \Delta, \hat{s})$ *such that:*

- $S = S_1 \times \ldots \times S_n$;
- $\Sigma = \{a \mid (e, a) \in \mathcal{R}\}$;
- $\Delta = \{((s_1, \ldots, s_n), a, (s'_1, \ldots, s'_n)) \mid \exists((e_1, \ldots, e_n), a) \in \mathcal{R} \bullet \forall i \in \{1 \ldots n\} \bullet$
  $(e_i = - \wedge s_i = s'_i) \vee (e_i \neq - \wedge (s_i, e_i, s'_i) \in \Delta_i)\}$;
- $\hat{s} = (\hat{s}_1, \ldots, \hat{s}_n)$.

We write $s \xrightarrow{e} s'$ iff $(s, e, s') \in \Delta$, and $s \xrightarrow{e}$ iff $\exists s' \bullet (s, e, s') \in \Delta$. There is a path from s to s' with the sequence of events $\langle e_1, \ldots, e_n \rangle \in \Sigma^*$, represented by $s \xrightarrow{\langle e_1, \ldots, e_n \rangle} s'$, if there exist $s_0, \ldots, s_n$ such that $s_0 \xrightarrow{e_1} s_1 \ldots s_{n-1} \xrightarrow{e_n} s_n, s_0 = s$ and $s_n = s'$. A state $s \in S$ is reachable iff $reachable(s) \triangleq \exists t \in \Sigma^* \bullet \hat{s} \xrightarrow{t} s$.

Henceforth, we use *system state* (*component state*) to designate a state in the system's (component's) LTS. Note a system state is a combination of component states that might not be reachable within the system's induced LTS. Also, for the sake of decidability, we only analyse machines with a finite number of components, which are themselves represented by finite LTSs with finite alphabets.

3   Related Work

The majority of the papers on incomplete/approximate verification techniques propose frameworks for deadlock-freedom analysis [1–3,5–8,10,15–18]. Most of these frameworks were designed around the principle that under reasonable assumptions about the system, any deadlock state would contain a proper cycle of ungranted requests amongst components. This characterisation, however, is rather imprecise [2], as a cycle of ungranted requests is only a necessary condition for a deadlock. Furthermore, this characterisation is inextricably linked to deadlock, so it does not generalise to other properties.

In [1–3], we improve on this by being imprecise only in terms of reachability. These frameworks characterise a deadlock as a system state that is blocked and passes a reachability test that over-approximates reachability. Roughly speaking, they look through an over-approximation of the system's state space and either show that no blocked state exists or they find a blocked state. Thanks to the over-approximation, in the former case the system has to be deadlock free, whereas in the latter the framework's result is inconclusive: the blocked state found might not be reachable. The reachability approximations in these works are completely independent from the fact that we are checking for a blocked state. So, they could be re-used to check other properties. The approximations proposed in these works are tailored to capture some common mechanisms employed by distributed systems to avoid "bad" states.

In [2], we approximate reachability based on the behaviour of pairs of components in the system. Broadly speaking, this approximation, captured by predicate $reach_{Pair}$[1], considers a system state $s = (s_1, \ldots, s_n)$ unreachable if there exists a pair of component states (s_i, s_j) that is not reachable considering the (sub)system that runs components i and j independently from the rest of the system. This technique can show that some systems that use a resource-allocation mechanism or a client-server architecture are deadlock free [16].

In [3], we combine global invariants (i.e. notions of consistency for component states) with information about how individual components participate on shared rules to approximate reachability. It proposes four approximations for reachability: $reach_{NC}$, $reach_{NA}$, $reach_{SC}$, $reach_{SA}$[2]. While $reach_{NC}$ tries to show that a system state is unreachable by showing that components cannot agree on the number of times they perform a given system rule, $reach_{SC}$ attempts to

---

[1] The predicate $reach_{Pair}$ corresponds to *pairwise_reachable* in [2]. This new name is introduced for uniformity.

[2] These predicates correspond to $reachable_N^C$, $reachable_N^A$, $reachable_S^C$, and $reachable_S^A$ in [3], respectively. This renaming is for uniformity.

demonstrate that a system state is unreachable by proving they cannot agree on the order in which they perform some system rules. $reach_{NA}$ and $reach_{SA}$ are techniques that mirror $reach_{NC}$ and $reach_{SC}$, respectively, and perform some additional data abstraction. These approximations can be used to prove deadlock freedom for some systolic-array-like and token-based systems.

In [1], we improve on [3] in dealing with token-based systems. We use SAT queries to detect implicit token invariants. These token invariants are in turn used as reachability definitions. While $reach_C$ uses SAT queries to find a token-conservation invariants, $reach_E$ synthesises a existential-token invariant. For instance, the technique in $reach_C$ assigns a boolean value to each state of each component that denotes whether the component holds a token at that point. This assignment is made in a way that if there is a system transitions from s to s', the number of tokens held by components in s and s' are the same. Thus, $reach_C$ can approximate reachability by ensuring that the state being tested has the same number of tokens as the initial state.

Theorem 1. *For $x \in \{Pair, NC, SC, NA, SA, C, E\}$ and s a state of the system, $reachable(s)$ implies $reach_x(s)$*[3].

Our reachability tests can be seen as *interaction invariants* in the sense of [10]. They seem to tackle a different class of systems when compared to the interaction invariant in [10], so they could complement it.

In this paper, we propose a framework to specify and check a general class of safety properties that we call static properties, generalising the above work. We build on these approximations to effectively verify such properties. In-depth knowledge of these reachability approximations is not required to understand the rest of this paper. It suffices to keep in mind that they can be more efficiently calculated in comparison to exact reachability, they can precisely tackle some interesting classes of systems (such as token-based, systolic-array-like, client-server, etc.), and they are sound reachability over-approximations as per Theorem 1.

4   Capturing Static Properties

In this section, we propose a framework to specify *static properties* of a distributed system. A static property takes the form: "the system can never reach a *bad* state". In our framework, bad states are described based on the system and its components' immediate possible behaviour. Hence the term static; it does not attempt to address things like traces.

4.1   Static Properties

A *static property* is described by a pair $(\mathcal{V}, \sim)$ where $\mathcal{V}$ is a *violation formula* and $\sim$ is a *satisfiability relation*. A *violation* for this property is a system state s such that $s \sim \mathcal{V}$. Roughly speaking, $\mathcal{V}$ describes some bad behaviour and

---

[3] Proofs are given in reports associated to original papers.

$\sim$ is a relation that captures whether a state behaves badly. A violation formula describes some immediate behaviour of a system by a propositional formula where atomic propositions correspond to system events.

Definition 4. *Let Σ be the alphabet of the system under analysis, which can include τ (invisible event) or $\checkmark$ (successful-termination signal), and $ev \in \Sigma$. A violation formula $\mathcal{V}$ is inductively constructed as follows.*

$$\mathcal{V} \,\widehat{=}\, \textbf{Event } ev \mid \textbf{Not } \mathcal{V} \mid \textbf{Or } \mathbb{P}(\mathcal{V}) \mid \textbf{And } \mathbb{P}(\mathcal{V})$$

The following formula is an example of a violation formula:

Violation formula 1. $\mathcal{V}_1 \,\widehat{=}\, \textbf{And } \{\textbf{Not Event } ev \mid ev \in \Sigma\}$

We propose two satisfiability relations that give rise to two different types of violations. The first relation is based on the overall system's behaviour. We call violations of this type *global violations*. For this relation, the atomic proposition "**Event** ev" holds for states in which the system can perform event ev.

Definition 5. *Let $\mathcal{V}$ be a violation formula, $\mathcal{S}$ a supercombinator machine, $(S, \Sigma, \Delta, \hat{s})$ its induced LTS, and $ev \in \Sigma$. A state s is a global violation for formula $\mathcal{V}$ iff $s \models \mathcal{V}$ holds. Let $\mathcal{V}'$ be a violation formula and $\mathcal{VS}$ be a set of violation formulas, $s \models \mathcal{V}$ can be calculated using the following clauses:*

$$s \models \textbf{Event } ev \text{ iff } s \xrightarrow{ev} \qquad s \models \textbf{Or } \mathcal{VS} \text{ iff } \bigvee_{\mathcal{V}' \in \mathcal{VS}} s \models \mathcal{V}'$$
$$s \models \textbf{Not } \mathcal{V}' \text{ iff } s \not\models \mathcal{V}' \qquad s \models \textbf{And } \mathcal{VS} \text{ iff } \bigwedge_{\mathcal{V}' \in \mathcal{VS}} s \models \mathcal{V}'$$

This relation and Violation formula 1 characterise the blocked states of a system, i.e. $\{s \in S \mid s \models \mathcal{V}_1\}$ for a system with states S.

The second relation is interpreted based on the behaviour of subsystems. We call violations of this type *local violations*. We analyse the behaviour of a subsystem through the following projection. Given a subsystem (i.e. a non-empty set of component indices), it restricts the behaviour of the system to the transitions involving components in this subsystem.

Definition 6. *Let $\mathcal{S} = (\langle L_1, \ldots, L_n \rangle, \mathcal{R})$ be a supercombinator machine where $L_i = (S_i, \Sigma_i, \Delta_i, \hat{s}_i)$, $ss \subseteq \{1 \ldots n\}$ such that $ss \neq \emptyset$ a subsystem, and e_i be the i-th element of tuple e. The projection of $\mathcal{S}$ on ss is given by $\mathcal{S}_{ss}$ defined as:*

$$(\langle L_1, \ldots, L_n \rangle, \{(e_{ss}, a) \mid (e, a) \in \mathcal{R} \wedge \exists i \in ss \bullet e_i \neq -\})$$

where e_{ss} is the tuple e' such that $e'_i = e_i$ if $i \in ss$, and $e'_i = -$ otherwise.

We use $s \xrightarrow{ev}_{ss}$ to denote the predicate $s \xrightarrow{ev}$ with respect to the LTS induced by $\mathcal{S}_{ss}$. For this local relation, a violation occurs when one subsystem engages in some bad behaviour. Hence, a violation formula is evaluated with respect to every subsystem ss of the system under analysis. The atomic proposition "**Event** ev", in particular, holds whenever a subsystem ss can perform ev.

Definition 7. *Let $\mathcal{V}$ be a violation formula, $\mathcal{S} = (\langle L_1, \ldots, L_n \rangle, \mathcal{R})$ a supercombinator machine, $(S, \Sigma, \Delta, \hat{s})$ its induced LTS, and $ev \in \Sigma$. A state s satisfies the formula $\mathcal{V}$ under the local interpretation iff $s \models \mathcal{V}$ holds, where $s \models \mathcal{V}$ is a shorthand for $\exists\, ss \subseteq \{1 \ldots n\} \mid ss \neq \emptyset \bullet s \models_{ss} \mathcal{V}$. Let $\mathcal{V}'$ be a violation formula and $\mathcal{VS}$ a set of violation formulas, $s \models_{ss} \mathcal{V}$ can be calculated as follows:*

$$s \models_{ss} \textbf{Event } ev \text{ iff } s \xrightarrow{ev}_{ss} \qquad s \models_{ss} \textbf{Or } \mathcal{VS} \text{ iff } \bigvee_{\mathcal{V}' \in \mathcal{VS}} s \models_{ss} \mathcal{V}'$$

$$s \models_{ss} \textbf{Not } \mathcal{V}' \text{ iff } s \not\models_{ss} \mathcal{V}' \qquad s \models_{ss} \textbf{And } \mathcal{VS} \text{ iff } \bigwedge_{\mathcal{V}' \in \mathcal{VS}} s \models_{ss} \mathcal{V}'$$

The second relation and Violation formula 1 characterise locally blocked states, namely, $\{s \in S \mid s \models \mathcal{V}_1\}$ are the states for which a subsystem is blocked.

We make a few remarks about these two satisfiability relations. Firstly, one should note that $\models$ is equivalent to $\models_{ss}$ when ss is the set containing all the component indices in the system under analysis. Secondly, we point out that for a given state s and a given violation $\mathcal{V}$, from our first remark and our definition of $\models$ it follows that if $s \models \mathcal{V}$ then $s \models \mathcal{V}$. So, the second relation gives rise to a much weaker/looser sort of violation compared to the first one; it only takes one violating subsystem to establish a violation. Thirdly, we point out to the fact that the task of analysing local violations should be more demanding as it involves the analysis of the behaviour of all subsystems of a system.

4.2   Checking Static Properties

A system without reachable violations satisfies the corresponding static property.

Definition 8. *Let $\mathcal{V}$ be a violation formula, $\sim \in \{\models, \models\}$ a satisfiability relation, $\mathcal{S}$ a supercombinator machine and S the set of states for its induced LTS. The system $\mathcal{S}$ satisfies the static property $(\mathcal{V}, \sim)$ iff $\neg \exists\, s \in S \bullet reachable\_violation(s)$ where $reachable\_violation(s) \,\hat{=}\, reachable(s) \wedge s \sim \mathcal{V}$.*

For instance, $(\mathcal{V}_1, \models)$ captures deadlock freedom, since reachable violations are deadlocks. $(\mathcal{V}_1, \models)$, on the other hand, captures local-deadlock freedom, as reachable violations represent local deadlocks.

Local static properties, i.e. static properties employing the local relation, should provide an interesting tool to show that a system respects a given property thanks to the good behaviour of its subsystems. Ensuring that all subsystems respect a given property might be more desirable than showing the property for the global system, and this fact is often neglected. For instance, let us examine the relationship between deadlock and local-deadlock freedom. Usually, deadlock freedom is checked as a first step to show that a system behaves as expected. A system, however, might be deadlock free, not because it behaves well, but because an individual component is always making the system progress, even though the rest of the system is blocked. So, in general, checking local-deadlock freedom, which ensures that no subsystem gets to a state in which it is forever stuck, seems like a better initial step in showing that a system behaves well.

We point out that a local static property is stronger than its global counterpart. The local satisfiability relation weakly defines that a violation occurs when one subsystem behaves badly but when plugged into a static property it requires all subsystems to be violation free. Note this generalisation to local properties does not scale well in most verification frameworks. For most frameworks, checking this property would entail carrying out exponentially many checks; one for each subsystem of the original system.

4.3 Capturing Some Other Static Properties

In this section, we move away from properties involving blocked states and show how to capture mutual-exclusion properties and a sort of safe-invocation property.

It is often the case that distributed systems implement a mutual-exclusion mechanism to ensure that the system behaves well. We capture a *general mutual-exclusion property* by the sets CS_i of component states, defining the *critical section* of component i. So, this property states that no two components can be simultaneously in their critical sections.

To capture this property, components' critical sections must be identified. The special (fresh) event mx_i annotates each state of component i that belongs to its critical section. This annotation is made with a self-loop transition using mx_i. Furthermore, we add some system rules that allow the system to perform this new special event so they can be used in static properties.

Definition 9. *Let* $S = (\langle L_1, \ldots, L_n \rangle, \mathcal{R})$ *be a supercombinator machine where* $L_i = (S_i, \Sigma_i, \Delta_i, \hat{s}_i)$, $(S, \Sigma, \Delta, \hat{s})$ *its induced LTS,* $CS_i \subseteq S_i$ *the critical section of component* i, *and* $mx_i \notin \Sigma_i$. *We use the modified system* $S_{MX} \cong (\langle L'_1, \ldots, L'_n \rangle, \mathcal{R} \cup \mathcal{R}')$ *to verify general mutual-exclusion properties.*

- $L'_i = (S_i, \Sigma_i \cup \{mx_i\}, \Delta_i \cup \{(s, mx_i, s) \mid s \in CS_i\}, \hat{s}_i)$
- $\mathcal{R}' = \{([i, mx_i], mx_i) \mid i \in \{1 \ldots n\}\}$
- $[i, e]$ *is the tuple of events where event* e *is in position* i *and* $-$ *is in all others.*

A violation occurs when any two components i and j are simultaneously in their critical sections. In our modified system, this corresponds to a state in which the events mx_i and mx_j can be performed, i.e. a state s satisfying $s \models \mathcal{V}_2$.

Violation formula 2. *For components* $\{1 \ldots n\}$:

$$\mathcal{V}_2 \cong Or\{And\{\textbf{Event } mx_i, \textbf{Event } mx_j\} \mid i, j \in \{1 \ldots n\} \wedge i \neq j\}$$

So, a system S satisfies the general mutual-exclusion property with respects to the critical sections CS_i iff the modified system S_{MX} satisfies $(\mathcal{V}_2, \models)$.

Many systems, however, implement a more fine grained type of mutual exclusion. For instance, concurrent access to read from a storage space is often not harmful but concurrent access to read and write or to write is. We propose a *read-write mutual-exclusion property* that is specified by the pairs of sets R_i and W_i, which represent the reading and writing sections of component i. We employ the same annotation method as before and use self-loops with events r_i and w_i to annotate the component states in the reading and writing sections, respectively, of component i.

Definition 10. *Let* $\mathcal{S} = (\langle L_1, \ldots, L_n \rangle, \mathcal{R})$ *be a supercombinator machine where* $L_i = (S_i, \Sigma_i, \Delta_i, \hat{s}_i)$, $(S, \Sigma, \Delta, \hat{s})$ *its induced LTS,* $R_i, W_i \subseteq S_i$ *the reading and writing sections of component* i, *respectively, and* $r_i, w_i \notin \Sigma_i$ *events. The modified read-write system is given by* $\mathcal{S}_{RW} \cong (\langle L'_1, \ldots, L'_n \rangle, \mathcal{R} \cup \mathcal{R}')$ *where:*

- $L'_i = (S_i, \Sigma_i \cup \{r_i, w_i\}, \Delta_i \cup \{(s, r_i, s) \mid s \in R_i\} \cup \{(s, w_i, s) \mid s \in W_i\}, \hat{s}_i)$
- $\mathcal{R}' = \{([i, r_i], r_i), ([i, w_i], w_i) \mid i \in \{1 \ldots n\}\}$

A violation to the read-write mutual-exclusion property occurs when a component i is in its writing section and another components j is either in its writing or reading section. Hence, such a violating state s satisfies $s \models \mathcal{V}_3$.

Violation formula 3. *For components* $\{1 \ldots n\}$:

$$\mathcal{V}_3 \cong \mathbf{Or}\{\mathbf{And}\{\mathbf{Event}\ w_i, \mathbf{Or}\{\mathbf{Event}\ r_j, \mathbf{Event}\ w_j\}\} \mid i, j \in \{1 \ldots n\} \wedge i \neq j\}$$

So, a system $\mathcal{S}$ satisfies the read-write mutual-exclusion property for sections R_i and W_i *iff* the modified system $\mathcal{S}_{RW}$ satisfies the static property $(\mathcal{V}_3, \models)$.

In addition to these two mutual-exclusion properties, we propose a way to ensure components only invoke services that are properly initialised. We describe a *safe-invocation property* by sets I_i. The set I_i contains pairs (ev, U): the event ev represents a service offered by component i and U the states of component i where this service has not been initialised yet. We identify component states in the sets U by annotating them with self-loops using events $si_{i,ev}$.

Definition 11. *Let* $\mathcal{S} = (\langle L_1, \ldots, L_n \rangle, \mathcal{R})$ *be a supercombinator machine where* $L_i = (S_i, \Sigma_i, \Delta_i, \hat{s}_i)$, $(S, \Sigma, \Delta, \hat{s})$ *its induced LTS,* $I_i \subseteq \Sigma_i \times \mathbb{P}(S_i)$, *where if* $(ev, U), (ev, U') \in I_i$ *then* $U = U'$, *the initialisation requirements for component* i, *and* $si_{i,ev} \notin \Sigma_i$ *events such that* $si_{i,ev} \neq si_{i,ev'}$ *if* $ev \neq ev'$. *We use the modified system* $\mathcal{S}_{SI} \cong (\langle L'_1, \ldots, L'_n \rangle, \mathcal{R} \cup \mathcal{R}')$ *to capture a safe-invocation property.*

- $L'_i = (S_i, \Sigma_i \cup \{si_{i,ev}\}, \Delta_i \cup \bigcup_{(ev,U) \in I_i} \{(s, si_{i,ev}, s) \mid s \in U\}, \hat{s}_i)$
- $\mathcal{R}' = \{([i, si_{i,ev}], si_{i,ev}) \mid i \in \{1 \ldots n\} \wedge (ev, U) \in I_i\}$

A violation to the safe-initialisation property occurs when a service ev is invoked but the corresponding provider component is uninitialised, namely, in a component state in U. Such a violating state s satisfies $s \models \mathcal{V}_4$.

Violation formula 4. *For components* $\{1 \ldots n\}$ *and sets* I_i:

$$\mathcal{V}_4 \cong \mathbf{Or}\{\mathbf{And}\{\mathbf{Event}\ ev, \mathbf{Event}\ si_{i,ev}\}\} \mid i \in \{1 \ldots n\} \wedge (ev, U) \in I_i\}$$

A system $\mathcal{S}$ satisfies the safe-invocation property for sets I_i if and only if $\mathcal{S}_{SI}$ satisfies the static property $(\mathcal{V}_4, \models)$.

Note that to capture these properties we systematically identify some special states of components and specify a violation based on some combination of these special states. So, as long as our violation formula is able to capture the desired violating behaviour for the system, this systematic process can be used to capture any such property. The design of our notation to capture static properties was driven by the properties presented here and our event-based system description. Nevertheless, we do not anticipate any difficulties in generalising this language to accommodate, for instance, special sets of marked states (which could replace our annotated states) or quantification in terms of specific subsystems. Note our annotation of states using self-loops with special events is already an implicit representation of a set of marked states, and handling quantification for specific subsystems should be simpler than handling quantification over all subsystems.

5   Approximate Verification of Static Properties

One way to check static properties is to explicitly look for a violation in the reachable states of the system. Explicit state exploration, however, tends to be very inefficient due to the state-space explosion problem. Many approaches have proposed the use of symbolic techniques to tackle this problem in the context of distributed systems but they have not significantly improved on the scalability of property checking. In this section, we introduce a verification framework that combines SAT checking with reachability approximations [1–3].

The framework we propose combines the reachability-approximating techniques in Sect. 3 to check static properties. So, it can tackle systems implementing a combination of the mechanisms captured by each individual technique.

Definition 12. *Let S be a supercombinator machine and $(S, \Sigma, \Delta, \hat{s})$ its induced LTS. For a $s \in S$, we define:*

$$reach_{Ap}(s) \cong reach_{Pair}(s) \wedge reach_{NC}(s) \wedge reach_{SC}(s) \wedge reach_{NA}(s)$$
$$\wedge reach_{SA}(s) \wedge reach_{C}(s) \wedge reach_{E}(s)$$

The combination of reachability approximations we use is itself an over-approximation. This follows from Theorem 1.

Theorem 2. *Let S be a supercombinator machine and $(S, \Sigma, \Delta, \hat{s})$ its induced LTS. For all $s \in S$, we have that reachable(s) implies reach$_{Ap}(s)$.*

Instead of looking through the reachable states of the system, our framework looks for a *candidate violation*, namely, a violating state that passes the reachability test $reach_{Ap}$.

Definition 13. *Let $(S, \Sigma, \Delta, \hat{s})$ be the induced LTS under analysis, and $(\sim, \mathcal{V})$ a static property. For $s \in S$, candidate_violation$(s) \cong reach_{Ap}(s) \wedge s \sim \mathcal{V}$.*

Our framework is imprecise as a candidate might pass our reachability test and yet be unreachable. Nevertheless, by conjoining these approximations, we tighten the state space analysed; it only takes one failed test to consider a state unreachable. Furthermore, as our framework over-approximates reachability (Theorem 2), it is sound in the sense that if no candidates are found, the corresponding static property must hold.

Theorem 3. *Given a static property, if a system is candidate-violation free it must also be free of reachable violations.*

5.1   Violation Candidate Search as a SAT Problem

We built upon [1–3] to create an efficient implementation for our framework. So, we encode the search of a candidate violation as a satisfiability problem to be later checked by a SAT solver. For the remainder of this section, let $S = (\langle L_1, \ldots, L_n \rangle, \mathcal{R})$, where $L_i = (S_i, \Sigma_i, \Delta_i, \hat{s}_i)$, be a supercombinator machine and $(S, \Sigma, \Delta, \hat{s})$ its induced LTS.

In our propositional encoding, $st_{i,s}$ is the boolean variable representing the state s of component i. The assignment $st_{i,s} = true$ indicates this component state belongs to a candidate, whereas $st_{i,s} = false$ means it does not. We propose SAT formula SP to look for a candidate violation for a static property. The combination of component states assigned to true in a satisfying assignment forms a candidate violation.

$$SP \mathrel{\hat{=}} State \wedge Reach_{Ap} \wedge Violation$$

Sub-formula $State$ holds if the combination of component states assigned to true forms a valid system state.

$$State \mathrel{\hat{=}} \bigwedge_{i \in \{1 \ldots n\}} \left(\left(\bigvee_{s \in S_i} st_{i,s} \right) \wedge \left(\bigwedge_{\substack{s,s' \in S_i \\ \wedge s \neq s'}} (\neg st_{i,s} \vee \neg st_{i,s'}) \right) \right)$$

To implement $Reach_{Ap}$, we reuse the propositional formulas presented in [1–3]. Each formula $Reach_x$ where $x \in \{Pair, NC, SC, NA, SA, C, E\}$ captures the corresponding reachability approximation[4]. So, the component states assigned to true in a satisfying assignment pass our reachability test.

$$Reach_{Ap} \mathrel{\hat{=}} Reach_{Pair} \wedge Reach_{NC} \wedge Reach_{SC} \wedge Reach_{NA}$$
$$\wedge\ Reach_{SA} \wedge Reach_C \wedge Reach_E$$

The sub-formula $Violation$ is encoded differently depending on whether the static property to be checked is global or local. For global static property $(\mathcal{V}, \models)$, $Violation$ captures that the state currently assigned to true satisfies $s \models \mathcal{V}$. To encode $s \models \mathcal{V}$, we only need to introduce a way to encode $s \models$ **Event** ev. Given an encoding for $s \models$ **Event** ev, the satisfiability of $s \models \mathcal{V}$ for any violation formula $\mathcal{V}$ is trivially encoded based on its propositional structure.

To encode $s \models$ **Event** ev, we need to encode the events available in a system state and, consequently, system rules. We use variable V_{ev}^i to encode that component i is in a state in which it can perform ev.

$$V_{ev}^i \Leftrightarrow \bigvee_{(s,ev',s') \in \Delta_i \wedge ev' = ev} st_{i,s}$$

---

[4] $Reach_{Pair}$ corresponds to the formula $Reachable$ in [2] where the pairs in NPR are calculated over sets S_i and S_j instead of $RequireSync_i$ and $RequireSync_j$. The sets $RequireSync_i$ represent an optimisation for checking deadlock freedom that is not valid to all static properties. $Reach_{NC}$, $Reach_{SC}$, $Reach_{NA}$ and $Reach_{SA}$ correspond to formulas $Reach_N^C$, $Reach_S^C$, $Reach_N^A$ and $Reach_S^A$ in [3], respectively.

Then, we capture that rule $r = (e, ev)$, where e_i is the element at position i, can be applied by variable V_r. This variable holds whenever the system in a state where components can perform their corresponding events, set in e.

$$V_r \Leftrightarrow \bigwedge_{i \in \{1...n\} \wedge e_i \neq -} V_{e_i}^i$$

Variable $V_{\text{Event } ev}$ holds for states in which the system can perform ev, namely, whenever a rule triggering event ev can be applied. r_{ev} denotes the system event performed by rule r. Finally, the sub-formula *Violation* is then constructed by replacing **Event** ev in $\mathcal{V}$ by $V_{\text{Event } ev}$.

$$V_{\text{Event } ev} \Leftrightarrow \bigvee_{r \in \mathcal{R} \wedge r_{ev} = ev} V_r$$

For local static property $(\mathcal{V}, \|\!\models)$, *Violation* captures that the system state s currently assigned to true satisfies $s \|\!\models \mathcal{V}$. We reuse the encoding for V_{ev}^i proposed for a global property. To encode quantification on subsystems, we introduce *participation variables* p_i. Variable p_i is true if and only if component i is part of the subsystem ss under analysis and add the clause $\bigvee_{i \in \{1...n\}} p_i$ to ensure that $ss \neq \emptyset$. As SAT checkers are designed to efficiently handle existential quantification, they should be particularly effective in tackling the sort of subsystem quantification we use in our local properties.

The encoding of rule variables V_r has to take into account subsystem projections. So, rule $r = (e, ev)$, where e_i is the element at position i, can be fired with respect to the system projection on the subsystem currently assigned to true (according to variables p_i) if and only if the following variable V_r holds. Note that if a component does not participate on a subsystem, its participation on rules is not required as per Definition 6. Hence, the disjunct $\neg p_i$.

$$V_r \Leftrightarrow \bigwedge_{i \in \{1...n\} \wedge e_i \neq -} (V_{e_i}^i \vee \neg p_i)$$

Variable $V_{\text{Event } ev}$ has to take into account the subsystem projections as well. For rule $r = (e, ev)$, r_C represents the components participating in r (i.e. components for which $e_i \neq -$) and r_{ev} denotes the system event performed by rule r, namely, ev. We encode variable $ron_r \Leftrightarrow \bigvee_{i \in r_C} p_i$ to represent whether rule r is on or off for the assigned subsystem: rules that do not involve the participation of any component in this subsystem must be disregarded, that is, they are off. So, event ev can only be performed by on rules.

$$V_{\text{Event } ev} \Leftrightarrow \bigvee_{r \in \mathcal{R} \wedge r_{ev} = ev} (V_r \wedge ron_r)$$

As SP captures candidate violations, if it is unsatisfiable, the system is candidate-violation free and, therefore, must satisfy the static property being checked. Otherwise, the solver returns an appropriate candidate violation.

6   Practical Evaluation

In this section, we evaluate our new framework. FDR4's ability to analyse CSP and generate supercombinator machines is used in generating our SAT encoding, which is then checked by the Glucose 4.0 solver [9]. Our framework is implemented in the *ApprOx* tool. For efficiency purposes, it incrementally constructs and makes use of the proposed reachability test. It initially queries the solver using only $reach_{Pair}$ as its reachability test, then it conjoins $reach_C$ and $reach_E$, then $reach_{NA}$ and $reach_{SA}$, and finally, $reach_{NC}$ and $reach_{SC}$. If at some point the combination of reachability predicates so-far conjoined is enough to prove the desired property, it can stop and save the time that would take to construct the following reachability predicates. ApprOx and the system models used in this section are available at [4].

We carried out two experiments: the first analyses how our framework fares in checking deadlock freedom and local-deadlock freedom, while the second evaluates how it fares for the verification of mutual-exclusion and safe-invocation properties. These experiments were conducted on a dedicated machine with a quad-core Intel Core i5-4300U CPU @ 1.90 GHz, and 8 GB of RAM.

6.1   Checking Deadlock and Local-Deadlock Freedom

We compare ApprOx to: CSDD and FSDD (which are implemented in Deadlock Checker [16]); FDR4's built-in deadlock freedom assertion [12], and its combination with partial order reduction [13] or compression techniques [21]. Note, only FDR4 techniques take advantage of the multicore setting.

We analyse 9 triple-disjoint local-deadlock-free systems: a distributed database (DDB), a matrix multiplication system (Mat), a token ring system with $N/2$ tokens (TkHF), the mad-postman routing network (Rout), a grid network implementing Tarry's algorithm (Tarry) [23], a central lock system (Lock), a central priority-queue-lock system (PrLock), a priority-token ring system (PrRing), and a grid network implementing a simplified implementation of Raymond's algorithm (Ray) [20]. Table 1 presents the results that we obtain for them.

While ApprOx proves that 8 of these systems are deadlock free and 7 local-deadlock free, CSDD and FSDD combine to check only 4 systems. We point out that CSDD and FSDD are examples of methods that try to prove the system's ungranted-request graph is acyclic. Hence, whenever a system passes their tests, it is free of deadlocks and local deadlocks. The difference in precision between our method and FSDD or CSDD can be justified by the fact that we exactly characterise blocked and locally-blocked states while these other methods imprecisely assume that a cycle of ungranted request characterises them. Also, the approximation that we use seems to be more precise than theirs. So, these results show that ApprOx can handle a larger class of systems while scaling similarly when compared to other incomplete frameworks. We have not compared ApprOx to the different versions of the DeadlOx tool [1–3], since it must be as efficient and more accurate thanks to code re-use and the incremental construction of our tighter reachability test. We point out that checking local-deadlock freedom

Table 1. Results for local-deadlock and deadlock freedom comparison.

	N	Incomplete		CSDD	Complete
		ApprOx		+FSDD	Best
		Deadlock	Local		
DDB	5	0.21	0.26	-	0.11
	10	3.27	3.37	-	*
	20	115.20	118.66	-	*
Mat	10	2.06	5.47	0.27	0.31
	15	10.43	39.89	0.37	4.42
	20	24.11	*	0.67	23.04
Rout	10	0.16	0.21	0.37	0.71
	20	0.66	1.21	1.28	4.42
	50	18.49	39.44	21.97	115.77
TkHF	50	1.16	1.36	-	*
	100	9.93	11.68	-	*
	200	124.32	136.39	-	*
Tarry	5	0.06	0.06	-	0.06
	10	1.46	-	-	0.11
	20	*	-	-	*
Lock	100	0.16	0.16	0.27	0.31
	200	0.41	0.46	0.67	0.11
	500	2.81	3.37	4.58	0.26
PrLock	5	-	-	-	0.86
	10	-	-	-	*
	20	-	-	-	*
PrRing	5	0.11	0.11	-	0.16
	10	0.61	0.61	-	*
	20	14.39	14.64	-	*
Ray	20	0.06	0.11	0.19	1.16
	30	0.11	0.16	0.22	290.20
	50	0.21	0.26	0.22	*

N is a parameter that is used to alter the size of the system. We measure in seconds the time taken to verify each system. * means that the method took longer than 300 s. - means that the method is unable to prove deadlock freedom. For ApprOx, **Deadlock** presents the time taken to verify deadlock freedom, whereas **Local** local-deadlock freedom. The column Best gives the fastest result amongst the complete methods we analysed. For the complete methods only deadlock freedom is checked, while FSDD and CSDD check a property stronger than local-deadlock freedom.

should be more difficult for systems where components are highly interconnected. The complex behavioural dependency between components in such systems complicates the sort of analysis we propose. So, verifying ring-like systems should be easier than verifying grid-like systems.

Note that for the Tarry example our tool only manages to prove local-deadlock freedom for $N = 5$. The components in this system are arranged in a $5 \times (N/5)$ grid that uses a token mechanism to construct a spanning tree for this grid. For $N = 5$, we have a 5×1-grid network where components can only communicate with their left and right neighbours, whereas for $N = 10$ and $N = 20$, we have a 5×2 and 5×4 grids, respectively, where components can communicate additionally with up and down neighbours. For $N = 5$, a pairwise analysis (carried out by $reach_{Pair}$) can keep track of the token and show that subsystems are never blocked. For $N = 10$ and $N = 20$, however, this added behaviour makes the identification of the underlying token structured required. The approximation $reach_C$ finds a conservative token structure but not the one that is required to prove local-deadlock freedom. The PrLock example is deadlock and local-deadlock free thanks to the fact that no two components can acquire a ticket with the same priority. This sort of invariant, however, cannot be captured by any of the approximations we use. We believe that an enhanced $reach_{Pair}$ approximation, where triples of interacting components are also analysed, could capture it, though.

For the complete approaches, i.e. FDR4 techniques, we only evaluate deadlock-freedom, as no built-in check for local-deadlock freedom is available in FDR4 and nor is it possible to formulate one efficiently. Approximate frameworks are consistently faster than complete approaches while being able to prove deadlock freedom for almost all analysed systems. The combination of FDR4's deadlock assertion with compression techniques comes closer to our approach in terms of verification time. We point out, however, that the effective use of compression techniques requires a careful and skilful application of those, whereas our method is fully automatic. For instance, a careful analysis of Mat's structure has pointed us to craft a compression strategy that is very effective. Slight modifications to this strategy, however, lead to compression strategies that are utterly inefficient. Unsurprisingly, FDR4's deadlock assertion outperforms our framework for the Lock and Tarry examples. For these systems, a single token/lock moves around the system and only components having a token/lock are allowed to perform actions. Hence, the state spaces of these systems are fairly small.

6.2   Checking Mutual Exclusion and Safe Invocation

To the best of our knowledge, our tool is the first one to propose an approximate approach to check mutual exclusion and safe invocation for distributed systems. So, we only compare our framework against refinement expressions that capture the same notions; verifying them using FDR4 creates a complete/precise approach. We check these expressions using FDR4's refinement-checking engine and its combination with partial order reduction or compression techniques.

We analyse 8 systems: a central lock system (Lock), a central priority-queue-lock system (PrLock), Milner's scheduler (Sched), a priority-token ring system

Table 2. Results for component-states other properties comparison

	N	Incomplete ApprOx	Complete Best			N	Incomplete ApprOx	Complete Best
	100	**0.51**	0.41			10	**0.11**	5.72
Lock	200	**20.52**	2.20		Grid	20	**0.11**	*
	500	**278.82**	17.29			50	**0.21**	*
	5	**0.16**	0.41			20	**0.16**	1.51
PrLock	10	**9.33**	*		Ray	30	**0.36**	244.41
	20	*	*			50	**1.51**	*
	50	**0.11**	171.84			5	**0.06**	0.06
Sched	100	**0.41**	143.90		RWLock	10	**0.36**	0.36
	200	**1.96**	*			20	*	*
	5	**0.11**	0.21			10	**0.11**	0.11
PrRing	10	**0.57**	*		SafeInv	20	**0.36**	*
	20	**14.09**	*			50	**5.34**	*

N is a parameter that is used to alter the size of the system. We measure in seconds the time taken to verify systems. * means that the method took longer than 300 s. The Best column shows the time taken by the fastest complete method to verify the refinement expression we propose.

(PrRing), a token-based message-passing grid system (Grid), and a simplified implementation of Raymond's algorithm (Ray), a central read-write lock system (RWLock), and root-based initialisation system (SafeInv). The first 6 systems implement general mutual-exclusion mechanisms, while the last two implement a read-write mutual-exclusion mechanism and a safe-invocation mechanism, respectively. The SafeInv system is designed so it passes from an initialising to a running phase via fairly loose coordination. Table 2 presents the results that we obtain for checking their corresponding properties.

ApprOx is able to verify for all systems their associated properties. Our implementation offers a more scalable approach if compared to the verification of the proposed refinement expression, at least for the systems tested, since it only exceeds the timeout set for two instances of the systems tested.

7   Conclusion

Motivated by the success of using reachability approximations for the verification of deadlock freedom, we have created a framework that can check static properties for distributed systems. Local-deadlock freedom, mutual exclusion, and safe invocation are some of the properties, other than deadlock freedom, that can be conveniently described in our framework. Unlike traditional frameworks, our approximative framework can effectively tackle local static properties. To the best of our knowledge, it is the first approximate approach to check this class of property for the kind of distributed system we tackle. Our experiments show that our framework can efficiently check static properties for some practical distributed systems that are out of the reach of complete methods. Thus, it represents a valid alternative to cope with the state space explosion problem. Finally, there is nothing CSP-specific in our methods, other than that we have a system described as a network of pairwise interacting LTSs. Therefore, the ideas in this paper should transfer to formalisms where systems are described as such.

Liveness properties do not seem to fit well with the kind of reachability approximations we use. To capture such properties, we would probably need to add complex regulator components to the system to transform the sort of path-based behaviour leading to a violation into a static property. The complex behaviour of such regulators, however, is likely to interfere and excessively damage the sort of analysis made by the approximations we use. A few approximate frameworks have been proposed to check liveness properties [11,19] but they use rather different types of system analysis.

We intend to extend this framework to check some of CSP's refinement relations. Also, we hope to add new reachability tests. For instance, to tackle the PrLock example in Sect. 6, we could create a new approximation that captures the fact that two components cannot acquire tickets with the same priority.

Acknowledgements. The first author is a CAPES Foundation scholarship holder (Process no: 13201/13-1). The other authors are partially sponsored by EPSRC under agreement number EP/N022777.

References

1. Antonino, P., Gibson-Robinson, T., Roscoe, A.W.: The automatic detection of token structures and invariants using SAT checking. In: Legay, A., Margaria, T. (eds.) TACAS 2017. LNCS, vol. 10206, pp. 249–265. Springer, Heidelberg (2017). https://doi.org/10.1007/978-3-662-54580-5_15
2. Antonino, P., Gibson-Robinson, T., Roscoe, A.W.: Efficient deadlock-freedom checking using local analysis and SAT solving. In: Ábrahám, E., Huisman, M. (eds.) IFM 2016. LNCS, vol. 9681, pp. 345–360. Springer, Cham (2016). https://doi.org/10.1007/978-3-319-33693-0_22
3. Antonino, P., Gibson-Robinson, T., Roscoe, A.W.: Tighter reachability criteria for deadlock-freedom analysis. In: Fitzgerald, J., Heitmeyer, C., Gnesi, S., Philippou, A. (eds.) FM 2016. LNCS, vol. 9995, pp. 43–59. Springer, Cham (2016). https://doi.org/10.1007/978-3-319-48989-6_3
4. Antonino, P., Gibson-Robinson, T., Roscoe, A.W.: Experiment package (2017). www.cs.ox.ac.uk/people/pedro.antonino/sppkg.zip
5. Antonino, P.R.G., Oliveira, M.M., Sampaio, A.C.A., Kristensen, K.E., Bryans, J.W.: Leadership election: an industrial SoS application of compositional deadlock verification. In: Badger, J.M., Rozier, K.Y. (eds.) NFM 2014. LNCS, vol. 8430, pp. 31–45. Springer, Cham (2014). https://doi.org/10.1007/978-3-319-06200-6_3
6. Antonino, P., Sampaio, A., Woodcock, J.: A refinement based strategy for local deadlock analysis of networks of CSP processes. In: Jones, C., Pihlajasaari, P., Sun, J. (eds.) FM 2014. LNCS, vol. 8442, pp. 62–77. Springer, Cham (2014). https://doi.org/10.1007/978-3-319-06410-9_5
7. Attie, P.C., Bensalem, S., Bozga, M., Jaber, M., Sifakis, J., Zaraket, F.A.: An abstract framework for deadlock prevention in BIP. In: Beyer, D., Boreale, M. (eds.) FMOODS/FORTE -2013. LNCS, vol. 7892, pp. 161–177. Springer, Heidelberg (2013). https://doi.org/10.1007/978-3-642-38592-6_12

8. Attie, P.C., Chockler, H.: Efficiently verifiable conditions for deadlock-freedom of large concurrent programs. In: Cousot, R. (ed.) VMCAI 2005. LNCS, vol. 3385, pp. 465–481. Springer, Heidelberg (2005). https://doi.org/10.1007/978-3-540-30579-8_30

9. Audemard, G., Simon, L.: Predicting learnt clauses quality in modern SAT solvers. In: IJCAI 2009, San Francisco, CA, USA, pp. 399–404 (2009)

10. Bensalem, S., Bozga, M., Legay, A., Nguyen, T.-H., Sifakis, J., Yan, R.: Component-based verification using incremental design and invariants. Softw. Syst. Model. **15**(2), 427–451 (2016)

11. Filho, M.S.C., Oliveira, M.V.M., Sampaio, A., Cavalcanti, A.: Local livelock analysis of component-based models. In: Ogata, K., Lawford, M., Liu, S. (eds.) ICFEM 2016. LNCS, vol. 10009, pp. 279–295. Springer, Cham (2016). https://doi.org/10.1007/978-3-319-47846-3_18

12. Gibson-Robinson, T., Armstrong, P., Boulgakov, A., Roscoe, A.W.: FDR3 — a modern refinement checker for CSP. In: Ábrahám, E., Havelund, K. (eds.) TACAS 2014. LNCS, vol. 8413, pp. 187–201. Springer, Heidelberg (2014). https://doi.org/10.1007/978-3-642-54862-8_13

13. Gibson-Robinson, T., Hansen, H., Roscoe, A.W., Wang, X.: Practical partial order reduction for CSP. In: Havelund, K., Holzmann, G., Joshi, R. (eds.) NFM 2015. LNCS, vol. 9058, pp. 188–203. Springer, Cham (2015). https://doi.org/10.1007/978-3-319-17524-9_14

14. Hoare, C.A.R.: Communicating Sequential Processes. Prentice-Hall, Englewood Cliffs (1985)

15. Lambertz, C., Majster-Cederbaum, M.: Analyzing component-based systems on the basis of architectural constraints. In: Arbab, F., Sirjani, M. (eds.) FSEN 2011. LNCS, vol. 7141, pp. 64–79. Springer, Heidelberg (2012). https://doi.org/10.1007/978-3-642-29320-7_5

16. Martin, J.M.R.: The Design and Construction of Deadlock-Free Concurrent Systems. Ph.D. thesis, University of Buckingham (1996)

17. Martin, J.M.R., Jassim, S.A.: An efficient technique for deadlock analysis of large scale process networks. In: Fitzgerald, J., Jones, C.B., Lucas, P. (eds.) FME 1997. LNCS, vol. 1313, pp. 418–441. Springer, Heidelberg (1997). https://doi.org/10.1007/3-540-63533-5_22

18. Oliveira, M.V.M., Antonino, P., Ramos, R., Sampaio, A., Mota, A., Roscoe, A.W.: Rigorous development of component-based systems using component metadata and patterns. Formal Aspects Comput. **28**(6), 937–1004 (2016). https://doi.org/10.1007/s00165-016-0375-1. ISSN:1433-299X

19. Ouaknine, J., Palikareva, H., Roscoe, A.W., Worrell, J.: A static analysis framework for livelock freedom in CSP. Logical Methods Comput. Sci. **9**(3) September 2013. https://doi.org/10.2168/LMCS-9(3:24)2013

20. Raymond, K.: A tree-based algorithm for distributed mutual exclusion. ACM Trans. Comput. Syst. (TOCS) **7**(1), 61–77 (1989)

21. Roscoe, A.W., Gardiner, P.H.B., Goldsmith, M., Hulance, J.R., Jackson, D.M., Scattergood, J.B.: Hierarchical compression for model-checking CSP or how to check 10^{20} dining philosophers for deadlock. In: TACAS, pp. 133–152 (1995)

22. Roscoe, A.W.: Understanding Concurrent Systems. Springer, Heidelberg (2010)

23. Tarry, G.: Le probleme des labyrinthes. Nouvelles annales de mathématiques, journal des candidats aux écoles polytechnique et normale **14**, 187–190 (1895)

Semantics and Languages

UTCP: Compositional Semantics for Shared-Variable Concurrency

Andrew Butterfield$^{(\boxtimes)}$ (iD)

Lero@TCD, School of Computer Science and Statistics,
Trinity College Dublin, Dublin 2, Ireland
butrfeld@tcd.ie

Abstract. We present a Unifying Theories of Programming (UTP) semantics of shared variable concurrency that is fully compositional. Previous work was based on mapping such programs, using labelling of decision points and atomic actions, to action systems, which themselves were provided with a UTP semantics. The translation to action systems was largely compositional, but their dynamic semantics was based on having all the actions collected together. Here we take a more direct approach, albeit inspired by the action-systems view, based on an abstract notion of label generation, that then exploits the standard use of substitution in UTP, to obtain a fully compositional semantics.

1 Introduction

In this paper we present a compositional semantics for a simple abstract shared-variable concurrent language, called the "Command" language presented in Fig. 1. The Command language is very simple, with sequential composition $(C_1 \,;; C_2)$, and only non-deterministic choices, for alternative execution paths $(C_1 + C_2)$ or deciding when to terminate a loop (C^*). The parallel composition $(C_1 \parallel C_2)$ allows arbitrary interference by each side on any variables, all of which are considered here to be global and shared. The semantics we present does not itself need to deal explicitly with any shared variables, but simply assumes a shared state s and the existence of atomic state-change actions a. This Command language corresponds directly to Concurrent Kleene Algebra (CKA) [14].

Our interest in this language stems from our general work within the Unifying Theories of Programming (UTP) framework [13], in which we seek to find ways to unify the semantics of a wide range of programming and specification languages, and language features, in order to be able to reason formally about systems built using a mix of such languages. The Command language in this paper is based on that introduced in the "Views" paper [10], which describes how a range of approaches to reasoning about shared-variable concurrency can

This work was supported, in part, by Science Foundation Ireland grants 10/CE/I1855 and 13/RC/2094 to Lero - the Irish Software Engineering Research Centre (www.lero.ie).

© Springer International Publishing AG 2017
S. Cavalheiro and J. Fiadeiro (Eds.): SBMF 2017, LNCS 10623, pp. 253–270, 2017.
https://doi.org/10.1007/978-3-319-70848-5_16

$$
\begin{array}{lll}
a \in \textsf{Atom} & \text{Atomic state-change actions} \\
C ::= \langle a \rangle & \text{Atomic Command} \\
\quad | \quad C \mathbin{;;} C & \text{Sequential Compostion} \\
\quad | \quad C + C & \text{Non-deterministic Choice} \\
\quad | \quad C \parallel C & \text{Parallel Compostion} \\
\quad | \quad C^{*} & \text{Non-deterministic Iteration}
\end{array}
$$

Fig. 1. Command language syntax

be mapped down onto CKA, and the Command language. Approaches covered in [10] include various Separation logics [8], type-theories, Owicki-Gries [20], and Rely-Guarantee [17], among others. Our intention in developing a UTP semantics of the Command language is to be able to use it as a foundation on which to build UTP theories of the above approaches that will be easy to link together. In effect we hope to use the results of the Views paper as a conceptual architecture to organise our work.

Another independent motivation for this work is a research collaboration that led us to give a UTP semantics to a process modelling language called PML [1], which has the notion of basic actions that require certain resources to run, and which provide further resources as a result. Actions can be combined using sequencing, selection, branching and iteration. We published initial work on a UTP semantics for PML [7], noting that it is essentially the same as the Command language. The semantics we gave in [7] was not compositional, however, and finding a fully compositional semantics was noted for future work.

Compositionality is important. By it we mean the property that the semantics of a composite construct can determined from the semantics of its parts, so for example, the meaning of the construct $C_1 \mathbin{;;} C_2$ would be determined by the meanings of C_1 and C_2, combined with the meaning of $\mathbin{;;}$. This property is desirable as without it both the semantics and any reasoning principle based on it would not scale up to large programs or systems.

The structure of the rest of this paper is as follows: we describe some related work (Sect. 2), followed by an introduction to the UTP methodology (Sect. 3). We then explain various aspects of our UTP semantics, touching on labels (Sect. 4), observations (Sect. 5), atomic actions (Sect. 6), and healthiness conditions (Sect. 7). We can then present the semantics in Sect. 8. Finally we discuss some calculations that contribute to the validation of the semantics (Sect. 9) and conclude in Sect. 10.

2   Related Work

Key work was done on concurrent semantics in the 80s and 90s, with a strong focus on fully abstract denotational semantics. Notable work form this period includes that by Stephen Brookes [5] and Frank de Boer and colleagues [3]. Both looked at denotations based on the notion of sets of transition traces, these being sequences of pairs of before-after states. In order to get compositionality the traces of any program fragment had to have arbitrary "stuttering" and "mumbling" state-pairs added to capture the notion of outside interference. Full abstraction meant that the semantics had to identify programs like $skip \;;\; skip$ with $skip$, while distinguishing between $x := 2$ and $x := 1 \;;\; x := x + 1$.

The first UTP theory in this area was presented in the UTPP paper [23]. This combined guarded commands [9] with the idea of action systems [2], interpreted in UTP as non-deterministic choice over guarded atomic actions, where disabled actions behave like the unit for that choice. This basic lattice-theoretic architecture for the UTPP semantics forms the foundation and inspiration for the UTCP semantics presented here.

More recently, also inspired by [10], the "UTP Views" paper by van Staden [21], starts algebraically, looking at Kleene algebras over languages. Languages here are sets of strings over an alphabet A. He then takes $A = \Sigma \times \Sigma$, which in effect encodes the Brookes model [5]. His semantics fits with the usual UTP approach to concurrency, in that it is based on traces as sequences of some notion of event.

All the compositional semantic frameworks we have discussed in this section are based on this notion of sets of transition traces, but we are seeking a semantics based on direct relations between before- and after-program states, without any explicit notion of traces. The reason for this is that the resulting UTP theory will have a form that will make it easier to link to concurrency approaches such as rely-guarantee, or separation logic, that are used with languages that are imperative and program-variable based.

There is however a semantics for shared-variable concurrency that is much closer in form to the one developed in this paper. This is the "actions with axioms" approach of Lamport [18]. In this, the semantics of each language construct is given by a set of axioms, that are predicates over both program variables, and additional "auxiliary" variables that manage flow of control. The meaning of a composite is given by taking the axioms that describe each of its components, and combining them with appropriate renamings. This requires being able to identify specific sub-components of any given component, and a syntactical method for doing this is described.

We were not aware of this work when we developed the UTCP theory in this paper, but there are very strong parallels between the features of our semantics and those in [18]. In some sense our semantics is a re-working of his within UTP. We shall point out specific correspondences as we proceed with our presentation.

3   UTP

The Unifying Theories of Programming framework [13] uses predicate calculus to define before-after relationships over appropriate collections of free observation variables. The before-variables are undashed, while after-variables have dashes. A simple approach would be to simply observe the values of program variables, in which case the before- and after-*values* of program variable v would be represented by observational variables v and v' respectively. For example, the meaning of an assignment statement might be given as follows:

$$x := e \quad \widehat{=} \quad x' = e \wedge \nu' = \nu$$

The definition says that the assignment terminates, with the final value of variable x set equal to the value of expression e in the before-state, while the other variables, denoted collectively here by ν, remain unchanged. This leads to a theory of partial correctness for imperative programs.

The theory can be extended to cover total correctness by introducing Boolean observations of program starting (ok) and termination (ok'). In this case, we find that we need a technique that allows us to identify predicates whose interpretation is nonsense, and eliminate them from any semantic theory we might construct. For example, the predicate $\neg ok \wedge ok'$ describes a situation in which a program has not started, but has terminated.

In UTP we use the concept of healthiness conditions to specify which predicates are meaningful in the context of our theory. For the total correctness theory to work, we need to ensure that all predicates have the form $ok \wedge P \implies ok' \wedge Q$, where P and Q do not refer to ok or ok'. This is interpreted as saying, if the program is started and P holds true at the start, then the program will terminate with Q being satisfied at the end.

A standard UTP approach is to define healthy predicates as being fixed-points of suitable idempotent, monotonic predicate transformers. For example, in the total correctness theory, we can define a predicate transformer $\mathbf{H}(P) \widehat{=} ok \implies P$. A predicate D that satisfies $D = (ok \implies D)$ is one that only asserts its behaviour once it is started $(ok = \mathbf{true})$. Our healthiness conditions (Sect. 7) are expressed in this fashion.

An important characteristic of both the UTP theories referred to above, is that their predicates are interpreted as a relation between the before-state and after-state of a *complete* program execution.

The "standard" treatment of concurrency in UTP [13, Chps. 7, 8], is focussed on local-state concurrency, without any mutable state variables. Here it becomes necessary to observe the program state at intermediate points in its execution, typically when the program is waiting for external events to occur. This necessitates another pair of Boolean observations, *wait* and *wait'* that indicate such waiting. We do not give any further details regarding these theories, but instead mention them simply to make the observation that here the predicates are interpreted as a relation between the before-state, and some *subsequent* intermediate or final state of the complete execution.

Our focus in this introduction on how the predicates are *interpreted* in terms of program state is important, because the theory presented in this paper involves yet more adjustments in interpretation, as explained in Sects. 5 and 9.

In order to present our UTP semantics of shared-variable concurrency, we have to address an issue that Lamport's semantics [18] faced, namely how to refer to sub-components and their semantics from within a composite. In particular

he enunciates a number of principles at the start of his semantics. One identifies
the need to know "who" carries out a specific action, while another says that
we need to be able to transform a statement about command C into one about
command C *within the context of some enclosing construct.*

In the next section we introduce labels and their generators, which are our
approach to addressing these concerns. We then follow-up with a description of
the observation variables for our theory, how we handle atomic actions, healthiness conditions, and then the semantic definitions.

4 Labels

In order to manage flow-of-control, we need to be able to identify when every
construct starts, is running, and ends. In some approaches in the literature, the
program syntax allows for and requires explicit labels which are used for this
purpose. In our semantics, and that in [19], these identifying labels are generated
in a systematic way from the abstract syntax tree. We adopt the idea from [23]
that flow of control is managed by an auxiliary variable whose value is the set
of all labels of constructs that are able to execute.

We adopted the idea of a label-generator. Given some notion of labels ($l \in Lbs$), we want a notion of a generator ($g \in Gen$) that supports two operations:
$new : Gen \rightarrow Lbl \times Gen$ that produces a new label and a new generator; while
$split : Gen \rightarrow Gen \times Gen$ splits a generator into two new ones. In all cases we
require that any labels obtained from new generators will not have been obtained
previously from any of their parent generators.

To avoid long nested calls of new, $split$ and projections π_1, π_2, we define the
following terse label and generator expression syntax:

$$g \in GVar \qquad \text{Generator variables}$$
$$G \in GExp ::= g \mid G_: \mid G_1 \mid G_2$$
$$L \in LExp ::= \ell_G$$

Here $G_:$ denotes the generator left once new has been run on G, with ℓ_G
denoting the label so generated. Expressions G_1 and G_2 denote the two outcomes
of applying $split$ to G. We use $labs(G)$ to denote all the labels that G can generate
and we require the following laws to hold:

$$labs(G) = \{\ell_G\} \cup labs(G_:) \cup labs(G_1) \cup labs(G_2)$$
$$\ell_G \notin labs(G_:)$$
$$\emptyset = labs(G_1) \cap labs(G_2)$$

The simplest model for a generator that satisfies the above constraints is one that
represents the label ℓ_G by the expression G itself. The reason for this shorthand
is that without it we would have to write something like the following[1]

$$\pi_1(new(\pi_2(new(\pi_2(split(\pi_2(new(\pi_1(split(g)))))))))).$$

---

[1] "Split g, take the first one, generate a label and take the resulting generator, split
it and take the second, take two new labels and give me the last one".

instead of $\ell_{g1:2:}$. This notation is compact, and may appear very contrived. However it has one very strong advantage: it makes generators and their labels "relocatable", in much the same way as some program code can be so considered. The variable g can be viewed as a sort of "base", with all of the labels generated from it being relative to that base. We can do this, in one way only, by substituting any generator expression for g. If we replace g with something different, then we "shift" all the associated labels accordingly. If γ and σ range over sequences of :, 1 and 2, then

$$(\ell_{g\gamma})[g\sigma/g] = \ell_{g\sigma\gamma} \tag{1}$$

In effect the substitution "relocates" generator g by running *new* and *split* on it as specified by σ, and any labels are in effect generated by this relocated generator using their γ specification. This simple use of substitution gives us a really easy way to compose program fragments in terms of their semantics. In fact this ability to "relocate" is how we manage Lamport's principle that we must be able to talk about command C in the context of an enclosing construct.

5   Observations

Any UTP theory has to clearly define its *alphabet*, that is, the set of observational variables that define its domain of discourse. The theory presented here is inspired by UTPP [23] and uses some of the observations presented there: the values associated with all (shared) variables are not mentioned individually, but instead are lumped together; and we assume that all actions are labelled and that we can observe the set of labels that are considered to be "active".

$$s, s' : State \tag{2}$$

$$ls, ls' : \mathcal{P}\,Lbl \tag{3}$$

Here s and s' denote the before- and after-values of the shared (variable) state, while ls and ls' denote the before- and after-values of the active label-set used for control-flow. In Lamport's semantics [18] a series of temporal logic axioms are provided to track the dynamics of which constructs are starting, in progress, or finishing. We achieve the same effect using the label-sets.

The role of label-generators is rather different, however. They will be used to generate labels for statements, and we do not want these to change during the lifetime of the program. We will also want to be able to refer in a general way to two key labels associated with any language construct, namely the label (in) that is used to enable the starting of a construct, and the label (out) that is used to signal that the construct has just terminated.

$$in, out : Lbl \tag{4}$$

$$g : Gen \tag{5}$$

These observations are *static*, in that their values do not change during program execution. Instead, these variables record context-sensitive information about how a language construct is situated with respect to its "neighbours", in a way that permits a compositional approach. For details of how this works, see Sect. 8.3.

In effect we are exploiting the fact that our language is block-structured with only one entry and exit point for each construct, in order to be able to decouple the semantics of an atomic action from whatever might come next. Dealing with that is the responsibility of the semantics of language composites.

To summarise, our semantics is will be built using observable variables $s, s', ls, ls', g, in, out$ to describe basic atomic state-change actions that modify global shared state s. The concurrent flow of control will be managed using the global dynamic label-set ls and the static association of a label generator g and two distinguished labels in, out, with every language construct.

This brings us to an important distinction between the usual approach taken by UTP regarding the distinction between syntax and semantics. The usual approach, inspired by the slogan "programs are predicates" [11,12], is to treat syntax and semantics as the same thing. A program's syntax is simply a shorthand notation for its semantics. So, the program text x := x+y *is* a predicate, a shorthand for the more verbose $x' = x + y \land y' = y^2$. in particular, the notation for sequential composition, $P; Q$, is a shorthand for $\exists obs_m \bullet P[obs_m/obs'] \land Q[obs_m/obs]$, where obs (obs') refers to all the before- (after-) observations. This "punning" between syntax and semantics largely works for theories of sequential programs or local-state concurrency, mainly because sequences of code lead to simple semantic sequencing. However, in global shared-variable concurrency, code sequences get broken up by interference from parallel execution threads, and there is no longer a simple correspondence between syntactical and semantic sequencing.

Here we shall use the notation $P; Q$ to denote *semantic* sequential composition, which means that the execution of P is immediately followed by the execution of Q, without any intervening external interfence. We define it as follows:

$$P; Q \mathrel{\widehat{=}} \exists s_m, ls_m \bullet P[s_m, ls_m/s', ls'] \land Q[s_m, ls_m/s, ls] \tag{6}$$

The key thing to note is that this definition makes no reference at all to g, *in* or *out*, as these are static observations.

We also define *semantic* skip (II), the unit for semantic sequential composition, as

$$\mathit{II} \mathrel{\widehat{=}} ls' = ls \land s' = s \tag{7}$$

6   Atomic Actions

An atomic action (a) is simply a global state transformer whose effects, once started, occur immediately and completely, without any external interference. We can consider it be a relational predicate that only mentions s and s'. Flow of control is managed by keeping a dynamic record of which labels are considered

---

[2] Assuming x and y are the only variables.

current, or "enabled". The behaviour of an atomic action is that it exhibits none until its label is enabled. Noting that many atomic actions can be enabled at once, what happens is that one of actions is selected non-deterministically to run. The action so selected transforms the global state, and then the control-flow management marks its label as disabled, and enables labels of atomic action that can immediately follow it according to the control-flow structure of the program.

As already stated, we use a to denote the predicate describing the core global state-changes, and use ls and ls' to record the set of enabled labels both before and after the atomic action has run. We can define a predicate that captures the basic behaviour of such "flow-controlled" atomic action:

$$in \in ls \wedge a \wedge (ls' = (ls \setminus \{in\}) \cup \{out\}) \tag{8}$$

In short: the action when its in-label is in ls, is that it performs the state-change specified by a, and replaces the in-label by the out-label, in the updated set ls' of enabled labels. If in is not in ls, or predicate a is not satisfied by the current value of s, then the semantic predicate reduces to **false**.

The semantics of a running composite program, as per the action systems approach used in [23], is to imagine all of the labelled atomic actions collected into one large non-deterministic choice, itself in a loop that runs until some distinguished stop-label appears in the enabled label-set. The whole thing is initialised by enabling at least one atomic action in-label. The result of initialising and running this loop once will be one possible complete execution sequence of the program (assuming it terminates). In effect, the meaning of a shared-variable concurrent program is all the interleavings of atomic actions that are consistent with flow-of-control restrictions, with each interleaving being a series of atomic actions sequentially composed *semantically*, using ; as defined in Eq. 6.

Given that we will be sequentially composing a lot of predicates like 8, we shall introduce a shorthand notation that we refer to as a "basic action", which refers to sets of labels called E (enablers) and N (new):

$$A(E \mid a \mid N) \,\hat{=}\, E \subseteq ls \wedge a \wedge ls' = (ls \setminus E) \cup N \quad \text{«·A-def·»}$$

The plan is to then produce some laws governing the semantic sequential compositions of basic actions ($A(E_1 \mid a_1 \mid N_1); A(E_2 \mid a_1 \mid N_2)$), but we quickly discover that in general the outcome cannot be expressed as a single instance of the form $A(E \mid a \mid N)$. Consider $A(l_1 \mid a \mid l_2); A(l_2 \mid b \mid l_3)$, in a starting state where both l_1 and l_2 are in ls. The overall result is a combined action that needs l_1 to start, and adds in l_3 at the end, but also removes both l_1 and l_2. So, in order to effectively calculate with the theory (see Sect. 9), we need to generalise the basic action idea to an eXtended basic action, where we explicitly identify the labels that we remove (R):

$$X(E \mid a \mid R \mid A) \,\hat{=}\, E \subseteq ls \wedge a \wedge ls' = (ls \setminus R) \cup A \quad \text{«·X-def·»}$$

Clearly $A(E \mid a \mid N) = X(E \mid a \mid E \mid N)$. We can now prove the following composition law:

$$X(E_1 \mid a \mid R_1 \mid A_1); X(E_2 \mid b \mid R_2 \mid A_2) \qquad\qquad \langle\!\langle \cdot \mathsf{X\text{-}then\text{-}X} \cdot \rangle\!\rangle$$
$$= E_2 \cap (R_1 \setminus A_1) = \emptyset$$
$$\wedge X(E_1 \cup (E_2 \setminus A_1) \mid a\,;b \mid R_1 \cup R_2 \mid (A_1 \setminus R_2) \cup A_2)$$

The condition $E_2 \cap (R_1 \setminus A_1) = \emptyset$ characterises all those cases were the second X is enabled immediately after the first X terminates (i.e., without any outside interference). This brings us to a very important aspect of how these predicates are to be interpreted. The semantic sequential composition of two basic actions captures the occurrence of both actions in sequence without any intervening interference, known as a *mumbling* step. This means that the first action once enabled, must be able to enable the second one without relying on some external agent. The expression $E_2 \cap (R_1 \setminus A_1)$ is all of the labels in E_2 that are removed (R_1) by the first action, but are not added back in (A_1). If this not empty then some of the labels from E_2 will not be present, and so the second action has been disabled by the first. So the whole predicate reduces to **false**, indicating that it is not possible to observe those two actions in sequence, unless some other execution thread manages to add in the missing E_2 labels in-between, as an interference step.

7 Healthiness

7.1 Wheels-within-Wheels

We are building a semantics based on predicates that define before-after relations on program state s, s' and label-sets ls, ls', using the static observations to put things in their syntactical context. In order to be able to extract the correct behaviour from this semantics, it was necessary to have a healthiness condition that effectively said that every program component, atomic or composite, has to be viewed as being willing to run as many times as necessary whenever its labels would appear in ls. At its simplest, the semantics required every construct to be embedded in its own infinite loop, to ensure it was always ready to "go". This lead to our use of the phrase "Wheels within Wheels" (WwW) to refer to this principle. This did not mean that everything ran forever, but that, in some sense, it should always be ready.

Technically we require any healthy UTCP program predicate to be equivalent to a non-deterministic choice of how many times it repeats itself, including zero, using UTP semantic sequential composition.

$$P^0 \cong II \qquad\qquad \langle\!\langle \cdot \mathsf{seq\text{-}0} \cdot \rangle\!\rangle$$
$$P^{i+1} \cong P\,;\,P^i \qquad\qquad \langle\!\langle \cdot \mathsf{seq\text{-}i\text{-}plus\text{-}1} \cdot \rangle\!\rangle$$
$$\mathbf{WwW}(P) \cong \bigvee_{i \in \mathbb{N}} P^i \qquad \langle\!\langle \cdot \mathsf{WWW\text{-}as\text{-}NDC} \cdot \rangle\!\rangle$$

Here we have introduced a *stuttering* step, denoted by UTP's *semantic* skip (II). We note also, that $\mathbf{WwW}$ is monotonic and idempotent.

It should be noticed that this theory underwent a large number of iterations before the WwW principle was finally elucidated properly and shown to give the right results. The number and complexity of the test calculations needed to debug, develop and validate the theory presented in this paper necessitated the development of a bespoke "UTP Calculator" [6].

7.2 Label-Set Invariants

The semantics we propose here depends on the careful management of when specific labels are, or are not, present in the global label-set ls. Key to the success of this semantics is a collection of label-set invariants which characterise proper label-set contents, which are preserved by all label-set manipulations performed by our semantic definitions. We have two kinds of invariants, both of which are concerned with the mutual disjointness, in some sense, of a collection of sets of labels. We introduce some shorthand notations to avoid excessively long predicates and expressions. We use '|' as a separator between things meant to be disjoint, and commas to list subsets and/or set- elements that should be unioned together. So the fragment $A, b \mid M, N \mid x, Y$ is shorthand for the mutual disjointness of $A \cup \{b\}$ and $M \cup N$ and $\{x\} \cup Y$. To assert mutual set disjointness, we use the following shorthand, where the L_i are label-sets,

$$\{L_1 \mid L_2 \mid \ldots \mid L_n\} \widehat{=} \forall_{i,j \in 1\ldots n} \bullet i \neq j \implies L_i \cap L_j = \emptyset$$
$$\text{《·short-disj-lbl·》}$$

We also want to assert that certain sets, necessarily mutually disjoint, can never have any of their elements in the global label-set, if any element from one of the other sets is present. Again, we have a shorthand:

$$[L_1 \mid L_2 \mid \ldots \mid L_n] \widehat{=} \forall_{i,j \in 1\ldots n} \bullet i \neq j \implies (L_i \cap ls \neq \emptyset \implies L_j \cap ls = \emptyset)$$
$$\text{《·short-lbl-exclusive·》}$$

The first invariant we have, Disjoint Labels (DL) is simply one that asserts, for every construct, that in, out and the labels of g are all different.[3]

$$DL \widehat{=} \{in \mid labs(g) \mid out\} \quad \text{《·Disjoint-Labels·》}$$

We shall simplify further by stating that in the shorthands presented here that we use just simple g to denote $labs(g)$, so DL can we written as $\{in \mid g \mid out\}$. We also need stronger Label Exclusivity invariants, regarding which labels can, or cannot, occur in the global label set at any one time. There is not one such

---

[3] The theory can be developed using only g as a static observation, and letting ℓ_g and $\ell_{g:}$ play the role of in and out respectively, in which case Disjoint Labels is automatically satisfied. However, while this results in an entirely equivalent theory, it is notationally more obscure making it harder to interpret and check.

invariant, but rather we have that some language constructs may define their own variation, in order to ensure that flow of control is correctly managed.

There is a general version of the invariant (LE) that holds for all language constructs that asserts that any point in time, only elements from of one of in, $labs(g)$ or out can be present in ls or ls' at any point in time:

$$LE \mathrel{\hat{=}} [in \mid g \mid out] \wedge [in \mid g \mid out]' \quad \text{《·Exclusive-Labels·》}$$

Note that $[in \mid g \mid out]'$ is simply indicates that it refers to ls' rather than ls.

So, in summary, we have that every healthy predicate describing a shared-variable concurrent program's behaviour is of the form $\mathbf{WwW}(C)$ for some predicate C and also satisfies DL and LE.

$$\mathbf{W}(P) \mathrel{\hat{=}} DL \wedge LE \wedge \mathbf{WwW}(P) \quad \text{《·W-def·》}$$

We note that many of the axioms for a given construct in the semantics of Lamport [18] exist to ensure the same properties regarding construct activation as the healthiness conditions described here.

8   Command Semantics

We present the full semantics of atomic commands first, then describe an important classification of expressions and substitutions, before describing the semantics of the four composite command forms.

8.1   Atomic Commands

The atomic command $\langle a \rangle$ can be very simply expressed as basic action with the addition of healthiness conditions:

$$\mathbf{W}(P) \mathrel{\hat{=}} DL \wedge LE \wedge \mathbf{WwW}(P) \quad \text{《·W-def·》}$$
$$\langle a \rangle \mathrel{\hat{=}} \mathbf{W}(A(in \mid a \mid out))) \quad \text{《·sem:atomic·》}$$

Here we would expect that if LE holds when this action starts, i.e. when $in \in ls$ and it gets to run, that LE' should also hold, with $out \in ls'$.

8.2   Grounded and Sound

Given that we have a distinction between static observations (g, in, out), and dynamic ones (s, s', ls, ls') it is worth extending this distinction to expressions and substitutions. The reason for this is to do with the fact that, by design, semantic sequential composition ignores the static variables. An expression or predicate is "ground" if the only variables present are static. The DL healthiness condition is ground, but LE is not, as it refers to ls and ls'. Ground predicates

K satisfy some important laws, and LE satisfies something similar:

$$K \; ; \; K = K$$
$$(K \wedge P) \; ; \; Q = K \wedge (P \; ; \; Q) \; = \; P \; ; \; (K \wedge Q)$$
$$K \wedge \mathbf{WwW}(P) = \mathbf{WwW}(K \wedge P)$$
$$(LE \wedge P) \; ; \; (LE \wedge Q) = LE \wedge ((LE \wedge P) \; ; \; (LE \wedge Q))$$

A substitution is also deemed "ground", if all the replacement expressions are ground, and the target variables are all static. A desired consequence of this is that ground substitutions γ will distribute through semantic sequential composition, semantic skip, both disjoint label-set notations, and $\mathbf{WwW}$.

$$(P \; ; \; Q)\gamma = P\gamma \; ; \; Q\gamma \qquad \text{《 seq-gnd-distr 》}$$
$$\mathit{II}\gamma = \mathit{II} \qquad \text{《 skip-gamma 》}$$
$$\{L_1 \mid \ldots \mid L_n\}\gamma = \{L_1\gamma \mid \ldots \mid L_n\gamma\} \qquad \text{《 DL-gamma-subst 》}$$
$$[L_1 \mid \ldots \mid L_n]\gamma = [L_1\gamma \mid \ldots \mid L_n\gamma] \qquad \text{《 LE-gamma-subst 》}$$
$$(\mathbf{WwW}(P))\gamma = \mathbf{WwW}(P\gamma) \qquad \text{《 WwW-gamma-subst 》}$$

Groundness is not enough, we also require substitutions to be "sound" in the sense that they cannot transform a situation that satisfies DL or LE into one that does not. A ground substitution ς, of the form $[labs(G), I, O/g, in, out]$ is *sound* if $\{labs(G) \mid I \mid O\}$ holds. We will see that all substitutions in the semantic definitions are sound, and that this is easy to check by inspection.

8.3   Composing Actions

The semantics of composite actions basically involves using the generator to produce a suitable number of labels, that are then used in zero or more "control-flow" actions of the form $A(E \mid ii \mid N)$, where ii is atomic skip that simply asserts $s' = s$. The left-over generator is then split as required, and then the components are "connected" into the relevant new labels and generators using sound substitutions. Finally the relevant healthiness conditions are applied. A key principle is to ensure that when any sub-component is "active", that is, at least one of its labels is present in ls, that none of the labels of the parent, other than those explicitly shared with the sub-component, are themselves in ls. This prevents a parent starting a spurious copy of a sub-component while that sub-component is actually running. The semantic definitions are listed in Fig. 2.

We will explain the semantics of parallel in more detail, aided by the diagram in Fig. 3. We take the generator g and split it to obtain g_1 and g_2. From g_1 we generate two labels ℓ_{g1} and $\ell_{g1:}$, and leftover generator $g_{1::}$. We then use a substitution to replace all references by P to g, in and out with $g_{1::}$, ℓ_{g1} and $\ell_{g1:}$, respectively. We do something similar with g_2 and Q. We also add a top-level control action that is enabled by label in, and adds both ℓ_{g1} and ℓ_{g2} into ls, so enabling both P and Q to start. We then have another control-flow action that waits for both of $\ell_{g1:}$ and $\ell_{g2:}$ to appear in ls, at which point they will be replaced by the top-level out label.

The similarity between our labels and the sub-statement notation of Lamport is quite striking. His parallel construct, called **cobegin**, labels the

$$P \mathbin{;;} Q \cong \mathbf{W}(P[g_{:1}, \ell_g/g, out] \vee Q[g_{:2}, \ell_g/g, in]) \qquad \langle\!\langle \cdot \mathsf{sem:seq} \cdot \rangle\!\rangle$$

$$P \parallel Q \cong \mathbf{W}(\; A(in \mid ii \mid \ell_{g1}, \ell_{g2}) \vee \qquad\qquad\qquad \langle\!\langle \cdot \mathsf{sem:par} \cdot \rangle\!\rangle$$
$$P[g_{1::}, \ell_{g1}, \ell_{g1:}/g, in, out] \vee$$
$$Q[g_{2::}, \ell_{g2}, \ell_{g2:}/g, in, out] \vee$$
$$A(\ell_{g1:}, \ell_{g2:} \mid ii \mid out)\;)$$

$$P + Q \cong \mathbf{W}(\; P[g_1/g] \vee Q[g_2/g]\;) \qquad\qquad\quad \langle\!\langle \cdot \mathsf{sem:NDC} \cdot \rangle\!\rangle$$

$$P^* \cong \mathbf{W}(\; A(in \mid ii \mid \ell_g) \vee \qquad\qquad\qquad\quad \langle\!\langle \cdot \mathsf{sem:star} \cdot \rangle\!\rangle$$
$$A(\ell_g \mid ii \mid \ell_{g:}) \vee$$
$$A(\ell_g \mid ii \mid out) \vee$$
$$P[g_{::}, \ell_{g:}, \ell_g/g, in, out]\;)$$

Fig. 2. Composite Semantics

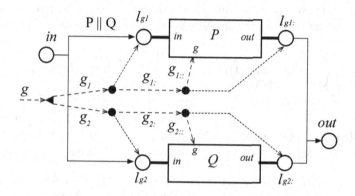

Fig. 3. Label and Generator "plumbing" for $P \parallel Q$.

subcomponents with numbers from 1 upwards. So he refers to P within **cobegin** $P \;\square\; Q$ **coend** as (**cobegin** $P \;\square\; Q$ **coend**, 1). We call it $P[g_{1::}, \ldots /g, \ldots]$. When for a construct P, we assert that $in \in ls$, he uses a predicate $at(P)$. In the parallel case here, an assertion by us that $\ell_{g1} \in ls$, corresponds to his assertion $at(\mathbf{cobegin}\; P \;\square\; Q\; \mathbf{coend}, 1)$.

Given that the invariant LE, which is $[in \mid labs(g) \mid out]$, is part of the definition of $\mathbf{W}$, then we have it satisfied, by definition, by any sub-components. From the perspective of the parent composite, this means that LE_ς also holds, where ς ranges over all the sound substitutions used in the definition of the parent's semantics. For example, for program sequential composition, we not only assert $[in \mid g \mid out]$, but can also infer $[in \mid g_{:1} \mid \ell_g]$ and $[\ell_g \mid g_{:2} \mid out]$.

In summary, we have predicate semantics for atomic and composite program constructs, in which everything at every level is wrapped in an infinite loop. This seems to be completely counter-intuitive: a program that consists of a single atomic action may wait for a while external interference rumbles on, but eventually it should get "scheduled", perform its atomic action and then effectively stop. How is this consistent with looping forever? To see the answer to this question, it helps to consider such simple examples, and this brings up the issue of *calculation*.

9   Calculations

Part of the validation of this semantic theory was by a series of test calculations done to ensure that it was making the right predictions about program behaviour. This typically involved taking small programs with a few atomic actions and trying to simplify their semantic predicates down to a non-deterministic choice of atomic action sequences. Some of the calculations proved to be very long, repetitive and tedious, motivating the UTP-calculator development [6].

We shall start by sketching out a test calculation for $\langle a \rangle$, where the objective is to reduce it down to a predicate involving just basic atoms.

$$
\begin{aligned}
&\langle a \rangle \\
&= \mathbf{W}(A(in \mid a \mid out))) && \langle\!\langle \cdot \text{sem:atomic} \cdot \rangle\!\rangle \\
&= DL \wedge LE \wedge \mathbf{WwW}(A(in \mid a \mid out)) && \langle\!\langle \cdot \text{W-def} \cdot \rangle\!\rangle \\
&= DL \wedge LE \wedge \bigvee_i A(in \mid a \mid out)^i && \langle\!\langle \cdot \text{WWW-as-NDC} \cdot \rangle\!\rangle
\end{aligned}
$$

At this point what remains is to compute $A(in \mid a \mid out)^i$ for $i \in \mathbb{N}$. The cases of $i = 0, 1$ are straightforward. Computing $i = 2$ is easy:

$$
\begin{aligned}
&A(in \mid a \mid out) \,;\, A(in \mid a \mid out) && \langle\!\langle \cdot \text{X-def} \cdot \rangle\!\rangle \\
&= X(in \mid a \mid in \mid out) \,;\, X(in \mid a \mid in \mid out) && \langle\!\langle \cdot \text{X-then-X} \cdot \rangle\!\rangle \\
&= \{in\} \cap (\{in\} \setminus \{out\}) = \emptyset \wedge X(\dots) && \text{set theory} \\
&= \mathbf{false} \wedge X(\dots)
\end{aligned}
$$

We see that $A(in \mid a \mid out)^2 = \mathbf{false}$, and as $\mathbf{false}$ is a zero for semantic sequential composition, we can deduce that $A(in \mid a \mid out)^i = \mathbf{false}$ for all $i \geq 2$. So our final result is

$$
\langle a \rangle = DL \wedge LE \wedge (II \vee A(in \mid a \mid out)) \tag{9}
$$

Ignoring the healthiness conditions, this boils down to two possible observations we can make of $\langle a \rangle$: either we observe stuttering—no change in state or label-sets (II) or we see the complete execution of the underlyng basic action $A(in \mid a \mid out)$.

Test calculations for simple usage of most of the composites is essentially the same. One slight complication is that the contents of $\mathbf{WwW}$ in theses cases is a disjunction of terms, rather than a single basic action, so we first simplify these out, applying all substitutions, to get a term Q of the form ($II \vee \textit{basic actions}$). We need to compute Q^i for $i \geq 2$, and sequential composition distributes through disjunction, so we obtain resulting terms of the same form, by repeated application of law $\langle\!\langle \cdot \text{X-then-X} \cdot \rangle\!\rangle$. A large number of these have results with the set side-condition that evaluates to $\mathbf{false}$, as per the $i = 2$ example above—these terms vanish. There are other terms produced that do not vanish, but some

$$\langle a \rangle \;;; \langle b \rangle = II \vee A(in \mid a \mid \ell_g) \vee A(\ell_g \mid b \mid out) \vee A(in \mid ab \mid out)$$
$$\langle a \rangle + \langle b \rangle = II \vee A(in \mid ii \mid \ell_{g1}) \vee A(in \mid ii \mid \ell_{g2}) \vee A(\ell_{g1} \mid a \mid out)$$
$$\qquad \vee A(\ell_{g2} \mid b \mid out) \vee A(in \mid a \mid out) \vee A(in \mid b \mid out)$$
$$\langle a \rangle \parallel \langle b \rangle = II \vee A(in \mid ii \mid \ell_{g1}, \ell_{g2}) \vee A(\ell_{g1:}, \ell_{g2:} \mid ii \mid out) \vee A(\ell_{g1} \mid a \mid \ell_{g1:})$$
$$\qquad \vee A(\ell_{g2} \mid b \mid \ell_{g2:}) \vee A(in \mid a \mid \ell_{g1:}, \ell_{g2}) \vee A(in \mid b \mid \ell_{g2:}, \ell_{g1})$$
$$\qquad \vee A(\ell_{g1}, \ell_{g2} \mid ba \mid \ell_{g1:}, \ell_{g2:}) \vee A(\ell_{g1}, \ell_{g2} \mid ab \mid \ell_{g1:}, \ell_{g2:})$$
$$\qquad \vee A(\ell_{g2:}, \ell_{g1} \mid a \mid out) \vee A(\ell_{g1:}, \ell_{g2} \mid b \mid out) \vee A(in \mid ba \mid \ell_{g1:}, \ell_{g2:})$$
$$\qquad \vee A(in \mid ab \mid \ell_{g1:}, \ell_{g2:}) \vee A(\ell_{g1}, \ell_{g2} \mid ba \mid out) \vee A(\ell_{g1}, \ell_{g2} \mid ab \mid out)$$
$$\qquad \vee A(in \mid ba \mid out) \vee A(in \mid ab \mid out)$$

Fig. 4. Some Test Calculation Results. Here ab (ba) is short for $a; b$ $(b; a)$, and we have omitted the DL and LE invariants for clarity.

of these can also be eliminated, because their enabling set violates the Label Exclusivity invariant. All remaining terms have the form $X(E \mid a \mid R \mid N)$, and some of these can be immediately re-written to $A(E \mid a \mid N)$, if $R = E$. In every test calculation we have done it turns out that the others, where $R \neq E$ can also be re-written, because LE says that none of $R \setminus E$ can be present in ls when anything from E is present, so the removal of those labels is ineffective, as they are never present when that action is enabled. So, the outcome is that we get final results where every basic action can be written in the A-form. All of these aspects of these test calculations are supported by current versions of the tool described in [6]. If there is no use of the iteration construct (P^*), then all calculations terminate because there is always some i for which Q^i evaluates to **false**. Any use of the language iteration construct however results in having terms for all values of i.

Some calculation results are shown in Fig. 4. If we look at the result for $\langle a \rangle \;;; \langle b \rangle$ we have II, the stuttering step, and $A(in \mid ab \mid out)$ which is the complete exection of both actions without interference (mumbling), and $A(in \mid a \mid \ell_g)$ that shows the execution of a, to an intermediate point where b has yet to occur. These three observations are consistent with the idea that our predicates are relations between a starting state and some subsequent or final state. However we also have action $A(\ell_g \mid b \mid out)$, which is an observation that begins after action a has already occured, and just observes the behaviour of b alone. What has happened with this UTP theory of concurrency is that it is now no longer insists that the "before" observation is pinned to be the start of the program. Now we are able to observe program behaviour that can both start and end at what are intermediate points in the lifetime of the program.

If we look at $\langle a \rangle + \langle b \rangle$, we also explictly see the control-flow "decisions", such as $A(in \mid ii \mid \ell_{g1})$ where the decision to execute a is made. This will remove in from ls if it runs, so disabling the other choice, denoted by $A(in \mid ii \mid \ell_{g2})$. By contrast, in $\langle a \rangle \parallel \langle b \rangle$ the initially enabled action is $A(in \mid ii \mid \ell_{g1}, \ell_{g2})$, which activates both a and b. The control flow action $A(\ell_{g1:}, \ell_{g2:} \mid ii \mid out)$ delays termination until both atomic actions are done.

Finally, we stress that the explicit inclusion of labels in the final results is essential in order to ensure compositionality. In [7] we had the explicit *run* form, and this reduced the semantics of $\langle a \rangle$ to a, that of $\langle a \rangle + \langle b \rangle$ to $a \lor b$ and $\langle a \rangle \parallel \langle b \rangle$ to $ab \lor ba$. While this looks cleaner, it has lost too much information, and we cannot compose these further to get correct answers. With the explicitly labelled semantics presented here for UTCP, we can, for example, correctly compute $(\langle a \rangle \;;; \langle b \rangle) \parallel \langle c \rangle$ by replacing the first ;; term by its expansion from Fig. 4.

10 Conclusions and Future Work

We have presented a compositional, denotational UTP semantics of shared-variable concurrency. It is "explicit" in the sense that it can enumerate all the observations that it is possible make of the program's own behaviour, in any time-slot. As already explained, our semantics has a lot of similarities to the axiomatic action semantics of Lamport [18].

The usefulness of this theory is that it is in a form that makes it very easy for us to specialise it to cover other approaches to concurrency in the Views paper [10], as that paper shows how thay all link to the simple concurrent language whose semantics we have just supplied. These concurrency approaches include Rely-Guarantee [15, 22], Owicki-Gries [20], and Concurrent Separation Logic [4]. This is precisely because it is formulated as a before-after relation, with the twist that before and after observations can occur at any time during program execution, with the obvious proviso that "before" precedes "after".

While careful inspection and test calculations give us a high level of confidence in the validity of our semantics, we still need to demonstrate that the algebraic laws of Concurrent Kleene Algebra [14] can be derived from our semantics. We also need to show how the standard operational semantics can be recovered.

We also hope to use this semantics as a baseline for a program to apply UTP to model the various linked approaches discussed in the Views paper [10]. Of particular interest is to explore the connection between UTCP and rely-guarantee [16] approaches. In particular, given our idea of "before" and "after" being able to refer intermediate execution points, and that we can explicitly provide all atomic actions and their mumblings, we see a good opportunity to explore how this can be exploited to analyse how well one or more program steps satisfy their guarantee obligation, given a reliable environment.

Given the similarities between our approach and that of Lamport, it also raises the possibility of bringing our observations and notation closer in line with his.

References

1. Atkinson, D.C., Weeks, D.C., Noll, J.: Tool support for iterative software process modeling. Inform. Softw. Technol. **49**(5), 493–514 (2007). https://doi.org/10.1016/j.infsof.2006.07.006

2. Back, R.J.R., Kurki-Suonio, R.: Decentralization of process nets with centralized control. In: Proceedings of the Second Annual ACM SIGACT-SIGOPS Symposium on Principles of Distributed Computing, Montreal, Quebec, Canada, pp. 131–142, 17–19 August 1983
3. Boer, F.S., Kok, J.N., Palamidessi, C., Rutten, J.J.M.M.: The failure of failures in a paradigm for asynchronous communication. In: Baeten, J.C.M., Groote, J.F. (eds.) CONCUR 1991. LNCS, vol. 527, pp. 111–126. Springer, Heidelberg (1991). https://doi.org/10.1007/3-540-54430-5_84
4. Brookes, S.: A revisionist history of concurrent separation logic. Electr. Notes Theor. Comput. Sci. **276**, 5–28 (2011). https://doi.org/10.1016/j.entcs.2011
5. Brookes, S.D.: Full abstraction for a shared-variable parallel language. Inf. Comput. **127**(2), 145–163 (1996). https://doi.org/10.1006/inco.1996.0056
6. Butterfield, A.: UTPCalc — a calculator for UTP predicates. In: Bowen, J.P., Zhu, H. (eds.) UTP 2016. LNCS, vol. 10134, pp. 197–216. Springer, Cham (2017). https://doi.org/10.1007/978-3-319-52228-9_10
7. Butterfield, A., Mjeda, A., Noll, J.: UTP semantics for shared-state, concurrent, context-sensitive process models. In: Bonsangue, M., Deng, Y. (eds.) TASE 2016 10th International Symposium on Theoretical Aspects of Software Engineering, pp. 93–100. IEEE, July 2016
8. Calcagno, C., O'Hearn, P.W., Yang, H.: Local action and abstract separation logic, pp. 366–378. IEEE Computer Society (2007). http://ieeexplore.ieee.org/xpl/mostRecentIssue.jsp?punumber=4276538
9. Dijkstra, E.W.: A Discipline of Programming. Series in Automatic Computation. Prentice-Hall, Englewood Cliffs (1976)
10. Dinsdale-Young, T., Birkedal, L., Gardner, P., Parkinson, M.J., Yang, H.: Views: compositional reasoning for concurrent programs. In: Giacobazzi, R., Cousot, R. (eds.) The 40th Annual ACM SIGPLAN-SIGACT Symposium on Principles of Programming Languages, POPL 2013, Rome, Italy, 23–25 January 2013, pp. 287–300. ACM (2013)
11. Hehner, E.C.R.: Predicative programming part i & ii. Commun. ACM **27**(2), 134–151 (1984)
12. Hoare, C.A.R.: Programs are predicates. In: Proceedings of a discussion meeting of the Royal Society of London on Mathematical Logic and Programming Languages, pp. 141–155. Prentice-Hall Inc., Upper Saddle River (1985)
13. Hoare, C.A.R., He, J.: Unifying Theories of Programming. Prentice-Hall International, Englewood Cliffs (1998)
14. Hoare, C.A.R.T., Möller, B., Struth, G., Wehrman, I.: Concurrent kleene algebra. In: Bravetti, M., Zavattaro, G. (eds.) CONCUR 2009. LNCS, vol. 5710, pp. 399–414. Springer, Heidelberg (2009). https://doi.org/10.1007/978-3-642-04081-8_27
15. Jones, C.B.: Developing methods for computer programs including a notion of interference. Ph.D. thesis, University of Oxford, UK (1981)
16. Jones, C.B.: Development methods for computer programs including a notion of interference (PRG-25), p. 265, June 1981
17. Jones, C.B.: Tentative steps toward a development method for interfering programs. ACM Trans. Program. Lang. Syst. **5**(4), 596–619 (1983). http://doi.acm.org/10.1145/69575.69577
18. Lamport, L.: An axiomatic semantics of concurrent programming languages. In: Apt, K.R. (eds.) Logics and Models of Concurrent Systems. NATO ASI Series (Series F: Computer and Systems Sciences), vol. 13, pp. 77–122. Springer, Heidelberg (1985). https://doi.org/10.1007/978-3-642-82453-1_4

19. Lamport, L.: Turing lecture: the computer science of concurrency: the early years. Commun. ACM **58**(6), 71–76 (2015). http://doi.acm.org/10.1145/2771951
20. Owicki, S.S., Gries, D.: An axiomatic proof technique for parallel programs I. Acta Inf. **6**, 319–340 (1976). https://doi.org/10.1007/BF00268134
21. Staden, S.: Constructing the views framework. In: Naumann, D. (ed.) UTP 2014. LNCS, vol. 8963, pp. 62–83. Springer, Cham (2015). https://doi.org/10.1007/978-3-319-14806-9_4
22. Staden, S.: On rely-guarantee reasoning. In: Hinze, R., Voigtländer, J. (eds.) MPC 2015. LNCS, vol. 9129, pp. 30–49. Springer, Cham (2015). https://doi.org/10.1007/978-3-319-19797-5_2
23. Woodcock, J., Hughes, A.: Unifying theories of parallel programming. In: George, C., Miao, H. (eds.) ICFEM 2002. LNCS, vol. 2495, pp. 24–37. Springer, Heidelberg (2002). https://doi.org/10.1007/3-540-36103-0_5

On Kleene Algebras for Weighted Computation

Leandro Gomes[1]([⊠]), Alexandre Madeira[1,2], and Luís S. Barbosa[1]

[1] HASLab INESC TEC, University Minho, Braga, Portugal
leandro.r.gomes@inesctec.pt
[2] CIDMA, University Aveiro, Aveiro, Portugal

Abstract. Kleene algebra with tests (KAT) was introduced as an algebraic structure to model and reason about classic imperative programs, i.e. sequences of discrete actions guarded by Boolean tests.

This paper introduces two generalisations of this structure able to express programs as weighted transitions and tests with outcomes in a not necessary bivalent truth space, namely graded Kleene algebra with tests (GKAT) and Heyting Kleene algebra with tests (HKAT).

On these contexts, in analogy to Kozen's encoding of Propositional Hoare Logic (PHL) in KAT [10], we discuss the encoding of a graded PHL in HKAT and of its while-free fragment in GKAT.

1 Introduction

1.1 Roadmap

Kleene algebra is pervasive in computer science: it arises in relational algebra, semantics and logics of programs, automata and formal language theory, and design and analysis of algorithms. In the specific context of program calculi, the axiomatisation of Kleene algebra forms a purely equational system to manipulate programs [8]. Its applications typically deal with conventional, imperative programming constructs such as conditional and loops. In order to reason equationally about them, a notion of test is required, which lead D. Kozen to define - *Kleene algebra with tests* (KAT) [9], which plays a major role in reasoning about programs.

Hoare logic (HL) was the first formal system proposed for verification of programs. Introduced in as early as 1969, its wide influence transformed Hoare's work in a cornerstone of program correctness, a reference for most current research in the area. HL encompasses a syntax to reason about partial correctness assertions (PCA) of the form $\{b\}p\{c\}$, also called a Hoare triple, and a

This work is financed by the ERDF – European Regional Development Fund through the Operational Programme for Competitiveness and Internationalisation - COMPETE 2020 Programme and by National Funds through the Portuguese funding agency, FCT - Fundação para a Ciência e a Tecnologia, within projects POCI-01-0145-FEDER-016692 and UID/MAT/04106/2013. The second author is also supported by the individual grant SFRH/BPD/103004/2014.

© Springer International Publishing AG 2017
S. Cavalheiro and J. Fiadeiro (Eds.): SBMF 2017, LNCS 10623, pp. 271–286, 2017.
https://doi.org/10.1007/978-3-319-70848-5_17

deductive system to reason about them [5]. In a PCA, b and c stand for predicates, representing pre and post conditions, respectively, and p is a program statement.

In particular, *propositional Hoare logic* (PHL) can be seen as a fragment of HL, in which PCAs are reduced to static assertions about the underlying domain of computation [10]. In [10] the authors show that this fragment can be encoded in a Kleene algebra with tests. The translation is based on equational logic, transforming PCAs into equations and the rules of inference into equational implications.

As originally presented, KAT is suitable to reason about classic imperative programs. In fact, such programs are particularly "well tractable": they represent a sequence of discrete steps, which can be modelled as atomic transition systems in a standard automaton. Moreover, the assertions about theses programs have an outcome in a bivalent truth space. However, current complex dynamic systems are based in new computing domains, namely probabilistic [15] or continuous [13], which entail the need for computing paradigms able to deal with quantitative program executions (e.g. weighted, valued, probabilistic). Moreover, the assertions about these programs can have a graded outcome. In this context, the development of algebraic structures to model weighted computations becomes a must. This work builds on such motivations to introduce two generalisations of KAT able to express programs as weighted computations and tests as predicates evaluated in graded truth space - the *graded Kleene algebra with tests* (GKAT) and the *Heyting Kleene algebra with tests* (HKAT). GKAT, for example, has a myriad of interesting examples, from continuous Łukasiewicz lattice to the discrete finite hoops. HKAT, on the other hand, allows to address full imperative languages.

In analogy to KAT [10], we intend to encode PHL into GKAT, in the context of a research agenda to extend the classical area of program correctness. However, we can only partially generalise such an encoding. More specifically, we can only encode *while*-free programs. To achieve a complete encoding of Hoare logic, we propose to refine the basic structure, obtaining HKAT as a generalisation of the classical KAT. HKAT is, indeed, a subclass of GKAT. As a consequence, however, its set of examples is smaller. It includes, in particular, the lattice **3** to deal with partial programs and uncertainty on tests, and Gödel algebra, a well-known basic structure used in logics whose truth values are closed subsets of the interval $[0, 1]$.

The remaining of the paper is organised as follows: Subsect. 1.2 recaps some fundamental concepts needed to understand the definitions and results presented in this work. Section 2 introduces graded Kleene algebra with tests as a generalisation of KAT, including its axiomatisation, a few examples and proofs of basic properties. It also presents a partial encoding of classical PHL in GKAT. Section 3 introduces Heyting Kleene algebra with tests as another generalisation of the standard KAT and a refinement of GKAT, enjoying of a complete encoding of PHL. Section 4 sums up some related research, concludes, and enumerates some topics for future work.

1.2   Preliminaries

Definition 1. *A* Kleene algebra with tests *(KAT) is a tuple*

$$(K, T, +, ;, ^*, ^-, 0, 1)$$

where $T \subseteq K$, 0 and 1 are constants, $+$ and $;$ are binary operators in K and T, * is a unary operator in K, and $^-$ is a unary operator defined only on T such that:

- *$(K, +, ;, ^*, 0, 1)$ is a Kleene algebra;*
- *$(T, +, ;, ^-, 0, 1)$ is a Boolean algebra;*
- *$(T, +, ;, 0, 1)$ is a subalgebra of $(K, +, ;, 0, 1)$.*

The elements of K, denoted by lower case letters p, q, r, s, x, y, z, stand for programs and the elements of T, denoted by a, b, c, d are called tests. Kleene algebra with tests induces an abstract programming language, where conditionals and **while** loops programming constructs are encoded as follows:

$$\textbf{if } b \textbf{ then } p \stackrel{\text{def}}{=} b; p + \bar{b}$$

$$\textbf{if } b \textbf{ then } p \textbf{ else } q \stackrel{\text{def}}{=} b; p + \bar{b}; q$$

$$\textbf{while } b \textbf{ do } p \stackrel{\text{def}}{=} (b; p)^*; \bar{b}$$

As stated in Sect. 1, Hoare logic allows to verify imperative programs by validating PCAs of the form $\{b\}p\{c\}$ through a deductive system [5]. The validity of a Hoare triple assures that whenever precondition b is met, after the execution of program p, if and when p halts, the postcondition c is guaranteed to hold. The set of logical rules is shown in Fig. 1. Although the importance of HL for reasoning about program correctness is unquestionable, proofs in PHL can be more easily done in terms of purely equational calculation on KAT, as presented in [10]. In fact, it is shown that PHL can be encoded in KAT, in such a way that the inference rules *Composition, Conditional, While* and *Weakening* become derived theorems of KAT.

- *Composition rule:*

$$\frac{\{b\}p\{c\} \quad \{c\}q\{d\}}{\{b\}p; q\{d\}}$$

- *Conditional rule:*

$$\frac{\{b \wedge c\}p\{d\}, \{\neg b \wedge c\}q\{d\}}{\{c\} \textbf{ if } b \textbf{ then } p \textbf{ else } q \ \{d\}}$$

- *While rule:*

$$\frac{\{b \wedge c\}p\{c\}}{\{c\} \textbf{ while } b \textbf{ do } p\{\neg b \wedge c\}}$$

- *Weakening rule:*

$$\frac{b' \rightarrow b, \ \{b\}p\{c\}, \ c \rightarrow c'}{\{b'\} \ p\{c'\}}$$

Fig. 1. Hoare logic rules

As presented in [10], the PCA $\{b\}p\{c\}$ can be encoded in KAT as $b; p; \bar{c} = 0$, which is equivalent to $b; p = b; p; c$. The first equation means, intuitively, that the execution of p with precondition b and postcondition $\bar{c}$ does not halt. Equation $b; p = b; p; c$, on the other hand, states that the verification of the post condition c after the execution of $b; p$ is redundant.

Moreover, the inference rules of Hoare logic can be encoded in KAT, as shown below:

- *Composition*:

$$b; p = b; p; c \wedge c; q = c; q; d \Rightarrow b; p; q = b; p; q; d$$

- *Conditional*:

$$b; c; p = b; c; p; d \wedge \bar{b}; c; q = \bar{b}; c; q; d \Rightarrow c; (b; p + \bar{b}; q) = c; (b; p + \bar{b}; q); d$$

- *While*:

$$b; c; p = b; c; p; c \Rightarrow c; (b; p)^*; \bar{b} = c; (b; p)^*; \bar{b}; \bar{b}; c$$

- *Weakening*:

$$b' \leq b \wedge b; p = b; p; c \wedge c \leq c' \Rightarrow b'; p = b'; p; c'$$

2   Graded Kleene Algebra with Tests

2.1   The Basic Structure

The approach proposed here, to reason about program executions in a many-valued context, is based on redefining the interpretation of the assertions about programs. Since such assertions take the form of tests, we start by modifying the part of the axiomatisation of KAT that deals with properties of tests, i.e., the Boolean algebra $(T, +, \cdot, ^-, 0, 1)$.

Instead of having a Boolean outcome, as happens in KAT, tests are graded, taking values from a truth space with more than two possible outcomes (0 and 1). As a consequence, the expression $b; p$ represents a weighted execution of program p, conditioned by the value of b. In order to reason about computations in this graded setting, we introduce the following generalisation of KAT:

Definition 2. *A graded Kleene algebra with tests (GKAT) is a tuple*

$$(K, T, +, ;, ^*, \rightarrow, 0, 1)$$

where K and T are sets, with $T \subseteq K$, 0 and 1 are constants and $+$ and ; are binary operations in K and T, * is a unary operator in K, and $\rightarrow$ is an operator only defined in T, satisfying the axioms enumerated in Fig. 2, where relation $\leq$ is induced by $+$ in the usual way: $p \leq q$ iff $p + q = q$. Note that $(T, +, ;, 0, 1)$ is a subalgebra of $(K, +, ;, 0, 1)$.

Again, programs are denoted by lower case letters p, q, r, s, x, y, z and tests by a, b, c, d. Note that, differently from what happens in KAT, negation is not explicitly denoted, although it can be derived as $a \rightarrow 0$, for $a \in T$. Indeed, this operator, along with a more relaxed subalgebra (which will replace the Boolean subalgebra of KAT) are introduced to support a proper truth space, for possible non bivalent interpretation of assertions.

$$p + (q + r) = (p + q) + r \qquad (1)$$
$$p + q = q + p \qquad (2)$$
$$p + p = p \qquad (3)$$
$$p + 0 = 0 + p = p \qquad (4)$$
$$p; (q; r) = (p; q); r \qquad (5)$$
$$p; 1 = 1; p = p \qquad (6)$$
$$p; (q + r) = (p; q) + (p; r) \qquad (7)$$
$$(p + q); r = (p; r) + (q; r) \qquad (8)$$
$$p; 0 = 0; p = 0 \qquad (9)$$
$$1 + p; p^* = p^* \qquad (10)$$

$$1 + p^*; p = p^* \qquad (11)$$
$$q + p; r \leq r \Rightarrow p^*; q \leq r \qquad (12)$$
$$q + r; p \leq r \Rightarrow q; p^* \leq r \qquad (13)$$
$$a; b \leq c \Leftrightarrow b \leq a \rightarrow c \qquad (14)$$
$$a \rightarrow b \leq a \rightarrow (b + c) \qquad (15)$$
$$b \leq a \rightarrow (a; b) \qquad (16)$$
$$a + 1 = 1 + a = 1 \qquad (17)$$
$$a; b = b; a \qquad (18)$$
$$a + (a; b) = a \qquad (19)$$

Fig. 2. Axiomatisation of graded Kleene algebra with tests

Some operators in GKAT play a different role when acting on programs or tests. Such is the case of "+" and ";". The former one plays the role of non-deterministic choice, when interpreting programs, and of logical disjunction, when acting on tests. The latter is taken as sequential composition of actions when applied to elements of K, and as a conjunction when applied to elements of T. In the domain of programs, the constants 0 and 1 refer to *halt* and *skip*, while when applied on tests, stand for false and true, respectively. However, there are operations specific to just one of these domains. For instance, while operation $*$ is taken as iterative execution of programs, operation $\rightarrow$ plays the role of logical implication over tests. Let us now discuss some instances of GKAT.

Example 1. (**2** - the Boolean lattice). Our first example is the well known binary structure

$$\mathbf{2} = (\{\top, \bot\}, \{\top, \bot\}, \vee, \wedge, {}^*, \rightarrow, \bot, \top)$$

with the standard interpretation of Boolean connectives. Operator $*$ maps each element of $\{\top, \bot\}$ to $\top$ and $\rightarrow$ is defined as logical implication.

Example 2. A second example is provided by the three-element linear lattice, which introduces an explicit denotation for "unknown" (or undefined).

$$\mathbf{3} = (\{\top, u, \bot\}, \{\top, u, \bot\}, \vee, \wedge, {}^*, \rightarrow, \bot, \top)$$

where

∨	⊥	u	⊤
⊥	⊥	u	⊤
u	u	u	⊤
⊤	⊤	⊤	⊤

∧	⊥	u	⊤
⊥	⊥	⊥	⊥
u	⊥	u	u
⊤	⊥	u	⊤

→	⊥	u	⊤
⊥	⊤	⊤	⊤
u	⊥	⊤	⊤
⊤	⊥	u	⊤

*	
⊥	⊤
u	⊤
⊤	⊤

Example 3. For a fixed, finite set A, let us consider the structure

$$2^A = (P(A), P(A), \cup, \cap, {}^*, \rightarrow, \emptyset, A)$$

where $P(A)$ denotes the powerset of A, $\cup$ and $\cap$ are set union and intersection, respectively, * maps each set $X \in P(A)$ into A and $X \rightarrow Y = X^C \cup Y$, where $X^C = \{x \in A | x \notin X\}$.

Example 4. This example is based on the well-known Łukasiewicz arithmetic lattice.

$$Ł = ([0,1], [0,1], max, \odot, {}^*, \rightarrow, 0, 1)$$

where $x \rightarrow y = min\{1, 1 - x + y\}$, $x \odot y = max\{0, x + y - 1\}$ and * maps each point of the interval $[0,1]$ to 1.

Example 5. Let us consider now the example given by the standard Π-algebra

$$\Pi = ([0,1], [0,1], max, ., {}^*, \rightarrow, 0, 1)$$

where . is the usual multiplication for real numbers and

$$x \rightarrow y = \begin{cases} 1, & \text{if } x \leq y \\ y/x, & \text{if } y < x \end{cases}$$

with/being the usual division for real numbers and * mapping each point of the interval $[0,1]$ to 1.

Example 6. Another example is provided by the Gödel algebra

$$G = ([0,1], [0,1], max, min, {}^*, \rightarrow, 0, 1)$$

where

$$x \rightarrow y = \begin{cases} 1, & \text{if } x \leq y \\ y, & \text{if } y < x \end{cases}$$

and * maps each point of the interval $[0,1]$ to 1.

Example 7. We consider now a GKAT endowing the finite *Wajsberg hoop* with a star operator, as presented in [1]. For a fixed natural k and a generator a, define the structure

$$\boldsymbol{W_k} = (W_k, W_k, +, ;, {}^*, \rightarrow, 0, 1)$$

where $W_k = \{a^0, a^1, ..., a^{k-1}\}$, $1 = a^0$ and $0 = a^{k-1}$. Moreover, for any $m, n \leq k - 1$, $a^m + a^n = a^{min\{m,n\}}$, $a^m; a^n = a^{min\{m+n,k-1\}}$, $(a^m)^* = a^0$ and $a^m \rightarrow a^n = a^{max\{n-m,0\}}$.

Example 8. The $(min, +)$ Kleene algebra of [6], known as the tropical semiring, can be extended to a GKAT by adding residuation $\rightarrow$. First let R_+ denote the set $\{x \in \mathbb{R} | x \geq 0\}$ and let ∞ be a new element. Thus, define

$$\boldsymbol{R} = (R_+ \cup \{\infty\}, R_+ \cup \{\infty\}, min, +, {}^*, \rightarrow, \infty, 0)$$

where, for any $x, y \in R_+ \cup \{\infty\}$, $x^* = 0$ and $x \rightarrow y = max\{y - x, 0\}$.

Note that in all examples considered, $T = K$, that is, the set of tests and the set of programs coincide.

For the purpose of this work, i.e., for reasoning about graded computations and assertions in a multi-valued truth space, Example 4 is particularly relevant. Indeed, this is a very well known model for fuzzy and multi-valued logics.

A main particularity of the GKAT axiomatization concerns rules (17)-(19), which form a weakened version of the axiomatization of a Boolean algebra. Note, however, that this is, in fact, a generalisation:

Lemma 1. *Any KAT is a GKAT.*

Proof. For a fixed KAT

$$\boldsymbol{A} = (K, T, +, ;, {}^*, \bar{}, 0, 1)$$

let us consider the structure

$$\boldsymbol{M} = (K, T, +, ;, {}^*, \rightarrow, 0, 1)$$

inheriting the operators $+$, $;$, * and constants 0 and 1 from $\boldsymbol{A}$. Define $a \rightarrow 0 := \bar{a}$ and $a \rightarrow b := \bar{a} + b$, for $a, b \in T$.
Actually, axioms (14)-(16) hold for $\boldsymbol{M}$, for all $a, b, c \in T$. For (14), assume $a; b \leq c$, i.e. by definition of $\leq$, $a; b + c = c$. Then,

$$
\begin{array}{ll}
a \rightarrow c & \\
= \quad \{ \text{definition of } \rightarrow \text{ and hypothesis} \} & = \quad \{ (1), \text{BA: } a + \bar{a} = 1, (17) \text{ and } (6) \} \\
\bar{a} + ((a; b) + c) & \bar{a} + b + c \\
= \quad \{ \text{BA } (+, ;)\text{-dist.} \} & = \quad \{ (2) \text{ and definition of } \rightarrow \} \\
(\bar{a} + (a + c)); (\bar{a} + (b + c)) & a \rightarrow c + b
\end{array}
$$

Thus, $a; b \leq c \Rightarrow b \leq a \to c$. Now, assume $b \leq a \to c$, i.e. by definition of M, $b; (\bar{a} + c) = b$, and reason

$$
\begin{aligned}
&a; b + c \\
&= \quad \{\, b; (\bar{a} + c) = b \,\} \\
&a; (b; (\bar{a} + c)) + c \\
&= \quad \{\, \text{BA } (+,;)\text{-dist.} \,\} \\
&a; b; \bar{a} + a; b; c + c
\end{aligned}
\qquad
\begin{aligned}
&= \quad \{\, \text{BA comm, } a; \bar{a} = 0, (9), (4) \text{ and } (8) \,\} \\
&(a; b + 1); c \\
&= \quad \{\, (17) \text{ and } (6) \,\} \\
&c
\end{aligned}
$$

Hence, $b \leq c \to c \Rightarrow a; b \leq c$. To prove (15), consider

$$
\begin{aligned}
&a \to b + a \to (b + c) \\
&= \quad \{\, \text{by definition of } \to \,\} \\
&(\bar{a} + b) + (\bar{a} + (b + c))
\end{aligned}
\qquad
\begin{aligned}
&= \quad \{\, (1), (2) \text{ and } (3) \,\} \\
&\bar{a} + (b + c) \\
&= \quad \{\, \text{by definition of } \to \,\} \\
&a \to (b + c)
\end{aligned}
$$

Axiom (16) is proved as follows:

$$
\begin{aligned}
&a \to (a; b) \\
&= \quad \{\, \text{definition of } \to \,\} \\
&\bar{a} + (a; b) \\
&= \quad \{\, \text{BA } (+,;)\text{-dist., BA: } a + \bar{a} = 1 \text{ and } (6) \,\}
\end{aligned}
\qquad
\begin{aligned}
&\bar{a} + b \\
&= \quad \{\, \text{definition of } \to \,\} \\
&a \to b
\end{aligned}
$$

We have that $b \leq a \to b$, so, by transitivity, $b \leq a \to (a; b)$, for all $a, b \in T$.

We concluded the proof that axioms (14)-(16) hold for any $a, b, c \in T$ in M. Since axioms (1)-(13), (17)-(19) are axioms of A, M is, indeed, a GKAT. $\square$

As stated above, while tests in KAT have an outcome of two possible values (0 and 1), GKAT deals with graded tests. This entails the need to weaken the Boolean subalgebra $(T, +, \cdot, {}^{*}, 0, 1, {}^{-})$ of KAT. In any GKAT, for any test $a \in T$, $a; (a \to 0) = 0$, which follows immediately from definition of $\leq$ and axiom (14). However, it is not necessarily true that $a + (a \to 0) = 1$. In order to show this, let us consider the following GKAT structure over the set $\{0, n, m, 1\}$, where $\{0, m, 1\} \subseteq T$ and $n \in K$, in which the operation $*$ maps all points to the top element of T, 1, and the remaining operations are defined as follows:

$+$	0	n	m	1
0	0	n	m	1
n	n	n	m	1
m	m	m	m	1
1	1	1	1	1

$;$	0	n	m	1
0	0	0	0	0
n	0	0	0	n
m	0	0	0	m
1	0	n	m	1

$\to$	0	n	m	1
0	1	1	1	1
n	m	1	1	1
m	m	m	1	1
1	0	n	m	1

In this structure, and considering $a = m$, we have $m + (m \rightarrow 0) = m + m = m \neq 1$. Recall that in KAT, a program execution is guarded by a test with only two possible outcomes: 0 or 1. Thus, an expression $b; p$ intuitively means that program p is executed when $b = 1$ and is not executed when $b = 0$.

It is therefore safe to state that GKAT has embedded a weakened Boolean subalgebra and, consequently, tests can assume other values besides 0 and 1, representing the truth degree of the statement "b is true". Consequently, the expression $b; p$ means that the execution of program p is guarded by that particular truth (graded) value.

2.2 Graded Propositional Hoare Logic

Kleene algebra with tests provides a theoretical basis to reason about classic imperative programs by using purely equational reasoning. Actually, its presentation in [10] aimed at the reduction of PHL to ordinary equations and quasi-equations, as mentioned in the introduction. In particular, the inference rules of Hoare logic are derived as theorems in KAT.

Following an analogous approach [10], mentioned in Subsect. 1.2, we now encode propositional Hoare logic in GKAT. Since this new structure deals with graded tests, both the meaning of PCAs and the inference rules need to be adjusted. This reinterpretation unfolds a generalised version of classic Hoare logic, that we call here *graded propositional Hoare logic* (GPHL).

In the presence of graded tests, the interpretation of a triple $\{b\}p\{c\}$, and hence, the correctness of a program, relies on the idea that whenever $b; p$ executes with a truth degree b, if and when it halts, it is guaranteed that $(b; p); c$ holds with at least the same degree of truth. By other words, correctness of a program can only grow with execution. Therefore, the encoding in GKAT is captured by the following inequality:

$$b; p \leq b; p; c$$

However, the equivalence

$$b; p \leq b; p; c \Leftrightarrow b; p = b; p; c, \tag{20}$$

also holds in GKAT, following immediately from (7), (17) and (6). Note, also, that the equivalence

$$b; p = b; p; c \Leftrightarrow b; p \leq p; c$$

does not hold in GKAT, as it does in KAT.

The inference rules of Hoare logic can also be encoded in GKAT, as presented in the following theorem.

Theorem 1. *The following equational implications are theorems in GKAT.*

1. Composition rule:
   $b; p \leq b; p; c \land c; q \leq c; q; d \Rightarrow b; p; q = b; p; q; d$

2. *Conditional rule:*

$b; c; p \le b; c; p; d \wedge (b \to 0); c; q \le (b \to 0); c; q; d$
$\Rightarrow c; (b; p + (b \to 0); q) \le c; (b; p + (b \to 0); q); d$

3. *Weakening rule:*

$b' \le b \wedge b; p \le b; p; c \wedge c \le c' \Rightarrow b'; p \le b'; p; c'$

Proof. 1. Let us assume that $b; p \le b; p; c$ and $c; q \le c; q; d$. By (20), these inequalities are equivalent to $b; p = b; p; c$ and $c; q = c; q; d$, respectively. So, we have

$$
\begin{array}{c|c}
b; p; q & = \quad \{ c; q = c; q; d\} \\
= \quad \{ b; p = b; p; c\} & b; p; c; q; d \\
b; p; c; q & = \quad \{ b; p = b; p; c\} \\
& b; p; q; d
\end{array}
$$

2. Assume $b; c; p \le b; c; p; d$ and $(b \to 0); c; q \le (b \to 0); c; q; d$.
First of all, observe that, for any $p, q, r, s \in K$

$$p \le q \ \& \ r \le s \Rightarrow p + r \le q + s \tag{21}$$

To prove this, assume that $p \le q$ and $r \le s$, i.e. $p + q = q$ and $r + s = s$. Then, by (1) and (2), $(p+r)+(q+s) = (p+q)+(r+s) = q+s$. So, by (21),

$$b; c; p + (b \to 0); c; q \le b; c; p; d + (b \to 0); c; q; d.$$
$$\Leftrightarrow \quad \{ (18), (7) \text{ and } (8)\}$$
$$c; (b; p + (b \to 0); q) \le c; (b; p + (b \to 0); q); d$$

3. Finally, for the Weakening rule, observe that, for all $b, c \in T$ and $p \in K$,   .

$$b; p \le b; p; c \Rightarrow b; p; (c \to 0) \le 0 \tag{22}$$

Using (20) to rewrite (22) as

$$b; p = b; p; c \Rightarrow b; p; (c \to 0) = 0 \tag{23}$$

and, assuming $b; p = b; p; c$, we have

$$
\begin{array}{l}
b; p; (c \to 0) \\
= \quad \{ b; p = b; p; c \text{ assumption}\} \\
b; p; c; (c \to 0) \\
= \quad \{ a; (a \to 0) = 0) \text{ and } (9)\} \\
0
\end{array}
$$

Using (23), the Weakening rule can be rewritten as

$$a \le b \wedge b; p; (c \to 0) = 0 \wedge (d \to 0) \le (c \to 0) \Rightarrow a; p; (d \to 0) = 0$$

which follows from the monotonicity of ";".   □

The attentive reader certainly noticed the absence of a While rule in the graded setting. In analogy with what was done before, such a rule would take the form:

$$b; c; p \leq b; c; p; c \Rightarrow c; (b; p)^{*}; (b \to 0) \leq c; (b; p)^{*}; (b \to 0); (b \to 0); c \quad (24)$$

However, this is not necessarily true for all $p \in K$ and $b, c \in T$.

To see this, consider the following GKAT structure over the set $\{0, n, m, 1\}$, in which the operator * maps all points to the top element 1 and the remaining operators are defined as follows:

+	0	n	m	1
0	0	n	m	1
n	n	n	m	1
m	m	m	m	1
1	1	1	1	1

;	0	n	m	1
0	0	0	0	0
n	0	0	0	n
m	0	0	0	m
1	0	n	m	1

$\to$	0	n	m	1
0	1	1	1	1
n	m	1	1	1
m	m	m	1	1
1	0	n	m	1

In this structure, $\{0, m, 1\} \subseteq T$ and $n \in K$. If $b = 0, c = m, p = 0$, the instantiation of $b; c; p \leq b; c; p; c$ becomes, using axioms (9) and (3),

$0; m; 0 + 0; m; 0; m = 0; m; 0; m \Leftrightarrow 0 = 0$

and that of $c; (b; p)^{*}; (b \to 0) \leq c; (b; p)^{*}; (b \to 0); (b \to 0); c$ becomes, by axioms (9), (10), (6) and (4),

$m; (0)^{*}; 1 + m; (0)^{*}; 1; 1; m = m; (0)^{*}; 1; 1; m \Leftrightarrow m = 0$.

Using these two equations, the equational implication which could represent the While rule (24) boils down to $0 = 0 \Rightarrow m = 0$, which is obviously false. In the next section we will discuss this problem, by presenting an alternative algebraic structure with complete Hoare logic encoding.

3 Heyting Kleene Algebra with Tests

3.1 The Basic Structure

By carefully looking at the while rule proof for the Hoare logic encoding in KAT it is easy to note that one cause for the failure of the analogous encoding in GKAT, mentioned in the previous section, is the impossibility of duplicating graded tests. Actually, in GKAT, we don't have that $b; b = b$, but only $b; b \leq b$. In fact, the duplication is a requirement for the proof of the While rule. The solution we propose here is to refine the GKAT structure with some additional properties, capturing two crucial aspects for the purpose of this work: allowing for a complete encoding of Hoare logic and, at the same time, capturing non-classical examples, with degrees of uncertainty in program executions and evaluation of tests. The idea is to use a Heyting algebra to model the tests, instead of the Boolean algebra implicit on KAT.

Definition 3. *A* Heyting Kleene algebra with tests *(HKAT) is a tuple*

$$(K, T, +, ; ,^* , \rightarrow, 0, 1)$$

where K and T are sets, with $T \subseteq K$, 0 and 1 are constants and $+$ and $;$ are binary operations in K and T, * is a unary operator in K, and $\rightarrow$ is an operator only defined in T, satisfying the axioms enumerated in Fig. 2 plus three axioms from KAT, listed in Fig. 3. The relation $\leq$ is induced by $+$ in the usual way $p \leq q$ iff $p + q = q$ such that:

- *$(K, +, ; ,^* , 0, 1)$ is a Kleene algebra;*
- *$(T, +, ; , \rightarrow, 0, 1)$ is a Heyting algebra;*
- *$(T, +, ; , 0, 1)$ is a subalgebra of $(K, +, ; , 0, 1)$.*

$$a; a = a \tag{25}$$
$$a; (a + b) = a \tag{26}$$
$$a + (b; c) = (a + b); (a + c) \tag{27}$$

Fig. 3. New axioms added to the axiomatisation of GKAT, to form the axiomatisation of Heyting Kleene algebra with tests

Note that, as in GKAT, negation is not explicitly denoted and can be derived as $a \rightarrow 0$.

Let us also enhance that HKAT is a subclass of GKAT. Examples 1, 2, 3 and 6 illustrate this structure. The set of examples discussed for GKAT and HKAT, as well as which ones are also KAT is summarised in Fig. 4.

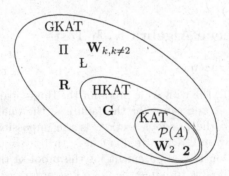

Fig. 4. Examples of KAT, GKAT and HKAT

In HKAT, we can think about the intuitive meaning of the execution of a program guarded by a test as an uncertain execution. For instance, in Example 2, if $b = u$, the expression $u; p$ means that we are not sure if program p could be executed or not.

Just as GKAT, HKAT is also a generalisation of KAT.

Lemma 2. *Any KAT is a HKAT.*

Proof. It suffices to show that axioms (14), (15) and (16) hold for all $a, b, c \in T$. The proof is the same as Lemma 1.

3.2 Heyting Propositional Hoare Logic

Let us now discuss how to encode propositional Hoare logic in HKAT. We call this generalisation *Heyting propositional Hoare logic* (HPHL). Differently from what happens in GKAT, the three encodings proposed by D. Kozen for Hoare logic are equivalent in HKAT:

$$b; p = b; p; c \Leftrightarrow b; p \leq b; p; c \Leftrightarrow b; p \leq p; c$$

Hence, the inference rules of Hoare logic can be encoded in HKAT as in classical propositional Hoare logic.

Theorem 2. *The following equational implications are theorems in HKAT.*

1. *Composition rule:*
   $b; p = b; p; c \wedge c; q = c; q; d \Rightarrow b; p; q = b; p; q; d$

2. *Conditional rule:*
   $b; c; p = b; c; p; d \wedge (b \to 0); c; q = (b \to 0); c; q; d$
   $\Rightarrow c; (b; p + (b \to 0); q) = c; (b; p + (b \to 0); q); d$

3. *While rule:*
   $b; c; p = b; c; p; c \Rightarrow c; (b; p)^*; (b \to 0) = c; (b; p)^*; (b \to 0); (b \to 0); c$

4. *Weakening rule:*
   $b' \leq b \wedge b; p = b; p; c \wedge c \leq c' \Rightarrow b'; p = b'; p; c'$

Proof. The proofs for rules 1, 2 and 4 are as in Theorem 1. To prove rule 3, consider

$$c; b; p \leq c; b; p; c \Rightarrow c; (b; p)^* \leq c; (b; p)^*; c.$$

Assuming

$$c; b; p \leq c; b; p; c \tag{28}$$

by (13), it is enough to show

$$c + c; (b; p)^*; c; b; p \leq c; (b; p)^*; c$$

But

$$
\begin{array}{ll}
c + c; (b;p)^*; c; b; p & \leq \quad \{\text{ by distributivity}\} \\
\quad \leq \quad \{\text{ by (28)}\} & c; (1 + (b;p)^*; c; b; p); c \\
c + c; (b;p)^*; c; b; p; c & \leq \quad \{\text{ by monotonicity}\} \\
\quad \leq \quad \{\text{ by B.A}\} & c; (1 + (b;p)^*; b; p); c \\
c; 1; c + c; (b;p)^*; c; b; p; c & \leq \quad \{\text{ by (11)}\} \\
& c; (b;p)^*; c
\end{array}
$$

Note that, as in classical case, for both encodings of PHL previously discussed, the way to reason about the correctness of a program is settled in a bivalent truth space.

4   Conclusion and Further Work

This paper aimed at generalising Kleene algebra with tests, to reason equationally about graded computations and assertions evaluated in a multi-valued truth space. Moreover, the propositional fragment of classic Hoare logic was revisited.

A similar attempt is discussed in [15], which introduces a complete theory of probabilistic KAT to deal with regular programs with probabilities. However, instead of focusing on the possible range of values for tests, or in adding an uncertainty concretisation to them, which have an immediate consequence on program executions, the authors add a new operator $+_\alpha$ to the algebraic structure, where α is a probability value. Thus, in their work, a *probabilistic Kleene algebra with Tests* is defined as

$$
(K, T, +, +_\alpha, \cdot, {}^*, 0, 1, {}^-)
$$

where expression $p +_\alpha q$ represents the probabilistic choice between executing a program p with probability α or a program q with probability $1 - \alpha$. More related work on this matter include references [3] and [12]. However, the main ideas behind these approaches is to introduce probabilities at the syntactic level, namely a new choice operator. Our approach, on the other hand, opted by redefining the notions of test and program execution.

The approach taken in this paper for GKAT, of adding a residual as a logical implication to capture a multi-valued setting, is based on previous work reported in [11], where an action lattice is adopted as the basic algebraic structure to generate many-valued dynamic logics.

Originally derived from *action algebras* [7], an action lattice entails both a generic space of computations, with choice, composition and iteration, and, supported by residuation, a proper truth space for a non bivalent interpretation of the assertions (as a residuated lattice). V. Pratt thought about residuation as a pure technicality to obtain a finitely-based equational variety [14]. Subsequently, the work of D. Kozen [7] extended this notion by adding and axiomatizing a meet operation, in order to recover the closure under matricial formation typical of the Kleene algebras [2].

The attentive reader may wonder about the lack of concrete illustrations for the introduced formalism, like simple imperative programs as in [10]. Note, however, that programs are interpreted here as weighted relations and tests as truth degrees. Hence, as it happens in propositional Hoare logic derived from standard KAT, there is no first-order structure to interpret program variables. Consequently, there is no assignment rule neither for GPHL nor for HPHL, as presented here. Extending the formalism in this direction, in order to deal with imperative fuzzy programs is, naturally, in our agenda.

Another important aspect to note is that, since both GKAT and HKAT are generalisations of KAT, as stated by lemmas 1 and 2, all the classical models of KAT, namely relational algebra over a set, languages over an alphabet and traces are naturally examples of our structures. In all these cases, the set of programs K and the set of tests T do not coincide, contrary to what happens with all the examples presented in this paper. Nevertheless, since the introduced structures intend to formalise over fuzzy programs, we want to go a step further: the tentative to formalise fuzzy relations and fuzzy languages, as they are presented in [4], as models of GKAT and HKAT is a priority in our agenda.

In all variants of dynamic logic discussed in the literature, even when some forms of structured computations are taken into consideration, the validity of assertions (for example, of Hoare triples annotating a program) is always stated in classical terms. This means that, even when the object of reasoning is e.g. a fuzzy program or a quantum system, the validity of an assertion over it is discussed in classical, two-valued logic.

In this work we assume, as in classic PHL, that a PCA is valid if $b; p = b; p; c$. In GKAT, this expression states that, after the execution of p guarded by the truth degree of precondition b, a state is reached where the truth degree of the post condition does not modify the value of the execution. In HKAT, for the case considered in Example 2, the variation from the classical case comes when $b = u$. Thus, the expression $b; p$ can be interpreted as "we are not sure if program p can be executed". Due to the nature of the expression (an equality relation), this is clearly tied to the classical, two-valued logic: despite the graded nature of the computations, their correctness is evaluated in a bivalent truth space.

This limitation motivates an approach to be addressed in future work: the intention is to go a step further and resort to the same algebraic structure used to specify the computing paradigm, in order to give semantics to the logic used to reason about it. This makes it possible to discuss the validity of an assertion over a fuzzy or a quantum program in terms of a logic capturing itself fuzzy or quantum reasoning, respectively.

References

1. Blok, W.J., Ferreirim, I.: On the structure of hoops. Algebra Univers. **43**, 233–257 (2000)

2. Conway, J.: Regular Algebra and Finite Machines. Dover Publications, New York (1971)
3. den Hartog, J., de Vink, E.P.: Verifying probabilistic programs using a Hoare like logic. Int. J. Found. Comput. Sci. 13(3), 315–340 (2002)
4. Guilherme, R.: A coalgebraic approach to fuzzy automata. Master's thesis, Faculdade de Ciências e Tecnologia - Universidade Nova de Lisboa, Lisboa (2016)
5. Hoare, C.A.R.: An axiomatic basis for computer programming. Commun. ACM 12(10), 576–580 (1969)
6. Kozen, D.: The Design and Analysis of Algorithms. Springer-Verlag, New York (1992)
7. Kozen, D.: On action algebras. In Logic and the Flow of Information, Amsterdam (1993)
8. Kozen, D.: A completeness theorem for Kleene algebras and the algebra of regular events. Inf. Comput. 110, 366–390 (1994)
9. Kozen, D.: Kleene algebra with tests. ACM Trans. Program. Lang. Syst. 19(3), 427–443 (1997)
10. Kozen, D.: On Hoare logic and Kleene algebra with tests. ACM Trans. Comput. Logic 1(212), 1–14 (2000)
11. Madeira, A., Neves, R., Martins, M.A.: An exercise on the generation of many-valued dynamic logics. J. Logical Algebraic Methods Program. 1, 1–29 (2016)
12. McIver, A.K., Cohen, E., Morgan, C.C.: Using probabilistic Kleene algebra for protocol verification. In: Schmidt, R.A. (ed.) RelMiCS 2006. LNCS, vol. 4136, pp. 296–310. Springer, Heidelberg (2006). https://doi.org/10.1007/11828563_20
13. Platzer, A.: Logical Analysis of Hybrid Systems - Proving Theorems for Complex Dynamics. Springer, Heidelberg (2010)
14. Pratt, V.: Action logic and pure induction. In: Eijck, J. (ed.) JELIA 1990. LNCS, vol. 478, pp. 97–120. Springer, Heidelberg (1991). https://doi.org/10.1007/BFb0018436
15. Qiao, R., Wu, J., Wang, Y., Gao, X.: Operational semantics of probabilistic Kleene algebra with tests. In: Proceedings of IEEE Symposium on Computers and Communications, pp. 706–713 (2008)

Capturing Stochastic and Real-Time Behavior in Reo Connectors

Yi Li, Xiyue Zhang, Yuanyi Ji, and Meng Sun[✉]

Department of Informatics and LMAM, School of Mathematical Sciences,
Peking University, Beijing, China
{liyi_math,zhangxiyue,jyy,sunm}@pku.edu.cn

Abstract. Modern distributed systems are often coupled with flexible architectures, composed of heterogenous components, and deployed on different execution nodes. Under such frameworks, connectors (or middlewares) are widely used to organize the separated components and make them functioning. Apparently, reliability of such systems highly depends on the correctness of their connectors. Reo is a channel-based coordination language where complex connectors are constructed from simpler ones through a compositional approach. In this paper, we propose a stochastic and real-time extension of Reo, including a set of new primitive channels and an expressive semantics named *Stochastic Timed Automata for Reo* (STA_r). With the support of STA_r, different coordination scenarios in existing Reo extensions can be easily encoded, integrated, and analyzed.

Keywords: Coordination · Stochastic · Real-time · Distributed systems

1 Introduction

Distributed systems have been booming everywhere in the past decades. On the one hand, The Internet of Things (IoTs) are bringing network systems to daily life. Conventional devices are replaced by smart terminals, and in turn collected by central controllers to construct 'Smart Cities'. On the other hand, high-performance computation is being adapted from local workstations and clusters to cloud platform and elastic computation frameworks like Amazon EC2 [15] and Microsoft Azure [12]. These architectures are so popular that even small companies are starting to deploy their own private cloud systems.

In modern systems, the component-based method is widely used to speed up the development process. Long-tested functional units are encapuslated as *components*, and get integrated in different systems through *connectors*. Under this developing model, a connector often implements the core software protocol, and consequently, suffers frequently from different kind of vulnerabilities.

Reo [2], as one of the most popular coordination languages, was designed to formalize the hierarchy and communication patterns between components. Based on channels and nodes, Reo provides a compositional approach where

S. Cavalheiro and J. Fiadeiro (Eds.): SBMF 2017, LNCS 10623, pp. 287–304, 2017.
https://doi.org/10.1007/978-3-319-70848-5_18

complex connectors are built from simpler ones. In this paper, we extend Reo with three primitive channels, *Map*, *StochasticChoice* and *pTimer*, to capture data evolution, real-time and stochastic behavior. A new semantics named STA_r is also provided as the theoretical basis of the primitive channels.

Compared with existing timed and stochastic (or probabilistic) semantics of Reo [4,7,13,14], our work provides a more powerful and universal solution.

1. *Both timed behavior and stochastic behavior are supported, but declared separately.* This makes it convenient to model various coordination scenarios by different combination patterns.
2. *Timelocks are avoided in this semantics, making the timed connectors fully implementable.* In the common semantics of timed Reo [3,13], *Timer* channels may get trapped in *timelock*. Under such cases, the behavior of *Timer* is undefined, which makes it impossible to obtain an equivalent implementation.

The paper is organized as follows. Section 2 introduces Reo, the coordination language, and shows how we extend this language by adding new primitive channels. Then, in Sect. 3 we provide an adapted stochastic timed automata STA_r as its formal semantics. Related work and comparison are discussed in Sect. 4. Section 5 presents several examples. Finally, Sect. 6 summarizes the paper and comes up with some future work we are going to work on.

2 Extending Reo for Stochastic and Timed Behavior

In this section, we introduce Reo, the channel-based coordination language, and its stochastic and timed extensions. These extensions are realized through adding new channels to the primitive channel set of Reo.

2.1 Reo

Reo is a channel-based exogenous coordination language proposed by F. Arbab in [2], where concurrency protocols are manifested as *connectors*. Basically, connectors are constructed through a compositional approach: complex ones are composed of simpler ones, where the atomic ones are called *channels*. Channels are glued on *nodes*, and they together perform the behavior of connectors.

Nodes. There are three types of nodes in Reo: *source nodes*, *sink nodes* and *mixed nodes*, as shown in Fig. 1.

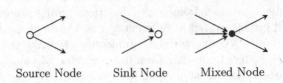

Source Node   Sink Node   Mixed Node

Fig. 1. Three types of nodes

Essentially, a *source node* performs *replicating* behavior. That is, any coming data values will be broadcasted synchronously if and only if all its successors are ready to accept. A *sink node* performs *merging* behavior, accepting data values from its predecessors randomly (this can be a non-deterministic choice if more than one predecessors are ready to write). And a *mixed node*, literally, performs both behavior at the same time, randomly picking one input and broadcasting it to all outputs.

Channels. As the basic functional units in Reo, channels are supposed to describe basic coordination behavior among *channel ends*. A channel ends can be either a *source end* or a *sink end*, indicating the direction of its data flow. A set of primitive channels can be found in Fig. 2, where we use arrows to indicate the type of channel ends.

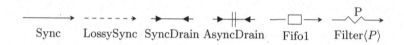

Sync   LossySync SyncDrain AsyncDrain   Fifo1   Filter⟨P⟩

Fig. 2. Primitive channels

Channels can be either *synchronous* or *asynchronous*. A channel is *synchronous* if and only if the read and write operations on its channel ends are always performed simultaneously. The behavior of the primitive channels shown in Fig. 2 are specified as follows, where the channels are denoted as *Name(Channel Ends)*.

Sync(A:source, B:sink) is a *synchronous* channel that delivers data values from its source end A to its sink end B if possible. A synchronous channel is fired only when A is prepared for reading and B is ready for writing.

LossySync(A:source, B:sink) is an *input-enabled synchronous* channel with a source end A and a sink end B. Such channels are always prepared to accept data from A. However, the transmission process could be unreliable. If B is also ready for writing, the received data will be sent to B. Otherwise the data will be dropped immediately.

SyncDrain(A B:source) is a *synchronous* channel with two source ends A and B. It only accepts input from both A and B simultaneously and drop them together after being received.

AsyncDrain(A B:source) is an asynchronous variation of *SyncDrain*. The most important difference is that it accepts data only from one end at a time. If both ends are ready to read, one of them (randomly picked) should wait.

FIFO1(A:source, B:sink) is an asynchronous channel with a source end A and a sink end B. A FIFO1 channel can temporarily store one data value from its source end A for an arbitrary duration, and deliver it anytime when B is ready to write. When the buffer is full, a FIFO1 cannot accept any more data values.

Filter⟨P⟩ (A:source, B:sink) is a synchronous channel with a source end A, a
sink end B and a boolean function P as its parameter. When data comes to
end A, first we have to check whether the it satisfies the filter predicate P.
If the answer is yes, the channel will behave just as *Sync*, otherwise the data
will be simply dropped.

Composition. Formalization of nodes sometimes becomes rather complicated,
especially when an arbitrary number of incoming and outgoing edges are
involved. Usually, we prefer using two ternary channels *Replicator*, *Merger* and
use their combinations to capture the behavior of mixed nodes (Fig. 3).

Fig. 3. Replicator and merger

Replicator(A:source, B C:sink) is a *synchronous* broadcast channel with a source
end A and two sink ends B, C. The channel accepts data values from A, and
broadcasts them to B, C iff both B and C are ready to write.
Merger(A B:source, C:sink) is an *asynchronous* channel that collects inputs from
either A or B and sends them to C simultaneously if C is prepared.

Replicators and *Mergers* can reduce the number of incoming and outgoing edges
for mixed nodes. For example, if we replace two outgoing edges with a *Replicator*
channel, the number of edges would be reduced by 1. After a finite number of
replacements, all the mixed nodes can be simplified as nodes with one incoming
edge and one outgoing edge, which are called *flow-through*. When processing the
semantics of connectors, we assume that all the mixed nodes are *flow-through*
ones. But in the figures we still draw the mixed nodes in their original form to
make it clear and easy to understand.

2.2 Capturing Timed and Stochastic Behavior

In this subsection, we come up with some primitive channels, which extend Reo
and make it capable to specify timed and stochastic behavior. Compared with
other formal languages, Reo provides a framework which can be easily extended
by adding new channel types to the primitive channel set. Usually, new channels
should be simple enough, and orthogonal to the existing ones. Following this
idea, here we propose three channel types, capturing *data evolution, stochastic
choice*, and *time delay*.

   In the following definitions, we use $⟨p⟩$ to denote the parameter of a channel.
Value of parameters should be provided while declaring the channel, and would
never be updated during the execution (Fig. 4).

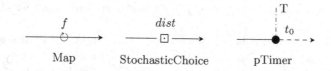

Fig. 4. Extended primitive channels

$Map\langle f\rangle$ *(A:source, B:sink)* is a synchronous channel with a source end A, a sink end B and a mapping function f as its parameter. A *Map* channel accepts incoming values from its source end A (only when B is ready for writing) and then it writes $f(dA)$ to B simultaneously (dA denotes the data accepted from A).

StochasticChoice$\langle dist\rangle$ *(A:source, B:sink)* is a synchronous randomizer channel that accepts data values from its source node A (only when B is ready for writing) and writes a random value to B simultaneously. The random value is sampled from the distribution parameter $dist$.

pTimer$\langle t_0\rangle$ *(A T:source,B:sink)* is a *parameterized* version of t-Timer in [13]. The channel accepts data values from its source end A and starts counting down. Then after a certain delay, it will send a TIMEOUT signal to B if writable, and otherwise do nothing. In both cases, the channel will reset itself and prepare to accept the next incoming value.

Value of the delay is initialized by the parameter t_0, and can be overridden by incoming values from the source end T. When the *pTimer* is not in counting down stage, an incoming value from T will simply update the delay value. Otherwise the incoming value will reset it, update the delay value, and write nothing to B. When the new delay value is provided exactly at the same time when counting down process terminates, the channel will still generate the timeout signal.

3 Stochastic Timed Automata for Reo

In this section, first we introduce the formal model STA_r that yields the basis for reasoning about timed and stochastic behavior of connectors. Then we define the new semantics for primitive Reo channels based on STA_r, and explain how to construct STA_r for complex connectors by applying the *product* and *hiding* operators to STA_r of simpler ones.

3.1 STA_r

Stochastic timed automata (STA) [8] is a powerful formalism to describe stochastic behavior and real-time behavior. Both continuous distributions and discrete distributions are supported in STA. In this paper, we slightly adapt STA as STA_r so that Reo channels can be depicted more naturally and clearly. Before touching the technical details of STA_r, we first introduce some notations that will be used later.

During the rest of this paper, we will use $\mathbb{D}$ to denote the *data scope*, which can be either *a) any finite set, b) the set of real numbers* $\mathbb{R}$, or their union. Namely, $\mathbb{D}$ is finite, or $\mathbb{D}\backslash\mathbb{R}$ is finite (if $\mathbb{R} \subseteq \mathbb{D}$). When the data scope is restricted to finite sets, stochastic assignments are no longer supported. For example, if $\mathbb{D} = \{1,2\}$, $v := norm(e,\sigma)$ is an invalid assignment while $v' := 1 + \text{B}(1,0.5)$ is acceptable, where *norm* and B stand for normal and binomial distribution respectively. We use $Dist(S)$ to denote the set of continuous or discrete distributions on S.

Definition 1 (Evaluations). *Suppose V is a finite set of variables, an evaluation on V is defined as a function $ev_V : V \to \mathbb{D}$ that maps a variable identifier to its valuation. Similarly, we can also define clock evaluations on C as $ev_C : C \to \mathbb{R}$, where C is a set of clock variables. Natually, we can use EV_V to denote the set of all evaluations on V, EV_C to denote the set of all clock evaluations on C, and EV to denote their combination, i.e.*

$$EV = \left\{ ev : V \cup C \to \mathbb{D} \cup \mathbb{R} | ev(v) = \begin{cases} ev_v(v) \ v \in V \\ ev_c(v) \ v \in C \end{cases}, ev_v \in EV_V, ev_c \in EV_C \right\}$$

In practice, evaluations are usually represented by a set of assignment statements. E.g., $\{a := TIMEOUT, b := 1, c := 0.5, \cdots\}$.

In STA_r, there is a very different concept named *adjoint variable*. That is, for each external action A, when it is provided by the environment, there must be a data value coming along, and assigned to its adjoint variable dA. Adjoint variables are used to describe the channels' behavior, where the basic idea is: channel ends are triggered iff data values come (or leave).

Definition 2 (STA$_r$). *Stochastic Timed Automata for Reo (STA$_r$) is defined as an 8-tuple $\langle L, l_0, Acts, V, V_0, C, Inv, E \rangle$ where:*

- *L is a finite set of locations,*
- *$l_0 \in L$ is an initial location,*
- *$Acts$ is a finite set of actions,*
- *V is a finite set of variables that satisfies $\forall A \in Acts, dA \in V$,*
- *$V_0 \in EV$ is an initialized function for variables,*
- *C is a finite set of clocks (we always assume that $V \cap C = \varnothing$),*
- *$Inv : L \to (EV \to Bool)$ is a function that maps locations to their corresponding invariants,*
- *E is a finite set of edges. An edge in E is defined as a 5-tuple $\langle l, acts, g, u, l' \rangle$ where*
  - *$l \in L$ is the source location,*
  - *$acts \in P(Acts)$ is a finite set of actions (internal action is denoted by the empty set),*

- $g : EV \rightarrow Bool$ is the guard constraint that maps an evaluation (for both variables and clocks) to a boolean value true or false,
- $u : EV \rightarrow Dist(EV)$ is a random assignment that updates the current evaluation with a random sample following a certain distribution of $Dist(EV)$,
- $l' \in L$ is the target location.

In the following, we write $l \xrightarrow{\mathbf{acts},g,u}_E l'$ instead of $\langle l, acts, g, u, l' \rangle \in E$, or simply $l \xrightarrow{\mathbf{acts},g,u} l'$ if it does not lead to ambiguity. Meanwhile, in a STA_r graph we use $[\mathbf{acts},\ g]u$ to label such a transition (see in Fig. 5). For simplicity reasons, tautology guards and internal actions are omitted.

3.2 Semantics of Primitive Channels

As mentioned before, the STA_r for a given Reo connector is constructed in a compositional way. In this subsection, we provide semantics of the primitive channels as STA_r, including both original and extended ones. The $[\![\cdot]\!]$ operator is used to denote *semantics map* which maps a Reo connector to its semantics as STA_r.

The following figures (Figs. 5 and 6) provide a graphical representations of the primitive channels' semantics (both standard and extended ones included). In these figures, we use the following notations:

- Initial location is decorated with double-line border.
- Actions of edges are denoted by bold font and embraced with '[ ]', e.g. [**A**, **B**]. If an edge is internal, i.e. its action set is empty, we will use '[ ]' instead.
- Guards of edges are denoted by an italic formula just next to the actions, e.g. $P(dA)$, $t > 0$. Tautology guards (e.g. *true*) are omitted.
- An update is denoted by a set of assignments. For example, $dA, dB := exp_1, exp_2$ is an update, in which the value of dA and dB are overwritten by exp_1 and exp_2 (both are calculated under the original evaluation).

$[\![Sync(A{:}source, B{:}sink)]\!]$ in Fig. 5(a) has only one single location and a self-loop edge with two actions [**A**, **B**], indicating that reading operation from its source end A and writing operation to its sink end B should be fired simultaneously. The data transform process is captured by the assignment $dB := dA$.

$[\![LossySync(A{:}source, B{:}sink)]\!]$ in Fig. 5(b) has one more edge than *Sync*. The extra edge with one action [**A**], capturing the lossy behavior, is fired only when A is ready to read but B is not ready to write.

$[\![SyncDrain(A{:}source, B{:}source)]\!]$ in Fig. 5(c), also has only one self-loop edge with label [**A**, **B**]. Compared with *Sync*, there is no assignment here because both A and B are source ends, i.e. from both ends the channel reads data values and simply drops them.

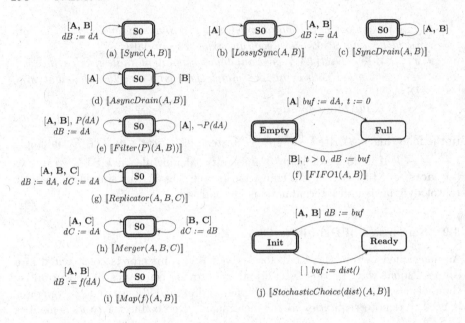

Fig. 5. Semantics of primitive channels

$\llbracket AsyncDrain(A{:}source, B{:}source) \rrbracket$ in Fig. 5(d) is an asynchronous variation of $SyncDrain$.[1] In its corresponding STA_r, there are two edges with single action $[\mathbf{A}]$ or $[\mathbf{B}]$, indicating that the channel is fired only one of the source end is ready to read. In other words, it only drops data values asynchronously.

$\llbracket Filter\langle P \rangle(A{:}source, B{:}sink) \rrbracket$ in Fig. 5(e) has two edges. One captures the data transfer process when the filter predicate is satisfied, and the other captures the data loss when the filter predicate is not satisfied. In the former case, with actions $[\mathbf{A}, \mathbf{B}]$ and guard $P(dA)$, the data transfer happens only when its source end A is ready to read, its sink end B is ready to write, and its incoming value dA satisfies the given predicate P. In the later one, it only reads from A and drops it.

$\llbracket FIFO1(A{:}source, B{:}sink) \rrbracket$ in Fig. 5(f) consists of two locations and two edges. The first location is the initial location, where the buffer is empty. And in the second one indicates the buffer is assigned. Local variable buf is used to store the value in the buffer. As mentioned earlier, data items are supposed to stay in the buffer for a positive delay, so we also need a clock t even if it's not a timed channel. The reading edge, with action $[\mathbf{A}]$, reads a value from A, stores it in buf and reset the delay t. This value will be written to B, through firing the writing edge with action $[\mathbf{B}]$, when the delay is large than 0 and B is prepared for writing.

---

[1] Different interpretations of $AsyncDrain$ have been proposed in [2,6]. For simplicity we choose the later one in [6], and don't consider fairness issues.

$[\![Replicator(A{:}source, B{:}sink, C{:}sink)]\!]$ in Fig. 5(g) has only one location and one edge. Actions of this edge include all of its ends [**A**, **B**, **C**], which shows that it is fired only when A is ready to read and both B, C are ready to write. The value from A will be broadcasted to B and C.

$[\![Merger(A{:}source, B{:}source, C{:}sink)]\!]$ in Fig. 5(h) has two edges for two cases, *transferring from A to C* (with actions [**A**, **C**]) or *transferring from B to C* (with actions [**B**, **C**]).

$[\![Map\langle f\rangle(A{:}source, B{:}sink)]\!]$ in Fig. 5(i) is a synchronous channel where the mapping function f will be applied to any flow-through data values. In the assignment of its only edge, it writes the calculated value $f(dA)$ to B.

$[\![StochasticChoice\langle dist\rangle(A{:}source, B{:}sink)]\!]$ in Fig. 5(j) is a synchronous channel including two locations, *init* and *ready*. In the *init* location, the channel accepts data values from its source end A but write random values (sampled just before) to its sink end B synchronously.

The basic idea is that the random sampling should not be performed simultaneously. Otherwise, you may meet the case where two edges can be triggered at the same time, but guard of the later edge relies on the random assignment of the previous one. It's hard to describe such semantics naturally, so we always assume that the random process is done before triggering the assignment.

$[\![pTimer\langle t_0\rangle(A{:}source, T{:}source, B{:}sink)]\!]$ in Fig. 6 consists of two locations and a large family of edges. Various border behavior is covered in this semantic model, making it capable to meet different requirements. When the channel is in *init* state, it is able to accept values from T and update its delay time, or accept values from A, jump to the *activated* state and start counting down process. In the *activated* state, the channel may accept values from A, B and T:

- *When counting down process is not finished yet,* only T is writable and any incoming values from T will reset the timer to *init* state.
- *When counting down finishes,* all combinations in $P(A, B, T)$ is acceptable. If B is writable, a TIMEOUT signal will be sent to B. If A has an incoming value, it will trigger a new counting down process immediately. And if T has an incoming value, the delay time will be overridden.

3.3   Composition of Connectors as STA$_r$

As mentioned before, connectors in Reo are constructed from simpler ones in a compositional approach. Now we show how connectors are composed by *product* and *hiding* operations on STA$_r$.

The *product* operator is used to combine two connectors by joining their *shared nodes* (*shared actions* in STA$_r$). In *product* operations, we always assume that shared actions have the same identifiers, while other variables and clocks are all named without repetition. Before showing the formal definition of the *product* operator, first we introduce a predicate *compatible*.

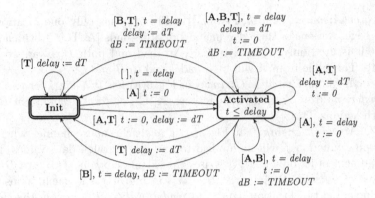

Fig. 6. Semantics of pTimer

Definition 3 (Compatible STA$_r$). Let $\mathscr{A}_i = \langle L_i, l_{0,i}, Acts_i, V_i, V_{0,i}, C_i, Inv_i, E_i \rangle$ be two STA_r $(i=1, 2)$, they are compatible if

- there's no conflicting initialization on shared variables, formalized as $\forall v \in V_1 \cap V_2, V_{0,1}(v) = V_{0,2}(v)$, and
- shared variables can only be assigned in one of them, i.e. if $v \in V_1 \cap V_2$ and $v := expr$ (expr is an expression) appears in the assignments of $\mathscr{A}_1$, then $\forall e \in E_2$, e should not contain any assignment on v, and vice versa.

In other words, we don't allow two connectors to write on the same node simultaneously.

Definition 4 (Product). Let $\mathscr{A}_i = \langle L_i, l_{0,i}, Acts_i, V_i, V_{0,i}, C_i, Inv_i, E_i \rangle (i = 1, 2)$ be two compatible STA_r, their product $\mathscr{A} = \mathscr{A}_1 \bowtie \mathscr{A}_2$ is defined as:

$$\mathscr{A}_1 \bowtie \mathscr{A}_2 = \langle L_1 \times L_2, (l_{0,1}, l_{0,2}), Acts_1 \cup Acts_2, V_1 \cup V_2, V_0, C_1 \cup C_2, Inv, E \rangle$$

where

- $V_0(v)$ is equal to $V_{0,1}(v)$ if $v \in V_1 \backslash V_2$, or $V_{0,2}(v)$ otherwise,
- $Inv(l_1, l_2)(ev) = Inv_1(l_1)(ev \restriction_{V_1 \cup C_1}) \wedge Inv_2(l_2)(ev \restriction_{V_2 \cup C_2})$, where $\restriction$ is used to restrict a function on certain domain,
- E is obtained through the following rules:

$$\frac{l_1 \xrightarrow{acts_1, g_1, u_1}_{E_1} l'_1, acts_1 \cap Acts_2 = \varnothing}{\langle l_1, l_2 \rangle \xrightarrow{acts_1, g_1, u_1}_E \langle l'_1, l_2 \rangle} \tag{1}$$

$$\frac{l_2 \xrightarrow{acts_2, g_2, u_2}_{E_2} l'_2, acts_2 \cap Acts_1 = \varnothing}{\langle l_1, l_2 \rangle \xrightarrow{acts_2, g_2, u_2}_E \langle l_1, l'_2 \rangle} \tag{2}$$

$$\frac{l_1 \xrightarrow{acts_1, g_1, u_1}_{E_1} l'_1, l_2 \xrightarrow{acts_2, g_2, u_2}_{E_2} l'_2, acts_1 \cap Acts_2 = acts_2 \cap Acts_1}{\langle l_1, l_2 \rangle \xrightarrow{acts_1 \cup acts_2, g, u}_E \langle l'_1, l'_2 \rangle} \tag{3}$$

In rule (3), guard formula is the logical conjunction of g_1 and g_2, formally $g(ev) = g_1(ev \restriction_{V_1 \cup C_1}) \wedge g_2(ev \restriction_{V_2 \cup C_2})$ is defined simply following Inv. However, the definition of u is much more complicated. For example, in Fig. 7 we may have $dB := dA$ as u_1, and $dC := dB$ as u_2. Their direct product is $dB := dA$, $dC := dB$. Obviously, we need an order here to resolve the dependency between variables (otherwise these statements could become a great mess), which is provided as follows.

1. Check all the assignment statements $v := expr$ in u_1, and use expression $expr$ to replace all the existence of v in both u_2 and g_2,
2. Reversely, check all $v := expr$ in u_2, and replace their existence in both u_1 and g_1 (note that this replacement will also affect g),
3. Repeat the previous steps until nothing can be replaced,
4. Suppose u_1' and u_2' are the resolved assignment statements, we have

$$u(v) = \begin{cases} u_1'(v) & v \text{ is assigned in } v_1, \\ u_2'(v) & otherwise \end{cases}$$

With the *product* operator, we can obtain a rough combination of Reo connectors (as STA_r). But there are still redundant statements that should have been simplified. We now introduce the *hiding* operator which can be used to omit such unnecessary parts.

Definition 5 (Hideable Action). *Let $\mathscr{A} = \langle L, l_0, Acts, V, V_0, C, Inv, E \rangle$ be a STA_r and $A \in Acts$ is an action. We say A is hideable in $\mathscr{A}$ if (a) all the assignment statements do not depend on the value of dA (i.e. dA never appears on the right-hand side of any assignment statement), and (b) dA doesn't appear in any guard or invariant.*

Definition 6 (Hiding). *Let $\mathscr{A} = \langle L, l_0, Acts, V, V_0, C, Inv, E \rangle$ be a STA_r and $A \in Acts$ is a hideable action in $\mathscr{A}$. The hiding operator $\mathscr{A} \backslash \{A\}$ is defined as*

$$\mathscr{A} \backslash \{A\} = \langle L, l_0, V \backslash \{dA\}, V_0 \restriction_{V \backslash \{dA\}}, C, Acts \backslash \{A\}, Inv, E' \rangle$$

where $E' = \{\langle l, acts \backslash \{A\}, g, u \restriction_{V \backslash \{dA\}}, l' \rangle | \langle l, acts, g, u, l' \rangle \in E\}$.

Hiding operation can be also used to remove multiple hideable actions at a time. For example, we introduce the following notation, and it easy to prove that this notation is well-defined, and satisfies the law of commutation (since all we do in hiding is to remove things from existing terms).

$$\mathscr{A} \backslash \{A_1, \cdots, A_n\} := \mathscr{A} \backslash \{A_1\} \backslash \{A_2\} \cdots \backslash \{A_n\}$$

We consider a simple example in Fig. 7, where we use *product* and *hiding* operators to combine a *Sync* and a *FIFO1* channel. In Fig. 7, we show the combined connector in different stages and its corresponding STA_r step by step.

Next we consider two Reo connectors both consisting of a *StochasticChoice* channel and a *FIFO1* channel but placed in a different order.

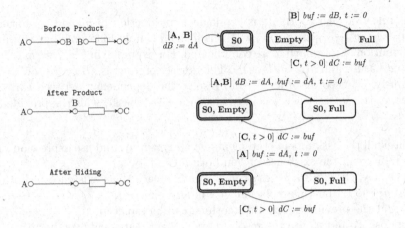

Fig. 7. *Product* and *Hiding* of *Sync(A,B)* and *FIFO1(B,C)*

Fig. 8. Composition of StochasticChoice and FIFO1 channel.

As *StochasticChoice* channel is a synchronous channel, here we omit the *Ready* state and the internal action. The two connectors are shown in Fig. 8, where *dist* is a random distribution.

In the first Reo connector, data items arriving in *B*1 are stochastic. Following that, whatever the data item is, it is stored into the buffer of FIFO1 deterministically. Nevertheless, in the second Reo connector, no matter what the data item taken from the buffer is, the output of the connector will totally depend on the parameter *dist* of *StochasticChoice* channel (Fig. 9).

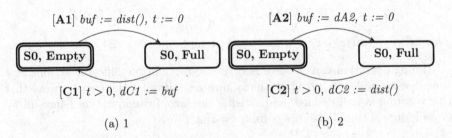

Fig. 9. Final product of StochasticChoice and FIFO1

3.4   Well-Definedness of Composition Operators

To specify the well-definedness of composition operators listed above, here we present the *commutative* law and the *associative* law for them. Before starting, first we introduce the *isomorphism* of STA_r.

Definition 7 (Isomorphism). *Two STA_r are isomorphic ($\mathscr{A}_1 \cong \mathscr{A}_2$, where $\mathscr{A}_i = \langle L_i, l_{0,i}, Acts, V_i, V_{0,i}, C_i, Inv_i, E_i \rangle$), if the 1-to-1 mappings $f_L : L_1 \to L_2$, $f_V : V_1 \to V_2$ and $f_C : C_1 \to C_2$ exist and satisfy:*

- $f_L(l_{0,1}) = l_{0,2}$,
- $\forall v \in V_1, V_{0,1}(v) = V_{0,2}(f_V(v))$,
- $\forall l \in L_1, Inv_1(l)$ *and* $Inv_2(f_L(l))$ *can be obtained from each other by variables' replacement specified by* f_V *and* f_C,
- $\forall e = \langle l, acts, g, u, l' \rangle \in E_1$, *we can find a corresponding exclusive edge* $e' \in E_2 = \langle f_L(l), acts, g', u', f_L(l') \rangle$ *where* g', u' *and* g, u *can be obtained from each other by variables' replacement specified by* f_V *and* f_C.

Informally speaking, two STA_r are isomorphic if they have the same graphical structure and homologous behavior, despite the slight difference of location labels or variable identifiers. The *commutative* and *associative* laws we present in the following are essentially based on the definition of *isomorphism*.

Theorem 1 (Commutative[2]).   *Let* $\mathscr{A}_1, \mathscr{A}_2$ *be two* STA_r, $\mathscr{A}_1 \bowtie \mathscr{A}_2 \cong \mathscr{A}_2 \bowtie \mathscr{A}_1$.

Theorem 2 (Associative). *Let* $\mathscr{A}_1, \mathscr{A}_2, \mathscr{A}_3$ *be three* STA_r, $(\mathscr{A}_1 \bowtie \mathscr{A}_2) \bowtie \mathscr{A}_3 \cong \mathscr{A}_1 \bowtie (\mathscr{A}_2 \bowtie \mathscr{A}_3)$.

From the two theorems above, it's clear that orders make only little difference in composition of STA_r. No matter how we label the identifiers and write the composing expression, finally the connectors we obtain have the same behavior. Similar to the isomorphism of graphs, these laws can be easily proved through a constructive approach.

4   Discussion

In the coordination community, Reo is well known for its variety on extensions and semantics [11]. This paper is not the first work on its timed or stochastic extension. Here we take *timed Reo*, *probabilistic Reo*, and *stochastic Reo* as examples to illustrate how our model differs from its predecessors.

---

[2] Proof can be found at https://github.com/liyi-david/ReoSTA.

Timed Reo. Time was natively involved in Reo from its very beginning [2], where *FIFO1* channel needs time constraints to ensure its retardancy. However, time was involved only implicitly in [2] instead of syntax. And in some other semantic models like *constraint automata*, time is even simplified as temporal order. A set of raw *t-Timer* channels was proposed in [3] to capture timed delays. This work was then followed and extended in [13,14] with different types of timed models.

The *pTimer* channel proposed in this paper is basically an improvement of *t*-Timer in [13]. A *t*-Timer channel accepts data values and produce timeout signals after a certain delay t. However, it does not describe what happens if the timeout signal fails to deliver. In some cases, this may lead to timelock.

Timelock has different meaning in different semantic models. Informally speaking, a timed model falls into timelock if and only if there is no possible evolution that satisfies the model constraints, and hence the model execution is forced to stop. From a practical perspective, a connector suffering from timelock can not be simulated or implemented.

Example 1 (Timelock in Timed Reo). The *t*-Timer channel may easily lead to timelock. Given two *t*-Timers, one is located between A and C, the other between B and D. According to the definition of *t*-Timer in [3,13] we knows,

$$\forall i \in \mathbb{N}, t_i(C) = t_i(A) + 0.5, t_i(D) = t_i(B) + 1, t_i(A) = t_i(B), t_i(C) = t_i(D) \quad (4)$$

where $t(X)$ indicates the time stream on node X. It is easy to derive that $t_i(C) = t_i(C) + 0.5$, which only For example, if A accepts the first value at time 0, and the second value at 1, then $t_0(A) = 0, t_1(A) = 1, \cdots$. From (4), it's easy to derive that $t(A) = t(A) + 0.5$. This connector will be trapped in timelock once A starts accepting values (Fig. 10).

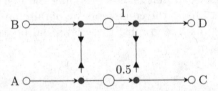

Fig. 10. Timelock caused by abuse of t-*Timer*

In comparison, *pTimer* channels are timelock-free. If its sink end is not ready, the timeout signal will be dropped, and it channel will become available to accept new data items again. Furthermore, *pTimer* channels also support reconfiguration of delays, which make it able to encode other timer channels (such as *EXP-Timer, OFFTimer and RSTTimer* in [13]) through simple combination patterns (refer to Example 3, Sect. 5).

Probabilistic Reo. A probabilistic extension of constraint automata was proposed in [5] to formalize the potential lossy behavior in connectors. In [5], probabilistic loss of data may happen while the data is being transmitted or waiting in the buffer. Definition of the former case is rather trivial, but in the latter one, the discrete time model is required. The authors assume that in each time unit, a buffer failure may happen with a probability τ, and data items may get lost due to this failure.

Probabilistic lossy behavior of connectors can be represented by combination of *StochasticChoice* channels and *SyncDrain* channels (an example of which can be found in Sect. 5). Actually, *pTimer* channels can also produce discrete time signals. Thus, we can use probabilistic lossy channels and discrete time counters to reproduce probabilistic connectors like the *LossyFIFO1* in [5].

Stochastic Reo. Baier and Wolf proposed the first stochastic extension for Reo in [7] based on Continuous-time Constraint Automata (CCA). The work was later extended with different semantics. For example, Quantitative Intentional Automata in [4] and interactive Markov Chain in [16].

Basically, most of those stochastic semantics are based on continuous-time Markov Chains. Delays and arrival rates are attached to primitive channels, giving them randomized or unreliable behavior. This approach has a defect that random behavior is bounded with time. We can produce random delays but not random values. That is the reason why we split off stochastic delays as *StochasticChoice*. *StochasticChoice* has nothing to do with time, but we can always combine it with *pTimer* to produce different timed connectors with stochastic behavior.

There are also other coordination models that supports stochastic and timed behavior except for Reo. For example, Probabilistic KLAIM in [17], Stochastic π-caculus in [18], etc. However, in most of them timed and stochastic behavior are supported in components, instead of coordinators. Compared with these approaches, our framework supports more complicated coordination behaviors and more intuitive modeling interfaces (graphical representation), which also keep connector designers away from potential failures.

5   Case Studies

With support of the composition operators, Reo can be used to capture various coordination scenarios in the real world. In this section, we present two examples: *Probabilistic Router* and *Expiring Timer*.

Example 2 (Probabilistic Router). *Router* is a widely used connector example [3,6]. As shown in Fig. 11(a), a *Router* uses two *LossySync* channels and a *SyncDrain* channel to make sure that a coming data value is only sent to one of its sink ends. This choice is made nondeterministically at C, where the *Merger* channel exists. Here we show how the nondeterministic behavior is resolved as probabilistic behavior through the *StochasticChoice* channel.

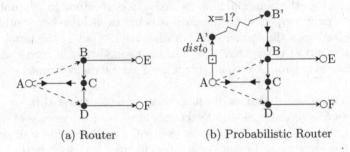

(a) Router   (b) Probabilistic Router

Fig. 11. From router to probabilistic router

We attach a new path $A \rightarrow A' \rightarrow B' \rightarrow B$ to the original *Router*, including a *StochasticChoice*, a *Filter* and a *SyncDrain*, as depicted in Fig. 11(b). When the *StochasticChoice* channel is triggered, numeric value 0 or 1 will be generated, and in turn passed to the *Filter* channel. If the value is 1, it will be sent to the *SyncDrain* channel BB'. In this case, the incoming value has to go through the path $A \rightarrow B \rightarrow E$. Otherwise, if the sampled value is 0, it will be dropped by the *Filter*, the incoming value will be sent to F as B cannot accept any data from A.

The corresponding STA_r of a *Probabilistic Router* can be deduced on the basis of primitive channels' semantics and product/hiding operators. There are two locations in the product STA_r, since only one primitive channel in the connector (*StochasticChoice*) has two locations. According to the *product* operator, the locations should be labelled as tuples like (*S0,..., Init,...*). Here for simplicity we use *Init* and *Ready* instead. The final result STA_r, after *hiding* all the internal nodes except A,E,F, is shown in Fig. 12.

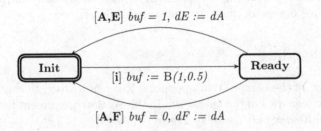

Fig. 12. STA_r of probabilistic router

Example 3 (Expiring Timer). In Timed Reo [13], different types of timer channels are proposed to capture real-time behaviors in different practical scenarios, including: *OffTimer* that allows the timer to terminate the counting process when a certain signal is received, *RSTTimer* that allows the timer to reset and restart its counting process, and *EXPTimer* that makes the timer produce the TIMEOUT signal immediately when a certain signal is received.

In this paper we take *EXPTimer* as an example to show how *pTimer* is used to encode the previous timers. In this example, the default delay time is denoted by t. (See Fig. 13)

Basically, this connector divide the incoming data values into two classes: expiring signals and normal values. For a normal value, it goes into the *pTimer* channel, and its copy is temporarily stored in the *FIFO1* channel to show that the *pTimer* is activated. When the counting process finished successfully without interruption, the buffered value will be dropped due to the *SyncDrain* channel, and a TIMEOUT signal will be sent to H.

On the other hand, when an expiring signal is caught, it will be replaced by the default delay value t and sent to the T end of the *pTimer*. According to the semantics, the *pTimer* will be reset immediately, and the buffered value will be dropped while sending out the TIMEOUT signal.

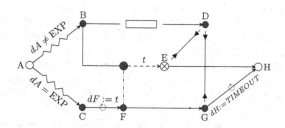

Fig. 13. Encode *EXPTimer* with *pTimer*

6   Conclusion and Future Work

This paper comes up with an approach using Reo connectors to capture stochastic and real-time behavior in distributed systems. With an extended set of primitive channels, stochastic choices and timed delays are encapsulated as individual channels. Theoretically, our approach supports partial reconfiguration (by rewritable *pTimer*) and various stochastic distributions (by highly customizable *StochasticChoice*). The case studies illustrate its capacity to formalize complex coordination scenarios in the real world. We use STA$_r$ as the formal semantics of stochastic and timed connectors, which is purely operational and timelock-free.

The framework, however, is still in its infancy. We need an implementation to make it compatible with existing popular tools for formal modeling and verification. Currently, our plan is to encode STA$_r$ in JANI (JSON Automata Network Interface) [1], which is a unified analysis framework including a shared model specification that covers STA, and a standard analyzing interface supported by various probabilistic model checking tools (Modest [10], IscasMC [9], etc.).

Acknowledgements. The work was partially supported by the National Natural Science Foundation of China under grant no. 61532019, 61202069 and 61272160.

References

1. The JANI specification of the jani-model format and the jani-interaction protocol. http://www.jani-spec.org/
2. Arbab, F.: Reo: a channel-based coordination model for component composition. Math. Struct. Comput. Sci. **14**(3), 329–366 (2004)
3. Arbab, F., Baier, C., de Boer, F.S., Rutten, J.J.M.M.: Models and temporal logical specifications for timed component connectors. Softw. Syst. Model. **6**(1), 59–82 (2007)
4. Arbab, F., Chothia, T., Mei, R., Meng, S., Moon, Y.J., Verhoef, C.: From coordination to stochastic models of QoS. In: Field, J., Vasconcelos, V.T. (eds.) COORDINATION 2009. LNCS, vol. 5521, pp. 268–287. Springer, Heidelberg (2009). https://doi.org/10.1007/978-3-642-02053-7_14
5. Baier, C.: Probabilistic models for Reo connector circuits. J. Univ. Comput. Sci. **11**(10), 1718–1748 (2005)
6. Baier, C., Sirjani, M., Arbab, F., Rutten, J.: Modeling component connectors in Reo by constraint automata. Sci. Comput. Program. **61**(2), 75–113 (2006)
7. Baier, C., Wolf, V.: Stochastic reasoning about channel-based component connectors. In: Ciancarini, P., Wiklicky, H. (eds.) COORDINATION 2006. LNCS, vol. 4038, pp. 1–15. Springer, Heidelberg (2006). https://doi.org/10.1007/11767954_1
8. Hahn, E.M., Hartmanns, A., Hermanns, H.: Reachability and reward checking for stochastic timed automata. Electron. Commun. Eur. Assoc. Softw. Sci. Technol. **70** (2014)
9. Hahn, E.M., Li, Y., Schewe, S., Turrini, A., Zhang, L.: ISCASMC: a web-based probabilistic model checker. In: Jones, C., Pihlajasaari, P., Sun, J. (eds.) FM 2014. LNCS, vol. 8442, pp. 312–317. Springer, Cham (2014). https://doi.org/10.1007/978-3-319-06410-9_22
10. Hartmanns, A.: Modest a unified language for quantitative models. In: Proceedings of FDL 2012, pp. 44–51. IEEE (2012)
11. Jongmans, S.S.T.Q., Arbab, F.: Overview of thirty semantic formalisms for Reo. Sci. Ann. Comput. Sci. **22**(1), 201–251 (2012)
12. Li, H.: Introducing Windows Azure. Apress, Berkely (2009)
13. Meng, S.: Connectors as designs: the time dimension. In: Proceedings of TASE 2012, pp. 201–208. IEEE Computer Society (2012)
14. Meng, S., Arbab, F.: On resource-sensitive timed component connectors. In: Bonsangue, M.M., Johnsen, E.B. (eds.) FMOODS 2007. LNCS, vol. 4468, pp. 301–316. Springer, Heidelberg (2007). https://doi.org/10.1007/978-3-540-72952-5_19
15. Newcombe, C., Rath, T., Zhang, F., Munteanu, B., Brooker, M., Deardeuff, M.: How amazon web services uses formal methods. Commun. ACM **58**(4), 66–73 (2015)
16. Oliveira, N., Barbosa, L.S.: An enhanced model for stochastic coordination. Electron. Proc. Theor. Comput. Sci. **228**, 35–45 (2016)
17. Pierro, A., Hankin, C., Wiklicky, H.: Probabilistic KLAIM. In: Nicola, R., Ferrari, G.-L., Meredith, G. (eds.) COORDINATION 2004. LNCS, vol. 2949, pp. 119–134. Springer, Heidelberg (2004). https://doi.org/10.1007/978-3-540-24634-3_11
18. Priami, C.: Stochastic pi-calculus. Comput. J. **38**(7), 578–589 (1995)

Author Index

Printed in the United States
By Bookmasters